LIVING KARMA

SHENG YEN SERIES IN CHINESE BUDDHISM

THE SHENG YEN SERIES
IN CHINESE BUDDHIST STUDIES

CHÜN-FANG YÜ, SERIES EDITOR

Following the endowment of the Sheng Yen Professorship in Chinese Buddhist Studies, the Sheng Yen Education Foundation and the Chung-Hwa Institute of Buddhist Studies in Taiwan jointly endowed a publication series, the *Sheng Yen Series in Chinese Studies*, at Columbia University Press. Its purpose is to publish monographs containing new scholarship and English translations of classical texts in Chinese Buddhism.

Scholars of Chinese Buddhism have traditionally approached the subject through philology, philosophy, and history. In recent decades, however, they have increasingly adopted an interdisciplinary approach, drawing on anthropology, archaeology, art history, religious studies, and gender studies, among other disciplines. This series aims to provide a home for such pioneering studies in the field of Chinese Buddhism.

Michael J. Walsh, *Sacred Economies: Buddhist Business and Religiosity in Medieval China*

Koichi Shinohara, *Spells, Images, and Maṇḍalas: Tracing the Evolution of Esoteric Buddhist Rituals*

LIVING KARMA

THE RELIGIOUS PRACTICES OF
OUYI ZHIXU

BEVERLEY FOULKS MCGUIRE

COLUMBIA UNIVERSITY PRESS
NEW YORK

Columbia University Press
Publishers Since 1893
New York   Chichester, West Sussex
cup.columbia.edu

Copyright © 2014 Columbia University Press
Paperback edition, 2020
All rights reserved

Library of Congress Cataloging-in-Publication Data
McGuire, Beverley Foulks, author.
Living karma : the religious practices of Ouyi Zhixu /
Beverley Foulks McGuire.
  pages cm. — (The Sheng Yen series in Chinese Buddhist studies)
  Includes bibliographical references and index.
ISBN 978-0-231-16802-1 (cloth)—ISBN 978-0-231-16803-8 (pbk.)—ISBN 978-0-231-53777-3 (e-book)
  1. Karma. 2. Zhixu, 1599–1655. 3. Spiritual life—Buddhism.
  4. Buddhist literature, Chinese—History and criticism. I. Title.
    BQ4435.M43 2014
    294.3'92092—dc23
                                                              2013036854

Cover design: Jordan Wannemacher

CONTENTS

Illustrations vii
Acknowledgments ix

INTRODUCTION   1

1. KARMA AS A NARRATIVE DEVICE IN OUYI'S AUTOBIOGRAPHY   17

2. DIVINATION AS A KARMIC DIAGNOSTIC   37

3. REPENTANCE RITUALS FOR ELIMINATING KARMA   53

4. VOWING TO ASSUME THE KARMA OF OTHERS   81

5. SLICING, BURNING, AND BLOOD WRITING: KARMIC TRANSFORMATIONS OF BODIES   93

CONCLUSION   125

Appendix 1. A Translation of Ouyi's Autobiography   133
Appendix 2. A Map of Ouyi's Life   143
Notes   145
Glossary of Terms, People, Places, and Titles of Texts   193
Bibliography   203
Index   221

ILLUSTRATIONS

Figure 2.1   Set of wheel tops used in the *Divination Sutra*.   44
Figure 3.1   Dizang Tower, Jiuhuashan.   56
Figure 5.1   Pillar from Qing dynasty stupa, Lingfeng Temple.   121
Figure 5.2   Rebuilt stupa, Lingfeng Temple.   123
Figure 5.3   Memorial Hall for Ouyi, Lingfeng Temple.   124
Figure AP2.1   Map of Ouyi's life.   143

ACKNOWLEDGMENTS

IT SEEMS fitting to begin a book on karma by acknowledging the causes and conditions that led to its production. I would first like to thank Dharma Drum Buddhist College and the Chung-Hwa Institute of Buddhist Studies for their support in the beginning stages of the project and its final completion: Dharma Drum Buddhist College hosted me as a visiting scholar while I was in Taiwan from 2007–2008, and the Chung-Hwa Institute awarded me a grant to revise my manuscript in 2010–2011. *Living Karma* builds on Master Shengyan's encyclopedic study of Ouyi Zhixu published in Japanese and translated into Chinese, and I have felt a particular "karmic affinity" with Master Shengyan and Dharma Drum Mountain because of this connection.

I am also profoundly grateful to colleagues who offered feedback and constructive criticism of the manuscript in its various iterations, including Robert Gimello, Anne Monius, Michael Puett, Michael Szonyi, Daniel Stevenson, Raoul Birnbaum, Lynn Struve, Walt Conser, Diana Pasulka, Justin Ritzinger, Eyal Aviv, Jason Clower, Ryan Overbey, Ching Keng, Wei-jen Teng, Alan Wagner, Brooks Jessup, Erik Hammerstrom, and my reviewers from Columbia University Press.

I would like to express my appreciation to several institutions that supported me during my research and writing. In the early stages of the project, the Fulbright Program (IIE) funded a year of research in Taiwan from 2007–2008; a Frederick Sheldon Travel Fellowship from Harvard

University allowed me to pursue two months of field research in mainland China during the summer of 2008; and a fellowship from the Andrew W. Mellon Foundation and American Council of Learned Societies supported my writing from 2008–2009. More recently, the University of North Carolina Wilmington awarded me a Summer Research Initiative Award and an International Travel Grant that supported writing and revisions during the summer of 2011.

Last but not least, I give special thanks to family and friends who encouraged and supported me throughout the process.

LIVING KARMA

INTRODUCTION

KARMA IS a fundamental idea in Buddhist ethics but a contentious topic for scholars of Buddhist ethics. Although it undergirds most academic introductions to Buddhist ethics,[1] scholars disagree on how best to approach the study of karma in Buddhist traditions. Those focused on systematizing Buddhist theories of ethical action and moral choice have approached karma through moral philosophy, and they have largely debated whether Buddhist ethics represents a form of consequentialism or virtue ethics.[2] A few scholars—notably Charles Hallisey, Anne Hansen, and Maria Heim—have advocated a different approach to Buddhist ethics that incorporates other methodologies including literary studies, anthropology, and ethnography, and they have examined particular Buddhist views of what it means to be a moral subject.

Although proponents of the philosophical approach argue it enables them to move beyond descriptive ethics to analyze Buddhist moral logic, patterns of justification, and ethical discourse, advocates of the latter approach contend that it overlooks significant aspects of Buddhist moral reasoning—such as feelings and motivations—and fails to attend to particular circumstances that impinge on moral decision making. As Charles Hallisey and Anne Hansen note, "The abstract analysis of the doctrine of karma gives us little insight into what it feels like to live in a world structured by karma."[3] Narratives allow for a portrayal of karma in all of its obscurity by sharing life experiences in all of their complexity and contradiction. Maria Heim echoes their concern: "To take seriously what it is to be human in a karmic reality is to be profoundly aware of a person in time, formed by past events and enmeshed in complicated entanglements with others in past and present."[4] Buddhists interpret their moral agency as having capacities and limitations according to their particular karmic heritage, stage of life, and history: one must attend to the conditioned reality of human experience to adequately capture their moral understanding.

This book gives a detailed account of how one particular Chinese Buddhist monk interpreted the capacities and limitations of his life and morality. His belief in karma shaped his everyday experiences, which in turn provide an incredibly rich portrait of his "world structured by karma"—one that was likely shared by many other Chinese Buddhists. The individual in question—Ouyi Zhixu (1599-1655)—is a seminal but largely overlooked figure in Chinese Buddhist history. Although he is typically recognized as one of the "four great Buddhist masters of the Ming dynasty,"[5] unlike the other masters Yunqi Zhuhong (1535-1615),[6] Zibo Zhenke (1543-1604),[7] and Hanshan Deqing (1546-1623),[8] there have been no in-depth studies of Ouyi in any Western language, and there is only one book written about him in Japanese.[9] This can be explained in part by the general neglect of scholarship of Buddhism in the Ming dynasty (1368-1644), a period previously considered one of decline for Buddhism[10] and recently reevaluated as a time of "renewal"[11] when lay associations were further developed and monasteries became sites for an emerging "gentry society."[12] Ouyi has also left an indelible print on modern and contemporary Buddhists such as Hongyi (1880-1942), considered one of the foremost Vinaya masters of the modern period, Taixu (1889-1947), an activist educator and promoter of Human Life Buddhism, and Shengyan (1930-2009), a Chan master and founder of one of the most prominent Buddhist organizations in Taiwan. Indeed, Shengyan considered Ouyi to be one of the four great modern Buddhist figures alongside Taixu, Ouyang Jingwu (1872-1944), and Yinshun (1906-2005).[13]

Instead of assessing his impact on Chinese Buddhism or offering a detailed chronology of life, I focus on the way Ouyi's religious practices and written works were influenced by his belief in karma. I base my discussion on Ouyi's ritual texts and personal writings, grappling with questions that cross a variety of disciplines including comparative religious ethics, religious studies, ritual studies, and literary studies, such as: What does it mean to be human and have a body? How does one make sense of experiences of illness and suffering? What does it mean to live in a karmic universe? How does karma operate as a lens for interpreting one's life? How does writing represent a karmic and religious practice?

Although he was a prolific writer and erudite scholastic, Ouyi lived a relatively quiet, uneventful life—one that was not especially dramatic or worthy of repentance. He expresses remorse for writing anti-Buddhist tracts in his youth, for not being a filial son, and for not receiving the precepts in accordance with monastic rules, even though he burned his anti-Buddhist writings soon after writing them, he ostensibly never mistreated his parents, and he shows perennial concern for the Vinaya. Nonetheless, his writing and religious practices frequently emphasize the need for penitence and self-discipline, suggesting a sense of guilt for things he may have done in a previous life. All of this is expressed in karmic terminology familiar to Chinese Buddhists.

Karma serves as an ideal "bridge concept" to consider the various ways that Buddhists make sense of themselves, their lives, and their world. Comparative religious ethicists have become increasingly concerned with viable categories of comparison,[14] and Aaron Stalnaker has proposed "bridge concepts" as relatively "thin" specifications of a given topic to guide comparison and enable interpreters "to thematize disparate materials and order details around these anchoring terms."[15] Although karma may initially seem too "thick" or culturally embedded to serve as a comparative category, in fact, it has already become a contested term in Buddhist ethics. There is no uniform cross-cultural or transhistorical understanding of karma in Buddhism, yet its prevalence and prominence in Buddhist studies scholarship suggests it may prove useful as a means of comparing how Buddhist practitioners view themselves and their worlds. We may discover not only that Buddhists understand karma differently according to their particular cultural, historical, and religious context but also that individual Buddhists hold multiple—even contradictory— understandings of karma simultaneously.

For example, Ouyi occasionally speaks of karma in retributive terms but more often portrays karma as organic and malleable. He uses divination as a karmic diagnostic technique, but he does not resign himself to his karmic fate. Instead of viewing karma as inevitable and inescapable, Ouyi tries to change his karma by performing repentance rituals to eliminate his karma, by pronouncing vows to bind him to a good karmic future, and by engaging in burning, blood writing, and other ascetic acts as a means of marking that future commitment. Ouyi views his body as a site for revealing and redressing past karma; just as bodily illness signals retribution for previous transgressions, bodily asceticism enables him to rectify his past karma.

This book examines the textual, ethical, and somatic dimensions of karma in Ouyi's ritual writings. First, it explores karma as a live option for Chinese Buddhists struggling to understand themselves and their world. Karma serves as an ethic to guide their behavior, a hermeneutic to interpret their lives, and a narrative device to structure their writing. Second, it considers the way karma impinges on Ouyi's religious and ethical life. Ouyi's ritual writings offer a glimpse into how karma is lived. Third, it analyzes the way in which Ouyi views his own body as a living result of previous karma. Instead of bifurcating thinking and doing—a tendency in ritual studies that has been deftly criticized by Catherine Bell[16]—Ouyi assumes an interdependent relationship between thought and action. By paying attention to the textual dimensions of his ritual writing—including genre, audience, and literary tropes—we unearth a nuanced ritual theory in which certain cognitive states enable ritual activity, and other ritual acts engender cognitive states. For example, divination rituals incite a profound belief in cause and effect, a cognitive state that plays a crucial role in repentance rituals, which in turn rouse emotions that can stimulate enlightened beings to transform a practitioner's karma.

RITUAL AND TEXT

By paying attention to the ritual and textual aspects of Ouyi's writings, I seek to redress the "Protestant bias" that has been identified within the field of Buddhist studies. Scholars have criticized how previous scholarship in the field has overlooked ritual practice and privileged textual analysis,[17] which applies to scholarship on Ouyi as well as to other studies of Ming Buddhism that often focus on the doctrinal issue of how Buddhist, Daoist, and Confucian teachings were integrated into a "syncretism" or "unity of the Three Teachings" (*sanjiao heyi*).[18] Although Ouyi certainly shared this tendency toward syncretism with other eminent monks from the late Ming dynasty, he also emphasized the importance of practice.[19] This study focuses especially on the ritual dimension of Ouyi's corpus that has been overlooked in previous scholarship. However, instead of overlooking textual dimensions entirely, it approaches texts as ritual objects and reading and writing as religious activities.

When one takes genres of texts into consideration, one discovers that Ouyi's writing on ritual cannot be limited strictly to ritual manuals—texts titled "methods of practice" (*xingfa*). Although Ouyi created divination rituals and repentance rituals of his own, he also used other genres including commentaries (*shu*) or "explanations" (*jie*) of certain texts to discuss ritual, its value, and its range of repertoires. Commentarial writing has been one of the prominent ways religious readers have expressed themselves discursively, and this is especially true within the Chinese context.[20] For Chinese literati, interlinear commentary was a dominant mode of philosophical discourse that enabled them to reflect upon the meaning and significance of religious classics for their own lives.[21] As Daniel Gardner points out, "commentary is a genre that gives interpretive elasticity to the Confucian tradition, permitting the tradition to reshape itself in response to changing times and audiences, to meet the intellectual and cultural challenges it confronts."[22] Ouyi capitalizes on the elasticity of the genre to read Chinese classical texts from Confucian and Buddhist perspectives. He also shows an acute awareness of the possibilities afforded by other genres, clearly illustrated in his *Collected Essays Refuting Heterodoxy*, where Ouyi positions himself as a Confucian, signals his audience as Confucian literati, and cites Confucian classics in order to criticize claims of Jesuit missionaries in China.[23] By couching his critique on Confucian grounds, he seeks to mask his Buddhist loyalties, which nevertheless rise to the surface when he discusses Jesuit confession rituals that bear too striking a resemblance to his own repentance rituals.[24] Although the polemical genre clearly demarcates audiences and allegiances, this study focuses on other, seemingly neutral, texts such as his poems, votive texts, and his autobiography to discern their assumed audiences and functions.

Ouyi's ritual writings draw from long-standing ritual concepts and repertoires within Chinese religions, cutting across a variety of religious traditions. Although his repentance rituals largely adopt the ritual parameters established within the Tiantai Buddhist tradition, his autobiography portrays his religious practice as consonant with Buddhism and Confucianism, his divination texts draw from Chinese Buddhist apocryphal texts, and his votive texts model themselves after Pure Land texts such as the longer *Sukhāvatīvyūha Sutra*. In this way, Ouyi positions himself within a variety of "textual communities"[25] organized around different "root texts," and although he occasionally innovates, he largely adopts previous liturgical patterns and warns that deviation may render the practice ineffective. As a result, his ritual theory cannot be reduced to a single Buddhist tradition or even Buddhism alone.

Although acknowledging the burgeoning field of ritual studies,[26] this book focuses on the ritual theory implicit within Ouyi's writings instead of applying Western theories to his texts. It responds to Michael Puett's call for scholars to learn from indigenous theories of non-Western cultures and to take them seriously as theory.[27] It uses the term "practice" not to suggest a dichotomy between practice and theory—what one does versus what one thinks—but to underscore the capaciousness of Ouyi's vision of religious activity. As Carl Bielefeldt notes, practices include not only rituals but also ethical observances and spiritual exercises.[28] The word "practice" also connotes a type of repeated activity or training, which reflects Ouyi's own estimation of such activities as means of cultivating bodhisattvahood and which also allows for a discussion of his writing as a type of religious practice. Because they entail certain assumptions about cosmology and soteriology, they are "religious practices." Analogous to the way Catherine Bell uses "ritualization" to describe "a way of acting that differentiates some acts from others,"[29] Ouyi underscores the fact that one should engage in such practices in a different way from ordinary activities, otherwise they are stripped of their efficacy.

Ouyi's religious practices entail more than saying—they entail doing, such as establishing a sacred space, making offerings, presenting prayers, engaging in prostrations, and participating in other types of activities.[30] When the practices do involve recitation of words or phrases, these are often fixed formulas or mantras, lending further force to the ritual frame. Only within ritualized settings can one properly summon Buddhas or bodhisattvas, who can then reveal past karma, eliminate present karma, or ensure a good future. The "doing"—the practice—in turn "does" something of its own, changing the state of those who perform it. Ouyi insists that each religious practice has the potential to transform the practitioner.

This transformation largely depends on three factors that characterize Ouyi's ritual theory. First is the notion of stimulus-response (*ganying*), a principle used to describe the relationship between practitioners and Buddhas or bodhisattvas, in which the former is able to "stimulate" (*gan*) a compassionate "response" (*ying*) from the latter. The concept of stimulus-response predates the arrival of Buddhism in China, appearing in Chinese cosmological and philosophical texts from the third century B.C.E. onward.[31] Described as "a theory of non-simultaneous, nonlinear causality"[32] by some scholars, and "a kind of sympathetic vibration in the force field of *qi* that pervades the cosmos"[33] by others, stimulus-response assumes that events taking place simultaneously, though separated in space, can subtly affect each other. Because everything in the universe was understood to consist of *qi* (which literally means "breath" or "air"), including our thoughts, feelings, and consciousness, they could resonate with each other. The paradigmatic example of *ganying* was the harmonic resonance between musical instruments—for example, when a string on one instrument was plucked and the corresponding string on a separate instrument would vibrate.[34] Chinese Buddhists used the term *ganying* alongside *baoying* ("retribution") and *yinguo* ("cause and effect") to refer to the functioning of karma—namely effects that derived from each action.[35] The notion of *ganying* was developed by Tiantai scholars such as Zhiyi (538–597), who specified that the ability to stimulate a response derived from the power of the impetus (*ji*), which depended on the practitioner's karmic accumulation of good deeds. As Robert Sharf notes, Zhiyi used stimulus-response to explain the efficacy of Buddhist ritual practice, identifying stimulus-response with causes and conditions (*yinyuan*).[36]

A second important concept in Ouyi's ritual theory is the crucial role that emotions play in religious practice, especially those of shame (*cankui*) and sincerity (*cheng*). In early China, emotions were understood to be movement of *qi* in response to external phenomena, and the sense of shame was considered a natural human manifestation.[37] Rituals were understood as effective means of guiding such emotions and improving one's dispositional responses to those surrounding them.[38] Sincerity appears in a variety of Chinese philosophical texts—especially neo-Confucian ones—to describe an honest or truthful stance toward one's nature as endowed by heaven.[39] For neo-Confucians, sincerity serves as a means of realizing the true nature of themselves, other humans, and the phenomenal world as a whole,[40] encapsulating the entire project of self-cultivation.[41] Ouyi emphasizes the importance of shame and sincerity when appealing to the mercy of Buddhas and bodhisattvas—only rituals performed with such dispositions will prove efficacious.

Ouyi also employs the distinction between "principle" (*li*) and "practice" (*shi*) to discuss the function of ritual; instead of prioritizing one over the other, Ouyi seeks to align the two in ritual activity. *Li* originally meant modifying an object according to its incipient patterns into an orderly form, as one might do when making jade implements from raw jade, but it gradually came to refer to the patterns or principles themselves.[42] For neo-Confucians such as Cheng Yi (1033–1107) and Zhu Xi (1130–1200), *li* and *qi* were understood to be two aspects of all phenomena, with *li* being "that which gives structure to its *qi*, directs its evolution over time, and defines its function in context."[43] In the Chinese Buddhist context, *li* was often viewed as synonymous with emptiness and distinguished from *shi*, which was understood to be activities, events, or things experienced as discrete items. Emptiness entailed the absence of self-nature, and for Chinese Buddhist traditions such as Huayan and Tiantai, it implied "nonobstruction" between differentiated parts of existence.[44] Ouyi similarly interprets *li* as emptiness, but he suggests that *shi* play an equally important role in the performance and efficacy of rituals.

Although ritual manuals convey this vision for how one should engage in such religious practices, his writing about his own religious practice discloses the extent to which Ouyi felt he upheld or violated these normative expectations. For that reason, I focus especially on his personal writings contained in the *Lingfeng Zonglun*, a compilation edited by Ouyi's disciple Jianmi Chengshi (died 1678). It consists of ten fascicles or scrolls (*juan*) that contain Ouyi's votive texts (*yuanwen*), Dharma talks, responses to questions, lectures, tea talks, miscellaneous writing, letters, discourses, discussions, historical accounts of texts and events, introductions, prefaces and postscripts, commentaries on certain events or occasions, biographies, congratulatory remarks, *stūpa* inscriptions, funerary texts, inscriptions, admonitions, prayers for rain, words of praise, and poems. Unfortunately, Jianmi Chengshi often removed their dates of composition, and he also frequently excised the names of other clerics or laypeople who performed rituals with Ouyi. Nevertheless dates remain for certain texts—especially his votive texts—which allows for speculation about possible developments in this particular practice in the fourth chapter.

The *Lingfeng Zonglun* is contained within the reprinted *Ming ban jiaxing dazangjing* (Ming edition of the Jiaxing Canon)[45] published from the canon at Jingshan and available in the Chinese Buddhist Electronic Text Association (J36nB348), and it is also included in the *Ouyi dashi quanji* (Collected works of Great Master Ouyi).[46] Because previous scholarship on Ouyi cites according to the former text, but the latter will likely be cited more frequently in future scholarly work, both citations are included here.[47] As we will see, the writings contained in the *Lingfeng Zonglun* show an overriding concern with karma: how one deciphers it, how one repents for it and evokes the power of bodhisattvas and Buddhas to erase it, and how one might change it by pursuing the path of bodhisattvahood.

OUYI'S UNDERSTANDING OF KARMA

In contemporary parlance, karma is typically understood as a mechanistic cause and effect relationship between previous or present actions and future repercussions. This is reflected in the definition of karma in the *Oxford English Dictionary Online*: "In Buddhism, the sum of a person's actions in one of his successive states of existence, regarded as determining his fate in the next; hence, necessary fate or destiny, following as effect from cause."[48] Karma is thus portrayed as iron clad, with each bodily, verbal, or mental action inevitably having an effect on one's later existence; a common contemporary Chinese translation for karma as simply "cause and effect" (*yinguo*) reflects this understanding.

However, one should be circumspect before assuming a mechanistic view of karma; it has expansive connotations that cannot be reduced to cause and effect. In technical Chinese Buddhist texts, karma is translated as "activity" or "action" (*ye*) or transliterated as *jiemo* from the Sanskrit term *karman*, meaning action or deed.[49] One of the foremost Chinese Buddhist dictionaries defines "karma" (*ye*) as bodily, verbal, or mental activities that can be classified as good (*shan*; Skt. *kuśala*) or bad (*e*; Skt. *akuśala*)[50] and that result in the corresponding retribution, unless they are indeterminate actions (*wuji ye*), which are neither good nor evil and not strong enough to bring about any effect.[51] Although this would suggest a uniform vision of karma as a type of retributive causality, underlying points of contention or debate surface when one reads further in parentheses "maturation," suggesting an organic understanding of karma. It also notes, "The sutras emphasize that while karma can be eliminated in an instant, the karma has already planted seeds in one's mental consciousness that will stimulate karmic retribution, and that owing to these seeds one will receive retribution."[52]

The entry speaks to a complexity we also see in Ouyi's writing: sometimes he suggests that certain religious practices can result in the instant elimination of karma, although at other times he suggests that karmic retribution will still come to fruition. In fact, this seeming contradiction can be explained by paying close attention to the genre and function of a particular ritual text. For example, Ouyi's discussion of karma in mechanistic terms in his divination texts stems largely from the requirements of the genre: the notion that one can divine one's previous karma assumes a correlation between past karmic causes and their impending effects. However, he espouses both views of karma in his repentance texts, where the tension between the mechanistic and organic understanding of karma plays a crucial role in how Ouyi understands the efficaciousness of repentance. By affirming that one will suffer karmic retribution, one gives rise to a state of shame and sincerity that can stimulate Buddhas and bodhisattvas to compassionately respond and change one's karma. When Ouyi envisions himself as a future bodhisattva in his votive texts, he extends compassion to those who are successful in stimulating such gracious responses as well as those who are less fortunate, by vowing to eliminate the karma of sentient beings, or in the event that they cannot escape their karma, vowing to substitute in their stead. This nuance and complexity in Ouyi's understanding of karma would be lost if one ignored the textual dimensions of his ritual corpus.

Ouyi's representation of karma remains unique among his contemporaries in late imperial China. Although there have been relatively few analyses of karma in Chinese Buddhism[53]—unlike the voluminous scholarship on karma in Indian Buddhism[54]—these studies emphasize that retributive notions of karma became prominent in late imperial China, when they merged with early Chinese notions of retribution. Jan Yün-hua identifies three features of early ideas of retribution: first, life and death were the decree of heaven (*ming*); second, a person's morality or virtue could possibly (though not inevitably) influence heaven; and third, retribution could result in a shortened lifespan or an unnatural death, or could affect one's family and descendants.[55] Although early Chinese Buddhists such as Xi Chao (circa 331–373) and Huiyuan (334–417) argued that karmic effects did not extend to relatives, seventeenth-century narratives portrayed the exact opposite—that one's relatives could suffer the consequences for one's own action—and suggested a correspondence between actions and their retribution.[56]

However, earlier Chinese Buddhists allow for more ambiguous notions of karmic retribution. Although Jan acknowledges potential misunderstandings of Huiyuan's use of the term "subtle" (*shen*) to describe the functioning of karma, Huiyuan's characterization of karma as subtle and mysterious suggests a complexity to the relationship between cause and effect. Huiyuan writes, "Ignorance is the abyss of illusionment; desire is the house of bondages. When these two principles wander jointly, they create invisible (*ming*) and subtle (*shen*) functions."[57] He suggests that the workings of karma are inscrutable, and although he admits a relationship between karmic cause and effects, it is not one of simple correspondence. Huiyuan writes, "The mind takes good and bad deeds as the cause, retribution takes crime and virtue as the outcome, (and their relation is like) form and its shadow, sound, and its echo."[58] Huiyuan's choice of metaphors—those of form and shadow, or sound and echo—suggests a more ambiguous relationship than a direct correspondence between cause and effect. Without the sun, forms do not cast shadows; likewise, barriers can muffle the echoes of sounds. Implicit in such metaphors is the idea that if one cultivates certain conditions one can intervene in the workings of karma. Similarly, Xi Chao portrays karma in his *Fengfa yao* (Essentials of religion) as a "hidden response" (*youdui*) with a "mysterious structure" (*minggou*). Xi Chao writes, "Ordinary thoughts that appear in the mind in every instant of thought receive retribution; although the phenomena has not yet taken form, there is a hidden response and mysterious structure."[59] Although he recognizes that thoughts and intentions have future repercussions, Xi Chao describes this karma as "hidden" and "mysterious."

Such articulations of karma differ from what we find in later writings—especially in the sixteenth and seventeenth centuries—where karma is typically depicted as a strict retributive causality, with an exact correspondence between past actions and future rewards or punishments.[60] Chinese Buddhist narrative literature predates this period, and there have been studies of karma in "miracle tales" (*baoji*),[61] "strange writings" (*zhiguai*),[62] "precious scrolls" (*baojuan*),[63] and narratives of dependent origination (*yuanqi*) from Dunhuang.[64] However, Stephen Teiser identifies a shift in the prominence of notions of karmic retribution following the Tang dynasty, when rituals such as the Ghost Festival (*yulan pen*), based on the sutra describing how Mulian seeks to rescue his mother from purgatory, became popular because of its vivid depictions of the torment of purgatory and its ties to mortuary practices.[65] The systematization and bureaucratization of the underworld into various courts and hells presided over by officials encouraged the idea that "fate and retribution could be figured and the divinatory arts could be practiced."[66]

A particular group of texts called "ledgers of merits and demerits" (*gongguo ge*) and "morality books" (*shanshu*) claimed to enable late imperial Chinese elites to master their fate by following specific guidelines for behavior.[67] Because such texts gave people control over their social destiny and a clearly defined moral code to follow, they were quite popular.[68] Such texts promoted the idea that people could "create their own destiny" (*zaoming*) by improving their moral status through good deeds. Urging readers to draw up an account of their merits and demerits each day, tally and record the results each month, and calculate the balance at the end of the year, ledgers encouraged a quantified measurement of morality in particular, concrete actions.[69] As scholars have noted, this promoted a type of "management of moral capital"[70] or "stockpiling of merit"[71] that differed significantly from earlier morality books, which portrayed karma as the fruit of many lifetimes and encouraged people to perform acts of devotion and entrust themselves to compassionate bodhisattvas who might relieve them of their karmic burden. Ledgers implied that one could influence and predict one's destiny and karmic retribution, and the eminent Buddhist monk Yunqi Zhuhong went so far as to assign relative weight to each action, with points from one to one hundred, in his *Zizhi lu* (Record of self-knowledge).[72]

Alongside these texts quantifying karma and fixing morality into controllable merits and demerits, we find an alternative understanding of fate and karma in Ouyi's writings. He occasionally portrays karma retributively as "cause and effect" (*yinguo*), but more frequently he adopts the term "action" or "activity" (*ye*) to discuss karma. For example, Ouyi uses the term *yinguo* six times in the first fascicle of the *Lingfeng Zonglun*, whereas he uses the term *ye* one hundred times. Not only is *ye* a more capacious term, but it avoids the retributive connotations of "cause and effect." In Ouyi's writing, "action" appears in general combinations such as "previous action" or is characterized as good or evil: "good action," "pure action," "evil action," "defiled action," "deluded action," and "dark action." He frequently uses the term in the compound "fixed karma" (*dingye*), connecting it to specific acts, especially breaking the five precepts by killing, stealing, being licentious, telling lies, or criticizing the Three Jewels of the Buddha, Dharma, and Sangha. Karma can be divided into various types—karma of the present in which present activity reaps retribution in the present, karma of the next life in which one's present activity reaps retribution in the next life, and karma of later lives in which retribution follows the third rebirth or later—all of which have a fixed duration; thus they can also be called "fixed karma" (*dingye*), whereas karma that does not have a fixed period is called "unfixed karma" or "karma whose retribution is not fixed."[73]

The term "action" (*ye*) allows Ouyi a certain degree of flexibility when it comes to determining the workings of karma—enabling him to portray karma as more mysterious and malleable than mechanical. It also accords with his promotion of religious practice as essential when responding to previous karma. Because karma is an "action" or "activity," any rectification of karma would call for religious activities. When Ouyi does discuss the "result" or "fruit" (*guo*) of karma, he either says simply, "one receives the fruit," or he specifies that it is the "fruit of suffering," "the fruit of truth," "the fruit of sages," "the ultimate fruit," or "the fruit of the Way." Whereas Ouyi clearly identifies actions as good or bad, he remains more ambiguous about the fruits of such action. Although evil actions clearly reap the fruit of suffering, and good actions eventually lead to the fruit of Buddhahood, he does not enumerate an explicit correspondence between actions and results. In this way, Ouyi suggests karma is a complex process, dependent on a variety of factors in addition to the action itself.

Although a mechanistic understanding of karma leaves people who have committed mistakes with no other recourse than to anticipate with dread what awaits them in future lives, Ouyi envisions a karmic process that allows for intervention of Buddhas and bodhisattvas. As an individual who battled illness throughout his life and engaged in what he later viewed as morally reprehensible conduct during his youth, Ouyi had a palpable sense of the bad karma he had accrued in his lifetime. Several passages in his writing illustrate Ouyi's anxiety about his future punishment, yet there are also instances in which he claims that repentance has the power to eliminate karma entirely, suggesting that one might be able to erase past actions instead of suffering their karmic consequences with the help of Buddhas and bodhisattvas. These beings have the power to erase karma, and Ouyi insists that one can summon them only in specific ritual contexts: one must engage one's body as "living karma"—using body, speech, and mind to stimulate the gracious response of Buddhas and bodhisattvas—if one hopes to reveal past karma, redress present karma, or benefit future karma.

PREVIOUS SCHOLARSHIP

This book puts itself in dialogue with scholars of late imperial China, Buddhist studies, religious studies, and comparative religious ethics. It builds on Shengyan's in-depth and encyclopedic account of Ouyi's life and thought, but it presents a different characterization of Ouyi based on his religious practice. Shengyan argues that Ouyi belongs to Tathāgata Chan (*rulai chan*)[74]—as opposed to the Chan of his time that emphasized *gong'an* (Jpn: *kōan*) practice—based on the fact that Ouyi took tonsure with the Chan Master Xueling, relied on the *Śūraṃgama Sutra* to attain enlightenment, admired the Chan figures Yongming Yanshou (904–975) and Zibo Zhenke (1543–1603), read the Vinaya Canon from a Chan position, adopted a Chan style of Pure Land worship, and used the *Śūraṃgama Sutra* as the basis of his philosophical thought about Chan and Pure Land.[75] Ch'en Ying-shan has raised several persuasive criticisms of Shengyan's position, arguing that one cannot take sutras to be an indication of doctrinal affiliation, nor can one compartmentalize Ouyi's thought from his practice because he viewed the two as being one and the same.[76] Although Shengyan admits the *Śūraṃgama Sutra* was important in Chan and Huayan traditions, he argues that because Ouyi drew more from the *Śūraṃgama Sutra* than the Lotus Sutra, he was therefore more oriented toward Chan than Tiantai; however, Ch'en points out that Tiantai was tied to a number of philosophical schools following the Tang and Song dynasties and that the *Śūraṃgama Sutra* was studied by a number of schools. Iwaki Eiki similarly notes that Ouyi's breadth of studies complicates any attempt to fix him within a particular tradition, and that although Ouyi supersedes Tiantai, it does not make sense to identify him as Chan.[77] Iwaki insists that Ouyi's influences are broader than either tradition, that Ouyi's ideas of "harmonizing the traditions" (*zhuzong ronghe*) transcend such distinctions.[78]

I show how Ouyi drew from various religious texts and traditions in his religious practice, which complicates any attempt to restrict him to a particular school or tradition. Unfortunately, as Ch'en notes, the foremost issue in previous scholarship on Ouyi has been determining whether or not he should be categorized within the Tiantai tradition.[79] Ouyi himself sought to eliminate such distinctions over the course of his life, and Ch'en describes Ouyi's intellectual development as moving from Chan, to Vinaya, to Teachings, and finally Pure Land.[80] However, movement implies that he left one tradition for another; a more apt analogy would be that of a repertoire: never discarding his Chan heritage, his concern for the Vinaya, or his Tiantai influence, but instead employing each as appropriate. This allows scholars to analyze why he may have drawn from certain traditions at certain places and times, and it challenges the notion that Ouyi "returned" to Pure Land at the end of his life. As we will see, his Pure Land practice in his youth differs from that which he pursued late in life.

With the exception of Shengyan's work, other scholarship on Ouyi has focused entirely on doctrinal matters.[81] The majority of articles focus on distinctive features of Ouyi's commentaries on particular sutras[82] or his Vinaya thought,[83] and there have been several studies of Ouyi's engagement with non-Buddhist thought, analyzing his commentaries on Confucian texts[84] or his writings against the Jesuits.[85] By contrast, this book examines karma as it is lived rather than as it is theorized. It considers how Ouyi understood karma as integral to his religious practice, his ethical outlook, and his bodily experience.

BOOK OVERVIEW

The book is divided into five chapters, each of which addresses a particular religious practice: writing, divination, repentance, vows, and bodily practices. Each chapter first offers a diachronic perspective about the history of each religious practice in the context of Chinese Buddhism and then provides a synchronic analysis of that practice based on close reading of Ouyi's writings.

The first chapter examines Ouyi's autobiography, in which he eschews identification with particular institutions (Buddhist or Confucian) of his day and instead broadly appeals to ritual and writing as means of religious development. It considers later biographical portraits of Ouyi, noting how some actually work against Ouyi's vision of an inclusive religiosity and seek to identify him as a master within particular Buddhist traditions. It then proposes an alternative interpretation of his autobiography as a karmic narrative that illustrates how Buddhist practitioners have the ability to change their karma through religious practices—including reading and writing.

The second chapter considers Ouyi's use of divination as a diagnostic technique for determining past karma. On the one hand, it reflects mechanistic views of karmic retribution, but on the other hand, reliance on such divination devices suggests a degree of opacity to karma and limits on one's ability to know oneself.

The third chapter examines Ouyi's repentance rituals (*chanhui*) that seek to extinguish karma. The crux of the ritual lies at the point in which Ouyi calls upon practitioners to recognize their inability to change their own karma and to admit their reliance on the power of salvific bodhisattva figures. He appeals to Dizang in particular as savior of the penitent.

The fourth chapter analyzes votive texts (*yuanwen*) in which Ouyi envisions his future potential as a bodhisattva. Engaging the future in a way that complements divination as a technique for diagnosing karma in the past and repentance rituals as a means of redressing karma in the present, votive texts allow Ouyi to present two visions of himself as a bodhisattva: one that can eliminate karma, and the other that can substitute on behalf of sentient beings in their specific retribution.

The fifth chapter explores various types of bodily practices that Ouyi engages in, including "filial slicing" to heal ailing relatives, burning his head and arms, and writing texts in his blood. His practices reflect diverse constructions of bodies as gifts from parents that require repayment, as products of previous karma, as sources of suffering, and as vehicles for karmic transformation. He advocates practices aimed at extracting practitioners from the cycle of birth and death and transforming their bodies into those of bodhisattvas. By suggesting that illness not only signals karmic retribution but also provides an opportunity for perfecting bodhisattva virtues of forbearance, Ouyi portrays bodies not only as sources of suffering but also vehicles for realizing the truth of suffering and thereby escaping such suffering.

ONE
KARMA AS A NARRATIVE DEVICE IN OUYI'S AUTOBIOGRAPHY

My vows are unfulfilled; for now I await later [beneficial] conditions (yuan). Once in my life I said, "Like a square piece entering a round hole, commentaries from the Han and Song dynasties are plentiful, but the teaching of the mind of the sages is unclear. Like water added to milk, the [Commentary on the Monk's] Behavior According to [the Four-Part Vinaya] has been written but study of the Vinaya has declined. Like a hole drilled into primordial chaos, discourse records circulate freely yet Chan is in shambles. Like someone who treats a critical illness with an outdated prescription, [Zhiyi's] Doctrine of the Four Teachings is transmitted but Tiantai is obscured. For this reason, whether it is Confucianism, Chan, Vinaya, or the Teachings, everyone considers it strange or hate it like an enemy." I smile and say, "Only Śākyamuni and Dizang know me; only Śākyamuni and Dizang judge me. I drift away alone, the circumstances of my death unknown."
—Ouyi Zhixu[1]

THESE ARE the closing remarks of Ouyi Zhixu in his autobiography, which he completed in January 1653—two years before his death. They evoke a sense of uncertainty in the face of the vagaries of karma and rebirth, with his present conditions lacking and his future destiny unknown. They also encapsulate one purport of his autobiography: his eschewing of any identification with specific contemporary institutions (be they Buddhist or Confucian). Perceiving himself as inhabiting an age of religious decline, instead of binding himself to a contemporary institution or locating himself within a specific Confucian, Chan, Vinaya, or Tiantai lineage, Ouyi portrays himself as beholden to two figures—the historical Buddha Śākyamuni and the bodhisattva Dizang (Skt. Kṣitigarbha). The latter is known for the vow he makes to save sentient beings who have been relegated to hell. Ouyi thereby connects himself with the past (founding figure of the tradition) and the future (one who has vowed not to seek enlightenment until all hell-dwellers have been liberated) without identifying himself with a particular Buddhist lineage or tradition.

However, later biographies of Ouyi—largely based on his autobiography—undermine if not oppose this message. Whereas Ouyi depicts himself as a "jack of all trades" drawing from multiple religious beliefs, his biographers largely portray him as a master within specific Buddhist traditions. Although Shengyan (1930-2009) admits that Ouyi cannot be limited to a particular tradition because of his systematic integration of a variety of religious thought, he identifies Ouyi as a Chan cleric—but as a "Chan of the Tathāgatas" (*rulai chan*) rather than as a "Chan of the Patriarchs" (*zushi chan*) of his day.[2] Similarly, most of the scholarship on Ouyi has focused on how one might categorize him—as solely Tiantai or as an amalgamation of Tiantai and other traditions.[3] Why have scholars characterized Ouyi in a way that runs contrary to the underlying message of his autobiography? Although this characterization may be due to his biographers' social, political, or religious locations, it also stems from approaching his autobiography as a historical document, disregarding its literary dimensions. Reading the events depicted in his autobiography as historical data, scholars have overlooked its stylistic and rhetorical features.[4]

This chapter attends to Ouyi's autobiography as a text, examining what claims it makes and what audience it assumes. After comparing the parameters and goals of Chinese autobiography to Western autobiography, a close reading of Ouyi's autobiography suggests that he was most likely trying to convey a message of a broad, nonsectarian religiosity to his intended readers. This chapter concludes by offering a second interpretation that, unlike his later biographies, is faithful to Ouyi's own intentions. Ouyi broadly appeals to ritual and writing as means of spiritual cultivation. By reading, commenting on, and writing texts (including the autobiography itself), Ouyi seeks to connect himself to traditions of the past and readers of the future, while distancing himself from religious institutions of his time. Karma serves as a narrative device in Ouyi's autobiography, triggering his enlightenment experience and undergirding his religious practices thereafter.

AUTOBIOGRAPHY AND/OR AUTOHAGIOGRAPHY: QUESTIONS OF GENRE

Ouyi's autobiography draws from two genres of writing: Chinese biography and Buddhist hagiography. In premodern China, autobiography (*zizhuan*) largely modeled the conventions of biography, beginning with a person's name, parentage, and ancestral heritage and then detailing the various official positions that they held during their lifetime. Buddhist hagiography typically follows the life story of the Buddha and relates the religious development of an eminent figure from birth through enlightenment. Ouyi adopts conventions from each genre to create a narrative that positions him within Confucian and Buddhist traditions.

The goals and stylistic parameters of Chinese autobiography differ markedly from Western autobiography. The former can be traced to the biographical writings of Sima Qian (ca. 145–90 B.C.E.), who wrote the first comprehensive history of China, while the latter typically takes Augustine's *Confessions* as its precedent and emerged as a genre in the late eighteenth and early nineteenth centuries. Philippe Lejeune, one of the foremost scholars of autobiography in the West, has defined the genre as "the retrospective prose narrative that someone writes concerning his own existence, where the focus is his individual life, in particular the story of his personality."[5] He argues that an "autobiographical pact" governs such texts, wherein the author explicitly proposes to the reader a narration about himself or herself.[6] It is the self-referential gesture that remains central and primary; instead of authentically or verifiably resembling some extratextual reality, Lejeune views autobiography as "a fiction produced under special circumstances."[7] Northrop Frye suggests that autobiographies are an important type of prose fiction that he called "the confession form, following St. Augustine, who appears to have invented it, and Rousseau, who established a modern type of it."[8] Although there are other approaches to the autobiographical genre in the West,[9] in general, it is understood to be a self-conscious narrative of self-expression tied to notions of "individuality" and "personhood."

Though some scholars maintain that one can find this type of autobiography in China dating to the sixteenth and seventeenth centuries,[10] such attempts to equate Chinese and Western autobiographical writing overlook significant differences. These scholars point to various self-referential writings to insist that autobiography is not strictly a Western phenomenon.[11] For example, Yves Hervouet argues that there are four primary sources of autobiography: autobiographical prefaces (*zixu*) in which the author tells about his or her life, travel journals or diaries, autobiography proper (*zizhuan*), and annalistic biography (*nianpu*)—a chronological list of life events—that he notes is "a historical *genre* specific to China."[12] However, even though one can find writing that expresses the self in China, this "self" differs markedly from Western notions of an autonomous individual.[13] In fact, Chinese autobiography often highlights social and cultural markers that Western autobiography typically effaces; it reconstructs a self that is more of a public model than a personality. Chinese autobiographies seek to provide models of proper intellectual development for others to follow, which often entails embodying the norms of tradition or society and cultivating oneself (*xiushen*).[14] Some contemporary scholars have argued that Augustine's *Confessions* serves a similar didactic or exemplary function. They consider its role in spiritual formation—how the text leads the reader along a certain itinerary so he or she can make spiritual progress,[15] how it emphasizes spiritual exercises aimed at personal and social transformation,[16] or how it promotes study of scriptures—"re-reading" of memories in one's life—and self-examination as a means for disciplining the body and leading an ethical life.[17] However, these approaches remain the minority; most scholars emphasize the fundamental role "personality" plays in Western autobiography.

If we acknowledge that premodern Chinese autobiographies do not share Western notions of "personality" or "individuality," we can salvage the remaining characterizations of the genre and constructively apply them to the Chinese context. First, autobiography is indeed retrospective: authors usually write later in their lives, looking back from birth to the present, as is the case with Ouyi. They may not necessarily assume a trajectory or self-development over time, but they do narrate their life in hindsight; literati write after they have attained various official positions, clerics after they have accomplished certain religious achievements. Second, readers do expect the author and the principal character or narrator of the autobiography to be one and the same person. Finally, autobiography has a creative or fictional impulse, which tends to be overlooked in scholarship on Chinese autobiography. Although Chinese autobiographies do not necessarily follow Frye's "integrated pattern" or an evolutionary process of self-development,[18] nevertheless they highlight certain features or events in a person's life and downplay others. They are narratives reflecting particular concerns from later periods in life. Though they typically follow a chronology, this does not mean they are disinterested or are historically accurate accounts of a person's life. They may seem virtually indistinguishable from a diary because they recount one experience or event after another, without the overt linkage or cohesive development found in Western autobiographies. However, one cannot automatically conclude that these types of narratives mainly aim to impress or to gain respect by listing achievements.[19] In the case of Ouyi's autobiography, we will see that this episodic approach actually mitigates against attempts to pigeonhole him in a single lineage or group. Though later biographers do precisely that, they can accomplish this only by disclosing certain parts of the autobiography and by concealing others.

Ouyi's autobiography features standard elements of Chinese biography (zhuan), which rarely delves into subjective or personal elements but instead serves as a more didactic recording of events that can be verified by public records or by secondhand sources. Official biographies begin with what Wendy Larson has called "circumstantial references" to kinship, ancestry, real times and places, proper names, and official positions. Larson distinguishes these from the "impressionistic references" in premodern autobiographies that allude to leisurely literati activities such as reading and writing for pleasure, drinking, and the use of figural names instead of socially or genealogically determined ones.[20] "Circumstantial" elements define the self in relation to institutions and structures signifying status and power, while "impressionistic" ones identify the self with a tradition that is atemporal, intertextual, and detached from notions of ancestry or position.[21] As we will see, Ouyi adds "circumstantial" details about his family and ancestry, but he suppresses references that would tie him to a specific institution, instead using dreams, divination, and self-constructed epithets to envision a religious community surpassing sectarian boundaries. In lieu of associating himself with a particular lineage, he recounts his travels from one temple to another, suggesting a peripatetic lifestyle that downplays the institutional role that he played at Lingfeng Mountain.[22] Instead, he emphasizes the texts that he reads and writes, placing himself in an intertextual tradition similar to that which Larson finds in literati "impressionistic" references. His writing allows him access to a textual community beyond his present historical moment; his texts draw from past writing (including sutras, commentaries, liturgical texts, etc.) and extend into the future. By listing the texts he writes, Ouyi does not solely seek to impress the reader with his erudition and scholasticism, he also hopes that his works will find a future audience and will prompt further writing to continue the intertextual tradition.

Ouyi's autobiography also bears the traces of hagiography, or what Buddhist studies scholars have labeled religious or sacred biography.[23] Religious biographies portray the ideal type or saint through the events of his or her life. In the Buddhist context, they tell stories of those who have achieved enlightenment and thereby provide models for others to follow. In the Chinese Buddhist context, biographies of eminent monks (*gaoseng zhuan*) were not meant to be exhaustive or accurate accounts but instead to praise the conduct of the deceased in order to edify the living.[24] Originally modeled on the life of the Buddha, they describe the religious instruction and evolution of an individual. As we will see, Ouyi includes early childhood indicators of his future spiritual eminence—for example, he describes being conceived following the manifestation of the bodhisattva Guanyin in a dream and becoming a vegetarian at the early age of six.

Autobiography and sacred biography were understood as providing models for readers to follow; therefore, by drawing upon tropes in historical and hagiographic writing, Ouyi represents himself as an exemplar for Chinese literati and Buddhist clerics. Specifically, his life story exemplifies the dangers of sectarianism and the rewards of a broader, inclusive religiosity. Ouyi warns against sectarian affiliations such as neo-Confucianism, which led him as a youth to denounce Buddhism, and he promotes a religiosity that does not cling to parochial or particular boundaries but instead embraces various traditions, illustrated by his own journey through Confucian, Vinaya, Chan, Tiantai, and Pure Land traditions.

Portraying sectarianism as rampant in his age, Ouyi depicts himself as a legitimate inheritor of Confucian and Buddhist traditions but simultaneously dissociates himself from his contemporaries. To do so, he emphasizes "vertical" allegiances with his Confucian and Buddhist predecessors over "horizontal" ties with his consociates. As Janet Gyatso has pointed out in the case of Tibetan life-story writing, this emphasis of "vertical" over "horizontal" allegiances can serve a polemical agenda of asserting the religious achievements of a master and his or her lineage against rival schools.[25] Although Ouyi avoids affiliating himself with a particular lineage, his autobiography uses similar strategies to promote a nonsectarian religiosity for the future.

THE AUTHOR: THE "FOLLOWER OF EIGHT NEGATIONS"

The title of Ouyi's autobiography—*Babu daoren zhuan* ([Auto]biography of the Follower of Eight Negations)—encapsulates its purport by positioning Ouyi squarely within Buddhist and Confucian traditions but on the most general of terms. Ouyi adopts the epithet "Follower of Eight Negations" at the end of his life, and the "eight negations" (or "eight 'noes'") has three possible allusions. In Nāgārjuna's *Madhyamaka-kārikā* (*Zhonglun*) and the *Fanwang jing* (Skt. *Brahmajāla-sutra*) (*Sutra of Brahma's Net*), it refers to "neither arising nor ceasing, neither eternal nor impermanent, neither unitary nor different, neither coming nor going" (T. 1564.30.1b14-1b17; T. 1484.24.1010a1-1010a21). Ouyi ascribes a third connotation to his eight negations as he writes, "In the past, there was Confucianism, Chan, Vinaya, and the Teachings, but I dare not [study them]. Today there is also Confucianism, Chan, Vinaya, and the Teachings, but I disdain [to follow them]."[26] In this way, Ouyi dissociates himself from past and present Confucian and Buddhist traditions—the latter of which was divided into Chan, Vinaya, and Teachings during the Ming dynasty. Refusing to be categorized as Confucian or Buddhist (in any particular tradition), Ouyi instead espouses the most general religious identification of "follower" or "a person on the path" (*daoren*).

One could also argue that the title "Follower of Eight Negations" exemplifies a merging of Confucian and Buddhist traditions, if one interprets the first two characters as alluding to the "eight negations" of the Buddhist texts mentioned earlier and the last two characters of *daoren* appealing to Confucian notions of the "way" (*dao*) that date back to the beginning of Chinese intellectual history. The first two characters would thereby link Ouyi to early Indian and Chinese Buddhist traditions (through the two different texts) instead of the Buddhist institutions of his day, while the second two characters would mark Ouyi as a follower of ancient Chinese sages as opposed to one who "learns" or "imitates" (*xue*) neo-Confucianism. We see this parallel rhetorical construction of Ouyi appearing throughout the course of his autobiography, up to his thirty-fourth year (thirty-fifth *sui*), when it shifts into listing the years in which he wrote particular works.

Finally, one could argue that Ouyi's epithet "Follower of Eight Negations" positions him beyond past or present and into the future. By saying "no" to past and present religious institutions, Ouyi makes it difficult to consign him to a particular sect. His "no" to such identifications implies a "not yet" for the broad, nonsectarian religiosity that he promotes over the course of his autobiography. Although he briefly mentions his socially and genealogically determined names at the beginning of his autobiography, his repeated use of his figural name gives greater weight to this underlying message. We can better appreciate the significance of this choice if we compare it with the names he uses in his polemical writing against Christianity, the *Pixie ji* (Collected essays refuting heterodoxy), the preface of which dates to 1643.[27] In this collection, the introduction is attributed to a Buddhist monk named Dalang and the essays to a Zhong Zhengzhi, and an appendix includes correspondence between the author and a Chan Master Jiming. In fact, each name refers to Ouyi himself—his surname being Zhong, his given name (*ming*) being Jiming, his style name (*zi*) being Zhenzhi, and his alternative style name (*hao*) being Dalang. By using names of his childhood, young adulthood, and lay life before he took tonsure—and conspicuously avoiding his monastic name (Ouyi Zhixu)—Ouyi can position himself as a Confucian literatus appealing to an audience educated in the Chinese classics. Given that Ouyi could have similarly adopted a variety of epithets in his autobiography, his choice of "Follower of Eight Negations" should not be viewed as simply arbitrary.

Ouyi's autobiography elaborates the nonsectarian and inclusive religiosity implied in the epithet "Follower of Eight Negations," as it depicts his journey through Confucian and Buddhist traditions. To briefly summarize the text, after listing Ouyi's various secular names,[28] it recounts how his ancestors were originally from Henan province and later moved to Jiangsu province, where Ouyi was born in a town called Mudu Zhen, which was formerly the state of Wu, not far from Suzhou, which was the heart of literati scholastic activity in the Ming dynasty.[29] He attributes his birth to his father's recitation of the *dhāraṇī* of the bodhisattva Guanyin (Skt. Avalokiteśvara) for ten years, after which he dreams that Guanyin delivered him a son.

Continuing from his birth to his childhood, the autobiography relates how Ouyi becomes a vegetarian at age six[30] and studies under Confucian tutors at age eleven—specifically those of the Cheng-Zhu school that formed the basis of the examination system and an integral part of orthodoxy in late imperial China.[31] He drinks, writes many essays against Buddhism and Daoism, and dreams of meeting Confucius, and dreams of meeting Confucius and Yan Hui. At sixteen, after reading the preface to Zhuhong's *Record of Self-Knowledge* and *Jottings Under a Bamboo Window*, Ouyi burns all the tracts he had written. At nineteen, he has an enlightenment experience to the teachings of the mind (*xinfa*) of Confucius and Yan Hui while writing a commentary on the twelfth chapter of the *Analects*.[32]

The autobiography describes Ouyi's Buddhist enlightenment experience at Jingshan. After the death of his father, Ouyi hears Dizang's sutra and aspires to escape the world, focusing on Buddha-recitation (*nianfo*) at twenty-one and finally taking tonsure with a disciple of Hanshan Deqing at the age of twenty-three, after he has three dreams of Hanshan. Engaging in meditation, Ouyi has an enlightenment experience at twenty-four in which "his body, mind, and the outer world suddenly all disappeared. He then knew that his body came from beginningless time and perishes in the very spot it is born. It is only a shadow manifested by entrenched delusion. Instant to instant, thought-moment to thought-moment, it does not abide. It certainly is not born of a mother or father."[33] At twenty-seven, after the death of his mother and a grave illness, he again seeks rebirth in the Pure Land. Ouyi reads the Vinaya three times, and at thirty-one he draws lots to determine whether he should write commentaries according to Huayan, Tiantai, Weishi, or "a school of his own" (*zili zong*).[34] Ultimately, he draws the lot of Tiantai. The next year his two closest friends die, and he returns to Lingfeng and tries to obtain a copy of the Buddhist canon. Thereafter, Ouyi travels to various sites in the Jiangnan region writing texts.

His autobiography includes all of the elements of conventional Chinese and Buddhist biographies that would place him squarely within either tradition. After including biographical conventions such as his name, parentage, and ancestral heritage, he immediately ventures into hagiographic territory by suggesting that his birth was occasioned by devotional rituals and auspicious dreams by his father of the bodhisattva Guanyin. He relates how he followed ancient Chinese sages but then read Buddhist texts; how he dreamt of Confucius but then had a dream encounter with the Buddhist master Hanshan Deqing.[35] He even describes two enlightenment experiences—one Confucian and one Buddhist—that similarly encourage the reader to view him as having attained significant progress in both traditions. Thus Ouyi conscientiously models himself within Confucian and Buddhist traditions. His autobiography includes details about his Chan meditation practice, Vinaya learning, and his commentaries in various Teaching schools (Huayan, Tiantai, and Weishi) that imply he was exceptionally gifted within particular Buddhist traditions.

This parallel recounting of his religious development in Confucian and Buddhist traditions portrays Ouyi as exemplifying the "harmonization of traditions" (*zhuzong ronghe*) and the "unity of the Three Teachings" (*sanjiao heyi*) that he espoused and widely promoted over the course of his lifetime. His decision to espouse a commentarial tradition based on drawing lots instead of lineage ties, meditative experiences, or doctrinal reasons suggests that such "traditions" (*zong*) could be understood as not only compatible but also interchangeable. The term *zong* is generally translated as "school"—which has generated scholarly debate about the degree to which one can identify strictly defined "schools" of Chinese Buddhism[36]—but here it might be better rendered as "school of thought" or "position." By including the possibility of establishing his own *zong*, and drawing the Tiantai lot but refusing to become a member of the Tiantai lineage, Ouyi implies that *zong* could be created and adopted without a founder, lineage, or exclusive affiliation.

The events that Ouyi narrates in his autobiography become evidence in support of his criticism of sectarianism and of the promotion of syncretism in late imperial Chinese Buddhism. Just as he begins his autobiography by describing himself as a "Follower of Eight Negations," he ends his narrative by lamenting how his contemporaries have not understood or upheld the Confucian teachings, Vinaya texts, Chan records, and Tiantai doctrines. Ouyi portrays himself as isolated and as biding his time until there are fruitful conditions for his religious practice. Implicit in Ouyi's criticism is the assumption that he *has* fathomed the depths of Confucianism and Buddhism, and that as a result, he stands apart from his contemporaries and is temporally removed from his predecessors.

If we consider his autobiography in light of this message, we find that seemingly insignificant details (such as long lists of commentaries) actually serve an important function. The same year that two close Dharma friends pass away, he first enters Lingfeng and seeks to obtain a copy of the canon; only afterward does Ouyi detail the dates, locations, and titles of his writing.[37] Having lost the company of family and friends, Ouyi turns toward an intertextual community and seeks guidance from texts. Just as he identifies reading Zhuhong as his entry into Buddhism, writing connects him to former writers and future readers. By locating himself outside of any particular tradition, Ouyi can (and does) write commentaries on texts from a variety of traditions. Although he laments the corruption of contemporary religious institutions at the conclusion of his autobiography, it is precisely because he positions himself as an outlier that he can espouse and encourage such a broad harmonization and unification of teachings.

TROPES: DREAMS, DIVINATION, DEATH

If we examine some of the prominent themes in Ouyi's autobiography and analyze their poetic instead of referential function, we find they serve as literary devices connecting and separating Ouyi from lineages, traditions, and communities. On a figurative level, dreams, divination, and death represent how threads are tied, broken, and bound again. In this way, the themes and figures of the autobiography pertain to its underlying message, showing how a person's connection to sects or to groups is more fluid than fixed, changeable rather than predetermined. There is a kind of imaginative consistency—what Hayden White calls a "tropology" of imaginative discourse—at play, as the various tropes draw attention to how associations are made and severed.[38] But dreams, divination, and death also symbolize that which is beyond Ouyi's control, and although they figure prominently in the beginning of his narrative, they gradually give way to themes of ritual and writing, which fall squarely within the realm of Ouyi's control and responsibility.

Ouyi presents his life as evidence in support of his idea of harmonizing Buddhist traditions (Chan, Vinaya, Tiantai, and Pure Land) and unifying Buddhist and Confucian teachings. His life story illustrates how one might draw from various traditions in the course of one's religious development and how associations that initially seem most fixed—such as one's parents, education, or lineage—can form or dissolve unexpectedly. Altogether we find four deaths, five dreams, and one divination recounted in his autobiography. His father's dream occasions his birth, while Ouyi's first dream links him with the Confucian tradition. The death of his father prompts Ouyi to engage in Pure Land practice. He then dreams of Hanshan Deqing and takes tonsure with one of his disciples in a Chan lineage. The death of his mother induces Ouyi to again seek birth in the Pure Land. Engaging in divination to determine a style of commentary on a Vinaya text, he chooses the lot of Tiantai. The next year his two closest friends pass away, occasioning a definitive turn toward reading and writing. Thus we see how death, dreams, and divination serve as tropes to connect or to dissociate himself from his family, from Pure Land, Chan, Vinaya, and Tiantai traditions, and from Buddhist and Confucian traditions.

Dreams in particular are vehicles for connecting Ouyi with Confucian figures and Buddhist teachers who are temporally or geographically remote.[39] Although his father's dream provides auspicious signs surrounding Ouyi's birth that indicate his religious potential, his own dreams—which appear before his enlightenment experiences—function as evidence of his religious progress.[40] Dreams are common tropes in religious biographies, as Serinity Young has observed: "the biography confirms the prophecy of dreams by dramatizing their fulfillment while prophetic dreams confirm that it is the biography of someone worthy, someone who possesses religious authority or charisma."[41] Not only do such dreams serve to confer authority or charisma on Ouyi, but they also enable him to establish ties with Confucius and Hanshan Deqing that would otherwise be impossible.

Dreams were an established part of the cultural repertoire for Confucian literati and Buddhist monks alike in late imperial China. Not only is there a lengthy history of dreams in Buddhist biographies,[42] but we also find instances of Ouyi's contemporaries dreaming of Confucius.[43] Dream interpretation and the sighting of portents in dreams became quite sophisticated cultural forms and were widely reported in the sixteenth and seventeenth centuries,[44] appearing not only in drama and fiction (classical and vernacular) but also in scholarly treatises, informal essays, autobiographical writings, poetry, and even in paintings and woodblock illustrations.[45] Stimulated by the growth of the publishing industry, several handbooks on dream interpretation were compiled during this period.[46] Although there were certainly competing theories of explanation for dreams,[47] Ouyi draws on long-standing views of dreams having prognosticatory power and enabling communication with gods and deceased people.[48]

Dreams are among the many parallels between the autobiographies of Ouyi and of the eminent Buddhist monk Hanshan Deqing (1546–1623), suggesting that Ouyi may have used the latter's autobiography as a model for his own. Just as Ouyi uses dreams to connect himself with Hanshan, Hanshan includes dream encounters with a Buddhist master in his autobiography.[49] Hanshan describes how his mother dreamt that the bodhisattva Guanyin brought a baby boy to her doorstep—much like Ouyi described the dream of his father.[50] Just as Ouyi recounts burning his Confucian writings to concentrate on recollection of the Buddha (*nianfo*) when he was twenty-one, Hanshan says that he burnt his books and writings at the age of eighteen to concentrate on the same devotional practice, and he soon dreamt of the Buddha Amitābha.[51]

In short, the trope of dreams allows Ouyi to "imagine a community" that does not follow established lineages or restrict itself to particular traditions.[52] Just as the construction of lineages and establishment of canons involve imagining certain aspects of the past and creatively forgetting others,[53] Ouyi likewise uses dreams to envision a community that had not materialized in his lifetime. Orphaned in his twenties, Ouyi repeatedly expresses frustration over the dearth of worthy teachers to instruct him in his religious development, and he positions himself as an outlier among his contemporaries. Although he certainly studied with teachers and friends, he emphasizes that these relationships did not result in a religious community. At forty-two, Ouyi writes, "It has been nineteen years since I became a monk in 1622; I studied with impermanent teachers and made impermanent friendships."[54] Elsewhere he says, "My teachers were of the past, not the present."[55] When he later constructs a list of those people whom he considers his teachers, it skips several decades and ends with Yongming Yanshou (904–975) from the Five Dynasties and Yunqi Zhuhong, Zibo Zhenke, and Hanshan Deqing from the Ming.[56] Although his later texts occasionally connect him to Hanshan Deqing via Master Xueling (a disciple of Hanshan Deqing with whom Ouyi took tonsure) or via letters exchanged between the two of them that were also facilitated by Master Xueling, his earlier texts refer to his dream encounter with Hanshan Deqing and de-emphasize the role that Master Xueling played in Ouyi's spiritual formation.[57]

Writing enables Ouyi to collapse the past into his present; by linking himself to past figures such as Hanshan Deqing through literary tropes, Ouyi can form his own lineage back to the original disciples of the Buddha. This gives him legitimacy without tying him to a particular Buddhist tradition. In Ouyi's autobiography, his own life story provides the narrative frame for envisioning a community that is religiously diverse and nonsectarian in nature. Although he suggests that his relationships with teachers and friends have been short-lived and does not restrict himself to a particular school or tradition, he does espouse a harmonization and unification of teachings that he largely encounters through texts. His autobiography uses tropes of divination, dreams, and death to imagine a religious community that Ouyi suggests he rarely encountered in his own life but sought to bequeath to future generations of readers.

A MASTER OF NONE BECOMES MASTER OF MANY: LATER BIOGRAPHIES OF OUYI

Ouyi deliberately eschews identification with a single tradition in his autobiography; however, the breadth of his religiosity allows for considerable malleability by later generations of biographers. As in the case of autobiographies, we cannot view such biographical records as containing historically accurate material or overlook their underlying biases and agendas. Instead we must acknowledge the circumstances under which they were written and the aims of the communities who sponsored them.[58] As scholars John Kieschnick and James Benn have emphasized, biographies of eminent Chinese Buddhist monks formed a distinct genre (*gaoseng zhuan*) that did not seek to exhaustively or accurately portray a monk's life.[59] Benn writes, "The compilations are then not innocent and inert repositories of data; they were designed by their compilers to fulfill certain agendas and are highly selective and carefully arranged."[60] Likewise, in spite of Ouyi's promotion of a harmonization of various traditions and teachings in his autobiography, later biographers are quite selective in what they extract from his autobiography to support their characterizations of Ouyi.[61] When we examine how they incorporate the autobiography and other sources, the types of rhetoric they employ, and the aims they seek to accomplish by adding, eliminating, elaborating or borrowing certain elements of the narrative,[62] we find they reflect the different biases and selective criteria of their authors: Jianmi Chengshi (died 1678), Peng Xisu (Dharma name: Jiqing) (1740–1796), Yu Qian (died 1933), and Hongyi (1880–1942).[63]

Jianmi Chengshi's biography, written in the year of Ouyi's death (1655) with a further supplement in 1658, seeks to underscore his master's power and charisma in order to admonish his fellow disciples. First, it emphasizes the role that Ouyi played as master to his disciples at Lingfeng monastery, including a poem in which Ouyi reminisces, "There are about two or three disciples, they comfort my life-long thoughts."[64] Second, after recalling how Ouyi explicitly instructed his disciples to cremate him and to scatter his ashes to animals and fishes, it then recounts how the disciples disobeyed their master's will and instead erected a stupa at Lingfeng. Jianmi suggests lingering unease surrounding this decision and vows that he will "grind my own corpse in his stead to fulfill my teacher's great vows."[65] This leads him to explicitly exhort his fellow disciples to continue following Ouyi's teachings: "Do not [think that] on account of the fact that the body is not here now, it is acceptable to be disloyal to his mind!"[66] Jianmi addresses Ouyi's disciples in his biography; he reminds them of their relationship with their master while alive, chastises them for disobeying his last will and testament, and insists that they now remain faithful to their master's teachings. Jianmi's biography is also interesting because it suggests that he had a similar sense of heavy karma like his master. In the supplement from 1658, Jianmi laments, "Indeed, it is because our karma is heavy and thus we cannot cause sagely people to abide for a long time that the elder's transmission has ended."[67]

Later biographers treat Ouyi's autobiography in the same way as Ouyi's disciples treated his remains: they completely disregard his wishes and his insistence that he did not belong to an exclusive school. Peng Xisu's biography of Ouyi Zhixu in the sixth fascicle of his *Jingtu shengxian lu* (Record of Pure Land sages), written in 1783, effaces those elements of the autobiography that would challenge its portrayal of Ouyi as a Pure Land master who falls squarely within that tradition.[68] First, it not only excises those entries that would suggest ties with the Confucian tradition or with any other Buddhist tradition such as Chan or Tiantai, but it also omits details such as Ouyi's secular names and his ancestral heritage in order to further its sectarian goal of claiming Ouyi as an eminent Pure Land master. Second, it includes lengthy quotations from Ouyi's Pure Land votive texts and Dharma talks—these constitute three-fourths of the entire biography—to argue that "Buddha recollection" (*nianfo*) represents the supreme practice that completes all the perfections of a bodhisattva. Challenging the Chan criticism of Pure Land as merely an expedient teaching, Peng writes: "Only Ouyi said that the teaching of name-recitation (*risong foming*) was equal to this tradition of the Sudden and Perfect[ly Awakened] Mind (*yuandun xinzong*)."[69] Third, he not only portrays Pure Land practices as vehicles for attaining Chan goals, he also appropriates the Chan practice of "thorough examination [of nondiscursive thought]" (*canjiu*) as a Pure Land practice.[70] Thus Peng significantly alters Ouyi's autobiography to fit him within a sectarian paradigm, and it is this depiction of Ouyi that reigns supreme in contemporary China. When one travels to the sites that Ouyi visited over the course of his life, one finds that monks and abbots unanimously identify Ouyi as a Pure Land master, and this is also how he is introduced in standard monastic curricula.

Yu Qian's "Biography of Ouyi at Huayan Buddhist Temple on Mount Jiuhua at the Beginning of the Qing [Dynasty]," contained in the *Xinxu gaoseng zhuan siji* (New continued biographies of eminent monks in four collections) that was completed in 1923, emphasizes Ouyi's shortcomings as well as his strengths, painting a portrait of Ouyi that is less glowing but more human.[71] First, Yu offers a more plausible and realistic representation of Ouyi's life not by excising hagiographic elements but by adding details to render such episodes more credible. For example, he specifies that it was at his father's behest that Ouyi became a vegetarian at the age of six, a decision that would otherwise seem incredible for a six-year-old.⁷² Second, he relates Ouyi's misgivings about failing to uphold the precepts and his performance of divination to determine whether he still qualified as a monk, in which Ouyi reputedly drew the lot of a nonordained novice monk (*shami youpose*; Skt. *upāsaka-śrāmanera*).⁷³ Yu offers his biography as a message of hope for those who struggle with their own shortcomings. This becomes clear at the end of his biography, when he cites the following passage from Ouyi's writings: "Over the course of my life, I have committed serious mistakes, but fortunately I have known to struggle within myself. From head to toe my flaws are extensive, but fortunately I dare not conceal them. Through these seeds of shame, I can direct my thoughts to the Land of Bliss; through true speech, I hope to deliver a warning in many directions."⁷⁴ Not only does Yu's biography address an audience that transcends sectarian boundaries, but it also resembles the confessional approach one finds in Western autobiography and may have been influenced by this Western genre.

Hongyi's *Ouyi dashi nianpu* (Annalistic biography of the Great Master Ouyi), published in 1935, is notable for its comprehensive scope and for how it reflects aspects of Hongyi's own religious and personal life.⁷⁵ Hongyi shows concern for presenting a balanced and accurate portrayal of Ouyi, drawing from multiple sources, giving information about the textual history of sources such as Ouyi's personal writings (the *Lingfeng Zonglun*),⁷⁶ and including details excluded from the autobiography.⁷⁷ Yet he seems to be particularly interested in those elements of Ouyi's life that resonate with his own, noting the prominence of Dizang in Ouyi's religious life, the prevalence of Ouyi's ascetic practice, the repeated illness Ouyi suffers over the course of his life, and the significance of the Vinaya in Ouyi's religious life.⁷⁸ Hongyi does not present a sectarian view of Ouyi as exclusively a Vinaya master but instead echoes Jianmi's description of Ouyi first professing bodhisattva vows, then identifying the deficiency of Chan in not respecting the code of the Vinaya precepts (*poluotimucha*; Skt. *prātimokṣa*), focusing his efforts on the Vinaya and Teachings—especially five monks living together according to the Dharma, a project that was ultimately unsuccessful, and finally seeking rebirth in the Pure Land by "riding the wheel of his vows."⁷⁹ Insofar as he presents an expansive view of his religious thought and practice, Hongyi best approximates Ouyi's own depiction of his life. Hongyi's enthusiastic recommendation of Ouyi's writings to fellow clerics and lay practitioners in Republican China prompted a layman named Jiang Qian (1876–1942) to try to implement

Ouyi's vision of uniting Buddhist and Confucian traditions.[80] Embracing a nonsectarian harmonization of various traditions, Jiang becomes the reader that Ouyi addresses in his autobiography.

A KARMIC NARRATIVE

Ouyi's autobiography could also be read as an example of how one might live in the face of karma and respond to karmic obstacles—through reading, writing, and ritual. Ouyi concludes his autobiography by acknowledging that Śākyamuni and Dizang have the capacity to know and to judge his past actions, while he remains uncertain about his future—subject as it is to the vicissitudes of karma. Ouyi displays a heavy sense of karma throughout his writing, so it is not surprising that karma figures in his autobiography—for example, in his choice to adopt a vegetarian diet at the age of six. However, the way the text associates karma with writing and reading allows for interesting analysis of the connection between writing and ritual—or writing as ritual. In Ouyi's narrative, reading and writing play a central role in his spiritual development. Reading prompts Ouyi to commit the most heinous of transgressions (denouncing Buddhism), but it also triggers the most profound of conversions (accepting Buddhism) and occasions the height of virtuous action (promoting Buddhism). Specifically, a sectarian and divisive reading of the Confucian tradition espoused by the Cheng-Zhu school, which was considered orthodox in late imperial China, prompts Ouyi to write essays against "heterodox" (*yiduan*) Buddhist and Daoist traditions at the age of eleven. However, after reading Zhuhong's texts, Ouyi accepts Buddhism (symbolically depicted by Ouyi's burning of his anti-Buddhist tracts), and after reading Confucius's *Analects* he discovers a more inclusive religiosity centered on ritual practice. Although his writings as a youth aim at denouncing Buddhism (which he later equates with the heinous crime of destroying the sangha), his writings as an adult promote an acceptance of Buddhism and a more inclusive approach to religion.

Examining Ouyi's depiction of his realization of Confucian teachings and his Buddhist enlightenment experience, we can better appreciate why autobiography was a particularly appropriate vehicle for promoting a broader religiosity. As aforementioned, Ouyi describes having a "great awakening" (*dawu*) to the teachings of Confucius after writing a commentary on the verse from *Analects* 12.1. In this passage, a disciple asks Confucius about benevolence or goodness (*ren*).[81] The standard rendition of Confucius's response is: "To restrain the self and return to ritual is true goodness. If for a single day someone restrains the self and returns to ritual, the whole world will submit to goodness." However, although the majority of commentators, including those of the Cheng-Zhu school, adopted the phrase "restrain the self" (*keji*), Ouyi glosses it in a way that directly challenges this interpretation, going back to a Han dynasty commentary that had been obscured for over a millennium. In his discussion of the commentarial tradition on this passage, John Kieschnick notes how Ouyi criticizes Zhu Xi without mentioning him by name, adopting the gloss that had been obscured by the Cheng-Zhu interpretation.[82] Ouyi writes, "To be able of oneself to return to ritual is called goodness. As soon as one perceives the body of goodness (*renti*), then all under heaven immediately dissolves into the essence of goodness, and there is nothing beyond goodness to be obtained."[83]

Ouyi's choice to gloss *keji* as "to be able of oneself" is significant for several reasons. First, it directly challenges the Cheng-Zhu school, which adopted a divisive rather than inclusive approach to other religious traditions and which Ouyi laments having followed in his youth.[84] Second, it emphasizes the ability of Buddhist practitioners to choose their ritual practices. Ouyi seizes upon such practice as having the capacity to ethically transform the world. Finally, by extension, if global change comes from an individual decision to return to ritual, only an autobiography describing such a return could prompt a universal transformation for its readers. Ouyi can effect a comprehensive change in the way people approach religiosity only by showing how he himself overcame his previous sectarianism.

Similarly, Ouyi's Buddhist enlightenment experience underscores the role of karma and asserts its primacy over seemingly entrenched familial bonds. Again, it is a reading of Buddhist sutras that occasions his awakening. Ouyi reports perceiving a conflict between the notions of "Dharma nature" (*faxing*) as it appeared in the *Śūraṃgama Sutra* and "Dharma characteristics" (*faxiang*) from the *Cheng weishi lun*. He discusses the matter with one of his teachers who says, "You are mistaken when you say that there is only this body. Are not karmic consequences acquired already when one enters the womb?"[85] This prompts Ouyi to perspire in shame and to have great doubts, and he engages in intense meditation at Jingshan, where he says at one point, "my body, mind, and the outer world suddenly all disappeared. I then knew that my body came from beginningless time and perishes in the very spot it is born. It is only a shadow manifested by entrenched delusion. Instant to instant, thought-moment to thought-moment, it does not abide. It certainly is not born of a mother or father."[86] Ouyi comes to understand karma by reflecting on his own body. He ultimately sees that the body results from karmic causes and conditions instead of biological conception—it is not born of parents but of previous actions that were committed in a deluded state of consciousness. Considered alongside Ouyi's realization of the importance of choosing ritual practice, his Buddhist enlightenment calls attention to a person's bodily, mental, and verbal actions as that which determine one's later rebirth. Analogously, Ouyi cannot report dreams, deaths, or divination to encourage harmonization of religious teachings and traditions, for they are beyond his control. He must also highlight how he personally took responsibility for its promotion—his own karmic steps toward its realization. Again, the autobiographical genre is indispensable: only by narrating his own actions can Ouyi model how others might similarly promote a nonsectarian religiosity through their body, speech, and mind.

In this way, karma serves as a narrative device in Ouyi's autobiography. Scholars have noted how autobiography affords the opportunity to see how individuals extrapolate lessons about religious doctrine through tensions they negotiate in the course of living.[87] For Buddhists, this would include lessons about karma occasioned by the various obstacles and tensions they have faced in their life. In Ouyi's autobiography, his karmic activity largely consists of an engagement with texts: reading them, writing commentaries on them, or writing liturgical and philosophical texts based on them. As we have seen, texts play a seminal role in Ouyi's spiritual development as a youth; writing becomes fundamental in his adulthood. Following the death of his friends, Ouyi suggests he wrote prolifically—producing commentaries on Buddhist and Confucian texts, ritual liturgies, and philosophical treatises. He does not mention his polemical critique of Jesuit missionaries in China, quite possibly because it would run against his message of a broad and inclusive religiosity. However, writing clearly plays a crucial role in the latter half of his autobiography, supplanting the function that dreams and divination had in connecting him with teachers and traditions. Writing becomes the present link between his predecessors and future readers; just as Ouyi suggests that he realized the error of sectarianism through reading Zhuhong, Ouyi writes his autobiography in the hopes that his readers will appreciate the danger of sectarian divisions and instead promote a broader religiosity. However, he can impress on them its importance only by offering his own life story as an example—as a warning of what to avoid and as a model of what to aspire to. Writing becomes his ritual and his vehicle for karmic transformation.

Based on a close reading of Ouyi's autobiography, we have seen how Ouyi sought to convey a message of broad religiosity to his intended readers. However, biographers conveyed very different messages to their readers by portraying Ouyi as a master of Lingfeng Mountain or a master in the Pure Land tradition. We also considered an alternative interpretation of his autobiography, which emphasizes the capacity of Buddhist practitioners to change their karma by returning to religious rituals—including reading and writing. As we will see, Ouyi typically begins with a particular reading of a sutra or commentary before writing his own ritual texts. The next chapter examines his divination texts, which are largely tied to his anxiety and uncertainty about his reception of the precepts.

TWO
DIVINATION AS A KARMIC DIAGNOSTIC

> Repentance rituals generally disclose various transgressions of sentient beings, but because people have their own particular biases from previous karmic habits, the [Divination] Sutra says one should first engage in divination with wheel marks.
> —Ouyi Zhixu[1]

KARMA NOT only operates as a narrative device in Ouyi's autobiography but also serves as a hermeneutic in his ritual texts. In this passage, Ouyi distinguishes between repentance and divination rituals according to the types of karmic activity addressed by each. Mahāyāna Buddhist repentance rituals involve confession of sins from present and past lives but because of the difficulty of discerning the latter, they typically incorporate a general repentance of sins. By contrast, divination rituals enable one to specifically discern one's past transgressions. Ouyi emphasizes the fact that people inherit particular legacies of karmic habits (*yexi*) that have accumulated from previous karma; however, because of the opacity of such karma, they must rely on divination rituals to diagnose it.

Although Buddhist monastic codes formally prohibit divination, astrology, and fortune-telling by Buddhist monks,[2] Ouyi describes engaging in such activities throughout his life.[3] Shengyan considers Ouyi's practice of divination anomalous among Buddhist scholastics, but he does not elaborate on its possible significance for Ouyi, which is one of the main criticisms raised by Jan Yün-hua in his review of Shengyan's work.[4] In fact, divination serves as a karmic diagnostic for Ouyi, enabling him to determine his karmic status by identifying past sins, signaling spiritual potential, or indicating future rebirths. Divination not only offers insight into how Ouyi understands karmic causality and cosmology, but it also reflects his own values and spiritual aspirations. Far from being a superstitious or degenerate practice, Ouyi's use of "wheel marks" (lunxiang)—the sides of a type of die that face up after being spun—to determine his past karma and future potential makes sense if one appreciates that, for Ouyi, such "marks" or "characteristics" (xiang) are integral with one's "nature" (xing).

Ouyi's casting of lots illustrates the creativity of his approach to divination. He describes engaging in the practice on two occasions: at thirty-one, he casts lots to determine which Buddhist school of thought he should adopt for his commentary on the *Sutra of Brahma's Net*, and at thirty-four, he casts eight lots to determine his karmic status. Although the term that Ouyi uses for lot—*jiu*—was used from the thirteenth century onward, a more common term was *qian*, which could also serve for "prophecy" (*zhan*).[5] As Michel Strickmann argues, the tradition of drawing lots in Buddhism can be traced back to the fifth-century *Guanding jing* (Consecration sutra, T. 1331), which instructs readers to write 100 eight-line stanzas on a slip of bamboo or silk and then pick several from a pouch.[6] This text established a "canonical" precedent for drawing lots, which became a conspicuous practice in Chinese Buddhism by the thirteenth century.[7] What is exceptional in Ouyi's practice of drawing lots is that he describes making (*zuo*) his own lots (*jiu*) to be drawn. This allows him considerable flexibility in addressing his particular concerns and anxieties.[8]

Ouyi frequently engages in divination to address uncertainty about his reception and upholding of Buddhist monastic precepts. After receiving the *bhikṣu* precepts in front of an image of Zhuhong at Yunqi temple on January 28, 1624, and receiving the bodhisattva precepts at the same site on January 30, 1625,[9] Ouyi spent several years studying the Vinaya and wrote *Pini shiyi yaolüe* (Essentials of the Vinaya) in 1625.[10] When his mother passed away the following year, Ouyi went into a two-year retreat during which he suffered a serious illness; afterward, he composed several texts pertaining to the bodhisattva precepts and the Vinaya.[11]

Ouyi's reading of the Vinaya made him aware of the general neglect and disregard for monastic codes among his contemporaries and prompted him to question his own reception of the precepts before an image of Zhuhong instead of a more conventional reception in the presence of Vinaya masters. Although it is permissible to receive the precepts in front of an image of the Buddha if there are no Vinaya masters within a hundred *li* (approximately fifty kilometers), Ouyi not only received the precepts in front of an image but also used an image of a Buddhist monk rather than the Buddha himself. After the death of two of his closest Dharma friends, with whom Ouyi hoped to establish a Vinaya society—in which five pure monks live together in accordance with the Dharma—Ouyi describes turning to a variety of religious practices including divination, arguably to redress what he perceived as serious transgressions and violations of the Vinaya. When he drew lots to determine the purity of his precepts before the summer retreat in 1633, he received that of bodhisattva *śrāmaṇera* (*pusa shami*)—that is, a novice monk who has taken the bodhisattva precepts.[12] This signaled to Ouyi that he had lapsed in his *bhikṣu* precepts, and he is said to have given back (*tui*) his *bhikṣu* precepts until he received a "wheel mark" indicating purity of body, speech, and mind twelve years later (1645).[13] Interestingly, Ouyi performed the ritual again in 1650 and received a "pure" wheel mark, which suggests that he may have had residual doubts concerning his moral status.[14]

Not only does Ouyi connect divination with ethics, but he also views the Vinaya—with its bodhisattva and *bhikkhu* precepts—as emblematic of all Buddhist practice. He writes, "Meditation, the Teachings, and the Vinaya—these three are strung together continuously. They are not just spring orchids and fall chrysanthemums. Meditation is the Buddha's mind, the Teachings are the Buddha's words, and the Vinaya is the Buddha's practice. How can this world have the mind but not the words or the practices?"[15] Whether because of his failure to uphold the precepts or some other impetus, Ouyi argues that a particular sutra provides means of redressing such transgressions of the precepts: the *Zhancha shan'e yebao jing* (Sutra on the divination of good and bad karmic retribution; T. 839.17.901c–910c; henceforth called the *Divination Sutra*). He describes how this particular text settled his anxiety and uncertainty—likely over his own karmic status—as he writes in his *Rituals of the Divination Sutra* (1634), "I grieve over the depth of obstacles; encountering this disarray of the Dharma. The Vinaya, the Teaching, and the Chan schools are all confused—there is no unity. Fortunately, I came across this teaching, and it dispelled my cloud of doubt."[16] He suggests that the *Divination Sutra* served as a guide and a means of restoring his faith and confidence.

Divination allows Ouyi to uncover karma that would otherwise be hidden, fulfilling its basic function as "the discovery of what is hidden or obscure by supernatural or magical means."[17] Although some scholars consider divination to be evidence of the degeneration of Buddhism in late imperial China, if we consider that karma was portrayed as something hidden or opaque in early Chinese Buddhist texts, it makes sense that divination could be used as a means of uncovering karma, especially given the prominence of divination rituals and texts such as the *Book of Changes* from the earliest dynasties of Chinese history to today.[18] Divination enables Ouyi to determine whether he has karmic obstacles impeding his spiritual progress.[19] Ouyi takes divination quite seriously, holding himself accountable for the lots chosen. For example, when he draws the lot of bodhisattva śrāmanera, he says he will peacefully follow Buddhas and bodhisattvas who "know [his] former worldly roots" and use whatever position to benefit sentient beings.[20] Likewise, he expresses anxiety over not fulfilling the lot that he chose at Jiuhuashan to read and write a commentary on the canon.[21]

This chapter examines three divination texts that serve as the primary basis for Ouyi considering divination to be a tool for understanding his karma.[22] Divination serves as a strategy for self-interpretation, enabling Ouyi to determine his future potential by shedding light on his karmic past. He acknowledges limitations that prevent him from knowing himself without such techniques as he asks rhetorically, "How can those of weak intelligence know themselves?"[23] Elsewhere he admits, "Although with the clarity of right mindfulness one can divine one's rebirth, my merit and wisdom are not yet complete."[24] Ouyi suggests that the only beings who need not engage in divination are Buddhas and bodhisattvas who have attained advanced states of mental concentration (Skt. *samādhi*) or those who have supreme mastery (*zizai*) and the five powers (*wutong*) including divine sight, hearing, and the ability to read other people's minds.[25] Those beings who lack such abilities cannot fully understand themselves because they have no access to their karmic past.

OUYI'S DIVINATION TEXTS

Ouyi builds upon a lengthy history of divination in China that begins with the use of oracle bones in the Shang dynasty, continues with milfoil stalks in conjunction with the *Zhouyi* (later known as the *Yijing* or *Book of Changes*), and also appears in the promotion of "stimulus-response" (*ganying*) as a framework for interpreting portents and omens linking heaven and humanity.²⁶ Following the advent of Buddhism in China, such omens became associated with karma. Kang Senghui is said to have associated Buddhist notions of retribution (*baoying*) and Chinese ideas of "stimulus-response" as he says, "When good deeds are performed there are auspicious omens, and when evil deeds are performed there are likewise responses. Therefore, he who does evil in secret is punished by the demons and he who does evil in public is published by men."²⁷ Yixing (684–727) was a particularly prominent Buddhist monk during the reign of Xuanzong who was skilled at fate extrapolation, physiognomy, and geomancy.

Not only has divination been a pervasive phenomenon throughout Chinese history, it also flourished especially in late imperial China, cutting across social divisions of education, privilege, and economic status.²⁸ Faced with increasing competition, examination candidates in the Ming and Qing dynasties frequently resorted to "reading fate" (*kanming*) because they sought auspicious signs regarding their prospects in the examination market.²⁹ Zhu Yuanzhang (Ming Taizu, r. 1368–1398) himself is said to have believed in divination as well as ghosts and spirits, and Western missionary accounts of the late Ming dynasty attest to the widespread practice of astrology and other forms of divination.³⁰

The uniqueness of Ouyi's practice of divination derives from his commentaries on two divination texts—the *Zhouyi* and the *Divination Sutra*—and the ritual he designs in response to the latter. Although the title *Zhouyi chanjie* (Chan explanation of the Zhouyi) might lead one to assume that his commentary on the *Zhouyi* is solely Buddhist, Ouyi insists that his text incorporates Buddhist and Confucian perspectives.³¹ The *Zhouyi* is a text consisting of sixty-four hexagrams (*gua*)—six-lined figures composed of solid (*yang*) and broken (*yin*) lines—each of which has its own name, its own statement (*duan*), as well as a line statement (*yao*). It is traditionally ascribed to sages Fu Xi and King Wen, the Duke of Zhou, and Confucius; Fu Xi was said to have invented the eight trigrams to communicate with Heaven and to categorize the dispositions of everything on earth, reflecting the belief that the cosmos could assist human beings in uncovering patterns underlying change.³² Spared from the burning of the books during the Qin dynasty (221–206 B.C.E.), the *Zhouyi* was combined with commentaries titled the Ten Wings (*shi yi*) and became the classic of the *Yijing* by the reign of Han Wudi (141–89 B.C.E.).³³

In his commentary on the *Zhouyi*, Ouyi considers three interpretive stances for each hexagram: worldly teachings (which he equates with a Confucian literati perspective) (*yue shi fa*), Buddhist teachings (*yue fo fa*), and a contemplative mind (*yue guanxin*).³⁴ In his preface to the commentary, written in 1641, Ouyi proposes two interpretive schema for his commentary as a whole: one could interpret it according to the four *siddhantas*—from a worldly point of view, an individual point of view, a therapeutic point of view, and an ultimate point of view—or according to the Mādhyamika "tetralemma" (*siju*; Skt. *catuṣkoṭi*), the notion that something "is," "is not," "both is and is not," or "neither is nor is not." Ouyi suggests his interpretation "is" the *Zhouyi* if it gives rise to joy (a worldly point of view); it "is not" the *Zhouyi* if it gives rise to a virtuous mind but does not use conventional Confucianism (an individual point of view); it "both is and is not" the *Zhouyi* if one knows that there must be a distinction but recognizes that it both "is" and "is not," thereby preventing excessive generality (a therapeutic point of view); and finally "it is neither the *Zhouyi* nor is not the *Zhouyi*" if one realizes that neither Confucianism nor Buddhism is fixed—they are only names—which is the "accomplishment of supreme truth." At the conclusion of his preface, Ouyi writes that he seeks to "use Chan to enter Confucianism and to entice Confucians into knowing Chan."³⁵

Yuet Keung Lo has argued against interpreting Ouyi's project as a Buddhist-Confucian syncretism or as a comparative study, stating that his Buddhist remarks are "like afterthoughts" and often have no connection to the *Yijing* text they explicate.³⁶ However, even though Ouyi does not seek to reconcile Confucianism and Buddhism in the text, Buddhism does play a prominent role in Ouyi's emphasis on the importance of obstacles and spiritual cultivation. Although Ouyi was certainly concerned about change (as Lo points out, he wrote his commentary between 1641 and 1645, during the same period of the Ming-Qing transition), Ouyi was concerned with how one lives in the face of such change—what spiritual practices are beneficial during such challenging times.

Before delving further into his work on the *Zhouyi*, let us turn our attention to Ouyi's two commentaries on what Whalen Lai has called the "Buddhist answer to the *Yijing*"³⁷—the *Divination Sutra*. Compiled in the late sixth century C.E. in China, the sutra was designed to enable one to divine karmic retribution from past good and bad deeds.³⁸ The first fascicle of the sutra describes divination and repentance rituals, while its second fascicle focuses on the philosophical theory of one mind, which once led scholars to believe it had inspired the *Awakening of Faith*. The text itself recognizes signs of the decline of the Dharma (*mofa*) and views Dizang as an appropriate savior for this time, and it advocates divination as a means to address such uncertainty.

There are three sets of wooden "wheels" (*lun*) used in the divination, each of which is the size of a pinky finger, with flattened sides and sharpened ends so that they can be spun like tops. The first set of ten tops reveals various good and evil deeds committed in the past; the second set of three tops measures the strength of these karmic forces; and the third set of six tops verifies the modes in which the retribution will be received in the past, present, and future.[39] The first set of ten tops has two opposing sides inscribed with a pair of one of the ten wholesome actions (*shishan*; Skt. *daśa-kuśala*) and its corresponding unwholesome action (*shi'e*; Skt. *daśa-akuśala*), and one leaves two sides unmarked (signaling neither a good nor bad action).[40] One casts the ten tops at the same time. If one receives wholesome actions, it foretells good retribution, unwholesome actions predict bad retribution, and if all ten lots are unmarked, it means that one is without further outflows (*wulou*; Skt. *anāsrava*). A mix of the two means either that one's karmic forces are weak or that they cancel each other out.

The second set of three tops measuring the strength of the karmic forces is divided among the three karmic activities of bodily action, speech, and thought (figure 2.1). The three wheels are used separately and rely on the results of the first set of ten tops: the first three of the ten wholesome and unwholesome actions being traditionally considered those performed by the body, the second four by those of speech, and the last three by those of the mind.[41] The strength is signaled by markings on the side of the top: the first long and thick, the second short and thin, the third thick and deep, and the fourth thin and shallow. The first two weigh the strength of goodness, while the second two weigh the depth of evil. The first means fortune is imminent, while the fourth means misfortune will manifest itself gradually over time.[42]

The third set of six tops—tied to sins committed by the six sense faculties, the six objects, and the six cognitions (*liugen liuchen liuyi*; Skt. *indriya, viṣaya, vijñāna*) that are the 18 sensations—are used to designate time of the karmic retribution. One writes the numbers 1–3 on the first top, leaving one side blank, 4–6 on the second, and so forth. The practitioner throws each wheel three times (for a total of 18 numbers). These numbers are then added, and there follows a list of 189 fates: 1–160 signaling

FIGURE 2.1 Set of wheel tops used in the *Divination Sutra*.

the present, 161–171 the past, and 172–189 the future.⁴³ If one receives 16 "blanks," one is said to have gained the "gainless" (*wusuode*; Skt. *anupalabdhi*) in the present; the number 189, also difficult to get because it involves receiving the highest numbers on each top three times each, signals that "after one has renounced one's body (*sheshen*), one will abide in the Mahāyāna."⁴⁴ These wheels are still used in conjunction with the *Divination Sutra*; for example, the contemporary Chinese Buddhist monk Mengcan includes a plastic set of such tops with his commentary on the *Divination Sutra*.⁴⁵

Scholars have debated whether the divination practices in the sutra derive from indigenous Chinese divination practices or Buddhist sources.⁴⁶ Although Whalen Lai insists that "karma doctrine should not normally predispose itself toward such fortune-telling, even though theoretically the Buddha has knowledge of the destinies of all men and is free to reveal it,"⁴⁷ Ouyi views divination as a diagnostic tool for revealing karma. In regard to the *Divination Sutra* in particular, Ouyi urges one to "briefly observe the good and bad [karmic retribution] from each mark of the divination wheel; repent for whatever sin is the strongest."⁴⁸ Herein lies the uniqueness of Ouyi's approach: unlike general repentance practices that characterize Mahāyāna rituals, Ouyi advocates that one choose the heaviest sin of which to repent. In his own practice of the ritual, he signals his failure to uphold the precepts as calling for repentance until he receives a good "wheel mark."

The sutra itself prescribes that a purification rite should precede the spinning of the top. Practitioners are instructed to first find a quiet place, and then adorn an altar with a Buddha image, banner, flowers, and incense. After bathing and wearing clean clothes, practitioners should worship the Three Jewels and make bodhisattva vows with a sincere mind, promising to fulfill the six *pāramitās*, the four infinite states of mind (*apramāṇya*), the knowledge of nonproduction (*anutpādajñāna*), and the selfsame (*samatā*). Practitioners are then told to worship Dizang a thousand times, asking for guidance, protection, and deliverance from all obstacles. The text insists that before engaging in contemplation, practitioners should examine good and bad actions performed during past lives, measuring their quality and quantity. If they find weighty evil actions, they should first practice repentance rituals;[49] such rituals can continue for 7, 14, 21, 49, 100, or 1,000 days.[50] After such periods of repentance, practitioners consult the set of three tops, and if their karmic activities are pure, then they have effectively removed the evil karma. The text notes that people will receive auspicious signs (*shanxiang*) or dreams (*shanmeng*), see lights, smell odors, or have visions of Buddhas, bodhisattvas, or their images in dreams, though it admits that they could be illusory and false if they occur before purification.[51] Efficacy of the divination depends in part on whether one's mind is sincere.

Ouyi Zhixu was the first to write a commentary to this Chinese apocryphal sutra, which was recommended to him by a layman from Wenling (contemporary Quanzhou, Fujian province) during the winter of 1631. Interestingly, it was also in Wenling that he wrote his commentary on the *Zhouyi*. He wrote his *Zhancha shan' e yebao jing xingfa* (Rituals of the divination sutra) in 1634, his commentary on the *Zhouyi* from 1638 to 1641, and his *Zhancha shan' e yebao jing shu* (Commentary on the divination sutra) in 1651, four years after he reports receiving the wheel of purity. As we have seen, it was immediately prior to his composition of the *Rituals of the Divination Sutra* that he had drawn the lot of bodhisattva-śrāmaṇera, and it was immediately before completing his commentary on the *sutra* that he performed the divination ritual again. Why was his divination activity tied to this particular place in Fujian province? In a Dharma talk,

Ouyi offers a possible explanation. Lamenting his failure to uphold the precepts, his drawing of the bodhisattva-*śrāmanera* lot in 1633, his severe karmic obstacles (*suzhang*), and his being plagued by serious illness, he describes how he overcame sickness at Jiuhuashan and traveled south to Fujian, where he says that he felt his false reputation was flourishing at the expense of true virtue. Renowned for his Vinaya texts, Ouyi felt a disjuncture between his fame and his own self-estimation. In the talk, he describes composing the divination ritual, performing it seven times that year, fourteen times the following year, and seven times the third year, all without receiving the wheel mark of purity. This leads to his decision to retreat even further from bodhisattva-*śrāmanera* to one that has taken only the three refuges.[52]

When considering why Ouyi may have written commentaries to the *Divination Sutra* and the *Zhouyi*, it is important to keep in mind their potential purpose. As Daniel Gardner notes, this is not always correlated with the functions and effects of the genre of commentary itself.[53] As we will see, his commentary on the *Divination Sutra* reflects a particular philosophical point of view that Ouyi sought to promote, but it also served to validate the legitimacy of the base text itself, suggesting its importance as meriting a commentary. This would not be a viable explanation for his *Zhouyi* commentary, which was accepted as a classic. Instead, the opportunity afforded by the *Zhouyi* is a malleability of interpretation, which allowed Ouyi to present Buddhist and Confucian interpretations of the divination text. As Gardner notes, those texts that are especially open to different readings can prompt commentators to delimit their meaning by giving them a certainty and stability. This was especially true of the *Yijing*, which was subject to a significant amount of commentarial activity during the Song dynasty.[54]

DIVINATION AS A KARMIC DIAGNOSTIC

Having discussed the various circumstances surrounding the composition of Ouyi's divination texts as well as their general content, we can examine how Ouyi specifically uses divination as a karmic diagnostic. As we mentioned earlier, Ouyi suggests that divination can reveal karmic obstacles from past sins, one's karmic potential, and one's future rebirth. Ouyi sees two positive functions for divination: by revealing karmic obstacles it guards against excessive pride, but by revealing karmic potential it enables one to dispel doubts and maintain confidence. Divination paradoxically serves to humble and to embolden practitioners; it draws to light one's evil deeds from the past, but after one knows the deeds for which to repent, one can then engage in religious practices designed to eliminate the karma resulting from such actions. We will also see that Ouyi's view of divination suggests a complex understanding of the workings of karma that is best described as an organic model of fruition rather than mechanistic cause and effect.

Ouyi argues that karmic obstacles revealed through divination can play an important role in spiritual formation, spurring one on in further self-cultivation. He suggests one should not become disheartened when one discovers one's karmic obstacles but instead become even more motivated to change one's karma. In his commentary to the Zhouyi, Ouyi suggests that the first hexagram "heaven" (*qian*) is a metaphor for Buddha-nature—the spiritual potential within humankind—that is "without obstacles" (*wuai*) like the sun in the sky or wisdom and righteousness on earth; yet it must be accompanied by practice (*xiu*) if such potentials are to be realized.[55] He describes the second hexagram "earth" (*kun*) as representing such practice: "Whereas *qian* is wisdom, *kun* is principle; *qian* is illumination, *kun* quiescence; *qian* is nature, *kun* is practice; wisdom amid cultivation is called *qian*, practice is *kun*. They are equal (one does not come before another), like a single ray of light, like the interpenetration of nature and practice, like the mutual adornment of wisdom and virtue."[56] He suggests that encountering "difficulties" (*tun*) or "small obstacles" (*xiaoxu*) can serve as the impetus for cultivating virtue,[57] playing an important role in spiritual formation. Ouyi notes that one can read "obstruction" (*xu*) as "cultivation" (*xu*), and he elaborates that if one encounters an obstacle but does not become resentful or fearful, this can be an occasion for virtue—such as a bell that rings when it is struck or a knife that cuts more quickly when it is sharpened.[58] Thus even when divination reveals karmic obstructions, Ouyi insists that this need not lead one to despair.

In fact, Ouyi suggests that repentance and regret can play a positive role in spiritual formation. Although the character "regret" (*hui*) is found in the Zhouyi itself, there it negatively signals problems;[59] whereas in his commentary, Ouyi suggests a positive and useful function for regret. Regret covers two different contexts—for ordinary people, regret can keep one humble when one makes spiritual progress; for bodhisattvas, it can cause them to remember the plight of sentient beings, turning back to be reborn into the realm of *saṃsāra*. Noting how Buddhas put forth ceaseless effort to benefit sentient beings, he writes, "In the state of ultimate realization, they do not enter *nirvāna* but flow among the nine realms [of hells, hungry ghosts, animals, *asuras*, humans, gods, *śrāvakas*, *pratyekabuddha*s, and bodhisattvas]; therefore, it is said there is regret."[60] Regret plays an essential role in the bodhisattva path because bodhisattvas "remember"[61] sentient beings and choose to return to the world of *saṃsāra* to liberate them instead of pursuing *nirvāna* for themselves. Ouyi considers arrogance a potential by-product of spiritual progress and promotes "regret" as a means of instilling humility in those advanced practitioners. Later in his commentary, Ouyi proposes another means of staving off pride, namely a sympathetic view of equality with other sentient beings. Ouyi describes the danger of becoming attached to *dharma*s and thereby entrenched in petty power struggles. He advocates equality in the hexagram "sameness with people" (*tongren*), suggesting that one mentally contemplate "entering into the nature of being born together, with those above harmonizing with the Buddha's compassionate power and those below seeking pity with sentient beings."[62]

For ordinary people, Ouyi suggests that punishment and self-reproach can cause one to give rise to shame, which then allows one to return to one's original Buddha nature.[63] In Buddhist terms, Ouyi admits that ideally one would use calming and contemplation (*zhiguan*), but that if karmic obstacles are strong, regret and repentance can serve important functions:

> If their afflictions and habits are strong, one cannot lack the skill of self-contention. As for contention, it means repentance, punishment, changing one's mistakes, and returning to goodness. If there is a mind of confidence but it is obstructed by those afflictions and evil karma, then being ashamed and anxious about oneself is beneficial. If one regrets endlessly, it is not a good expedient means; one is stifled by regret, and it is ultimately inauspicious. It is useful to see a great person in order to decisively choose to give rise to [*bodhicitta*] and eliminate doubts and regrets. It is not useful to cross the great river of affliction and *saṃsāra* and ultimately drown oneself.[64]

Here, Ouyi suggests that shame can cut through such layers of obscuration to reveal one's essential nature, but one must not be overly regretful, lest one become stifled by it. Instead, he says, "One need only eliminate sins and then stop."[65] Regret is a slippery slope: if one becomes overwhelmed with it, one can be led astray from the path. At this point, as Ouyi puts it, "the arrow of regret has entered the heart, which then causes a great loss,"[66] namely being debilitated by exhaustion and plagued with doubts about one's ability to act. But when one properly reflects on oneself to cultivate virtue, one realizes that obstacles and dangerous situations are created and manifested from one's mind, not from external causes; thus one should not blame other people or one's fate.[67]

Ouyi argues that divining one's karmic potential can carry one on the spiritual path by removing doubts and instilling confidence. In his *Zhancha shan'e yebao jing xuanyi* (Profound meaning of the divination sutra) Ouyi espouses the view that the "three realms are mind only" (*sanshi weixin*; Skt. *citta-mātra*) and praises the efficacy of this particular divination for eliminating doubts and engendering faith:

> Delusion and enlightenment seem distinct, [but] if one is deluded, then one is deluded about that which is enlightened; if one is enlightened, then one is enlightened about that which is deluded. This sutra is the essential ferry that points to delusion but returns to enlightenment. "Divination" is the wisdom that is able to observe; "good and evil karma" is the object that is observed. The observer is simply the three wisdoms of the one mind; the observed is the three truths of the one realm. It eliminates doubts and obstacles, strengthens pure faith, shows the expedient means to advance toward one's destiny, and it comforts and makes one no longer weak or fearful.[68]

Ouyi defends divination from charges of degeneracy by arguing that even if one criticizes the object (*suo*) of divination (good and bad karma), the subject (*neng*) or act of divining itself is not blameless if performed with wisdom; moreover, it can sometimes contribute to one's spiritual development, erasing doubts and bolstering faith in one's spiritual potential. Because one can use divination for others, it can also cause other people's virtue to increase and resolve their doubt and regret.[69] Ouyi specifies that one need not have supernatural powers to accomplish divination for others: "If one wishes to divine for others, one need not have divine vision, knowledge of past lives, or the ability to read the minds of others; one need only have the mark of the wheel."[70]

In his discussion of the *Divination Sutra* as particularly efficacious for bringing to light causes and conditions that have yet to manifest—such as one's future rebirth—we see that Ouyi does not reduce karmic retribution to simple causes and effects.⁷¹ Ouyi describes various causes (*yin*) that can give rise to retribution, but he states that three factors determine karmic retribution: "first the type of good and evil action from which it is incurred, second the type of object, and third which of the ten realms it belongs to."⁷² He also notes that direct and indirect retribution can be said to arise or to be manifested from causes and conditions (*yinyuan*) but like all *dharmas*, they are empty, provisional, and middle.⁷³ When the mind is good and evil in a continuity of thought-moments, Ouyi describes how karma accumulates following the mind, marks appear, and retribution necessarily arises: "good and evil karma also does not perish, like noise responds to sound, and shadow follows form, thus it is no different from mutual response (*xiangying*)."⁷⁴ Ouyi admits, "Although karma itself is empty, retribution is not lost; therefore, one must use the force of goodness to repent of *vāsanas*, causing the seeds of evil to be revealed, transformed, and weakened, also not to increase. Only then can one cultivate meditation and wisdom without encountering evil [thoughts] and worries."⁷⁵ Here, we should pay special attention to the process by which seeds can be weakened: they must first be "revealed" (*zhan*). In his commentary on the *Zhouyi*, Ouyi advises advanced practitioners to keep their virtue hidden, being bright on the inside but dark on the outside. Here he prescribes the reverse: those who have accrued evil karma are told to reveal or bring to light these misdeeds. Divination is a method for revealing karma; it represents the first stage for weakening one's seeds of evil.

Again, we see the importance of "revealing" or "manifesting" bad karma as Ouyi extols practitioners to either confess evil actions committed in one's present life or the evil karma that appears in the wheel mark. He insists that these misdeeds be "disclosed" (*pi chen*) and "laid open" (*fa lu*). Reading his description of the process in which bad seeds are uprooted, one is struck by the natural metaphors of growth that imply a more complex, organic process in the ripening (and weakening) of karma, instead of a mechanistic cause and effect relationship:

> In regard to the manifestation of evil actions of the past, it has already disappeared in an instant, but the perfuming seeds (*xun zhongzi*; Skt. *vāsanā bīja*) are stored in the eighth [storehouse] consciousness, and owing to the strength of attachment to self (*wozhi*; Skt. *ātma-grāha*) in the sixth and seventh consciousnesses, each instant of thought assists in permeating and causes [the seeds] to increase. If one now reveals them (*fa lu*), this eliminates the aforementioned seeds of attachment to self. Just as

the seeds of grass and trees lie dormant in the ground, one must expose the roots and stems. If one now digs up and reveals [them], one destroys oneself; moreover as regards the old seeds, even if one has exposed them, if one does not forever cut off the continuity of mind, then new perfuming seeds transform and increase with the old ones. When they do not yet exist, one must therefore vow never again to commit them.[76]

Here, Ouyi suggests that the act of revealing or manifesting one's evil karma, when done in a penitent state, can eliminate an attachment to the self that perpetuates the sixth and seventh consciousnesses (which are fertile ground for the growth of seeds of evil karma). Just as Ouyi warns against arrogance among those who are spiritually advanced in his commentary to the *Zhouyi*, here he suggests that an "attachment to the self" contributes to the growth of evil seeds. By revealing one's transgressions, divination enables one to break any attachment to oneself.

This organic vision of karma has positive and creative potential, illustrated in Ouyi's discussion of virtuous seeds that can result from "rejoicing in sympathetic joy." Ouyi writes, "If one sees another person carrying a lamp, one is also covered by its light; if another person burns incense, one is also transformed/perfumed (*xun*) by it. The roots of good with their same essence are clearly like this; why is there this obstacle of delusion? Not knowing this support, one mistakenly gives rise to jealousy. If one is able to rejoice in joy, then one knows that the good roots cultivated by Buddhas and bodhisattvas are originally shared with all sentient beings."[77] He then quotes the *Śuraṃgama Sūtra*, "Limitless merits, like bunched seeds, in the same place perfume cultivation and they are never scattered."[78] Ouyi suggests that sentient beings, sharing the nature of Buddhas and bodhisattvas, can better their karmic conditions by perfuming (*xunxi*) themselves via cultivation, contemplation, and hearing the Dharma, as well as by avoiding seeds of affliction.

Thus we have seen how Ouyi considers divination as a diagnostic tool for determining karma, so that one might then repent for one's previous misconduct and commit oneself anew to the Buddhist path. We also see ideas in his divination texts that become more important and pronounced in his repentance texts, namely the role of "stimulus-response" (*ganying*) and "confidence" (*xin*) in stimulating the compassionate response of Buddhas and bodhisattvas. Ouyi suggests that the interaction between Buddhas and sentient beings is one of "unity" (*xian*): if sentient beings are singularly focused on stimulating the Buddha, then the Buddha responds by teaching the Dharma.[79] He writes, "When *samādhi* and *prajñā* are balanced, one attains the correct path of stimulus-response; therefore, it is auspicious and problems disappear.... [I]f one attains correct stimulus-response, one can stimulate for an entire day and not break the essence of stillness and quiescence."[80]

Ouyi often uses stimulus-response to characterize the relationship between students and teachers: in order to create an appropriate stimulus, students seek out teachers with the right intention, at the appropriate time and occasion. He writes that students must aspire "to thoroughly penetrate (*gantong*) and only then can [teachers] respond, just as water must be clear before it can reflect the moon."[81] In addition to having the right intention,[82] Ouyi suggests that time plays a crucial role in bringing about stimulus and response as he writes, "In Buddhism, it is said that when the time arrives, the principle manifests itself, occasions (*ji*) and stimuli join together, and it is called 'one time.'"[83] Elsewhere, he insists that one cannot rush one's instruction of students: "One must wait for timely causes and conditions. If the time is appropriate, then the principle will manifest itself. However, it is important that the causes be true if the effects are to be correct. If [the students] have confidence (*fu*), light will be bright and auspicious."[84] Given the right intention, time, and occasion, Ouyi claims that "stimulus-response" can result in one's karmic obstacles being entirely eliminated by Buddhas and bodhisattvas.

Ouyi suggests that divination serves the important function of removing doubts (*chuyi*), while repentance can enable one to eliminate sins (*miezui*).[85] Although Ouyi recognizes that many Buddhas and bodhisattvas strive to liberate sentient beings, he argues that only Dizang can liberate those without conditions for liberation (*wuyuan*; Skt. *an-ālambana*) because of the permeation of his original vow not to attain awakening until the hells are empty. Ouyi states, "Because of the vast name and manifold virtues of Dizang, who summons true virtues of superior effects, he is able to increase superior conditions for sentient beings, causing obstacles to be removed and sins eliminated in every instant of thought."[86] The next chapter examines Ouyi's view of repentance, especially how he singles out Dizang in particular as savior of the penitent.

THREE
REPENTANCE RITUALS FOR ELIMINATING KARMA

One light in a room can break a thousand years of darkness. The power of repentance can undo karma.

—Ouyi Zhixu[1]

ALTHOUGH OUYI portrays divination as a vehicle for diagnosing his karma, his repentance rituals aim to eliminate karma entirely. He outlines procedures for performing such rituals in three texts—two that are based on apocryphal sutras and one centered on the bodhisattva Dizang: the repentance ritual from the *Zhancha shan'e yebao xingfa* (Procedure for performing the sutra of divining good and bad karmic retribution, 1633; hereafter referred to as Divination repentance),[2] his *Fanwang jing chanhui xingfa*[3] (Procedure for performing the repentance of the *Sutra of Brahma's Net*, 1633; hereafter referred to as Brahma's Net repentance),[4] and his *Zanli Dizang pusa chan yuan yi* (Ritual of repentance and profession of vows to venerate the Bodhisattva Dizang, 1637; hereafter referred to as Dizang repentance).[5] This chapter considers the formal features of such rituals, the broader context surrounding their creation and performance, and their underlying soteriological goals.[6] Ouyi designs these repentance rituals largely according to the formal structure and approach of his Tiantai predecessors—including Zhiyi, Zhanran, Zunshi, and Zhili—but slightly adapts them to accomplish his particular goal of eliminating his karmic retribution for having disparaged the Three Jewels in his youth, which violates one of the ten major precepts (*shi zhong jie*)[7] of the *Sutra of Brahma's Net*. In Ouyi's eyes, such karma is "fixed" or "ineluctable" (*dingye*), meaning that retribution will assuredly happen either in his present or future lives, unlike "unfixed karma," in which either the time or the result of karmic retribution remains undetermined. Ouyi's repentance texts are prescriptive, stipulating a protocol that he views as capable of redressing the gravest of transgressions. The crux of the ritual lies at the point in which Ouyi calls upon practitioners to recognize their inability to change their own karma, to admit their reliance on the power of salvific bodhisattva figures like Dizang, and to put their trust and confidence in them.

In Ouyi's repentance rituals, there is a clear tension between the affirmation of karmic cause and effect and the assertion that repentance can eliminate karma entirely. This serves as the linchpin for transformation, which is further heightened by the type of karma that Dizang is said to eliminate—namely the ineluctable karma that would otherwise relegate serious transgressors to hell. Shengyan argues that Ouyi saw no conflict between the notion that "one cannot escape fixed karma" and Dizang's ability to "eliminate fixed karma."[8] But Ouyi *does* perceive a conflict; in fact, the conflict is fundamental for the efficacy of his repentance rituals. It is precisely because one cannot escape fixed karma—because of the inevitability of one's actions having future karmic retribution—that repentance rituals afford incredible and rare moments of grace and transformation. In all three of Ouyi's repentance rituals, we see this climactic moment highlighted in the transformation of the "Ten Mentalities" (*shixin*).[9]

Because of his palpable sense of living in an age when the Dharma is in decline (*mofa*), Ouyi places a greater emphasis on the role that auspicious signs and divinatory wheel marks play in repentance. They are not mere practical aids but instead are fundamental elements of repentance in Ouyi's manuals. This may distinguish Ouyi from his predecessors, in that he admits that the realization of emptiness and recognition of interdependence can prompt one to pursue good conduct, but he suggests that one cannot fully overcome one's karma without external help. Because of this reliance, the affective state of shame (*cankui*) becomes extremely important, for Ouyi argues that this stimulus of suffering prompts bodhisattvas such as Dizang to mercifully respond. Although Ouyi views people as capable of attaining a cognitive understanding of emptiness, he thinks they are unable to understand the working of karma and thus are dependent on the grace of bodhisattvas if they wish to extinguish their karma. Because of Dizang's vow to save all sentient beings relegated to hells and his *dhāraṇī* that has the power to eliminate "fixed karma," Ouyi particularly appeals to this bodhisattva as a savior of the penitent.[10] Three years after composing his repentance ritual based on the *Sutra of Brahma's Net* and his ritual based on the *Sutra of Divining Good and Bad Karmic Retribution* in 1633, he traveled to Jiuhuashan, which became the central site of Dizang devotion in the late imperial period.[11] It was during his stay, after entering into seclusion (*dunji*) at the Dizang tower in Jiuhuashan, that he composed his repentance and votive text to the bodhisattva Dizang[12] (figure 3.1).

Although Ouyi began composing his own repentance texts in 1633, prior to that time he practiced primarily Tiantai repentance rituals but included special praise of the precepts and the bodhisattva Dizang in his performance of such rituals. In 1630, performing a repentance ritual attributed to Emperor Wu of the Liang kingdom—the *Cibei daochang chanfa*[13]—Ouyi esteems the precepts as "teachers that clarify and instruct" and "the foundation of purity,"[14] and he identifies the bodhisattva Dizang as his main object of veneration (*benzun*), praising him for his vow "to transform my fixed karma."[15] Even though he performs rituals to the bodhisattva Guanyin, his devotion to Dizang gradually becomes more prominent as he expresses increasing concern over his considerable karmic obstacles and the impurity of his practice.[16] In 1632, several texts describe him performing the Great Compassion repentance and reciting the Great Compassion *dhāraṇī*,[17] but he also shows continued interest in the bodhisattva Dizang—especially his *dhāraṇī* that can extinguish fixed karma—in another text from that same year.[18] In this text, Ouyi laments having already created fixed karma, being covered in ignorance, having criticized and slandered the true Buddhist teachings, and being morally deficient. He writes, "How can I blame others for the fruits (*guo*), since I myself created the original cause (*yin*)?"[19] After regretting his mistakes, he praises Dizang and his mantra to "eliminate karma" (*mieye*).[20] Reciting Dizang's *dhāraṇī* many times, he seeks Dizang's hidden empowerment (*mingjia*)[21] and, at the end of the text, he himself vows to "eliminate fixed karma of the three evil destinies."[22] Other texts from 1632 reflect Ouyi's respect for Dizang, the Vinaya, and Guanyin, as he vows to extinguish his own and

FIGURE 3.1 Dizang Tower, Jiuhuashan.

others' fixed karma, to renew the Vinaya, and to recite the Great Compassion *dhāraṇī* 108,000 times.[23] He also performs the Tiantai *Jinguangming* repentance (*Jinguangming chan*) in 1632 and Pure Land repentance (*zan jingtu chan wen*) the following year.[24] Thus Ouyi follows the Tiantai liturgical tradition, but he also recognizes the Vinaya and the bodhisattva Dizang as worthy of particular veneration and worship prior to composing his own repentance texts.

In this chapter, the English word "repentance"[25] covers a constellation of concepts that connote regret for negative actions done in present or previous lives: not only the Chinese Buddhist term that is typically translated "repentance" (*chanhui*)[26] but also phrases that could literally be translated "performing repentance" (*zuo chan*), "veneration and repentance" (*li chan*), "regret one's mistakes" (*huiguo*), or "regret one's sins" (*huizuo*). The word "repentance" has been used in lieu of combinations previously adopted—such as "confession-contrition"[27] or "confession/repentance"[28]—not only because it is less awkward but also because the term "confession," which implies a verbal telling of one's sins, applies best to Chinese expressions such as "stating one's sins" (*shuozui*). Repentance rituals certainly include a section for confessing one's sins (either in specific or general terms), but they also include ritual expressions of remorse and a demonstration of one's commitment to abstain from such actions in the future.[29]

As for what one repents, Ouyi uses the general terms "crime" or "sin" (*zui*), "mistake" or "transgression" (*guo*),[30] and "action" or "karma" (*ye*). He also cites specific lists of bad karma that derive from Buddhist doctrine such as the "five heinous sins" (*wuni*)[31] that lead one to the Avīci hell,[32] the "ten evil deeds" (*shi'e*),[33] the "four grave crimes" (*siqi*; Skt. *pārājika*)[34] for ordained monks that entail expulsion from the monastic order, and the "eight grave crimes" (*baqi*)[35] for ordained nuns adding four proscriptions against relationships with males and monks.[36]

Ouyi underscores a dimension of repentance that has been overlooked in previous comparative studies such as that of Amitai Etzioni and David Carney, who identify three elements of repentance: true remorse, doing penance or making amends, and restructuring one's life accordingly.[37] For Ouyi, repentance does entail these three elements; it requires not only confession of sins but also an affective feeling of regret, a practice in which one demonstrates that regret, and a forswearing of such action in his future life. However, this scheme omits a crucial aspect of repentance for Ouyi, namely the role that bodhisattvas play in the ritual process. In order for bodhisattvas to intervene on behalf of practitioners, the latter must express their devotion through worship and acknowledgment of their utter reliance on these salvific figures. Ouyi implies a direct relationship between the devotion of the practitioner and the response of the bodhisattva—the greater one's shame and self-abnegation, the more merciful the response. Ouyi portrays this intervention as having the potential to transform (*zhuan*) one's entire existence in the present and future.[38]

REPENTANCE IN CHINESE BUDDHISM

Repentance rituals are a common feature of Chinese Buddhist liturgical and devotional practice, but this chapter focuses primarily on their development in Tiantai because Ouyi bases his own practice of repentance within this tradition. In Indian Buddhism, repentance rituals addressed specific violations of monastic rules by monks, and they occurred during the *pravāraṇā*[39] at the end of the summer retreat and in the bimonthly rite of *poṣadha*.[40] Although it is uncertain when the *poṣadha* rite began to be observed in China, we can assume that it was followed after the eminent monk Daoan (312–385) placed his authority behind it in the fourth century.[41] If we examine repentance rituals in early Chinese Buddhism, we find several features that lack precedent in Indian Buddhism. First, there is evidence of lay participation in practice and creation of repentance rituals. Collections of Chinese Buddhist devotional literature from the fifth and sixth centuries include public repentance rituals written by laypeople such as Xiao Ziliang, Emperor Wu of Liang (r. 502–549), and Emperor Wen of the Chen (r. 560–566).[42] Second, repentance changes from an admission of specific misdeeds to a more generic or abstract confession of sins.[43] Most confessions are formulaic and prearranged, beginning by lamenting one's karmic obstacles, then stating a generic list of sins, and finally confessing that one has committed sins; variation comes only when practitioners insert their names at certain parts.[44]

Although there is scholarly debate over whether Chinese Buddhist repentance rituals developed in response to Daoism or were an indigenous growth from Buddhism,[45] Daniel Stevenson demonstrates that there were repentance rituals and meditative practices as early as the first half of the fifth century that served as the basis for the Tiantai patriarch Zhiyi's (538–597) Four Forms of Samādhi, and that Huisi and Zhiyi were representative of a broader base of Chinese Buddhist devotional practice beginning in the sixth century.[46] In his study of the biographical and institutional records of the early Tiantai community, Stevenson identifies three ritual valences for repentance rituals.[47] First, they could be featured in general monastic procedures such as daily worship at the six intervals during the day: morning, noon, late afternoon (or sunset), early night, midnight, and late night. Second, they could be integrated into an individually defined cult, occurring only occasionally, following spatial and temporal prescriptions, and undertaken by spiritual elite due to their rigorous character. Third, they could be large public ceremonials that use drama and pageantry instead of being intensive and meditative. Stevenson emphasizes that the first two were consciously demarcated in the Tiantai monastic institution in the ritual cycle of the main hall (*liushi li fo*) and "repentance in a separate sanctuary" (*bie chang chanhui*), respectively.[48]

Two of Zhiyi's most important repentance texts are designed for the second context: his *Fahua sanmei chanyi* (Procedure for performing the Lotus samādhi repentance, T. 1941)[49] and his *Fangdeng sanmei xingfa* (Procedure for performing the Fangdeng samādhi repentance, T. 1940).[50] The *Fangdeng Repentance* includes what later became characteristic features of Tiantai repentance: the three types of karmic obstacles (*sanzhang*)—namely, the obstacle of affliction (*fannao zhang*) from the three poisons of lust, anger, and delusion; the obstacle of retribution (*baozhang*), that is, obstructions posed by one's environment or bodily illness; the obstacle of karma (*yezhang*), especially acts that violate codes of discipline—and the two types of repentance in "practice" or "principle" (*shi li chan*). Intended as a purificatory rite for *bhikṣu*, *bhikṣuṇī*, *śrāmaṇera*, *śrāmaṇerikā*, or holders of the bodhisattva precepts who have committed any of the four grave crimes or five heinous sins, it is performed by as many as ten people in a secluded hall that has been carefully purified for the ritual.[51] Participants must undergo a week of purification beforehand, seeking an auspicious dream from one of the twelve Dream Kings (*mengwang*) who protect the *Fangdeng dhāraṇī sutra* (*Fangdeng tuoluoni jing*), a text that allows individuals to perform the repentance; the ritual itself consists of a repeated liturgical cycle of eleven stages, including offerings to the Three Jewels, summoning the Three Jewels and figures from the text, praise of the Buddhas' virtues, veneration by invoking names and prostrating, confession and vows, circumambulation and recitation of the *dhāraṇī*, and seated meditation.[52] Zhiyi describes two ways of approaching the repentance, according to the practitioner's level of meditative discernment: (1) repentance based on practice (*shi chanhui*) for novice or unskilled practitioners, which focuses on fixing one's attention on the practical features of the ritual, or (2) repentance based on principle (*li chanhui*) for advanced practitioners who can remain aware of the "principle" (*li*) of emptiness throughout the ritual.⁵³ Only the latter removes obstructions of vexation and liberates the practitioner from *saṃsāra*. Such repentance practices enable the practitioner to engage in "discernment of principle" (*liguan*)—namely the intrinsic emptiness of mind and phenomena. However, Zhiyi emphasizes that this does not lessen the importance of the practical techniques—the diversity of such disciplines enable practitioners of all levels to engage in spiritual formation.⁵⁴ Repentance rituals can reveal one's karmic capacities and propensities, thereby enabling the practitioner to determine the appropriate course of spiritual development; they can eliminate obstacles such as illness or demonic interference; and they ultimately enable one to establish a sympathetic resonance so that Buddhas and bodhisattvas can respond (*ying*) to the practitioner's needs.

The *Lotus Samādhi Repentance* is a twenty-one-day practice of intense worship and recitation of the Lotus Sutra that includes a "Repentance of the Six Sense Faculties"—repenting sins that have accumulated from misuse of the six sense faculties in past and present lives—within its liturgical cycle. The ten stages of the liturgy form the outline for later Tiantai repentance rituals: (1) salutation and presentation of offerings to the Three Jewels, (2) summoning of Three Jewels, (3) praise of Three Jewels, (4) veneration of Buddhas and figures from the Lotus Sutra, (5) repentance of the six sense faculties, (6) imploring the Buddhas to remain in the world to teach, (7) sympathetic rejoicing in the merits of others, (8) dedication of merit, (9) vows to liberate all beings, and (10) closing praise of Three Jewels and a recitation of the Three Refuges.⁵⁵ The fifth through ninth steps—repentance (*chanhui*), imploring the Buddhas (*quanqing*), sympathetic rejoicing (*suixi*), dedication of merit (*huixiang*), and professing vows (*fayuan*)—constitute the "fivefold repentance" (*wu hui*) that is later elevated as the core of repentance in the Tiantai tradition.⁵⁶ Zhiyi emphasizes the importance of generating a sense of shame and anxiety during the course of the ritual, and that one should visualize the bodhisattva Samantabhadra as if he were before one's very eyes. Similar to the *Fangdeng* repentance, one can approach the ritual with a focus on the practical activities (*shi*) of prostrating, reciting, and so on, or with a focus on the principle (*li*) of the fundamental emptiness of mind and characteristics (T. 1941.46.950a2-15). Such causes and conditions can enable the practitioner to come into responsive accord with *samādhi* and, through *samādhi*, apprehend Samantabhadra and the Buddhas of the Ten Directions before him (T. 1941.46.954b6-8).

Zhiyi discusses "repentance in practice" (*shi chanhui*) and "repentance in principle" (*li chanhui*) not only in his ritual protocols but also in his *Mohe zhiguan* (Great calming and contemplation; T. 1911), stating that the former aims at repentance for specific sins, while the latter addresses a general misconception about the principle of emptiness. In "Explanation of the Sequential Dharma Gates of the Perfection of Meditation" (*Chan boluomi cidi famen*),[57] Zhiyi lists three types of repentance: (1) "repentance by performing rituals" (*zuofa chanhui*), (2) "repentance by observing signs" (*guanxiang chanhui*) that, when they appear, signal that one has been purified of the transgression, and finally (3) "repentance by contemplating nonarising" (*guan wusheng chanhui*). The first category addresses sins that form obstacles because they violate moral rules, or "sins that block the way" (*zhangdao zui*); the second category redresses sins committed by the sense faculties or "sins of an essential nature" (*tixing zui*); and the third confronts "the fundamental sins of ignorance and attachment" (*wuming fannao gen benzui*). As we saw in the case of the Fangdeng and Lotus repentances, here Zhiyi claims that only by meditating on the true nature of reality—namely emptiness—can one overcome obstacles of attachment and attain enlightenment. In a sense, once one realizes the emptiness of all actions, there is no need to repent for any action in particular.

Yet the fact that Zhiyi includes multiple approaches to repentance signals a need to accommodate for diverse spiritual capacities and devotional interests even within a single tradition such as Tiantai, and it should caution against the assumption that "repentance on the contemplation of nonarising" or "repentance in principle" is the best approach for practitioners.[58] Instead, if we examine Zhiyi's philosophy—such as his idea of "the perfect interfusion of the three truths" (*yuanrong sandi*)[59] and "three thousand realms in a moment of thought" (*yinian sanqian*)[60]—we instead find that Zhiyi pays special attention to the mutual inclusion of principle and practice, that he in fact does not privilege the former over the latter. If we examine how repentance functions in the context of spiritual development, we can appreciate Zhiyi's inclusion of a variety of repentances that can be applied in different situations.

Kuo Liying and Daniel Stevenson emphasize the role that Buddhas and bodhisattvas play in Mahāyāna Buddhist repentance—becoming what Stevenson calls "the confessor par excellence" not only because they know the karmic destinies of sentient beings but also because their salvific power extends even to those transgressions—such as the four grave crimes, the five heinous sins, and even the sin of slandering the teachings (which some claim cuts off all access to liberation)—that would call for expulsion from the sangha or endless retribution in hell.[61] The Mahāyāna rituals often emphasize performance "face to face" before visualized images of Buddhas and bodhisattvas, and they include prayers calling for them to "confirm" (zhenming) or "witness" (zhengzhi) their repentance. Stevenson argues that the moment of repentance is pivotal; the practitioner juxtaposes his sin and limitations against the ideals of the Buddhas and bodhisattvas that he has summoned, and this generates a sense of urgency in that his future depends on their decision. As we will see, Ouyi conveys a similar sense of urgency about the future, but he suggests that one should channel feelings of shame and self-abnegation toward devotion to Buddhas and bodhisattvas.

Early Chinese Buddhist ritual protocols often emphasize the importance of this sense of urgency: the more intense and profound the regret, the greater stimulus (gan) generated. Zhiyi and other Chinese Buddhist writers emphasize the emotional dynamics of repentance, especially as it functions in this mechanism of sympathetic resonance (ganying). Zhiyi suggests that if the practitioner's heart is genuine and free of deceit, then he can stimulate the Buddhas to shine on him and remove his obstacles (T. 1911.46.92a9). He encourages practitioners to express these interior states by weeping profusely, by being stricken with remorse, and by throwing themselves at the Buddha's feet.

Following this initial establishment of ritual meditative practice in Zhiyi's liturgical manuals, with the exception of Zhanran's (711–782) commentaries on these liturgies, it is not until Siming Zhili (960–1028) and Ciyun Zunshi (964–1032) produce a series of new manuals for repentance rituals that we see substantive development in liturgy within the Tiantai tradition. As Daniel Getz argues, they were not simply conservators of Zhiyi's legacy but instead innovators in their own right.[62] All of the rituals were developed from a Tiantai perspective and largely followed the liturgical pattern set forth in Zhiyi's manuals—especially his Lotus repentance—but not all were simply expansions of Zhiyi's rituals. There were others—such as the Zunshi's Amitābha repentance (Mituo chanfa) and Zhili's Great Compassion repentance (Dabei chanfa)—that drew from Pure Land elements outside the Tiantai tradition. Although Zunshi is recognized for his contributions to liturgical practice, Daniel Getz argues that Zhili also played a significant role in the development of liturgical practices.

As we have seen, repentance represents a significant part of the meditation system that Zhiyi developed, so much so that some viewed the terms "repentance ritual" (*chanfa*) and *samādhi* (*sanmei*) to be essentially synonymous, though strictly speaking, the former was only part of the meditative system. Getz argues that Zhili sought to integrate the Pure Land visualizations set forth in the *Guan wuliangshou jing* (Contemplation sutra) with Tiantai's discernment of principle (*liguan*), and his own practice of repentance reflected this soteriological vision. Of the five types of repentances that he practiced over the course of his life, Ouyi performed Zunshi's Amitābha repentance fifty times—five times more than any other repentance.[63] In addition to holding bodhisattva precept assemblies every year and performing rituals of releasing living creatures (*fangsheng*) on the Buddha's birthday—a rite performed by Zhiyi and made famous by Zunshi—Zhili also drafted an announcement of a Pure Land society (*nianfo jingshe*) in 1012. Not only did it involve people from all social strata, but its central practice was reciting Amitābha's name a thousand times, repenting one's transgressions, and making vows, and practitioners were given a calendar chart so that they could record their practice, which Getz notes has become an important aspect of contemporary lay Buddhist practice.[64]

Zunshi also created repentance rituals for monks and laypeople, and his title "repentance master" (*chanzhu*) reflects the essential role he played in promoting such practices in the Song dynasty. Not only did he amend some of Zhiyi's repentance rituals, he also developed new repentance rituals including the *Wangsheng jingtu chanyuan yi* (Ritual of repentance and vows for rebirth in the Pure Land) and the Amitābha repentance incorporating repentance of transgressions alongside vows to be reborn in the Pure Land.[65] Zunshi draws on Zhiyi's notions of "ritual deportment" (*shiyi*) and "discernment of principle" (*liguan*) as equally necessary for purifying the three karmic activities of body, speech, and mind, and he also emphasizes the role of sympathetic response in his opening to the *Rite for the Invocation of Guanyin Samādhi*, when he suggests that it is when these three karmic activities form a "causal nexus" (*ji*) in one's practice that principle will surely respond (*ying*) and bring about purification.[66]

Although there is little discussion of the development of such Tiantai rituals following the Song in canonical materials, there is evidence to suggest that rituals developed by Zhiyi, Zhili, and Zunshi continued to be practiced and promoted in the Yuan and early Ming dynasties.[67] In a brief examination of repentance rituals in the Ming dynasty, Shengkai mentions the *Deyu Longhua xiu zheng chan yi* (Ritual of repentance, confirmation, and cultivation of encountering Longhua) composed in 1606 by a Tiantai monk named Ru Xing, a Maitreya repentance that follows the ritual protocol of Zhiyi's Lotus repentance (much like Zhili and Zunshi did in their own rituals) but adds elements of Maitreya worship—such as contemplation of Maitreya's ascent and descent—during certain parts of the ritual.[68] Thus, there is evidence (albeit scarce) that people continued to compose repentance rituals based on the ritual cycle set forth in Zhiyi's manuals but adapted the ritual to reflect their particular religious or soteriological interests.

OUYI'S REPENTANCE RITUALS

Ouyi follows the precedent set by his Tiantai predecessors who expanded upon the repertoire of repentance rituals developed by Zhiyi, whose fourfold samādhi allowed for considerable adaptation according to their particular liturgical interests.[69] As Daniel Stevenson argues, the Tiantai masters in the Song dynasty accorded their new repentance rituals "an interritual and intertextual cohesion" that brought about "a normalization of liturgical structure and literary form that seems to have been far more ramified and exacting than that of earlier periods."[70] In particular, the tenfold sequence for practice remained quite stable in its terminology, activities, and organization, and it became a kind of ideal framework for ritual performance—a "template" that could be adapted to various liturgical settings. As Stevenson further notes, the authoritative template for such routinized Tiantai ritual was Zhiyi's *Fahua sanmei chanyi* (Procedure for performing the repentance for the Lotus samādhi) together with Zhanran's *Fahua sanmei xingshi yunxiang buzhu yi* (Supplementary procedures for the visualizations [that accompany] the practical activity of the Lotus samādhi), and in his table of intertextual references comparing Tiantai repentance rituals, he shows that Ouyi frequently borrows from these two texts.[71]

Like his predecessors, Ouyi adopts the structure of the ten-part ritual formulary, but he adapts the ritual according to his particular concerns about his "fixed karma" from criticizing the Three Jewels as a youth and his devotion to the bodhisattva Dizang. Although the steps in the sequence vary slightly among his rituals, the overall structure remains the same, as illustrated by this table comparing the Brahma's Net and Divination repentances:

COMPARISON OF BRAHMA'S NET AND DIVINATION REPENTANCES

BRAHMA'S NET REPENTANCE	DIVINATION REPENTANCE
Adorn the place of practice	Adorn the place of practice
Purify one's body, speech, and mind	Purify one's body, speech, and mind
Make offerings of incense and flowers	Sit and contemplate marks of truth
Praise, venerate, and take refuge	Summon the Three Jewels and mundane gods
Confess and repent	Praise and venerate the Three Jewels
Make vows and recite the precepts	Cultivate repentance
Venerate the Buddha	Make vows and prayers
Renew one's vows and practice	Celebrate merit
Circumambulate and take refuge	Transfer merit
Sit and contemplate marks of truth	Make vows and recite the Buddha's name while seated in a quiet room

In addition to adopting the ten-part ritual formulary, Ouyi also lifts entire passages word for word from earlier Tiantai texts, just as his Song predecessors Zunshi and Zhili had done before him. For example, describing the need for "sympathetic resonance" in order to see Buddhas and bodhisattvas "face to face," Ouyi adopts a passage originally from Zhanran's *Supplementary Procedures for the Visualizations that Accompany the Practical Activity of the Lotus Samadhi* (T. 1942.46.956a2–956a3)—that later appears in Zhili and Zunshi's ritual texts[72]—as he encourages the practitioner to think, "The nature of the worshipper and the worshipped is completely empty. Mutual interaction (*daojiao*) and sympathetic resonance (*ganying*) are incredible. My place of practice is like a divine pearl: all the Buddhas' forms are manifested within it, and my own form is manifested before the Buddhas."[73] Ouyi emphasizes that for those like himself who live in a time when the Dharma is in decline (*mofa*), it is exceedingly difficult to achieve such purity; but if one can maintain purity and embody the appropriate affective and emotional state, one can stimulate the response of Buddhas and bodhisattvas.

For these reasons, Ouyi is even more emphatic about practitioners being ritually pure and emotionally sincere, which influences his recommendations for where and by whom the ritual should be performed. In general, Ouyi advocates solitary over communal practice to avoid the risk of having one's stimulus compromised by one's fellow practitioners. Although Ouyi is not alone in esteeming individual cultivation as a superior path,[74] it is significant that none of his repentance rituals are aimed at larger groups. Ouyi urges practitioners to perform the Brahma's Net repentance during the six periods of day and night—a characteristic associated with general monastic procedures in the main hall. But he also says that it should be performed ideally by one person—or two to three people at most, either novice monks (*shami*; Skt. *śrāmaṇeras*) or advanced laymen (*yuposai*; Skt. *upāsakas*) but not fully ordained *bhikṣus*—in a quiet room that has been swept clean, which signals it was a special ritual not to be generally practiced. Similarly, the other two repentances should be performed by few people—if not alone—in a ritually purified place, indicating that they too are special repentance rituals meant for intense and serious practitioners.

THE BRAHMA'S NET REPENTANCE

Ouyi's innovation lies in the way he develops extensive rituals from fairly brief references to repentance in the *Sutra of Brahma's Net* and the *Divination Sutra*. Although the sutras themselves allow for repentance by those who have committed the heinous and grave sins, they do not elaborate on the details of how one might go about engaging in such repentance.

As we have seen, Ouyi shows perennial concern for the purity of his own precepts. In a text written immediately before his summer retreat in 1633, Ouyi emphasizes the centrality of the precepts in his own life and the life of the sangha. He writes that he takes the precepts as his teacher, that he considers them to be the foundation of the three practices of *śīla*, *samādhi*, and *prajñā*, that he engages in *prātimokṣa* (*jiemo*)—that is, the bimonthly recitation of precepts—as instructed, and that by relying on the Vinaya and following its instruction, one can ensure that the Third Jewel, the sangha, will not vanish.[75] Appreciative of the opportunity to join other monks for a brief period in a solitary place (*lanruo*; Skt. *araṇya*) and to discuss the Vinaya, he asks that demons and obstacles not plague him and that because of pure precepts he might enter into the Pure Land.[76] Thus we can see that the precepts, for Ouyi, represent not only the foundation for religious practice in this life but also a means for rebirth in the Pure Land—a soteriological necessity. In a second text written the day before the retreat, he recalls slandering the Dharma but then hearing Dizang's sutra, arousing the aspiration to liberate sentient beings, and engaging in repentance. Ouyi describes casting lots to determine the purity of his precepts "according to his mental stimulus (*xin gan*)."[77]

Ouyi says that he cast the lot of bodhisattva-śrāmaṇera on that day, and he writes his repentance ritual based on the *Sutra of Brahma's Net* that same summer. He previously focused on this sutra in the *Xue pusa jiefa* (Ritual of practicing the bodhisattva precepts) that he first wrote in 1628 and revised in 1631. In his postscript to the revised edition, Ouyi states that the *Sutra of Brahma's Net* has been eclipsed by other texts on the bodhisattva precepts, and he admits that there is contention about the ceremony in the various sutras and commentaries,[78] as opposed to the Vinaya, which Ouyi claims has a "fixed pattern" (*dingshi*).[79] The *Sutra of Brahma's Net* advocates repentance for those who have violated the ten major precepts, but it does not specify the exact procedure for going about such repentance. It simply states that the practitioner should recite the bodhisattva precepts before the images of Buddhas and bodhisattvas in the six periods of day and night—for a week, two weeks, three weeks, or even a year—until he observes auspicious signs that signal the eradication of his transgressions. If he does not see such signs, then it means that he still lacks the precepts, but that he has increased the chance that he will receive the precepts in the future.[80] If we consider the fact that Ouyi expands these five lines of the sutra into a fifteen-page ritual, we can appreciate the degree to which Ouyi was not simply elaborating but altogether creating a new ritual—one that draws heavily on features of Tiantai repentance—as a prescription for how to repent for particular violations of the bodhisattva precepts.

Ouyi offers two reasons for designing a repentance ritual based on this sutra: not only is it particularly efficacious for those who have transgressed the ten major precepts, but it accommodates those who do not have an instructor within a thousand *li*, a circumstance he perceived to be increasingly common.[81] Although he admits that there are other ritual procedures (*xingfa*), such as the Lotus repentance, the *Fangdeng* repentance, and the Great Compassion repentance, that can eliminate sins, he emphasizes the unique value of the *Sutra of Brahma's Net* for bestowing mental calm on those who have committed major transgressions or who lack the support of Vinaya instructors. It describes two methods for transmitting the bodhisattva precepts: receiving them from a master who received his own through an unbroken lineage of teachers or receiving the precepts alone. In order to receive the precepts alone, one must first repent before the Buddha and see auspicious signs. Ouyi emphasizes that the repentance not only eliminates sins but completely restores the essence of the precepts (*jieti*).[82] Ouyi writes, "By sincerely seeking mercy, they will certainly succeed in closing the door to evil destinies and planting the seeds for liberation."[83] Only with the appropriate affective state of sincerity and penitence can one ensure the efficacy of the ritual.

Like his predecessors, Ouyi portrays the practitioner's mental and emotional state as being as important for ensuring the purity of the ritual as the ritual space or ritual implements. Thus he emphasizes the need for evoking appropriate feelings of shame and fear, and he also stresses that one must not be slipshod or stingy (such as relying on almsgivers) in one's adornment of the ritual site because these become the "conditions" (*suiyuan*)[84] under which one seeks forgiveness. Reflecting on the inherited good karma (*sushan*) that has enabled one to receive the precepts and the evil obstacles (*ezhang*) that have led one to violate them, Ouyi describes the single-mindedness that one should bring to the ritual as analogous to one stuck in prison or caught in a toilet who singularly seeks escape, or one whose hands are filled with oil and fears any trickling out. It is for this reason that Ouyi emphasizes that it would be better not to have companions in the ritual, unless there are one or two other transgressors who are remorseful, fearful, and have the same aim as oneself.[85] The more urgent and deprecating the practitioners are, the greater the stimulus and efficaciousness of the ritual.

Purifying the ritual space and one's karmic activities (of body, speech, and thought) creates those conditions conducive for mutual interaction and influence between the practitioner and Buddhas and bodhisattvas. Buddhas and bodhisattvas already know and see all of one's transgressions, but because of ignorance and attachment, the practitioner cannot see them. Ouyi likens the practitioner to a blind person in a large group: the practitioner, veiled by ignorance, has violated the precepts in the presence of Buddhas and bodhisattvas. Thus one cannot simply perform the ritual without the appropriate cognitive disposition—only by removing ignorance can one achieve a transparency in which one can see Buddhas and bodhisattvas as if they were directly in front of oneself. In order to accomplish this, the practitioner must perform the ritual with an attention to this principle of emptiness.[86] Both practice (*shi*) and principle (*li*) play crucial roles in creating an environment in which the practitioner can not only "be seen" but also "see."

In order to accomplish this transformation, in the section for eliminating sins, Ouyi prescribes the Tiantai notion of the "Ten Mentalities That Oppose [the Flow of Saṃsāra] (*shi ni xin*)" to combat "Ten Mentalities That Promote [the Flow of Saṃsāra]" (*shi shun xin*), which originate in the writing of Zhiyi (T. 1950.976c19–c24).[87] Ouyi encourages a transformation or "turning" of thoughts (*yunxiang*), criticizing the ten mentalities that further contribute to *saṃsāra*, including (1) assuming that one has a self, (2) accumulating false friendships, (3) not rejoicing in the good of others, (4) promoting the three karmic activities, (5) always having an evil mind, (6) retaining this evil mind continuously day and night, (7) concealing (*fu*) one's faults or mistakes, (8) not fearing evil realms of rebirth, (9) not being ashamed (*cankui*), and (10) challenging that there is no cause and effect. The list of sins begins with mental activities—attachment, views of selfhood, selfishness—that might qualify as cognitive sins, and then proceeds to certain affective tendencies—the tendency to conceal one's faults, not fearing evil, and lacking a sense of shame or regret—that are equally pernicious. The crucial mentality is the mistaken view that there is no cause and effect—this tenth mentality serves as the linchpin for transformation, becoming the first of the ten mentalities that oppose the flow of *saṃsāra*.

Thus, transformation centers on one's view of karma; ironically, in order for one's karma to be eliminated, one must have the profound belief in the inevitability of karmic retribution. Ouyi urges the practitioner to cultivate (1) faith in cause and effect, (2) a sense of shame, (3) fear of evil realms of rebirth, (4) a willingness to reveal (*falu*)[88] one's sins, (5) cutting off the mind-stream (*xiangxu xin*), (6) arousing the aspiration to seek enlightenment and breaking from evil and cultivating good, (7) reflecting on past heavy sins with body, speech, and mind (as a novice monk), (8) sympathetically rejoicing in the slightest good deed of an ordinary or sagely person, (9) maintaining mindfulness of Buddhas in the ten directions whom Ouyi esteems for their ability to rescue from the "sea of two deaths" and place on the "shore of the three virtues,"[89] and (10) knowing that *dharmas* in their original nature are empty. Whereas we saw a movement from the cognitive to the affective in the mentalities promoting the flow of *saṃsāra*, here we see the opposite movement from the affective to the cognitive; but instead of the constricted view of selfishness and ego, there is an appreciation of good deeds of ordinary and extraordinary people, an expansive awareness of all the Buddhas everywhere, and a grasping of the principle that all *dharma*s are empty of self-nature. The dynamics of transformation rest upon the central faith in cause and effect.

It is interesting to note the places where Ouyi diverges from Zhiyi in this latter list, for it reflects his anxiety that is tied to the purity of his precepts. In Zhiyi's list, the seventh and eighth mentalities are (7) cultivating merit and repairing one's mistakes and (8) resolving to protect the True Dharma. Here Ouyi specifies that the novice monk recalls his mistakes (there is no mention of merit-making) and substitutes "sympathetic joy" instead of protecting the Dharma. By highlighting the need to redress one's mistakes and including sympathetic joy, Ouyi may be seeking to redress his own mistakes. As we saw earlier, Ouyi thought he was guilty of slighting others, which violates the seventh major precept in the sutra—prohibiting self-praise and disparaging others and emphasizing that a bodhisattva should not boast of his own virtue or conceal the good works of others.[90] Although the change is slight, it sets the stage for an individualized confession by the practitioner, whom Ouyi instructs to kneel, to put his palms together, and to reveal his violations by copiously weeping, confessing:

> I, the disciple of so-and-so, repent with a focused mind (*zhixin*). Sentient beings and I have original natures that are pure; but veiled by ignorance, we do not ourselves realize and know [this]. Because of these causes and conditions, I have long been caught in *saṃsāra*, but now I have reached the true Dharma and hold true to observance of the Vinaya. Mental afflictions (*fannao*; Skt. *kleśa*) disturb my mind and also obstruct my training. I have committed acts such as. . . . (One should confess according to the transgression, be it killing, stealing, licentiousness, or lying.) Without rituals of shame (*xiuchi fa*) when facing the sea of the Buddha's teaching, I will be abandoned forever and fall to the Avīci hell, into its great prison of fierce, scorching fires, receiving immeasurable suffering, perhaps even successive evil rebirths with no chance for liberation. Thus do sins obstruct; cause and effect is not empty.[91]

Again, we can see the seminal role played by the practitioner acknowledging karmic cause and effect: the consequences of sin are very real. Without repentance rituals—"rituals of shame"—humans who violate the ten major precepts will inevitably fall to hell. The passage continues by recognizing that Buddhas and bodhisattvas know all and see all;

thus practitioners dare not conceal their transgressions but instead must leave their crooked ways, repent of their transgressions, and seek mercy so that "together with sentient beings, [they] will be washed of future karma (*wangye*) that will follow from previously committed action."[92] The practitioner finishes by vowing (*shi*) never again to transgress and hoping that the Buddhas and bodhisattvas will "uproot my roots of sin and give me pure precepts."[93] The entire confession speaks to the degree to which obstacles can present very real impediments to liberation, even relegating one to hellish torment without hope of escape. Only repentance can prompt a transformation; by confessing previous sins, upholding the Vinaya, and vowing never to transgress again in the future, one hopes that Buddhas and bodhisattvas will mercifully respond by eliminating one's karma. Yet in order to accomplish this, the ritual itself specifies that the practitioner's cognitive and affective state—as well as his surroundings—must be focused, sincere, and pure.

Thus Ouyi largely adopts the structure and features of Tiantai repentance, but because he considers purity a rare commodity in the age of the decline of the Dharma, he encourages practitioners to practice alone or in very small groups (unlike Zhiyi, Zhili, and Zunshi, who typically allow for up to ten practitioners on special repentance rituals and even create rituals for large public gatherings); he emphasizes the importance of maintaining a single ritual aim; and he portrays repentance as necessitating a particular cognitive disposition in which one realizes the emptiness of all *dharmas* (including sin) as well as a certain affective and somatic state in which one emotionally and physically demonstrates one's regret and deprecation (in the face of hell, which is framed as the inevitable result of sin) in order to stimulate the gracious response of Buddhas and bodhisattvas.

THE DIVINATION REPENTANCE

These same themes appear in his other repentance ritual written that same year, in which Ouyi singles out the bodhisattva Dizang as a merciful savior who can fully uproot one's karma. The ritual is ostensibly based on the *Zhancha shan'e yebao jing* (Sutra on the divination of good and bad karmic retribution), but like the Brahma's Net repentance, the ritual sequence in the sutra is brief in comparison with Ouyi's ritual manual. The sutra itself describes two rituals, one for divining good and bad karma through wheel marks (*mulun xiang*) and another for confession, both of which are recommended as means of purifying the mind before taking the bodhisattva precepts. In his ritual, Ouyi again follows the liturgical cycle of Zhiyi, adding two sections entirely absent from the original sutra.[94]

The ritual shares the soteriological goal of purification and elimination of karma, but it promotes Dizang as the bodhisattva best equipped to eradicate karma. The text begins:

> Now then, Buddhas and bodhisattvas pity those who are lost, even more than a mother cherishes her son. Thus they use various kinds of expedient means to teach them how to escape *saṃsāra*. But sentient beings do not understand the causes and conditions (*yinyuan*) of karmic retribution. They do not know the extinguishing of evil and cultivation of good. Pure faith daily diminishes, and the five defilements of the world (*wuzhuo*)[95] increase. From this stimulus—these occasions of severe suffering (*juku ji*)—all the more there arises the response of gratuitous mercy (*wuyuan ci*). Therefore when there are suitable conditions, this we call to strengthen pure faith. We earnestly entreat the World-Honored One to condescend to mercifully save us. Thus does Buddha broadly praise the merits of Dizang, and brings it about that he establish expedient means.[96]

Although the portrayal of bodhisattvas as maternal figures is commonplace,[97] it is interesting to note the emphasis that Ouyi places on sentient beings not fully understanding the workings of karma. Ouyi suggests that this opacity renders humans less capable of eliminating evil and cultivating virtue—the mistaken view of karma is the crux of the problem. Although in this instance Ouyi is likely referring to those who disregard cause and effect entirely, he may also be acknowledging the possible antinomian interpretation of "all *dharmas* in their original nature are empty" or the principle of emptiness. If this leads one to conclude that karmic retribution is inoperative, then it obstructs the cultivation of virtue. Because humans have certain cognitive limitations and cannot fully understand the logic of karmic retribution, they must rely on the compassion and concern of Buddhas and bodhisattvas to escape the suffering of death and rebirth. Again, Ouyi draws on the notion of "stimulus-response" (*ganying*) to suggest that extreme suffering can prompt Buddhas and bodhisattvas to mercifully respond.[98]

Ouyi views repentance as particularly necessary for those who live in the age when the Dharma is in decline. As faith diminishes and defilement increases, these maternal figures respond with even more grace and concern for sentient beings. Ouyi writes:

[The scripture] warns that people with heavy karma cannot first cultivate *samādhi* and *prajñā*. They must rely on repentance rituals in order to purify themselves. Afterward they can practice the two methods of contemplation, and they will have no difficulty engaging in self-discipline (*kehuo*). Truly, this miraculously serves as the particular antidote to the latter-day (*moshi*); it is the foremost expedient means among expedient means.[99]

Although some might consider repentance rituals merely preparatory, Ouyi instead portrays them as foundational. No spiritual achievement can be accomplished without them. He suggests a variety of reasons that one would participate in repentance rituals, including removing karmic obstacles, eliminating even the most heinous crimes that would relegate one to Avīci hell,[100] achieving various meditative states, or being reborn in the Pure Land.[101] Ouyi's list is exhaustive—all three elements of the Buddhist path (*śīla, samādhi, prajñā*) depend on the practice of such repentance rituals, and the efficacy of such rituals relies on the saving power of the bodhisattva Dizang. He writes, "This is the extraordinary and vast compassion of the Tathāgata Śākyamuni [and] the compassionate vow of the admired bodhisattva Dizang. There is no suffering that he does not uproot. There is no happiness that he does not bestow. By this practice, pure faith is strengthened and made firm."[102] Ouyi's choice of the word "extract" or "uproot" (*ba*) is significant for it implies that Dizang does not simply eliminate those obstacles resulting from karma, but that he even gets rid of the root of sins—the seeds planted from karmic action that will later come to fruition.

The actual ritual protocol follows previous Tiantai rituals, but Ouyi makes additions that are specific to the sutra, such as consulting divination wheels to determine purification or praising the bodhisattva Dizang. Ouyi again emphasizes the importance of regulating the participants for the repentance ritual. He insists that all who participate must have a single purpose or goal—that it would be better to practice alone than to have many people repenting for different reasons. Ouyi states it plainly: "If there is not a unity of purpose, solitary practice is better."[103] Thus one must first determine one's purpose for repenting—whether it is following the protocol of monastic codes or seeking meditative states, rebirth, or the realization of enlightenment.[104] One can simultaneously seek multiple goals, but all participants must be of like mind. Not only must one have a singular purpose for the ritual, one must also maintain decorum throughout. Ouyi emphasizes that one must strictly select fellow practitioners: they must be "vessels suited to [receiving or carrying] the Dharma (*faqi*)."¹⁰⁵ He writes, "In ritual deportment (*shiyi*) and discernment of principle (*liguan*), refinement (*weixi*) is appropriate; do not be rushed even if one does ascetic practices."¹⁰⁶ His emphasis on ritual propriety is especially stringent: if one is not careful, one lapse can ruin the ritual entirely. Ouyi writes, "Do not for an instant think of random worldly things but instead consider the great matter of life and death, impermanence, and strengthen one's effort, then one can succeed and cross over [into *nirvana*]. If one slightly contravenes ritual purity, then in vain all is ruined and lost."¹⁰⁷

Dizang is particularly suited for such repentance rituals because of his ties with the three lower realms of rebirth—especially the hells. Ouyi singles out Dizang as "the master of repentance." Although he recognizes that Guanyin is also capable of liberating those in doubt and has power equal to Dizang, he writes that because of Dizang, "there is no evil that is not extinguished, there is no goodness that does not arise."¹⁰⁸ If we recall how Ouyi associates these two qualities with a proper understanding of karmic retribution, we can appreciate why Dizang is especially venerated in the ritual. Elsewhere he calls Dizang "the true savior of the world . . . who quickly eliminates obstacles and increases pure confidence."¹⁰⁹

The Divination repentance is especially aimed at using the wheel mark to divine the gravest sins to confess—the graver the sin, the greater the need to inculcate a feeling of penitence. In the section "Repentance," Ouyi again reminds the practitioners of the evil retribution that inevitably awaits those who have committed such transgressions. Ouyi writes:

> Now then, although your sins may be immeasurable, nevertheless, those revealed by the wheel mark are the gravest. They can incur evil fruition; they can be obstacles to the spiritual path. Thus one must be ashamed (*cankui*) and shed tears. Each of these [actions] in their different ways manifests this. With great effort, repent of your mistakes (*huiguo*). Pray that it will cause them to be extinguished (*xiaomie*). Throw yourself to the ground in prostration after you have related your gravest sins, then make this intention.¹¹⁰

The intention includes acknowledging that one has been obstructed by the six sense faculties as well as the three karmic activities of body, speech, and thought, that one has not seen Buddhas nor known how to escape the world but instead has continued in the realm of *saṃsāra*, not knowing the "wondrous principle" (*miaoli*). Ouyi even admits that although he knows this principle, he is still obstructed: "Now before Dizang and all Buddhas, for all sentient beings, I surrender myself to repentance and only pray for divine protection (*jiahu*) to enable my obstacles to be extinguished."[111]

The Ten Mentalities serve the same seminal function as they did in the Brahma's Net repentance—namely a transformation based on the recognition of karmic retribution—but here Ouyi especially focuses on the implications of karmic obstacles for one's religious practice. Ouyi acknowledges that sentient beings have an originally pure nature similar to the realm and bodies of Buddhas but because of ignorance (*wuming*), delusion (*chi*), darkness (*an*), and subliminal karmic impressions (*xunxi*),[112] they have false perceptions about the world, give rise to thoughts of attachment, and wrongly distinguish between subject and object. This misperception leads to all sorts of sins—including those most evil and heinous—that later become obstacles to meditative attainments. As Ouyi writes, "it leads one to be engulfed in a sea of suffering."[113] Even if one desires to practice spiritual cultivation, one becomes "vexed by external demons," "surrounded by erroneous views," or "lacks beneficial conditions" for practice.[114]

Only Dizang instills Ouyi's confidence that he can succeed in his religious practice, and Ouyi calls upon Dizang to "Dispel my cloud of doubt, wash away my anxieties, and clean my mind."[115] Asking Dizang to witness, protect, and care for him, Ouyi repents and vows never again to commit such mistakes.[116] He then prays that all sentient beings have innumerable eons of sins eliminated—including the most serious transgressions and heretical stances. Ouyi writes, "Thus even though the nature of sin—in its essential nature—is empty, nevertheless from such deception (*xuwang*) arises a perverted (*diandao*) mind. There is no true meditation that one can attain. I pray that all sentient beings quickly reach the origin of their mind and forever extinguish the root of sin."[117] Ouyi acknowledges that the nature of sin is empty, yet he claims that its consequences can be disastrous by hindering one's religious practice. Because the roots of sin are formidable obstacles, only by repenting and relying on bodhisattvas such as Dizang can one ever hope to progress on the religious path.

THE DIZANG REPENTANCE

In this way Ouyi explicitly borrows from the Tiantai liturgical tradition in his own repentance rituals—which center on purification tied to the bodhisattva precepts—and he focuses on the bodhisattva Dizang as a compassionate savior figure particularly suited to those living in the age when the Dharma is in decline. Four years later, in 1637, Ouyi travels to Jiuhuashan, the sacred Buddhist mountain where Dizang is said to abide, even though it is far from the main areas of Ouyi's religious activity.[118] It is here that he writes the Dizang repentance, in which there is evidence of development in Ouyi's devotion toward Dizang; he specifically appeals to Dizang as a "savior of the penitent" who can eliminate "fixed karma." In the text, Ouyi writes:

> [Dizang] illuminates the practice of virtue like a bright sun; he lights the path of destruction like a blazing torch. He eliminates the heat of affliction like a cold full moon. He delivers [us] from the four currents [that disturb a quiet mind—namely desire, existence, views, and ignorance—by making himself a bridge or beam; he hastens [us] to the shore by making himself a raft; he conceals non-Buddhist paths like a lion king; he defeats heavenly demons like a large elephant; he protects those who are fearful like a friend or relative; he guards against those who resent or oppose one like a moat or wall; he saves from calamity like one's parents; he hides those who are afraid like a thicket or forest; he ensures that good roots of sentient beings never decay; he makes manifest a miraculous realm causing everyone to be joyful. He urges sentient beings to increase their conscientiousness and shame (*cankui*) and causes them to be endowed with the adornments of merit and insight. He can turn the great wheel of the Dharma without exertion. One cannot measure his special and excellent virtues. For a long time firm in practice, he made a great vow with great compassion, with effort and energy, surpassing other bodhisattvas.[119]

Not only does Ouyi consider Dizang a savior figure, he attributes a particular role to Dizang—one who encourages people to feel regret and shame. Later in the same text, Ouyi writes, "With one mind I worship the bodhisattva-*mahāsattva* Dizang who is endowed with ample shame (*cankui*), *samādhi*, and *prajñā*."[120] He thereby substitutes the affective state of shame into the normal position of *śīla* (*jie*) within the traditional set of three practices (*sanxue*; Skt. *śikṣā-traya*). Although wisdom (*zhi*; Skt. *prajñā*) and contemplation (*ding*; Skt. *samādhi*) are stock traits associated with Buddhas and bodhisattvas, shame is rarely attributed to such figures. In short, Ouyi portrays Dizang as a savior of the penitent, and he associates the bodhisattva with the particular trait of regret and repentance.¹²¹

The actual protocol for the ritual is an abbreviated version of the tenfold Tiantai sequence. Ouyi omits the first three steps of adornment, purification, and binding the ritual, but he includes giving offerings, offering praises, bowing in worship, performing repentance and making vows, circumambulation, and dedication of merit. He likely omitted the three steps because the manual is meant as a mnemonic device or general outline—purification is implicit when he writes that practitioners should arrive before Dizang's image with "pure thought, speech, and mind." For the most part, Ouyi follows previous Tiantai repentance texts but focuses on Dizang and Dizang's texts such as the *Dizang pusa benyuan jing* (Sutra on the original vow of the Bodhisattva Dizang), the *Dacheng daji dizang shilun jing* (Sutra of the ten cakras of Kṣitigarbha in the Mahāyāna great collection), and the *Zhancha shan'e yebao jing* (Sutra on the divination of good and bad karma).

Physically, the ritual consists of first standing before the image of Dizang and chanting in worship to the Three Jewels; kneeling while offering incense and flowers in the hopes that they perfume all Buddha lands; chanting praises of Dizang with one's palms together; bowing in worship to various Buddhas, bodhisattvas, and sutras; fully prostrating with one's head to the ground as one recalls one's sins; kneeling and chanting in repentance; standing and circumambulating while chanting to the Buddha, Dharma, Sangha, Śākyamuni, Dizang, as well as the three Dizang sutras either three or seven times—however long it takes to return before the Dharma seat; offering verses of dedication; and concluding with three prostrations to the Three Jewels. At the end of the ritual, Ouyi insists that if one goes into a quiet room, or recollects the name of Dizang, or recites Dizang's *dhāraṇī* for eliminating fixed karma, or contemplates his *dharmakāya*, then one will be able to eliminate karmic obstacles.

Although the confession begins abstractly with the Ten Mentalities, as is the case in the Brahma's Net and Divination repentances, we soon see Ouyi's personal anxieties surface as he begins specifying various sins that apply to his own life, such as slandering the teachings and ridiculing lay and ordained Buddhist followers. Ouyi draws analogies between his anti-Buddhist writings and physical violence as he writes:

> I concealed the good and spread the bad; with harsh, evil speech for a time I cut them down, hit them with clubs to hurt them, stole their

clothes and bowls, stole their resources. I cut off their food and drink, forcing them to retire to ordinary life. I took off their monk's robes, binding them with cangues and shackles, throwing them in a prison.[122]

He likens the karma of such acts with the five heinous crimes (*wuni*) and ten evil deeds (*shi'e*) and fears that for future eons he will sink into evil realms of rebirth, passing through the three evil destinies (*santu*)—the fires of hell, the hell of blood, and the hell of swords—and experience all kinds of suffering and unspeakable pain.

Although we might find his tone extreme, Ouyi finds proof of residual karma in his inability to progress along the religious path. He writes, "These karmic obstacles, of which there is a surplus not yet exhausted, make us still unable to realize peace or *nirvana* and unable to realize states of meditative absorption or attain superior virtues."[123] Resolving to spread the Buddhist teachings and extinguish the hardships of sentient beings, Ouyi then asks that Dizang and all Buddhas "pity (*aimin*), protect (*fuhu*), and save (*jiba*) us, causing all of our karmic obstacles to be eliminated, and [allowing us] to never suffer the painful retribution (*kuguo*) of the evil destinies."[124] Following this prayer for protection and deliverance, Ouyi vows never again to slander the teachings, harm the sangha, or hinder the ability of sentient beings to receive Buddhist teachings.

Ouyi views Dizang as capable of erasing his karma, not merely allowing him the opportunity to gain good merit to offset his previous sins. In the text, we see the tension between Ouyi's resolution to profoundly believe in cause and effect and his view that Dizang can undo karmic effects. Ouyi clearly fears the repercussions from his early denouncement of Buddhism—he imagines not only the possibility of evil rebirth but also the likelihood of spending time in various hells—yet he also claims that Dizang has the power to erase such "fixed karma."[125] As Bruce Williams notes, there is something unsettling about the claim that repentance can remove the future karmic consequence of sins that have been committed. He writes, "Should the performance of relatively simple rituals be able to eliminate future, undesirable karmic retribution, this would disturb not only the cosmic balance of retribution and reincarnation, but might also serve to undercut the practice of the moral life altogether."[126] Although one might question whether repentance rituals are as "simple" as they seem,[127] nevertheless there seem to be antinomian implications underlying the view that karma can be undone.

By investing Dizang with the power to intervene in human affairs Ouyi suggests that in rare and exceptional cases, "fixed karma" can be undone. Ouyi recognizes the importance of emptiness—and he himself espouses the three types of repentance outlined by Zhiyi, namely repentance by performing rituals, repentance seeking marks, and repentance meditating on emptiness—but here he suggests that cognitive understanding alone is insufficient for erasing karma. In fact, in the Dizang repentance text, he states that emptiness sometimes leads people to erroneously conclude that there is no such thing as karmic retribution:

> With an ignorant and veiled mind I did not know the importance of escaping [saṃsāra]. I yearned for intelligence and showed conceit; I was truly foolish. I heard the Mahāyāna teachings, and I erroneously gave rise to an understanding of emptiness and questioned whether there was any cause and effect, thereby eliminating my good roots.[128]

Ouyi warns against relying solely on the intellect, for it can lead one astray if one thinks that because everything is empty, there is no karmic retribution. Recognition of the emptiness of sin does not render transgressions inconsequential. Here Ouyi suggests quite the opposite, that one cannot overlook karmic fruition. Ouyi regrets his previous intellectual conceit, which led him to deny karma and thereby cut the "good roots" (shangen) of his previous virtuous actions.

Instead of viewing emptiness as a license to behave immorally, Ouyi describes how emptiness compels a person to engage in virtuous acts. Emptiness (kong; Skt. śūnyatā) is a distinctive Mahāyāna Buddhist view of reality, in which all phenomena are said to arise in dependence upon each other (yuanqi; Skt. pratītya-samutpāda) and to lack an unchanging self-nature (zixing; Skt. svabhāva). Ouyi recounts how he committed sins because he was ignorant about the emptiness of his self. He writes, "Now I know about emptiness; because I seek enlightenment for the sake of sentient beings, I vastly cultivate these good deeds and everywhere cut off evil acts."[129] How are emptiness and virtue connected? After realizing that his self is empty—that it arises dependent on various causes and conditions—Ouyi can get rid of self-conceit and acknowledge the interdependence of all sentient beings. In order to liberate himself and other beings, he must engage in religious practices and thereby cultivate good merit. Emptiness alone cannot undo karma; it can only inspire one to engage in virtuous behavior. Ouyi allows for the possibility that "one's previous transgressions [can] be destroyed, scattered, and eliminated,"[130] but this requires external intervention. One can rectify one's mind by recognizing the emptiness of self, but this does not destroy previous karma; that is the domain of the bodhisattva Dizang.

In this instance, we see how Ouyi's view of repentance may differ from his predecessors in that he admits that the realization of emptiness and recognition of interdependence can prompt one to pursue good conduct, but he suggests that one cannot fully overcome one's previous sins without external help. Because of this reliance, Ouyi calls for practitioners to cultivate an affective state of shame and to engage in veneration and devotion of Buddhas and bodhisattvas, so that they might mercifully respond to such stimuli. Although Ouyi views people as capable of attaining a cognitive understanding of emptiness, he deems them incapable of understanding the workings of karma and thus dependant on bodhisattvas who can extinguish their karma.

Having examined three repentance rituals designed by Ouyi—two based on brief passages in apocryphal sutras and one stemming from his devotion to the bodhisattva Dizang—we have seen how the crux of such rituals occurs when Ouyi calls upon practitioners to affirm karmic cause and effect but also acknowledge that repentance can eliminate karma entirely. Buddhas and bodhisattvas play a crucial role in the ritual process; only by recognizing their reliance on such salvific figures and cultivating an appropriate sense of shame and devotion can practitioners cause them to mercifully respond and eliminate karma. Drawing from a rich legacy of repentance rituals in the Tiantai tradition, Ouyi adapts the Tiantai ritual protocol to reflect his concern for those who have committed grave transgressions. He singles out Dizang in particular because of his vow to save all sentient beings—including those relegated to the lowest of hells.

FOUR
VOWING TO ASSUME THE KARMA OF OTHERS

With one stick [of incense] I regret my severe deficiencies and karma, giving rise to murderous acts and licentious tendencies, the sin of slandering the Three Jewels, faults of speech, and evil thoughts, as well as defilements and illnesses. According to the Dharma, these various [crimes] cannot be eliminated; let these vows completely eliminate them.

—Ouyi Zhixu[1]

JUST AS Ouyi esteems Dizang for his vow to erase the fixed karma of humankind, Ouyi himself makes vows throughout his life. His votive texts (*yuanwen*) form the first fascicle of his collected writings in the *Lingfeng Zonglun*, which was compiled by his disciple Chengshi. The designation of the section as "votive texts" belies the actual diversity of the types of texts that are included—"oaths" (*shiwen*), "repentance texts" (*chanwen*), "invitations" (*qiwen*), "addresses" (*gaowen*), "verses" (*jie*), and "texts of dedication of merit" (*huixiang wen*)—but Jianmi Chengshi was not entirely misguided in grouping them under this larger theme because many of these texts include a series of vows.

Votive texts are often structured as follows—first, an invocation of certain Buddhas, bodhisattvas, or scriptures; second, a recollection of past crimes and misdeeds for which Ouyi repents and seeks divine compassion; third, a temporal shift demarcated by the words "now" (*jin*), "therefore" (*yuan*), or some other word signaling a turn from the past to the present, followed by a description of the types of actions performed as part of the ritual, be it repenting for mistakes, burning incense, reciting *dhāraṇī*, purifying the boundary for the ritual, and so on; fourth, an aspiration for some future condition, usually the salvation of sentient beings or the pronouncement that Ouyi himself will not gain enlightenment until others attain either enlightenment or rebirth in the Pure Land; and finally, some closing sequence in which Ouyi asks that Buddhas and bodhisattvas protect and envelop him and all sentient beings.

Unlike Ouyi's divination and repentance texts, which were either commentaries or prescriptive protocols for performing divination and repentance rituals, his votive texts were composed on specific dates to commemorate specific ritual activities and occasions. Each includes the year in which it was composed (many specify the month and day) and some occasionally mention the names of people who either participated in or sponsored such rituals. In many respects, they serve a similar function as Chinese Buddhist poems, celebrating social occasions such as parting from friends, ending retreats, engaging in rituals, and lamenting the death of friends, which have a rich tradition of "occasional writing" in Chinese secular poetry. Just as Chinese poems carried strong autobiographical dimensions and were vehicles through which poets sought to make themselves known, as has been argued by Stephen Owen,[2] votive texts similarly carry autobiographical dimensions and enable clerics to make themselves known as future bodhisattvas. Like poems, votive texts were written down, they could be circulated and preserved, and they could be effective ways of promoting a particular vision of oneself as an eminent cleric and bodhisattva-to-be.

This chapter employs such reading strategies when examining Ouyi's votive texts, paying attention to the way in which Ouyi uses these texts to promote a certain vision of himself as a future bodhisattva. Votive texts engage with future possibility in a way that complements divination as a diagnostic for karma in the past and repentance as a means of redressing karma in the present. Votive texts enable Ouyi to not only project himself into the future but to also write his future by presenting himself as a bodhisattva and solidifying that characterization in the eyes of his readers. This is not to suggest that Ouyi solely wrote such texts for purposes of self-promotion. His particular vision of bodhisattvahood actually compels him to portray his own life—particularly his sins as a youth and his failure to uphold the precepts—in an especially damning light. He occasionally revels in the dramatic possibilities of this moral turpitude, envisioning the various hells and torment that faces him because of his transgressions.

Ouyi presents two visions for himself as a future bodhisattva. On the one hand, he models himself after Dizang as a bodhisattva who eliminates fixed karma; on the other hand, he acknowledges cases in which sentient beings, because of their fixed karma, must be reborn in the evil rebirths of hells, animals, or hungry ghosts. In such instances, Ouyi makes the vow as an aspiring bodhisattva to substitute (*dai*) for such beings.[3] At one point, he even uses the word "atone" or "ransom" (*shu*) to describe this act of compassion. Thus Ouyi presents two future roles for himself as a bodhisattva: one that eliminates karma entirely in instances of sincere repentance, and another that assumes the karma of those who have committed particularly heinous sins, substituting for them and suffering karmic retribution on their behalf.

This chapter first examines the genre of votive texts, which allows Ouyi the creative license to project himself into the future role of a bodhisattva. Although there were certainly precedents for these vows detailed in scriptures such as the *Sukhāvatīvyūha-sutra*s, the genre allowed considerable flexibility for people to imagine what they would do as bodhisattvas. Next, this chapter considers a theme that becomes particularly prominent in Ouyi's votive texts, namely the ability of bodhisattvas to affect people's karma. It concludes by considering his two visions of bodhisattvahood: one having the power to eliminate karma, and the other able to substitute for people in their various karmic predicaments, taking on their evil karma so that they might attain enlightenment before him.

THE GENRE OF "VOTIVE TEXTS": IMAGINING FUTURE BODHISATTVAHOOD

Before discussing the role of "substitution" in Ouyi's votive texts, we should first attend to issues of genre vis-à-vis votive texts. As a Western scholar approaching the genre of votive texts, one is immediately tempted to use "speech-act theory"[4] to analyze the force and effects of such vows, but Chinese literary theory provides a more fruitful avenue of analysis, particularly Stephen Owen's work on Chinese poetry. Western scholars might also draw to mind vows that appear in the Hebrew Bible[5] or vows in

Christian sacraments such as baptism and marriage when they hear the word "vow," but one must be cautious about such associations. In Ouyi's case, such vows are not promises to any particular Buddha or bodhisattva but are instead formal pronouncements of his commitment to the bodhisattva path—specifically the resolution to save all sentient beings.[6]

The Chinese character for "vow"—*yuan*—has a variety of connotations including vow, aspiration, desire, prayer, and request. The most general vow of a bodhisattva—"I vow to attain Buddhahood for the sake of all sentient beings"—can be augmented by emphasizing various elements of the bodhisattva path.[7] The most famous vows in the Chinese Buddhist tradition are the forty-eight vows pronounced by the bodhisattva Dharmākara, who later becomes the Buddha Amitābha, in the longer *Sukhāvatīvyūha Sutra*. In fact Ouyi's earliest extant votive text titled *Forty-Eight Vows* explicitly models itself on these vows. Dharmākara's vows all begin with the phrase "May I not gain possession of perfect awakening if . . ." and then describe the various qualities of his purified or created land. We can appreciate the imaginative possibilities of the genre of votive texts when we read that Dharmākara not only views his Pure Land as a utopia the inhabitants of which possess supernatural powers but also envisions personal benefits that will accrue from his profession of vows, such as an infinite lifespan (vow 13) and Buddhas everywhere praising him and proclaiming his name (vow 17). The sutra indulges in great creative flourish in its description of the Pure Land.[8] Dharmākara's vows guarantee and create the possibilities in which salvation can be realized for sentient beings. Dharmākara's creativity sets a precedent for Ouyi and other writers of votive texts.[9]

Ouyi clearly models his first votive text on the forty-eight vows of Dharmākara, but his vision of bodhisattvahood differs in one important respect. If we consider the famous eighteenth vow that paves the way for later practices of recollection of the Buddha (*nianfo*; Jpn: *nembutsu*; Skt. *buddha-anusmṛti*) in East Asia, we see that Dharmākara vows:

> May I not gain possession of perfect awakening if, once I have attained Buddhahood, any among the throng of living beings in the ten regions of the universe should single-mindedly desire to be reborn in my land with joy, with confidence, and gladness, and if they should bring to mind this aspiration for even ten moments of thought and yet not gain rebirth there. This excludes only those who have committed the five heinous sins and those who have reviled the True Dharma.[10]

Although this vow—along with the nineteenth vow offering the same assurances to those who single-mindedly aspire for rebirth in the Pure Land on their deathbed—has often been interpreted as signaling an easy path toward liberation, we should note that Dharmākara excludes those who have committed the five heinous sins (*wuni*) of matricide, patricide, killing an *arhat*, wounding the body of the Buddha, or destroying the harmony of the sangha. Indeed, the only figures excluded from rebirth in the Pure Land are those who revile the Dharma and bodhisattvas who make vows on behalf of sentient beings. Dharmākara excludes the latter because they have already put the liberation of other sentient beings before their own salvation: "Because of the vows they took in the past to effortlessly bring all living beings to spiritual maturity, [they] don the armor of the Great Vows, amass the roots of virtue, and liberate all these beings."[11] It is precisely because of their vows that bodhisattvas cannot be reborn in the Pure Land.

These passages clearly made an impression on Ouyi, for he writes in a later Dharma talk that he felt that because he slandered the Three Jewels as a youth, "this should result in my falling into Avīci Hell. I am not even accepted in the forty-eight vows of Amitābha!"[12] Ouyi writes his own *Forty-Eight Vows* in 1621[13] and confidently projects himself into the position of bodhisattva as he promises that there be no difference between himself and the bodhisattvas Guanyin and Dizang (vow 19)[14] and writes, "Let the wheel of my vows horizontally spread in all directions, and also vertically exhaust the three limits [of past, present, and future]."[15]

In direct contrast to Dharmākara, Ouyi not only makes vows to save beings in every realm of rebirth but he also appeals to save demons and heretics (vows 25, 42), those who dwell in lands without Buddhism (vow 32), and those who have committed the five heinous sins, the ten evil deeds, the four *pārājika*, the eight *pārājika*, and those who have fallen into the hells. He vows that they will "know to seek pity, to repent (*chanhui*), and accordingly the marvelous *rūpakāya* will appear, lay his hand on their head in comfort, and cause the roots of their sin to be forever uprooted, and they will give rise to *bodhicitta* (vow 43)."[16] Although the title ostensibly refers back to Dharmākara's vows, we can see that Ouyi was not simply modeling himself as a similar bodhisattva but was instead using the title as an explicit signal that he envisions himself as a future bodhisattva. This vision differs markedly from that of Dharmākara because it appeals to those very constituents excluded from the latter's Pure Land paradise.

KARMA LOOMS LARGE: DRAMATIC FLOURISH IN OUYI'S VOTIVE TEXTS

Having discussed the general contours of the genre of votive texts, we can now turn to Ouyi's votive texts in particular. If we survey the types of vows that Ouyi makes, we find that he frequently makes them to the Three Jewels (Buddha, Dharma, and Sangha) and Buddhas and bodhisattvas such as Amitābha, Guanyin, and Dizang,[17] for his father and mother, especially on the anniversary of their deaths,[18] to eliminate *saṃskāras* and karmic stains,[19] to be born in the Pure Land,[20] to relieve those in all types of rebirth,[21] to eliminate karma,[22] to substitute for other sentient beings,[23] and finally, to receive prediction of Buddhahood.[24] The elimination of karma and its corollaries (*vāsanā, saṃskāra*, etc.) occupies the bulk of Ouyi's writing—it appears in two-thirds of the votive texts included in the *Lingfeng Zonglun* (40 of 63 total votive texts). Karma looms large in Ouyi's votive texts because it remains integral to the way Ouyi envisions himself as a potential bodhisattva.

Because votive texts were written, and like poems had the potential to be circulated, it is important to note that when Ouyi refers to his karmic guilt, he does so publicly. In the context of his votive texts, his public profession of sins cannot be limited to penitential purposes, for it also serves to bolster his two visions of bodhisattvahood. In the first instance, his present feelings of shame, when juxtaposed with himself as a bodhisattva like Dizang, spotlight his future potential to erase shameful karma; in the second case, if Ouyi can persuade his audience that he might end up in Avīci, he can present a convincing vision of himself as a karmic substitute—as one who takes on the karma of others after being reborn in the lowest realms of rebirth. In this way, personal details that emphasize his moral failure strengthen his future bodhisattva image. In addition to lamenting his defamation of Buddhism as a youth, Ouyi admits he abandoned his mother when she was a widow and expresses general anxiety about being unfilial toward his parents. In a votive text from 1629 marking the third anniversary of his mother's death, Ouyi writes:

> Only an unfilial son abandons his mother. Already it has been three years, and I have examined myself. There is no virtue that can be rewarded; I am truly and deeply ashamed, I am in anguish, regretful, and blame [myself].... I only vow that vast *bodhicitta*, vast vows of enlightenment, and vast practices of enlightenment will spread over sentient beings in the *dharma-dhātu*, and [if] my father and mother have already been

reborn, [that they] in the course of a *kalpa* personally have causes [for rebirth in the Pure Land].²⁵

Here we see a contrast between Ouyi's feelings of regret and his bodhisattva vows, the former highlighting his present sense of shame and the latter his future potential to liberate others. Interestingly, Ouyi's decision to abandon his mother enabled him to become a Buddhist cleric. In this way, his regret serves to further underscore the sacrifice he made to become a monk and will make as a bodhisattva.

His early votive texts present a vision of himself as a bodhisattva who can eliminate karma and its resultant stains (*lou*) and karmic impressions (*yexi*).²⁶ Ouyi continues to view devotion and affective states of shame as means of stimulating the compassionate response of a Buddha or bodhisattva through the mechanism of stimulus-response (*ganying*), but he also suggests the reverse—that a bodhisattva's light of compassion can reach various beings, stimulating them to respond in penitential ways. In his *Forty-Eight Vows* he promises to eliminate karmic impressions entirely, and in seven of these vows, he details how his compassionate light might illuminate the various realms of rebirth (hells, animals, hungry ghosts, sentient beings, humans, *śravaka*s, and *pratyekabuddha*s) such that all who contact or receive it (*chu* or *meng*),²⁷ when they respond might renounce (*sheshen*) in order to be reborn in the Pure Land.²⁸ The karmic implications of such illumination become clear in vow 43, where Ouyi pledges:

> By the strength of my compassionate mind, cause those sentient beings who, having committed the five grave crimes, the ten evil deeds, the four *pārājika*, and the eight *pārājika*, and who must fall into the great hells, to seek pity and repent. Accordingly, the marvelous *rūpakāya* will appear and lay his hand on their head in comfort, causing the roots of their sin to be forever uprooted, thus giving rise to *bodhicitta*.²⁹

Here we see a back-and-forth between the compassionate mind of Buddhas and bodhisattvas and the penitent response of sentient beings. Although it is the strength of the compassionate mind that causes sentient beings to repent, this affective response stimulates the appearance of Buddhas and bodhisattvas, who touch sentient beings and cause the roots of their sin to be eliminated.

He suggests a similar dynamic at work in another votive text from 1629 where he describes how bodhisattvas can "unfurl" (*shu*) brilliance of fearlessness, purity, *samādhi*, and *prajñā*.³⁰ By disclosing the virtue of the Buddhist path, bodhisattvas lessen fear of the prospect of evil rebirth, remove the stain (*gou*; Skt. *mala*) of having broken the precepts, and ultimately exhaust the taint (*lou*; Skt. *āsrava*) of ignorance. In addition to such references of bodhisattvas touching or illuminating sentient beings and thereby enabling liberation, Ouyi frequently ends his votive texts by entreating Buddhas and bodhisattvas to "witness, know, collect, and protect" or "graciously pity, collect, and protect" him and other sentient beings.³¹ Although one might be tempted to disregard this closing phrase as simply formulaic (analogous to a Christian "Amen"), it reveals Ouyi's understanding of the capacity of Buddhas and bodhisattvas to realize the plight of sentient beings³² and to compassionately "cover" (*fu*)³³ and "embrace" (*yong*)³⁴ them. Recalling how his own confidence or faith in Buddhism was due to the secret empowerment of Dizang,³⁵ he notes how the three bodies of the Buddha (*sanshen*; Skt. *trikāya*) always cover (*fubi*) [him]; therefore, he says, "I now humbly beg and give rise to profound sincerity, praying that the *mahāsattva* compassionately rescue [me]. Although I have limitless sins, the *mahāsattva* can cause them all to vanish. Although I have no roots of goodness and excellence, the *mahāsattva* can cause them all to be endowed."³⁶ When considered in the context of a votive text, the virtues he claims for the *mahāsattva*—the ability to make limitless sins vanish—also apply to his future self because he is the one who is professing such bodhisattva vows.

Ouyi's illness also serves as a means of drawing attention to the potential of bodhisattvas—and himself as a future bodhisattva—to mercifully intervene on behalf of sentient beings. Decrying himself and other beings for being deluded, ungrateful toward the Buddha's loving kindness, and damaging their merit, he says that as a result they have caused themselves myriad illnesses, their minds are twisted (*rao*), darkened (*hun*), and foolish, and they have met the latter-day fate in which they are surrounded by the armies of Mara. He writes, "Our fortune befits the profound compassion [of the Buddhas] because our karma is heavy, our obstacles deep, our virtue slight and our understanding superficial. We fully harbor shame (*cankui*) in our hearts and hope for [the Buddha's] empowerment (*jiachi*; Skt. *adhiṣṭhāna*)."³⁷ Illness highlights his moral failures, and Ouyi repeatedly embellishes his feelings of disconsolation, illustrated in the recurring trope of him "examining his conscience" (*menxin*) and "wringing his hands" (*ewan*).³⁸

In one votive text, he describes being deceived about karmic causes and unclear about karmic effects, and how he feels his retribution will be to suffer painfully in the three evil destinies (*santu*); so he prostrates, repents, and prays that the bodhisattva's vow will eliminate all of his karma, not only so he can realize his accumulated merit but also so that his body will not be plagued by illness.[39] In this way, Ouyi calls upon Buddhas and bodhisattvas to compassionately touch him with their illumination.[40] Elsewhere he suggests that it is not only the salvific action of Buddhas and bodhisattvas but the vows themselves that are delicate threads keeping him tied to the bodhisattva path; he suggests that *bodhicitta* protects him from falling into hell,[41] and he finds solace in the four extensive vows in his heart.

Occasionally, Ouyi seems to revel in the dramatic possibilities of his moral turpitude, writing how he has accumulated more evil karma than Mount Sumeru.[42] At another point, after distinguishing between two kinds of excellent people—those who do not commit faults and those who can repent afterward and never commit them again—he says, "I am like a person who has fallen into a toilet: my body, mouth, ears, and nose are all sunken in excrement."[43] In a votive text written in 1638, explicitly aimed at revealing his sins and seeking the pity of bodhisattvas, Ouyi describes his seven great "burdens" or "defeats" (*fu*):[44] (1) not having repaid the kindness of his birth (*sheng'en*), (2) not having realized his nature and soul (*xingling*),[45] (3) the deficiencies of the Chan school,[46] (4) his inability to reform or improve the state of the sangha, (5) his failure to uphold the precepts and serve as a model for others, (6) not having gathered others with similar ambitions and renewed the true Dharma;[47] and finally, what he calls the "greatest defeat," (7) a failure to repay the profound kindness of the emperor's protection.[48] Ouyi writes:

> Alas! I am burdened by these seven grave sins. Again they flood over me . . . I can barely breathe . . . I am on the brink of death. Half of my body has been pathetic for over ten years. For the past three days, I have been violently ill with fever; having suffered from illness for the past three years, suddenly I am at the gates of hell![49] I concede my past mistakes—even though they are strong, yet one thread of the powerful vows of illumination can protect the Dharma and a suffering mind. May it slightly stimulate (*gan*) a single ray of compassion and wisdom, causing a transformation in the heavy retribution from previous lives, so that it lightens the evil to be received. I curl up in fear and shame. I do not know the past depths of my [misdeeds]. A compassionate form [appeared] in my dream while I was asleep, [its] sighs penetrating my parents' quarters. I rely only on the thread of mental vows that I have not yet forgotten, but it is [like]

wishing to save a burning cart with a cup of water. I am increasingly fearful. Thus the Buddhas sincerely say: the treasure of the bodhisattva mind is incredible; it is like a little *vajra* that can make a hole in the earth; like a lion's milk that can leave an ocean of milk. If one breath remains one dare not be pained but instead exert oneself.[50]

Ouyi portrays himself on the brink of death and at the gates of hell, while his bodhisattva vows represent a lifeline of sorts, connecting him to the compassionate vows made by all bodhisattvas before him. By dramatizing the depths of his physical and mental suffering, he heightens the miracle of a "single ray" of a bodhisattva's compassion being able to transform one's karmic retribution. Repeatedly likening his vows to "threads" (*xian*), he connects his own bodhisattva vows with those "single rays" that will liberate others in the future. However, we also see an uncertainty about whether his vows will be efficacious in keeping him from the fires of hell—comparing them to a cup of water trying to stop a blazing fire—which contributes to his second vision of bodhisattvahood, that of a karmic substitute.

BODHISATTVAHOOD AS KARMIC SUBSTITUTION

Alongside this view of bodhisattvas as those who can eliminate karma by touching or illuminating sentient beings, Ouyi suggests that as a bodhisattva he might "substitute" (*dai shou*) for those sentient beings suffering the effects of karmic retribution. This first appears in his *Votive Text on Receiving the Bodhisattva Precepts*, which Ouyi wrote at the beginning of 1625.[51] In this text marking the occasion of his reception of the bodhisattva precepts, Ouyi writes:

> Using the merit from practicing these precepts, I vow that the various sins (*zui*) that sentient beings and I have accumulated since beginningless time will all be extinguished. For all those sentient beings who because of their fixed karma must receive retribution, I will replace them in receiving (*dai shou*) [retribution] everywhere in defiled worlds and successive evil births. Without loathing or regret, to the very end [I will] enable these sentient beings to first realize Buddhahood.[52]

As we saw in the previous chapter, Dizang similarly vows to extinguish the karma of sentient beings—even those relegated to the hells—but the notion of "substitution" is somewhat novel and controversial.[53]

On the one hand, Ouyi suggests it is possible to "stimulate" a compassionate response from Buddhas and bodhisattvas; on the other hand, by offering to substitute for others in evil rebirths, he implies that some may be unable to accomplish this task. Ouyi clearly views the former as preferable; for example, in one votive text, Ouyi makes an offering on behalf of a teacher, repents of various crimes against Buddhism on his behalf, and he then states, "All of these sins, I vow to eliminate. Those which cannot be eliminated, I vow that I will act as a substitute, causing all those who presently suffer from illness to swiftly recover and have peace."[54] He views the elimination of karma as primary; in cases where this is impossible, he then vows to substitute himself for others.

This theme of "substitution" appears consistently throughout Ouyi's votive texts. He suggests that those who commit evil actions "must receive retribution" (*ying shou bao*), and he goes into elaborate detail about what "substitution" entails, namely experiencing immeasurable suffering during "an ocean of unspeakably numerous *kalpa*s, fully tasting poisons and the whipping rod."[55] In another votive text, he embellishes the types of retribution even further. For murderers, he will endure the hells of mountains of knives and trees of swords; for thieves, he will pay back their stolen goods with great offerings; for the licentious, he will be relegated to an iron bed or copper pillar; for liars, he will have his tongue removed or cut open; for drunkards, he will drink rivers of lava or bubbling excrement.[56] Again, we see the dramatic flourish with which Ouyi envisions himself as a future bodhisattva.

Ouyi emphasizes his own moral turpitude—sometimes going to great lengths to describe the depth of his sin and depravity—and we see how this bolsters his second vision of bodhisattvahood as Ouyi writes, "If I attain liberation in this life, I vow everywhere to have influence; or if I myself sink [to evil rebirths], I vow forever to replace them in various suffering."[57] Ouyi suggests that his heavy karma may enable him to be reborn in lower realms and simultaneously assume the karmic burden of others while suffering his own retribution. Similarly, we see Ouyi making vows to substitute for other people and hoping that he remembers these vows if he is reborn in lower realms:

> Supposing that there were only one being in the *dharma-dhātu* who had not yet realized true awakening, I am willing to substitute in various poisons in immeasurable hells, fully for every *kalpa*, without loathing or fatigue. Today I make vows similar to those made by the Buddhas and bodhisattvas in all ages—add them all to [those of] all bodhisattvas

and Buddhas. If because of evil karma from beginningless time I must fall into destinies of great suffering, my divine consciousness be lost in darkness, and I be separated from the great practices, vows, and mind of today, I look to the original teacher Sakyamuni and the compassionate Father [Vai]rocana, Amitābha the king of vows, and the compassionate mother Dizang to pity and protect me, enlighten me, and cause me to recall today's original vows in that suffering, not abandoning suffering, but liberating sentient beings.[58]

Ouyi hopes that he might remember his vows to substitute for other beings while he himself suffers in hell, welcoming the suffering on their behalf. Elsewhere, he even uses the character meaning "atone" (*shu*)[59] to describe his assumption of their karma, as he vows "to save and atone for sentient beings, spreading compassionate causal conditions (*yuan*) throughout the *dharma-dhātu*."[60] Yet at other times, Ouyi implies that heavy karma will delay his completion of such vows. In the votive text he writes before the Dizang tower at Jiuhuashan, Ouyi hopes that if his heavy karma relegates him to hell that Dizang will awaken him, causing him to "always consider the bodhisattva mind and cause it to continue unceasingly," but that if his karma is light, that he swiftly attain states of *samādhi*, be born in a Pure Land, and then "ride the power of the original vows, through boundless oceans, transforming sentient beings completely in future times without any exhaustion."[61] Here, Ouyi suggests that only by following meditative attainment and rebirth in a higher realm can he complete his bodhisattva vows.

Thus we see how Ouyi uses votive texts to promote a certain vision of himself as a future bodhisattva. Votive texts engage with future possibility in a way that complements divination as a diagnostic for karma in the past and repentance as a means of redressing karma in the present. Ouyi envisions two primary bodhisattva roles: eliminating fixed karma by spreading his light so that it touches sentient beings and stimulates them to repent, or even substituting on behalf of those whose fixed karma relegates them to the lower rebirths. Yet there is an additional way in which Ouyi seeks to present himself as a bodhisattva in a very public way: he burns his head and arms, and he writes sutras in his blood. In the next chapter we examine these somatic dimensions that appear in Ouyi's writing, how they reflect a particular ideal of bodies as means to transform karma, and how the depiction of painful, ascetic acts further contributes to Ouyi's presentation of himself as a future bodhisattva.

FIVE

SLICING, BURNING, AND BLOOD WRITING

Karmic Transformations of Bodies

Having seen how Ouyi portrays divination as a karmic diagnostic, views repentance as having the potential to extinguish karma, and professes vows to substitute for others in their karmic retribution, we will now consider the role Ouyi's body[1] plays in presentations of himself as a future bodhisattva. As Paul Williams notes, bodhisattva bodies are the medium for fulfilling bodhisattva vows because their bodies become "being-for-others" or physical expressions of their commitment to save other sentient beings.[2] Bodies are vehicles for instantiating bodhisattva ideals.

Susanne Mrozik contends that bodhisattva bodies are not only the medium for fulfilling generic bodhisattva vows but also the product of particular and individualized vows—that vow-making is one of many practices that can produce bodhisattvas with bodies capable of "ripening" or transforming others.[3] In her study of "embodied virtue,"[4] Mrozik argues that Buddhist traditions do not easily or absolutely distinguish between physical and moral dimensions of living beings; thus ethical development includes cultivation of desired physical qualities as well as affective or cognitive states. Bodhisattva practices create bodies that not only serve as markers of virtue but that can also have profoundly transformative effects on other living beings.[5]

This chapter examines the variety of "bodily practices"[6] in which Ouyi describes engaging—such as cutting himself, burning his head and arms, and writing texts in his own blood—and how such acts further contribute to the vision of Ouyi as a bodhisattva. It draws largely from Ouyi's votive texts, which as we have seen were written to commemorate specific ritual activities and occasions yet were also subject to a degree of embellishment and rhetorical flourish. For example, Ouyi does suffer from illness in the course of his life, but in his votive texts, illness becomes a means of highlighting the gracious response of bodhisattvas toward suffering sentient beings. Here we will consider how bodily practices contribute to Ouyi's representation of himself as a future bodhisattva and his view of his body as a site of karmic retribution and transformation.

Ouyi's discussion of his body and bodily practices suggest a view of bodies (*shen*)[7] as sites for revealing and redressing karma. Ouyi describes his illness and disease as signaling direct retribution for karma from previous lives, but he also envisions its potential for marking his commitment to future bodhisattvahood. Just as repentance rituals include a term marking the temporal shift from the past to the future (often marked by a "now" or "so") one can understand bodies as presently embodying the results of past karma and the potential for future rebirth; just as illness indicates moral degeneration, burning and blood writing demonstrate ethical cultivation. Ouyi represents his body as a site of such karmic transformation. The skin that is scarred and blood that is drawn make visible and palpable that which Chinese Buddhist discourse portrays as obscure and hidden. In this way, Ouyi sees such practices as not only marking his body—his karmic inheritance—for all to see but also transforming it—by removing past karmic effects and using his body for meritorious purposes.

Ouyi portrays his body as playing a crucial role in his own spiritual development. As we saw in his autobiography, Ouyi writes that his enlightenment experience centers on an awareness of his own body as direct retribution for previous karma—when he realizes that his body is not born of his parents but instead results from previous karma. Ouyi calls it "a shadow (*ying*) manifested by entrenched delusion." His body arises from seeds in his consciousness; like all phenomena, it is empty and impermanent. Nevertheless, we continue to read how three years later, when his mother falls ill, Ouyi cuts his arms four times but cannot save her and becomes severely distraught. Ouyi describes the traditional filial practice of feeding ill parents part of one's own flesh, an act which apparently causes consternation for his disciple Jianmi Chengshi, who writes in an annotation, "He already realized that this body is not born from a father and mother, so why did he then cut his arm to save his mother? Examine (*can*) [this as one would a *gongan/kōan*]." His disciple finds it problematic that Ouyi would view his body as insubstantial but also as a means of saving his mother: the two positions seem contradictory. In order to appreciate the complexity of Ouyi's understanding(s) of his body, let us first examine three of his bodily practices: filial slicing, burning his head and arms, and writing texts with his blood.

FILIAL SLICING: REJUVENATING THE SOCIAL BODY[8]

In his autobiography, Ouyi describes slicing a piece of flesh from his arm (*kuigong*) during his mother's grave illness, ostensibly to make medicine for her. Jimmy Yu has coined the phrase "filial slicing" to describe such practices, which became a culturally accepted expression of filial piety in the sixteenth and seventeenth centuries.[9] Insofar as it symbolized using one's body to nourish one's parents in return for what one received during pregnancy and childhood, and it was eulogized and praised by literati in order to criticize social customs and reaffirm or challenge social hierarchy, it represents a different type of practice from burning oneself or writing texts in one's blood, which find more explicit precedent in Buddhist texts.[10] In Ouyi's autobiography, "filial slicing" rhetorically signals his filial devotion toward his mother and preservation of Confucian social relationships, which furthers his autobiographical message of a broad religiosity that spans Confucian and Buddhist traditions.

"Filial slicing" involves cutting flesh from one's arm, thighs, or liver to make a healing broth for sick relatives (especially parents). It appeared prominently in popular and didactic texts, such as Guo Jujing's (fl. 1295–1321) *Poems on the Twenty-Four Filial Exemplars*, which was popular among commoners as well as educated literati in the Ming dynasty.[11] Although "filial slicing" ostensibly contradicts the Confucian injunction against harming the body, the practice was sanctioned because it served the filial purpose of securing a family's reputation for posterity. The *Xiaojing* (Classic of filial piety) explicitly proscribes damaging one's body (even one's hair or a bit of skin) that is bequeathed from one's parents, but it also encourages glorifying one's parents by making one's surname famous. As Keith Knapp illustrates in his study of filial piety tales in medieval China, stories of extreme filial piety not only played a didactic role of promoting Confucian values, but it also boosted the family's reputation, which opened possibilities for public service and concomitant social and economic rewards.[12]

Given that Ouyi mentions "filial slicing" for his mother in the context of his autobiography, we can surmise that he describes himself engaging in such filial acts for didactic and social purposes. Although he may have actually cut himself to rejuvenate his mother and extend her life, he recounts his tale of "filial slicing" that characterizes him as a filial son and may have also strengthened his family's prestige and reputation. He cannot carry on his familial lineage with offspring, yet his writing boosts his family's status for posterity.

Interestingly, "filial slicing" also appears in a poem that Ouyi writes for an ailing Dharma brother. In a poem titled "Cutting My Thigh for Brother Xinggu," Ouyi says that he aimed to cut off part of his thigh (*gegu*) when his friend Xinggu Daoshou (1583–1631) fell ill in 1631 but only managed to scrape a few pieces of skin, which suggests he may not have actually engaged in the practice but used it for rhetorical purposes. The poem reads: "Receive this body with its gathered illusory conditions / I hoped to scoop out a thousand sores (*chuang*)[13] but shamefully cannot / I have scraped a few superficial bits of skin as a small offering / Use the reward of loving kindness from my solemn and dreadful cutting."[14] Ouyi supplants his flakes of skin with Buddhist understandings of the body as insubstantial and defiled, but his gesture toward "filial slicing" intimates the depth of his relationships with his other clerics and implies that his monastic community was analogous to his natal family.[15]

BURNING HEADS AND ARMS: MA(R)KING THE BODHISATTVA BODY

Ouyi also describes engaging in a bodily practice common among Buddhist clerics, namely burning incense on his arms and head.[16] Shengyan insists it is not a painful practice but simply letting incense fall on the head and arms, noting that Ouyi uses the term *ran* to describe how he "burns incense" (*ranxiang*), "burns his arms" (*ranbi*), or "burns his head" (*rantou*), which is not as extreme as *shao*—another character used for burning as well as cooking and cremating.[17] Nevertheless, burning does leave traces in the form of scars, and it can certainly cause a degree of discomfort, if not pain. Previous scholarship on such bodily mortification typically begins by relating the precedent for such acts in Buddhist scriptures such as the Lotus Sutra or narrative tales about bodhisattvas who go to extremes by feeding hungry animals with their own flesh, or who gouge out their eyes and chop off their arms to save sentient beings or propagate the Buddhist teachings.[18] Many eminent clerics appealed to such precedents when engaging in acts of bodily mortification that were chronicled in biographies and emulated by later figures.[19]

Ouyi's burning serves a variety of functions in addition to offering; it can mark a temporal transition from previous to future bodily states, seek to redress past bodily actions, or represent a concrete instantiation of otherwise abstract Buddhist doctrines. In his votive texts Ouyi frequently burns incense as offering to the Three Jewels (Buddha, Dharma, Sangha)[20] or various bodhisattvas,[21] and he occasionally dedicates it to "a certain cleric (*biqiu moumou*)" or "virtuous friends (*shanyou*; Skt. *kalyāṇa-mitra*)."[22] In these instances, burning connotes his devotion toward salvific figures or intimate friends. However, Ouyi also describes burning incense for certain states of being—to repent (of sins), purify (sinful states), or protect (virtues or virtuous beings). In one text, though he does not specify whether he burns incense on his head or arms, he describes burning incense (*ranxiang*) for a variety of purposes:

> [I]—the cleric [Ouyi] Zhixu—having written the Buddha's names, [now] burn incense and make vows (*fayuan*). With three sticks [of incense] I give offerings to the Three Jewels, vowing that together with sentient beings of the *dharma-dhātu*, I will hand down the seeds of Buddhahood, enter into the storehouse of wisdom, and realize the gates of liberation. With six sticks [of incense], I repent for sins of my six sense faculties, vowing that with sentient beings of the *dharma-dhātu* I will always see the form of the Buddha (*fose*), hear the sound of the Dharma, smell the fragrance of the Dharma, and taste the flavor of the Dharma, wearing the cloak of shame (*cankui yi*) and awakening to the womb of the Tathāgata (*rulai zang*; Skt. *tathāgata-garbha*). With two sticks [of incense], I pray for the conditions of my father and mother and for people of the land, that they enter the embryos (*baotai*) of the nine lotus [levels of rebirth in the Pure Land] and receive blessings from the Three Jewels. With four sticks [of incense], I protect the eternally abiding sangha, the communal recitation of the precepts, good friends with pure karma (*jingye*), Vinaya that is pure and adorned, pure groups in the meditation hall, Mahāyāna that is perfumed by practice (*xunxiu*), teachers who oversee affairs, and lotus stamens and branches. With three sticks [of incense] I protect a certain cleric and all

good friends: that they have healthy bodies, prosperous fortunes, and turn toward *bodhi*. I universally offer such merits to sentient beings, that together we are born in [the Pure Land] paradise.[23]

The text underscores the variety of functions that burning can serve: offering, repentance, prayer, and protection. In light of the multifarious roles Ouyi ascribes to the act, we cannot solely interpret burning as a form of offering. Instead, we see that Ouyi attributes a creative potential to the burning of incense and to the profession of vows. Somatic and generative images appear prominent throughout the text: seeds of Buddhahood, wombs of Tathāgatas, embryos of the Pure Land, healthy bodies, and rebirth in the Pure Land. If we focus particularly on the penitential burning of incense, we see Ouyi focuses on the importance of seeing the physical form of the Buddha, on covering himself in a cloak of shame, and on recognizing that he embodies the capacity for Buddhahood: the womb of the Tathāgata. Ouyi suggests a value to *seeing* the Buddha and *being seen* by others as clothed in shame. Although repentance entails the transformation of all six sense faculties, Ouyi places special emphasis on its visual aspects. Burning incense serves a creative purpose; it aims toward transformation and rebirth. It marks his body with a "cloak" of shame and uncovers a "womb" of awakening.

As illustrated in the previous chapter, burning also marks a transition from repentance of the past toward bodhisattvahood in the future. It further bolsters Ouyi's presentation of himself as a bodhisattva-to-be. In a text written for a ritual before the Dizang tower at Jiuhuashan, Ouyi says that he burns three sticks: one regretting his past, one making vows for the future, and one resolving doubts about his present condition. With the first stick, he regrets (*hui*) mistakes from the three karmic activities (*sanye*) of body, speech, and mind, including licentious tendencies, slandering the Three Jewels, erroneous speech, evil thoughts, and various diseases and illnesses.[24] With the second stick, he seeks (*qiu*) the four great bodhisattva vows, pure monastic conduct, to cut off delusion and realize truth, to live a long life without illness, and to perform meritorious actions.[25] The third stick he dedicates toward resolving (*jue*) his net of doubts about his present condition that vary according to the type of practice: pure conduct for repentance, no afflictions for meditation, wisdom and understanding for reading the canon, and vast merit for practices.[26] In this way, burning demarcates the past from the future, accentuating the image of himself as a future bodhisattva. In his *Text Reciting Mantras*, before burning incense as offerings, Ouyi first acknowledges his profound karmic obstacles, his heavy afflictions, and his depressed and scattered thoughts. He confesses that each time he violates the proper conduct for monks, he restrains himself (*keji*), examines himself (*xinggong*), and becomes increasingly ashamed and fearful. Therefore, he says, he again gives rise to compassion and reveals his sincerity, seeking to "transform his anxiety," "cleanse his mind," "punish himself for previous [misdeeds]," and "begin future [action] (*chuanghou*)."[27] The character *chuang* means not only "to begin" but also "to wound" and "to create." Ouyi describes the shift from his previous wrongdoing to his future potential as simultaneously punitive and creative. Immediately following this phrase, he describes burning seven sticks of incense for his seven daily recitations of the mantra of the *Śūraṃgama-sutra* and three sticks of incense for the mantra of Dizang. He concludes the text by acknowledging that if one recites with sorrow and sincerity, they will empower one's pursuit of pure precepts, meditation, and wisdom. He concludes with a general vow to transform sentient beings and together be reborn in the Pure Land. The act of burning incense signals a change from past to future, demarcating his previous wrongdoing from his present merit making and future bodhisattvahood. Burning entails a simultaneous destruction (of his former self) and creation (of a bodhisattva).

Especially in votive texts tied to the recitation of mantras or verses, one can fruitfully use the notion of the "three karmic activities" of body, speech, and mind to interpret the significance of burning in his texts: burning redresses bodily action, mantras or verses rectify verbal action, and vows cultivate proper mental states. At times, Ouyi explicitly states that he burns incense to remedy his karmic activities, but often he simply acknowledges his karma before he burns his body, professes his vows, and recites his mantra or verses. In one text, Ouyi writes how he burns incense to the Three Jewels, vowing that he and sentient beings will eliminate all karma, and how he also burns three sticks of incense out of regret (*hui*) for evil bodily, verbal, and mental actions.[28] He represents burning as a means of purging himself of evil and paving the way for future goodness. Elsewhere he describes his physical body wracked with illness and pain as clear retribution for previous wrongdoing, suggesting that the flesh he describes burning is not a simple blank slate. He writes: "My karma is as profound as the ocean / With effort, I strive for *samādhi* in meditation / Half my body feels sharp pain / Truly it comes from the roots of the three poisons / Now with shame I punish [myself] (*keze*) / Burning my arms with three sticks of incense."[29] The "three poisons" refer to the three basic afflictions: desire (*tanyu*; Skt. *rāga*), anger (*chenhui*; Skt. *dveṣa*), and ignorance (*yuchi*; Skt. *moha*). Ouyi portrays his body as a manifestation of the effects of his previous sins: burning his arms with three sticks of incense signals a castigation of his body and eradication of sins.

We have seen how Ouyi says he burned three sticks for the Three Jewels or three poisons, six sticks for the six sense faculties, or seven sticks for his seven-day recitation of certain mantras; these illustrate the way in which burning can also serve to concretely instantiate otherwise abstract Buddhist doctrines. Ouyi portrays his body as a body of doctrine: a *dharmakāya*. For example, in one text he writes:

> I am ashamed and give rise to *bodhicitta* / Entering the [ritual] boundary, I recite divine *dhāraṇī*s / Many are sufficient, [but] my mind is scattered / And my conduct (*weiyi*) is not yet pure / Within I feel anxiety and dread / Vow-making is a difficult task to complete / Thus I burn ten sticks of incense / And repent of my ten evil afflictions (*shi'egen*)[30] / Additionally I recite 10,000 [*dhāraṇī*s] / To eliminate 50,000 fixed karma (*dingye*) / I also burn my arm with six sticks / To empower my mind to be like my vows / Moreover for 11 friends / I recite the *dhāraṇī* to extinguish fixed karma / Altogether that makes 900,000 [times] / I offer seven sticks of incense on my arm / For a mind that continuously aspires to repay kindness / For a mind in pursuit of making offerings [for the deceased] to hereafter seek liberation / For a mind entrusted to turning [the wheel of] the Dharma and rejoicing in joy with others / For a mind that gets rid of mistakes of heterodoxy and compassionately liberates [sentient beings] / For a mind that propagates the salvific [Dharma] on behalf of companions / For a mind that protects and propagates the Dharma on behalf of [ritual] boundaries / For a mind that always compassionately recites [the name of the Buddha] together in groups / For the ritual boundaries I protect and propagate the mind of Dharma / Hoping to recite [the *dhāraṇī*] 3,200,000 [times] / I burn my arm with incense again with seven sticks / Causing my seven consciousnesses to all be realized.[31]

Here we see a clear correspondence between burning, reciting, and vowing as bodily, verbal, and mental actions, as Ouyi repents for his ten defilements by burning himself with ten sticks of incense, recites mantras to eliminate karma, and tries to empower his mind to conform to his vows. Ouyi seeks a mind that continually looks outward to benefit others: to repay kindness, to seek liberation, to protect and spread the Dharma, to rejoice in joy with others, to rectify heterodox beliefs, and to compassionately recollect and recite the name of the Buddha. In other words, he aspires to become a bodhisattva by engaging in liturgical rituals on behalf of all sentient beings.

Similarly, in a votive text for performing a Pure Land repentance ceremony, Ouyi says he burns three sticks of incense not only to give offerings to the Three Jewels but also to expel the three karmic obstacles and give rise to the three minds. He writes, "I burn three sticks of incense to the Three Jewels in the two lands [of the Pure Land and the defiled *sahā-loka*], vowing to perfectly give rise to the three minds and suddenly eliminate the three obstacles."[32] Although the three minds have various referents depending on Buddhist texts and traditions, the three obstacles likely refer to the three poisons mentioned earlier. Thus three sticks of incense simultaneously serve as offerings to the Three Jewels, as penance for the three hindrances, and as production of the three minds; a single act creates three scars that evoke many layers of significance when they are seen. Such scars, as Roy Rappaport notes, are "irreversible, indelible, and ever-present, distinguishing those who have suffered them from those who have not in contexts outside of ritual as well as in."[33] Ouyi can make abstract doctrines concrete, and he himself is predicated by such doctrine; others can attribute qualities of bodhisattvahood to Ouyi because of such scars.

Burning makes a bodhisattva body by leaving traces that visually symbolize the sacrificial activity of bodhisattvas. Such scars are meant to be seen: they appear on the head and arms, which are visible on robed clerics. Ouyi acknowledges the exhibitory element of burning as he writes in another text, "I burn my head with four sticks of incense, clearly displaying my profound mind [seeking enlightenment].... I keep the four extensive vows in my heart."[34] Burning serves to "clearly display" (*chenbai*) Ouyi's innermost desire to become a bodhisattva who makes the four extensive vows (*sishi*) to liberate all sentient beings. In the omitted portion, he relates his considerable karmic obstacles as well as his numerous shortcomings and mistakes, which implies that burning also lays bare karma that might otherwise be concealed. By burning himself, Ouyi signals his dedication to liberate sentient beings and reveals his commitment to the bodhisattva path. The conclusion of the text underscores the transformative potential of such practice. Ouyi vows that sentient beings all have sufficient resources and opportunities for study so that:

> All can complete their vows, transform the three poisons [of desire, anger, and ignorance] into the three liberations, turn the six paths of rebirth into the six supernatural powers, see the Pure Land before their

eyes, realize instant enlightenment and the nonduality of nature and cultivation, possess all sorts of practices such that principle and affairs merge and produce successive *dharmas* of transformation.[35]

Ouyi draws upon the familiar dyad of "principle" (*li*) and "practice" (*shi*) to emphasize the transformative potential of religious practices (*xingmen*). *Li* connotes doctrinal teachings or theories, while *shi* includes things, phenomena, and practical matters. Here Ouyi suggests that religious practices—when performed correctly—have transformative power. He uses the characters *hua* and *zhuan*—both of which connote transformation, transition, and change—to describe the process of becoming a bodhisattva. Sentient beings with their three karmic obstacles and six realms of reincarnation become endowed with the three liberations and six magical powers that they can employ in their "wonder-working" salvific activities.[36]

As was briefly mentioned in the previous chapter, these votive texts occasionally include the names of those who participated alongside Ouyi in rituals. One example is a text in which Ouyi describes being in a group of clerics who read the Vinaya, make vows in repentance (*chanmo*), draw lots, and burn their heads with three sticks of incense and their arms with varying numbers of incense sticks. The text gives the impression that burning could move from display to spectacle, as Ouyi says that he burns his arm with twenty-eight sticks, while others vary from four to fourteen.[37] Although we have no way to determine whether Ouyi *actually* burned himself with twenty-eight sticks on a single occasion, the fact that Ouyi *wrote* that he burnt himself with twice as many sticks as other participants does suggest that he sought to distinguish himself among his contemporaries. In this particular text, the clerics burn themselves for three types of bodies: familial, political, and religious. Before they burn themselves, they promise to assemble, interpret, and complete a collection of Vinaya texts. They repent for karma, for either not knowing the precepts or for receiving the precepts but not upholding them, for being ungrateful for the Buddha's loving kindness, and for damaging their meritorious roots, which has resulted in bodies suffering from myriad illnesses, minds that are confused and ignorant, and being born in the latter-day (*moyun*).[38] After expressing gratitude for being fortunate enough to encounter the Buddhist teachings, the group vows to protect the Dharma and burns three sticks of incense on their heads: one for rulers and ministers, one for the condition of their parents, and a third for the Buddha, Dharma, and Sangha. In this way, they use their bodies to express gratitude for their family, their country, and their religion.

Ouyi's additional twenty-five vows extend his gratitude toward others who have fostered his religious development: Buddhas and bodhisattvas through their vows, and clerics through their specific acts of kindness. Ouyi describes burning his arms to give offerings to those of the past, to repay the kindness (*bao'en*) of those in his present life, and to accompany vows for teachers and virtuous friends (*shanyou*; Skt. *kalyāṇa-mitra*) with similar practices in the future.[39] In his final vow directed to all sentient beings, he hopes that they break through the twenty-five wheels of existence, manifest the twenty-five self-natures, and together enter the Pure Land and realize the path toward Buddhahood. The text embodies each of the characteristics highlighted in this section: not only does burning serve a variety of functions—offering, repaying kindness, redressing karma, signaling a transition from past to future states, and creating three scars to their family, country, and religion—but Ouyi implies that his body instantiates his transition from twenty-five previous rebirths to future bodhisattvahood.

BLOOD WRITING: KARMIC PRODUCTS AND KARMIC PRODUCERS

Like burning, blood writing (*xieshu*)—writing texts or copying scriptures with one's own blood—can also serve a variety of functions, correlating with the associations of blood with birth, the *yin* manifestation of vitality, and power.[40] Blood and *qi* were essentially identical in Chinese medicine, representing different aspects of a singular vitality: the former *yin* and the latter *yang*.[41] Blood writing required practitioners to inflict substantial pain on themselves that in turned garnered veneration and respect.[42]

Although Jimmy Yu argues that Ouyi used blood writing to secure a sense of religious authority and publicly criticize unorthodox Chan practice,[43] we will see that Ouyi does not limit blood writing to this single purpose, instead employing it for different reasons in various contexts.[44] He also draws on blood writing to repay a "birth debt" to his mother, to honor his teachers, to promote Pure Land recitation of the Buddha's name, and to ensure the vitality of the Vinaya.

As Yu notes, blood writing has complex origins in blood covenants, sacrificial rites, and apotropaic talismans; drawing on views of blood as sanctifying and authenticating sincerity, performers of blood writing breach the boundaries of their bodies, graphically transferring their life force to texts in order to authenticate, animate, and sacralize them.[45] In early Chinese rituals, blood was spilled as a form of self-sacrifice for heaven, or used to demonstrate one's sincerity in covenant rituals, or sometimes smeared on ritual implements to sanctify them; in later practices such as the production of Daoist and Buddhist talismans, performers substituted blood with vermillion ink, cinnabar, or animal blood.[46] Blood was a multivalent concept, associated with vitality but never reducible to a material fluid.[47] Influential Chinese Buddhist sutras including the Lotus Sutra, the *Sutra of Brahma's Net*, and the Huayan Sutra extol the meritorious practice of copying Buddhist scriptures in one's own blood, a practice which Yu notes persisted even after the printing boom of the sixteenth and seventeenth centuries, suggesting a value to the form and the meaning of the text.[48] The Huayan Sutra, which describes the Vairocana Buddha peeling his skin as paper, drawing his blood for ink, using his marrow for water, and breaking his bones for pens, was particularly popular among late imperial practitioners of blood writing. Yu speculates this was due to the length of the sutra instead of its doctrinal content, pointing out that its approximately six million characters far exceed the six thousand of the Diamond Sutra, another popular text for copying.[49]

Ouyi does acknowledge the length of the sutra, whose eighty-one fascicles require at least eight months of blood writing to complete, but he also emphasizes its doctrinal appeal by recounting how Sudhana witnesses numerous tiny Buddha fields in a single pore of Samantabhadra's body, which has incredible corporeal characteristics (*shenxiang*).[50] Ouyi underscores the primacy of bodies, which are themselves products of bodhisattva vows: by using one's body to write blood texts, one can produce a body like that of Samantabhadra.[51] Or, as he writes in another text about blood writing, "Every drop of blood flows from the pores of Samantabhadra; each drop contains thousands of scrolls of scriptures."[52] Each drop of blood that one draws—especially for copying the Huayan Sutra—recalls the pore of Samantabhadra that emanates numerous Buddha lands. Such bodily acts evoke bodhisattvas' bodies.

The mechanics of blood writing underscore how painful and prolonged a process it could be, distinguishing it from practices of filial slicing or burning incense on one's arms or head. Blood writing typically begins by preparing the body with a diet to counteract congealing, then sitting upright, cutting one's fingers or the underside of one's tongue, draining the blood into a bowl, and perhaps using wood to grind the blood to remove the fibers that may have come out with the blood; blood writers occasionally mix blood with cinnabar, the toxicity of which prevents insects from eating away at the paper and thereby ensures its preservation.[53] One could write only a few pages a day because blood congeals rather quickly, thus as Yu points out, longer scriptures would entail longer enduring of the pain of pricking one's body to draw blood.[54] Because of the mechanics of blood writing, Yu contends that blood written texts were not only read but revered as objects of worship because they materialized pain; their materiality asserted a sanctity that demanded public recognition.[55]

Yu argues that Ouyi engages in blood writing to convey his spiritual authority and to defend Buddhist orthodoxy from Chan heterodoxy. He first cites a text called a *Cixie shujing yuanwen* (Votive text on drawing blood to write scriptures), in which Ouyi vows to prick his tongue to copy Mahāyāna scriptures and the Vinaya in his blood. Yu notes how Ouyi seeks to benefit his parents and all parents by severing their afflictive and cognitive hindrances that prevent their attainment of Buddhahood: the first being an attachment to self (*wozhi*), the second an attachment to phenomenon (*fazhi*).[56] He argues that Ouyi overcomes the two hindrances himself by inflicting violence on his own body, which demonstrates detachment from the self, and vowing that all sentient beings "destroy the two attachments," which signals detachment to phenomena.[57] However, one need not conclude that blood writing signals detachment to the self because of the pain inflicted; one could also argue that he is directing his acts toward that which he perceives to be the karmic result of his past attachments.

This interpretation becomes especially plausible when we examine another text in Yu's discussion—Ouyi's preface for a lay disciple who copied the Lotus Sutra in his own blood.[58] In this text and others, Ouyi esteems blood writing as encompassing all the practices of Samantabhadra, even though "Crazy Chan" (*kuang chan*) belittles it as "having form" (*youxiang*).[59] Ouyi writes:

> As for the root causes of beginningless birth and death, none is deeper than the view of the body (*shenjian*). Of the wonderful world-transcending Dharmas, there is none prior to [that which] destroys the mountain of the "view of self" (*sajiaye*; Skt. *satkāya*). When this view breaks, then the wheel of birth and death is forever stilled. This is called revering the correct Dharma; this is called giving Dharma offerings to the Tathāgata. The *Lotus* and *Śuraṃgama* [sutras] profoundly praise burning one's arms and fingers, as well as the merits of burning [incense on one's body]. Some say, "How can cutting off the arm of affliction or burning the body of

ignorance reside in mere flesh and blood?" They do not know the profound karmic habits produced by sentient beings, or that flesh and blood is as empty as a flower (i.e. "floaters") in one's eye. This very body (*dangti*) is this affliction and ignorance.⁶⁰

Ouyi clearly portrays bodies as products of karma: they are produced by karmic habits but also ultimately empty. Only by recognizing that one's body results from previous karma can one rid oneself of views of self that perpetuate the cycle of birth and death. Bodily practices of burning oneself or writing texts with one's blood do not necessarily imply detachment toward oneself; they can also signal a perception of bodies as sites of karmic transformation. Burning marks and makes a bodhisattva body; blood writing extricates one's vital essence to demonstrate the profundity of one's sincerity and commitment.

This interpretation of bodies as karmic products becomes particularly useful for understanding how blood writing enables bodies to become karmic producers. It is because blood writing entails a karmic transformation that Ouyi enjoins Chan practitioners to engage in the practice. In a text extolling the writing and recitation of mantras, Ouyi writes, "If today's Chan practitioners give rise to a sincere mind and write the mantra in their blood, their contributory cause (*yuanyin*) [toward enlightenment] will not be superficial; the essence (*ti*) of their contributory cause is this direct cause (*zhengyin*) [of Buddhahood], and reaching this direct cause is also called the illuminating cause (*liaoyin*) [of wisdom]. The three causes are neither the same nor different."⁶¹ Here Ouyi frames the bodily practice of blood writing within a broader discussion of karma; their bodily act not only serves as a contributory cause for enlightenment but also a direct and illuminating one. Blood writing can encompass all of these causes because it extracts the bodily essence (*ti*) of blood to convey a verbal mantra and signal a sincere mental state: all three karmic activities of body, speech, and mind thereby converge and become causes for enlightenment. In this way, we can understand the body as a karmic product as well as a karmic producer.

Ouyi also describes blood writing as a filial practice aimed to repay the debt owed to his mother. He uses blood to write a letter to his mother on February 21, 1624, that focuses especially on the debt owed to his mother for giving birth to him. In this respect, blood writing can also seek to repay a "birth debt": a range of kindnesses that mothers provide during infancy, such as giving birth and breast-feeding.⁶² As Alan Cole has argued, many

Chinese Buddhist texts shifted from a Confucian emphasis on a father–son dyad to the mother–son relationship, introducing a new complex of sin, guilt, and indebtedness so that sons would be anxious about "repaying the kindness" (*bao'en*) of their mothers and also ensuring that they not suffer in hell for the sin of childbirth.[63] In his letter, Ouyi not only expresses his desire to repay his mother's kindness, but he also discloses his anxiety over his lingering affection for her and his fear that she will suffer in hell for his sins. Identifying himself as a man who lives a monastic life (*fangwai*), Ouyi writes that he reverently burns his arms, cuts his tongue until it bleeds, kneels before his mother and says that as a boy he heeded his parent's instruction, studied the Way (*daoxue*), and was raised by his mother after his father suddenly died, but he was terrified when he pondered the universality of "birth and death" (*shengsi*). Thinking of his maternal uncle who died suddenly, he realized that one could be healthy yet die at a young age—that life was impermanent and death inescapable. Pained at the thought of his deceased father and elderly mother, Ouyi writes that if one does not plan early to escape the world (*chushi*), it would be truly frightening to later regret and have no possibility of transcendence. Ouyi then recalls how at twenty years old, he learned from an astrologer that his mother would die at sixty-one or sixty-two, which prompted him to make a vow before the Buddha to shorten his own life and weaken his own merit in order to lengthen his mother's life. He then writes:

> Now all my thoughts transcend worldly affairs: if I develop an attentive mind, how can this thought seek to improve my mother's life? How can I ensure she will not die prematurely? The single act of giving birth is the origin of worldly suffering. Alongside fame, it has a fixed duration. Even high office and success cannot match birth and death. How can the example of my maternal uncle compare to the *mahāsattva* Dizang? The venerable Mulian accumulated *kalpa*s of kindness from his parents, and their liberation became his filial [repayment]. In my youth, I reviled the *mahāsattva* and relied on my mother suffering torturously below. Now I have corrected my mistakes and follow goodness: my aim is escaping the world. I fear my feelings of love for my mother will be difficult to sever, but I must harden my heart. I secretly practice expedient means and also fear for my mother's welfare day and night. Thus before the Three Jewels, I burn incense [on my body], cut myself until I bleed, and send a letter from far away. I pray that nothing burden my mind and that I only engage in recollection of the Buddha (*nianfo*) and seek escape from the wheel of rebirth.[64]

Ouyi portrays birth as the cause of suffering, expresses guilt over sins that potentially relegate his mother to hell, and depicts liberation of one's parents as the ultimate expression of filial piety. In this way, he evokes the symbiotic relationship between mothers, sons, and monasteries that Cole sees perpetuated in many Chinese Buddhist texts.[65] By engaging in devotional acts of burning and blood writing, Ouyi seeks to repay his debt and to sever his lingering attachment to his mother. In this text, blood takes on a significance that differs from his blood writing against corrupt Chan practices. There, it connotes inner vitality and sincerity, whereas here it symbolizes the debt owed to his mother. Equating childbirth as the root of suffering, Ouyi engages in a similarly painful practice by burning himself and cutting his tongue, and he uses the blood to write a letter to his mother explaining his decision to become a cleric. Although he admits that in his youth he sought to extend his mother's life and was frightened by his uncle's death, he describes how his thoughts now transcend such worldly concerns, and how salvific figures such as the bodhisattva Dizang supersede his familial relatives. His decision to escape *saṃsāra*—literally "birth and death" (*shengsi*)—displaces previous concerns about his mother's life and his uncle's death; now he fears only that his feelings for his mother will impede his spiritual progress. In the hopes that he might end his affection for his mother, Ouyi uses the blood given to him in childbirth to symbolically repay the kindness of his own birth.[66] He makes the blood of his conception the means of terminating his maternal ties.

In addition to criticizing certain Chan practices and repaying the debt of his mother's kindness, Ouyi uses blood writing to promote Pure Land recitation of the Buddha's name and to emphasize his commitment to Tiantai. Oftentimes he criticizes "Crazy Chan" in order to promote these other traditions; for example, in a poem commemorating a gathering of friends in which he cut his tongue (*cishe*), Ouyi insists that the Pure Land practice of reciting the Buddha's name surpasses all other practices—especially the practice of concentrating on a head phrase (*canjiu*) that is part of *gongan* (Jpn. *kōan*), which he views as especially difficult for those of his generation.[67] Blood writing underscores the efficacy of this Pure Land practice, especially when juxtaposed with Chan practices.

In another text, blood writing serves a penitential function. After regretting how he succumbed to "Chan sickness" while visiting the Tiantai master Youxi Chuandeng in 1623, Ouyi describes repenting for this mistake in front of his Tiantai brother Guiyi Shouchou, burning his body, and writing a blood text for his teachers and friends, which he then sends to Mount Tiantai.⁶⁸ We can appreciate the significance of his blood writing as we later read: "Like an inferior disciple, among my young mistakes were poisonous schools (*zongmen*) and self-indulgent habits that soaked me to the bone. Although I have now painstakingly reformed, some remaining habits are difficult to eliminate. Thus I personally study under Tiantai masters, but dare not explicitly claim this Dharma lineage. I honestly fear that my writings will occasionally have discrepancies and instead invite ridicule for being 'Shanwai' and turning their back on the [Tiantai] school."⁶⁹ Ouyi portrays his prior mistakes as penetrating his very bone and marrow: this previous karma has become part of his body. By extracting blood from his body and by burning his flesh, he can draw out the embodied forms of such mistakes and use them for meritorious ends.

Ouyi also suggests that blood writing can ensure the vitality of the Vinaya, again framing the practice as an attempt to quell the tides of "Crazy Chan."⁷⁰ In a text explaining his reasons for revoking the precepts, Ouyi narrates the story of his monastic career from his service at Yunqi to his meditation at Shuangjing, his visit with friends at Tiantai, and his return to Yunqi to receive the precepts.⁷¹ Admitting that he was then ignorant about which way of receiving the precepts accorded with the Dharma, Ouyi says he took Master Gude as his preceptor, faced an image of the monk Yunqi Zhuhong, bowed his head, and received the Four-Part Vinaya (*Sifen lü*; Skt. *Dharmaguptaka-vinaya*) on January 28, 1624, and returned to Yunqi to receive the bodhisattva precepts on January 30, 1625. That spring after reading the Vinaya canon and writing *Shiyi yaolüe* (Brief essentials outline of [Vinaya] rituals), he says he read the Vinaya a second time with Xuehang Zhiji and began his *Essentials* in four volumes during the spring of 1628. The following year he writes that when he sent the text to the Chan master Wuyi, the latter wanted to print it, but Ouyi said it was incomplete. He then says he went into winter retreat at Longju where he again read the Vinaya with Guiyi Shouchou, and then on February 12, 1630, he burned his arms with incense and cut his tongue so it bled and sent the text to Xinggu Daoshou (1583–1631), who three months later came with Rushi Daofang (1588–1639) to Longju, where they both received the precepts with the requisite instructors. After reading the Vinaya a third time, Ouyi writes that he realized what reception of the precepts accorded with the precepts, and that even Vinaya Halls were not in accordance with the Dharma. When he drew the lot of "bodhisattva-*śrāmanera*" (*pusa shami*) in 1633, he says he vowed to always be a Dharma protector and serve as a *bhikṣu* (*biqiu*) in accordance with the Dharma.

In this same year, he writes he increasingly suffered from illness, and fearing death was near, thought he would be unable to accomplish his first aspiration as a monk, that his life would be in vain, and his death a waste. Resolving to enter into solitary retreat and end his cruel life, he says he gave his handwritten copy of the *Essentials* to the monk Cheyin Hai and decried the decline of the Buddha Dharma, the unraveling of the Vinaya, and the chaotic state of Chan and the Teachings. Noting that some receive the precepts but fail to carefully practice or uphold them, he writes that if one hears the *Essentials*, they will personally practice the heavy and the light precepts. Noting how he suffered various illnesses and misfortunes from 1630 to 1634, he emphasizes the necessity of cultivating understanding and practice, and he writes, "With the appearance of my suffering body and the strength of my firm vows, I rely on the object of mindfulness and earnestly practice the Way; I take the Vinaya canon to be my *dharmakāya* parents (*fashen fumu*)."[72] However, even though Ouyi portrays Vinaya texts as his parents, he admits difficulty in forming any sort of family: "My fate (*yun*) is having innumerable suffering thoughts, pronouncing innumerable vows, and exerting innumerable minds and strengths. If I cannot bring five *bhikṣus* together to live according to the Dharma, this is predestined (*tianding*), thus how can I abandon these thoughts, vows, minds, and strengths?"[73] Considering Ouyi's blood letter in the context of his described efforts to rectify the state of the Vinaya, we can see how he uses blood not only toward filial or doctrinal ends but also to bring together Dharma brothers and teachers. Just as Ouyi speaks of the Vinaya texts as his parents, we can understand Vinaya brothers as his family, which is further substantiated by a blood text that he wrote to Xuehang Zhiji on February 7, 1629.[74] Although he ultimately fails to form a Vinaya community, he acknowledges the efforts that he has taken in his body, speech, and mind to benefit the Vinaya.

Just as scars are visible traces of burning, blood texts are visible reminders of blood writing. Lamenting how pure practices (*fanxing*) have become all but impossible at a time like his when the Dharma has declined, Ouyi emphasizes the merit of such acts of blood writing: "Like the essence of the precepts, this text will not perish but universally cause those in the future to see and hear, and together realize their own nature is the pure essence of the precepts."[75] Ouyi views texts produced by blood writing as especially efficacious at transmitting the Dharma; the blood extracted from one's body (*ti*) materially represents the essence (*ti*) of the precepts. By seeing the blood, future readers will look inward and discover their essence as similarly reflecting the precepts. In another text extolling blood writing as the supreme offering and the Lotus Sutra as king of all scriptures,⁷⁶ Ouyi notes that if a single line or word can plant seeds leading to Buddhahood, even more merit accrues from copying the entire sutra. He writes, "We find it difficult to renounce (*she*)—especially when it comes to our own body—and when it comes to cutting [one's tongue] and using blood as ink, one feels extreme pain and one's views of self are destroyed. How can it be second to the Medicine King's burning of his arm?"⁷⁷ Here Ouyi uses a parallel construction that links the feeling of extreme pain and the destroying of a sense of self. Although some may question the degree of pain that results from burning incense on one's arm or head, the pain involved in cutting the back of one's tongue is clearly conveyed by the Chinese character *ci* that means "stab," "prick," and "prod." Ouyi suggests that the pain involved in blood writing can prove instrumental; by extracting one's blood prick by prick, and drip by drip, one repeatedly inflicts pain upon oneself and reinforces a view of the body as the source of suffering.

Ouyi's blood writing and blood texts exemplify the convergence of writing and ritual that characterizes Ouyi's ritual texts. As we saw in his autobiography, Ouyi sees ritual and writing as playing fundamental roles in self-cultivation. If writing were less important than such bodily acts, how can we explain his decision to write all of the ritual texts that we have examined? In one of his letters, Ouyi acknowledges engaging in many penitential practices, which he describes as "hundreds of refining" (*bailian*) and "thousands of rubbing" (*qianmo*) that did not fully eliminate his confusion; whereas when it came to teachings and traditions, he did not have the slightest doubt or torpor and as a result "wrote a considerable amount, all of which could be verified with [past] Buddhist patriarchs and await a hundred [future] generations."⁷⁸ As we saw in the first chapter, his writings enable him to extend beyond his present moment into the past and future; only by writing about his ritual activity can he reach future practitioners. In one of his Dharma talks, Ouyi portrays writing as a type of embodiment. Arguing that "to write, one must understand meaning (*yi*)," he says that one must "sincerely read and recite, unfolding the scrolls as if you were facing the living Buddha (*huo fo*), receiving the scrolls as if he were right before your eyes, for thousands and thousands of times, until it sinks into your marrow. . . . [Y]our contributory causes (*yuanyin*) [toward enlightenment] will be profound."⁷⁹ Though we have focused largely on the extraction of blood and marrow for the purposes of writing blood texts, here Ouyi characterizes reading and recitation as bodily practices in their own right. If one sincerely receives scriptures, they should become part of one's own body and also contribute to one's journey toward enlightenment.

BODIES OF GENERATIVITY AND BODIES OF TRANSFORMATION

We have seen how Ouyi's bodily practices reflect various constructions of bodies: as gifts from parents that require repayment, as products of previous karma, as sources of suffering, or as vehicles for karmic transformation. Other views of bodies surface in Ouyi's commentaries. For example, in his commentary on the *Zhouyi*, Ouyi first details the human body. He states that human bodies consist of the five sense organs (*wuguan*)—the ear, eye, mouth, nose, and heart—that are in front and governed by the five internal organs (*wuzang*)—the heart, liver, spleen, lungs, and kidneys—that reside in the body cavity and contact the back.⁸⁰ This reflects common medical views of the body, where the five organs, linked with the five phases, were considered *yin* because they were associated with interior and deeper layers of vital function, such as the preservation and nourishment of the vitalities of *qi* as either blood or essence.⁸¹ Ouyi explains that when one faces the colors black, yellow, red, purple, and white, then feelings arise, but if the colors appear in back, then they are concealed and one is unaware of them. As a result, people consider the back to be stillness, and a still back can cause the five sense organs to be tranquil even when they are excited by feelings and cravings.

Following this description of bodies that largely echoes medical constructions Ouyi immediately deconstructs this view of the body and argues that such stillness and movement are nondual. He contends that bodies are insubstantial:

> The body originally is not true; only when entangled by feelings and desires do we mistakenly perceive that there is a body. Now if we observe it calmly, [we find] its solid parts belong to earth, its moist ones belong to water, its warm ones belong to fire, and its moving ones belong to wind. The eyes, ears, nose, and tongue differ in their function; the four limbs,

the head, and feet differ in their names, the 360 bones and ligaments, the 84,000 hairs and orifices, how can these ultimately make up the body? Since the body cannot be grasped, upon experiencing ten thousand transformations, how can the characteristic "personhood" be grasped?[82]

Ouyi supplants his previous discussion of the body drawing from strains of Chinese medical texts—namely a correspondence between internal organs, sensory organs, and the five colors—with a Buddhist understanding of the body as essentially untrue and impermanent. Because the body can be further and further broken down into its constituent parts, Ouyi concludes that one cannot cling to the notion of "personhood." Here Ouyi engages in a typical deconstruction of the body into the four great elements (*si da*; Skt. *mahābhūta*) of earth, water, fire, and wind that is found in many Buddhist meditations on the body. These themes also appear prominently in his Dharma talks, where he urges his audience not to be defined by this "deceptive form" (*xuwang xingzhi*), which arises and ceases, can never become immortal, and is produced by "illusive karma" (*huanye*). He writes, "One's bodily form is not self but is only that which is formed by borrowing the four great elements; the mind also has no characteristics, and it is only because of feelings and defilement that false views arise and cease."[83] He urges practitioners to exhaust such feelings in order to turn away from defilement and toward awakening.

Whereas medical constructions of the body in the Ming dynasty emphasize generativity, Ouyi advocates practices to extract people from the cycle of birth and death and to transform their bodies into those of bodhisattvas. As Charlotte Furth has argued, late sixteenth- and early seventeenth-century medical texts exhibit a preoccupation about "multiplying descendants" and increasing longevity by "nourishing life" (*yangsheng*).[84] Such "bodies of generativity" are characterized by the ability to originate, produce, or procreate, whereas Ouyi's "bodies of transformation" result from an undoing, extirpation, and uprooting aimed at producing bodhisattva bodies. As scholars note, the collections of biographies of eminent monks contained special sections for those who engaged in suicide, self-immolation, and other ascetic practices in which they "abandoned their bodies" (*shishen, yishen,* or *wangshen*) for the sake of the Dharma.[85] Ouyi appeals to this ideal in his bodily practices of burning and blood writing, which involve substantial pain, seek to eliminate karma, and remove vital life forces from his body. In contrast to a generative body that draws attention to "how the functions of generation and gestation related to the social transitions of kinship identity involved in becoming a mother or a father."[86] Ouyi criticizes the generative body as further binding people to the cycle of birth and death and instead promotes bodily practices aimed at disrupting this cycle.

We see evidence that Ouyi consciously challenged ideals of "generative bodies" in his Dharma talks, where he supplants the ideal of "nourishing life" with that of "nourishing virtue" (*yangde*) and recommends weakening one's vital forces instead of strengthening them. Advocating strengthening one's intentional desires (*zhi yu*) and weakening one's vital ones (*qi yu*) Ouyi writes, "If one's intention is not strong, one cannot realize the character of the thousand ancient [sages]; if one's *qi* is not soft, one cannot mold the many karmic impressions (*xiqi*)."[87] Ouyi uses "mold" or "shape" (*tao*)—as a potter molds clay—to describe the process of transforming one's karmic habits by weakening one's vital energy. Ouyi clearly views bodies (with their life forces) as products of karma, which one can transform by focusing one's intention on ritual activity. Whereas the male ideal seeks to strengthen vital energies to promote longevity and fertility, Ouyi advocates weakening one's vital energy and strengthening one's aim toward transformation. In another Dharma talk, he says that those who follow the path should have strong bones and soft *qi* as well as great intentions and slight courage; they should not indulge in decadent thoughts when pleased or concede to melancholy paralysis when disappointed and should be simple in their attire and eat only that which staves off hunger, stating: "They should always examine this world and ask what merit from previous lives did they do to be able to sit and enjoy the sandalwood offerings."[88] Ouyi emphasizes the preciousness of being born as a human, for it allows one to engage in ritual practices—such as sitting in meditation and giving offerings—that can lead to enlightenment. Finally, in a third Dharma talk, Ouyi warns that desires can prompt one to plot to kill one's father or have sex with one's mother, and he urges his audience to thoroughly sever their feelings, as one vows when one first becomes a monk: "I will be a dried up and decaying skeleton, and not exhaust the source of life, old age, sickness, and death."[89] He says one can say one possesses "strong bones" only when one has resolved not to be caught up in karmic circumstances (*yejing*).[90] Here Ouyi urges his audience to focus less on physical vitality and more on religious energies; by weakening those desires that perpetuate "bodies of generativity," they can strengthen their resolve to engage in religious practices that ultimately produce bodhisattva bodies.

Scholars have recently analyzed the relationship in Buddhist traditions between positive and negative discourse on bodies. Reiko Ohnuma has argued that a negative fixation on the "worthlessness" of bodies as impure, impermanent, fragile, and as fueling passions and deluded thoughts appears frequently in body-focused meditations, which Buddhist clerics use to overcome their attachment to the body, such as meditation on thirty-two loathsome parts of the body, meditation on the nine stages of decomposition of a corpse, or meditation on the ten types of dead bodies found in cremation grounds.[91] However, Ohnuma also acknowledges another line of Buddhist thinking that sees bodies as having "worth" as the locus and vehicle for enlightenment, and she suggests that the worthlessness of the body is used to overcome attachment to self, while the worth of the body seeks to inculcate proper care of bodies detailed in Buddhist monastic discipline.[92] Only by realizing the body's utter worthlessness can one abandon it entirely: "In that moment of sudden realization, the negative worth involved in merely *abandoning* the body is transformed into the positive worth involved in *using* the worthless body in a religious act, one which paradoxically transforms the body into a precious 'treasure.'"[93] Only by properly abandoning one's body can one turn it into something of worth.

In a similar vein, Susanne Mrozik has argued that a negative discourse or "ascetic discourse" can often contribute to a positive discourse or "physiomoral discourse" that seeks to produce bodhisattvas with virtuous bodies and minds. She acknowledges that bodies are products of an individual's karma and therefore "pliable"—or subject to transformation because of one's actions.[94] Theories of karma often refer to one's body as "direct retribution" (zhengbao) for previous actions, as opposed to one's social status and geographic location, which are considered "circumstantial retribution" (yibao). Karma dictates whether one is healthy or sick, male or female, and so on, but one can shape one's body through particular kinds of practices such as bodhisattva discipline, which aims toward materially transforming bodies into something that can be enjoyed by all sentient beings.[95] This "productive paradox" lies at the heart of Buddhist conceptions of the body: only those who cultivate to the point of sacrificing their bodies for others can receive the best body—that of a Buddha, which is adorned with thirty-two "marks of a great man" (dazhangfu xiang; Skt. mahāpuruṣalakṣaṇa) that are the karmic result of particular moral virtues cultivated in his former lives.

We see evidence of a more positive or "physiomoral discourse" as Ouyi describes Buddha bodies and human bodies in ethical terms. In one of his Dharma talks, he notes how people know that Chan is the Buddha's mind and the Teachings the Buddha's speech, but they do not realize that the monastic precepts are the Buddha's body, recalling how the Vairocana Buddha took the precepts as his body, such that there was no evil that he could not stop nor good that he could not perform.[96] Elsewhere Ouyi notes how the *Mahāprajñāparamitā-sutra* states the thirty-two marks of a great man result only from upholding the precepts: "If one does not uphold the precepts, one cannot even attain the body of a jackal, much less a Buddha's body."[97] On several occasions Ouyi admits his inability to uphold the precepts, suggesting he is unworthy of gaining a bodhisattva's or Buddha's body. In one of his extant letters, Ouyi admits his discomfort with others viewing him as the best at upholding the precepts, especially because he acknowledges having wet dreams and lying.[98] Particularly after withdrawing (*tui*) to the status of *śrāmanera*, Ouyi says he lacks the principle of promoting the precepts, and he writes, "I only have ascetic practice (*kuxing*) in the mountains and substitution for all beings that seek to eliminate previous karma and remove obstacles. I dare not be secure."[99]

Because he views the monastic precepts as equivalent to Buddha bodies, he urges clerics to uphold them in order to preserve their precious human bodies, which allow them the opportunity to attain enlightenment. He identifies three potential obstacles to upholding precepts: anger, pride, and laziness.[100] In light of such threats, he urges another cleric, "Prepare your body as a venerable jewel of the sangha," and that if he continues in his former ways without reforming, each action will result in numerous sins: "Once the winds of karma blow, your robe will be lowered and you will lose this human body."[101] Ouyi views human bodies as exceedingly special, and he laments how "those who now attain a human body are not worthy of the true Dharma."[102] Ouyi similarly upholds negative and positive discourses about bodies, urging people to recognize the precious opportunity of having human bodies that can perform religious rituals that can lead to liberation from the cycle of birth and death.

THERAPEUTIC ILLNESS: PERFECTING FORBEARANCE THROUGH SUFFERING

Having examined some of the various constructions of bodies in Confucian, Buddhist, and medical traditions, we now turn to an examination of how Ouyi describes the experience of pain and illness. Whether one believes pain eludes language entirely[103] or can be captured only in metaphor,[104] one cannot dispute the challenge pain poses to communication. Ouyi writes about bodily practices in which pain is controlled and embedded in public activities that can be witnessed by or shared with others.[105] He attributes creative or transformative potential to them, which starkly juxtaposes his description of the destructive and disintegrative effects of pain in illness. As Ariel Glucklich argues in his study of "sacred pain," religious practitioners often convert accidental pain or illness (sometimes conceived as punishment) into a positive force acting on behalf of passage, healing, or other advantages.[106] As we have seen, Ouyi warns against attachment to the body that fuels mistaken conceptions of having a self; in this respect, the disintegrative and disruptive effects of illness can serve as a helpful means of mitigating against self-attachment.[107] Ouyi also envisions a therapeutic potential to illness: by enduring sickness, one can perfect the virtue of patience or forbearance.

Although Ouyi portrays bodies as products of karma and sources of suffering, he views bodily illness as having the potential to be spiritually beneficial. After describing a grave illness that drove him to hide away at Jiuhuashan, Ouyi says that it then became "good medicine."[108] He explains elsewhere, "Nothing beats illness as good medicine for sentient beings; when illness is extreme, one's form becomes withered and one's mind also ashen."[109] He says that his own illness caused his form and spirit to become withered, such that when clerics or laypeople encountered him, they called him an "emaciated god" (shen qu).[110] He suggests a connection between illness and holiness because his desiccated form prompts others to attribute sanctity to him.[111]

In letters to laypeople, Ouyi suggests that illness has therapeutic value because it enables one to cultivate patience. In a letter he says, "I honor the sending of phlegm, sickness, and melancholy.... All kinds of adversities can move the mind toward the nature of forbearance."[112] In another letter, he writes:

> Illness is good medicine for our generation. It consumes defilement and deluded thoughts, and it breaks through the illusion of this body. It profoundly clarifies suffering, emptiness, impermanence, nonself, and the contemplative gates. This all depends on there being the condition of sickness. I vow to have an expansive mind and a patient intention, to calmly

endure [illness] without loathing, and I set my thought on eliminating old karma according to circumstances, on transforming the heavy sensation and perception and causing them to lighten, and on substituting for sentient beings in receiving suffering. I truly do not consider it shameful to be inferior to another.[113]

Illness can play beneficial physical and cognitive roles: by attacking the body (itself a karmic product) it consumes defilement, and by revealing the body as impermanent and a source of suffering, it challenges mistaken views of the body. Illness can be a powerful tool for instructing about Buddhist doctrine. In addition, Ouyi suggests it can provide an opportunity for cultivating the perfection of forbearance (ren; Skt. kṣānti) because he vows to endure his own illness by not generating hatred or disgust but instead focusing on eliminating past karma, transforming his present karmic actions, and substituting for others in their future karmic retribution. He suggests that one can use illness as an occasion for transforming one's karma.

Thus Ouyi portrays bodies not only as sources of suffering but also vehicles for realizing the truth of suffering and thereby escaping such suffering. In a Dharma talk, he says one should think of one's present body and mind as "tools of suffering" (ku ju). He writes, "Because one does not know suffering, one again creates causes for suffering; now, by observing the body with the four great elements and the mind with the four *skandhas*, one understands there is no self or object but only delusory conditions and useless rebirths."[114] By deconstructing one's body and mind, one can understand the origin of suffering. In another Dharma talk, he uses bodies to convey the Four Noble Truths, contending that one must pass through defilement in order to reach enlightenment. He advocates engaging in the four foundations of mindfulnesses (sinian): contemplating one's body (shen; Skt. kāya), one's feelings (shou; Skt. vedanā), one's mind (xin; Skt. citta), and dharmas (fa). He suggests that the five *skandhas* of reward and retribution (guobao wuyin) are the first truth of suffering; mistakenly fueling desires for permanence, joy, self, and purity is the second truth of the origin of suffering; understanding impermanence, emptiness, and nonself is the third truth of the cessation for suffering; and finally, not giving rise to mistaken thoughts and thus not inviting birth and death is the path leading to cessation of suffering.[115] Bodies play a significant role in the Four Noble Truths: birth, old age, sickness, and death exemplify the bodily experience of suffering.

In another Dharma talk, Ouyi suggests that "suffering bodies" and "truth bodies" (*fashen*; Skt. *dharmakāya*) differ only because of perception. Ouyi emphasizes the importance of "a single moment of thought" (*yinian*) in determining how one experiences one's particular realm of rebirth. Insisting upon the similarities of the essential direct cause (*zhengyin*), the nature of contributory causes (*liaoyin*), and the karmic functioning (*yeyong*) of causes and conditions in all ten realms of rebirth,[116] he argues that the realms only differ in "a single moment of thought." Turning one's back on awakening and joining with defilement turns the *dharmakāya*, *prajñā*, and liberation into suffering, delusion, and karma.[117] Interestingly, Ouyi pairs the *dharmakāya* with the suffering body, suggesting that a single thought can transform a body of suffering into one of truth, just as it can turn delusion into wisdom and karma into liberation. By extension, we can understand bodily practices of burning or inscription as instantiating a single moment when one focuses on enlightenment instead of defilement, creating the *dharmakāya* from one's suffering body.

SCATTERED ASHES OR PRESERVED RELICS: DISPUTING THE DISPOSAL OF OUYI'S BODY

As we noted in the previous section, the cycle of birth and death consists of four kinds of suffering: birth, old age, sickness, and death. When he writes about facing death, Ouyi says he frequently turned to Pure Land practices, which characterizes standard Buddhist monastic death practices from the seventh century to the present day.[118] When we examine Ouyi's death as recounted in Jianmi's biography, we find it also reflects Buddhist beliefs about the efficacy of practices at the time of death to determine one's future rebirth. Jianmi states that Ouyi instructed his disciples to cremate his body and distribute his remains to the fishes and birds. Even though he could have asked himself to be buried or mummified (and wrote inscriptions for fellow monks who did so), Ouyi is said to have "ordered that after his cremation (*duwei*)[119] they grind his bones and mix them with flour and divide it into two groups, one given to birds and beasts and one given to fishes and shellfish, that they all rejoice in the Dharma, and together be born in the Pure Land."[120] Jianmi then describes how Ouyi formed a Pure Land society (*jingshe*), wrote several votive texts, and after falling ill twenty days after the Chinese New Year, awoke the following day to find himself well; but at noon, he sat cross-legged on the corner of his corded seat and, facing west, he lifted his hands and died. Ouyi's practices in preparation of his death seek rebirth in the Pure Land: he forms a group, writes vows, assumes a seated posture, and faces westward toward the direction of the Pure Land.

Unlike Ouyi's bodily practices aimed at transforming his body into that of a bodhisattva, his cremation seeks to turn his body into ash that might then be given to other sentient beings in the hopes of being reborn together in the Pure Land.[121] Cremation of monks became increasingly common following the eighth century[122] though there is no evidence of laypeople being cremated prior to the tenth century.[123] Instead of the customary burial of bodies in coffins, cremation involved burning the body and either scattering the ashes in water, storing them in urns above ground, or burying them in the earth. Another development in the tenth century was the establishment of a "purgatorial" period during the forty-nine-day interim between death and rebirth (or liberation), in which the deceased was understood as traveling through a series of ten tribunals presided over by kings who functioned like magistrates in a Chinese bureaucracy, meting out rewards and punishments and determining his or her next rebirth.[124] Buddhist liturgies that resonated with Chinese mortuary traditions also became quite popular at this time, such as the "Assembly of Water and Land" (*shuilu hui*) conducted for the salvation of "all the souls of dead on land and sea." By the twelfth century, most major monasteries had sites for practicing this rite, which was performed by Buddhist monks and typically took seven days to complete.[125] The ritual began with offerings and prayers to temporarily release creatures from the heavens, earth, and underworld, and it then summoned "unenlightened beings" from Buddhist realms and indigenous Chinese cosmologies who they stripped of defilements by bestowing the Buddhist refuges and precepts and to whom they later distributed food.[126]

In light of such mortuary practices in late imperial China, Ouyi's request that his ashes be distributed to fish in water and animals on land would place him among the dead that are cared for in "Assembly of Water and Land" rituals. Ouyi ostensibly hopes his ashes might enable all beings to be born together in the Pure Land,[127] but the distribution of his ashes would effectively ensure others would care for him during his postmortem transition. However, Ouyi's disciples are said to have disobeyed his will; three years later, when they prepared to cremate him, they opened the shrine of his remains and found his hair long, his teeth undecayed, his legs crossed, and his face as if it were alive.[128] Instead of grinding his

FIGURE 5.1 Pillar from Qing dynasty stupa, Lingfeng Temple.

bones, they erected a reliquary or *stūpa* (*guta*) for his bones, to the left of the Great Buddha Hall at Lingfeng Mountain (figure 5.1).

Chengshi admits his unease about their decision to keep Ouyi's remains instead of scattering them, vowing to grind and scatter his own ashes in his master's stead. Nevertheless, they kept his bones as relics (*sheli*; Skt. *śarīra*)[129] for the Lingfeng community, and we can speculate on various reasons for doing so: Ouyi's relics could render Lingfeng Mountain more worthy of pilgrimage,[130] or they could provide some solace to his remaining disciples by serving as a locus for his enduring charisma, apotropaic power, and presence.[131] By placing Ouyi's relics at the center of their temple complex at Lingfeng Mountain, his disciples establish presence in his absence and provide a compelling stimulus for continuing their rituals and worship. As Robert Sharf has emphasized, "relics were powerful forces to be approached not conceptually or philosophically, but rather through the medium of worship and ritual."[132] Relics were often construed as animate entities capable of intentional actions not merely signs or representations. Their "allure" derives from how they distill the essence of the body, which in turn derives from how they are physically or ritually framed.[133] As Gregory Schopen has emphasized, "Relics, then, are defined as much by where they are located and what people do with them as they are by what they physically are."[134]

We have seen how Buddhist, Confucian, and medical traditions construe bodies in different ways, and how Ouyi viewed his own body as wracked with illness, which he approaches therapeutically as a way to perfect patience and transform his body into that of a bodhisattva. When facing his own death, he instructs his followers to grind his ashes into food for other sentient beings, which can be understood as a sacrificial offering characteristic of a bodhisattva or another type of Pure Land ritual ultimately seeking rebirth in the Land of Bliss. However, Ouyi has no control over his body after death; instead, his disciples have the last word about the disposal of his body, and they choose to incorporate his remains into their community.[135] They "frame" them in a reliquary and thereby add another layer of significance to his somatic existence—that of a master of the Lingfeng community—which continues to this day. His *stūpa* (figure 5.2) still sits to the left of the main hall at Lingfeng Temple, now locked and surrounded on all sides by a large cement wall, and they have added a memorial hall with a full-size statue and painting of Ouyi (figure 5.3): both sites remain hidden from the sight of pilgrims, but are occasionally used for rituals and worship by temple monks and lay devotees. Ouyi's presence is very much alive despite his absence—Lingfeng Temple is flourishing because of its reputation as Ouyi's home temple.[136]

As we have seen, Ouyi directs his bodily practices to various ends, using "filial slicing" to repay his mother's debt and thereby sever his connection with her but also referencing the practice in a poem for a sick Dharma brother; he burns his body in various ways—repentance, gratitude, or

FIGURE 5.2 Rebuilt stupa, Lingfeng Temple.

supplication—to mark his commitment to the bodhisattva path; he writes in his blood to repay a "birth debt," honor his teachers, criticize certain Chan practices, promote Pure Land practices, and to ensure the vitality of the Vinaya. His body instantiates his karmic retribution; by performing actions that scar his flesh and extract his blood, Ouyi suggests he can change his karma in material and public ways. Moreover, he ensures that

FIGURE 5.3 Memorial Hall for Ouyi, Lingfeng Temple.

such bodily practices will be witnessed by future readers by writing ritual texts to include in his corpus.

Ouyi draws from a variety of constructions of bodies—social, medical, and Buddhist—in his writing, and throughout he acknowledges the potential for bodies to change for better or for worse. Illness illustrates how bodies are far from "fixed" or "stable" and instead serves as further evidence in support of Buddhist notions of karma, emptiness, and impermanence. He acknowledges social views of bodies as binding sons to parents as he seeks to fulfill his filial obligations and thereby extricate himself from such relationships. He acknowledges medical understandings of bodies having vital essences and feelings, and he challenges male ideals of generativity with ascetic goals of abandonment and transformation. Finally, he prepares his own body for death by engaging in practices seeking rebirth in the Pure Land; however, his disciples seal his remains in a reliquary that further binds him to their community at Lingfeng Mountain.

CONCLUSION

In a world structured by karma, every experience—however trifling—becomes infused with greater significance. Anti-Buddhist writings that could easily be attributed to youthful naïveté become tantamount to disparaging the Three Jewels—the Buddha, Dharma, and Sangha—and worthy of rebirth in the lowest realms of hell. Leaving home to become a monk equates to a failure in one's filial duty and negligence that will result in an unfavorable rebirth. Receiving the precepts in front of the image of an eminent Buddhist monk instead of the Buddha nullifies their reception altogether and contravenes the monastic rules, which has its own karmic repercussions. Minor mistakes have the potential to precipitate major karmic effects.

In addition, karma opens up everyday challenges to reinterpretation. Each obstacle can be understood as retribution for some previous transgression—either in this life or the previous one. The political tumult of the seventeenth century, the fall of the Ming dynasty, and the Manchu conquest in karmic terms become "circumstantial retribution" (*yibao*) for previous misdeeds. Political instability is attributed to moral failure, and dynastic change is interpreted as evidence of the "decline of the Dharma" (*mofa*). Although such circumstances imply one's culpability, they also fall outside of one's sphere of control, thereby contributing to a sense of powerlessness.

Social ties are signs of karmic affinity, with close relationships indicating bonds in previous lives. By extension, the passing of friends and loved ones—and the subsequent suffering—can be understood as karmic retribution. A dearth of teachers and preceptors—which prompts monks to receive the precepts alone—also constitutes one's "circumstantial retribution" and can create difficult situations for monks hoping to receive the precepts in accordance with the monastic rules. Without adequate mentors to ordain them, those who aspire to become monks may feel uncertain about the validity of their ordination. When embedded in a larger karmic structure, opportunities for social connection (or lack thereof) are seen to be circumstantial results of previous karma, leaving one to feel morally responsible for any isolation, loneliness, or insecurity.

Intellectual and religious environments can similarly be understood within this framework of "circumstantial retribution." Educated in a Confucian tradition that establishes orthodoxy by vilifying Buddhism, and ordained in a Buddhist tradition suffering from sectarianism, one can be pulled into partisan allegiances. Writing and reading become karmic acts, and the texts produced have karmic implications. One misstep can leave one wary of affiliating oneself with any tradition and yearning for a community that overcomes such biases.

In sum, one's political, social, intellectual, and religious circumstances can be understood as karmic consequences for actions in previous lives. Finally, since one's body is "direct retribution" (*zhengbao*), any illness signifies moral degeneracy in a previous life. Even the slightest abnormality can be magnified under the karmic lens because physical weakness is understood to have a moral cause, while repeated bouts of sickness suggest more serious transgressions from previous lives. Occasioned by karma, somatic states can be deciphered ethically rather than physiologically.

One might think that living in a karmic universe would engender a state of fatalism, insofar as circumstantial and direct retribution seem to explain all aspects of one's present situation and to leave one little recourse for changing it. However, karma also functions as a mechanism for changing one's fate through religious practices. For Ouyi, such practices include writing, divination, repentance, profession of vows, and bodily practices of slicing, burning, and blood writing. When politics seem precarious, he takes solace in the possibility of cultivating himself in solitude. When social ties dissolve, texts become his interlocutors and writing his form of communication. To counteract religious sectarianism, he promotes a syncretistic vision in his autobiography and commentaries. Instead of resigning himself to chronic illness, he seeks to transform his body into that of a bodhisattva who might save sentient beings relegated to hell.

KARMIC OBSTACLES BECOME KARMIC OPPORTUNITIES

In this way, every obstacle becomes an occasion for spurring on further spiritual cultivation. Drawing inspiration from Confucian sources including the *Analects* and the *Yijing*, Ouyi cites the former when he insists that people have the ability "of themselves" to engage in rituals that can morally transform the world, and he interprets the first two hexagrams of the latter as symbolizing one's unobstructed spiritual potential, which can be accessed through religious practice. Even the smallest difficulty can stimulate one to cultivate virtue, as long as one does not resent such difficulties. Divination becomes a karmic endeavor, revealing the underlying causes of such obstructions, which should not lead one to despair but instead to further commit oneself to spiritual development.

Within Ouyi's karmically structured world, people can also call upon Buddhas and bodhisattvas for assistance. His repentance rituals invoke the aid of such beings—in particular the bodhisattva Dizang—for those facing the severest of karmic fates. By demonstrating the requisite shame and contrition, people can stimulate such beings to respond with grace and mercy. Devotion enables a karmic intervention, which in turn brings about karmic transformation. Emotions play a crucial role in this transformative process.

Not only can individuals appeal to Buddhas and bodhisattvas, but they can also aspire to become bodhisattvas themselves. Votive texts are replete with such aspirations that plant virtuous seeds one hopes will later come to fruition. Ouyi projects himself into the role of karmic savior as well as karmic substitute, as he vows to either eliminate the karma of sentient beings or to substitute in their place. He engages in all three karmic activities—that of body, speech, and mind—by burning his body as he professes such vows and by exsanguinating himself as he writes his votive texts. Burning and blood writing employ his body—his karmic inheritance—in virtuous ways in order to render it a bodhisattva body dedicated to the liberation of all sentient beings.

Finally, Ouyi suggests that certain views of karma can impede one's spiritual progress—if not derail it altogether. Specifically, he points out the implicit dangers of viewing karma in mechanistic term, or of misunderstanding the emptiness of karma. The former position—promoted in morality books and ledgers of merit and demerit—implies that one can definitively determine karmic causes and effects; the latter one—prevalent in many Mahāyāna texts—suggests that karma, like all phenomena, is ultimately empty. Both perspectives run the risk of encouraging a spiritual arrogance if people are led to believe they can completely control their fate or that their actions have no consequences. For these reasons, Ouyi emphasizes that unlike Buddhas and bodhisattvas with their supernatural powers, human beings cannot discern the workings of karma. He promotes an organic view of karma in which karmic seeds depend on a variety of conditions to come to fruition—many of which may be inscrutable to humans. The obscurity of karma in turn fosters a sense of humility among Chinese Buddhists, whose only recourse is to engage in religious practices in the hopes of changing their karma. Because certain ideas about karma can hinder one's religious development, Ouyi typically espouses the view with the least potential for deleterious effects.

In a world structured by karma, the cognitive, expressive, emotional, and physical dimensions of human experience are intertwined, which allows for a myriad of ways to address one's karma. Although divination allows one to ascertain one's karma (to a certain extent), penitential practices enable one to change that karma. For Ouyi and many Tiantai Buddhists, the linchpin of transformation is acknowledging karmic retribution yet seeking its elimination. This seeming contradiction opens up the possibility for Buddhas and bodhisattvas to intervene on people's behalf. Instead of resigning themselves to their fate, people can experience grace. Moreover, they can aspire to become bodhisattvas themselves by professing vows committing themselves to liberating others and engaging in activities befitting a bodhisattva. Once they begin using all of their faculties—mental, verbal, and physical—toward karmic transformation, their religious practice takes on a global dimension aimed at ethically transforming the world.

THE INSCRUTABILITY OF KARMA

When compared to the idea of a strict retributive causality prevalent in China during the sixteenth and seventeenth centuries, Ouyi's vision of karma may seem unique, but it is far from unprecedented. Earlier Chinese Buddhists such as Huiyuan and Xi Chao similarly understood karma as working in obscure and inexplicable ways: the former emphasizing the "invisible and subtle functions" created by ignorance and desire, and the latter describing how there is "a hidden response and mysterious structure albeit in indecipherable ways." They too acknowledged that karma could operate in enigmatic ways and that karmic retribution was more complex than an exact correspondence between past actions and future rewards or punishments.

In Ouyi's ritual writings, we see the possibilities afforded by this understanding of karma. If one accepts that karma is unfathomable, instead of speculating about the possible karmic causes of one's present condition, one can welcome every circumstance as providing the opportunity for karmic transformation. Every coincidence can potentially signal a karmic connection. Every obstruction can facilitate further opening and humility. Every ache can allow for the cultivation of patience. Every being can inspire commitment to becoming a bodhisattva.

Ouyi's ritual writings have resonated with later generations of Chinese Buddhists who similarly grapple with their own karma and how to live in the face of such karma. Alongside depictions of karma as knowable and mechanistic, Ouyi suggests a more obscure and organic view of karma, one subject to the intervention of Buddhas and bodhisattvas. However, such intercession depends upon the way one performs rituals. Ouyi acknowledges the potential for divination to decipher one's karma, repentance to evoke the power of bodhisattvas and Buddhas to erase one's karma, and vows and bodily acts to mark one's commitment to the bodhisattva path, but he insists that one can achieve such karmic transformations only when one properly engages in religious practices. His association of karma with religious practice should caution us against the assumption that one can separate thought from practice, or doctrine from ritual. Instead of approaching karma solely conceptually, we have considered it in practice—how one might live in the face of karma, or alternately, use one's body as living karma—an approach that has allowed us to uncover an organic view of karma that may have otherwise been overlooked.

CONSTRUCTIVE POSSIBILITIES

Appreciating the complexity of Ouyi's approach to karma—especially his emphasis on karmic inscrutability and karmic opportunities—we can move from describing Ouyi's karmic worldview to exploring its normative implications. Although some scholars have questioned whether local descriptive research can inform global and constructive discourses on ethics,[1] Ouyi's understanding of karma has much to contribute to constructive discussions about karma in Buddhist traditions.[2]

First, Ouyi's karmic worldview challenges the assumption that a metaphysical understanding of karma necessarily promotes an indifference to injustice in this life while speculating about the next life, a fixation on external rewards for our actions (wealth or status) instead of construction of character in this life, and an individual rather than collective conception of our lives. Dale Wright raises these objections in his argument for a naturalized concept of karma—one disconnected from metaphysics of rebirth and therefore persuasive for Western Buddhists.[3] As we have seen, Ouyi recognizes that his life depends on larger forces of nature, society, and history. He also focuses on the internal rewards of karma in shaping his character and his future possibilities. His "lived karma" underscores the importance of ordinary daily practice and customs of behavior—habits that constitute who we are and who we might become. He engages in disciplined practices of daily self-cultivation to ethically and spiritually transform himself into a being that might liberate other beings.

Second, far from obviating the need for disciplinary practice, Ouyi's supernatural beliefs—his devotion to bodhisattvas and acceptance of rebirth—motivate such practice. Wright assumes that a belief in rebirth would cause one to ignore the gravity and responsibility of one's present life, but for Ouyi, it heightens his sense of both. Ever cognizant of his own limitations, his devotion to the bodhisattva Dizang and his expectation of rebirth instills a sense of confidence in the possibility of transformation. In lieu of becoming a morally upstanding person solely in his present life, Ouyi seeks to develop himself into a being for others—a bodhisattva—who might aid sentient beings in his present and future lives. Instead of encouraging passivity or sanctioning inequality, karma motivates Ouyi to dedicate himself to the bodhisattva path.[4] Keenly aware of how habits condition behaviors, he engages in religious practices in order to habituate himself to endure illness with patience and to dedicate himself to others with selflessness. Ouyi lives his karma on a daily basis.

Third, karma not only motivates his religious practice but also has transformative potential. In this respect, Ouyi's vision of karma resonates with that of Peter Hershock who writes, "karma is also the inflection of things as-they-are-coming-to-be"[5] and "karma is always *playing out live*, in ways that are open to significant improvisation."[6] Although a deterministic understanding of karma runs the risk of fixating on past causes for present events, an organic and malleable approach to karma sees future possibility in the present moment. Ouyi's votive texts and bodily practice underscore this potentiality as he uses his body, speech, and mind to strengthen his resolve to become a bodhisattva who might liberate other sentient beings. His votive texts record the time and place of such practices, suggesting that each specific situation might become an opportunity for karmic transformation.

Finally, and perhaps this is the most powerful normative implication of Ouyi's karmic worldview, karma is best understood within the context of one's own life, not that of others. In other words, Ouyi applies karma to himself and his own circumstances; he does not presume to judge the karma of others. As he admits at the conclusion of his autobiography, only Buddhas and bodhisattvas (namely Śākyamuni and Dizang) have the power to judge him. Because karma is inscrutable, only those with supernormal powers have the ability to see other people's karma. Although Ouyi certainly speculates about karmic causes for his present conditions, he does not use karma as an explanation for evil or the suffering of others. As Eric Sean Nelson has noted, "Buddhist karma is primarily about the moral status of an action. It does not aim at excusing, justifying, or normalizing suffering as a necessary good."[7] For Ouyi, karma is primarily about the moral status of *his* actions. Neither a theodicy nor a license to judge other people's actions, karma provides a means of confronting and responding to the reality of his own life and morality. Thus, in response to Brian Victoria's question of whether modern Japanese Buddhists and others who have used karma in socially reactionary ways "got it wrong,"[8] Ouyi would respond, "they did." Because one cannot decipher karma, Ouyi implies that the most honest stance toward other people's suffering is that of extreme humility.

In other words, karma is best personalized. From Ouyi's personal writings, we have created a karmic biography and reconstructed his own karmic worldview. Although one might assume that his vision of karma—its capacity to motivate religious practice, its inscrutability, its transformative potential, and its appropriate scope—would have nothing constructive to offer Buddhist ethicists, in fact it cautions us against concluding that abstract theoretical discussions of karma trump detailed personal or local accounts. Might we consider an alternative, in which we interrogate what "karma" means to a variety of Buddhists in a range of times and places, how these Buddhists "live" their karma, and whether they too view their bodies as "living karma"?

APPENDIX 1
A TRANSLATION OF OUYI'S AUTOBIOGRAPHY

[AUTO]BIOGRAPHY OF THE FOLLOWER[1] OF EIGHT NEGATIONS[2]

(*The elder himself wrote [these] words; [which are] supplemented at three points [by Jianmi Chengshi]. [His name] is taken from the essential purport (zhi) of the eight negations of the Madhyamaka-śāstra and the Sutra of Brahma's Net.*)

I am a recluse from China. In the past, there was Confucianism, Chan, Vinaya, and the Teachings,[3] but I dare not [study them]. Today there is also Confucianism, Chan, Vinaya, and the Teachings, but I disdain [to follow them]. Thus I am called the "Eight Negations."[4]

My common surname is Zhong; I am called Jiming, also called Sheng. My style name is Zhenzhi. My ancestors were from Bianliang (in Henan); when my first ancestors immigrated south of the river, the family took residence in Mudu Zhen in Old Wu.[5] My mother's maiden name was Jin. I was born because my father Qizhong recited the *dhāraṇī* of the White-robed and Greatly-compassionate [Guanyin] for ten years and dreamt that the Great One sent him a son. This was the twenty-seventh year of the Wanli reign, in the *jiwei* year [1599] on June 24, between 9 and 11 P.M.

At the age of six (seven *sui*), I became a vegetarian.

At the age of eleven, I already had non-Buddhist (*wai*) tutors. I heard the teachings of the [Confucian] sages and assigned myself to the thousand ancients, vowing to destroy Buddhism and Daoism. I began eating meat and drinking. I wrote dozens of tracts attacking [non-Confucian] heterodoxy (*yiduan*). I dreamt that I met and spoke with Confucius and Yan Hui.

At the age of sixteen, I read the preface to [Zhuhong's] *Record of Self-Knowledge* and *Jottings under a Bamboo Window*. Then I did not criticize the Buddha but [instead] took the tracts I had written criticizing the Buddha and burned them.

When I was nineteen years old, I wrote a commentary on the *Analects*. When I reached [the verse] "the whole world will submit to humaneness" (*tianxia guiren*),[6] I could not put brush to paper; for three days and nights, I neither slept nor ate. I had a great enlightenment to the teachings of the mind (*xinfa*) of Confucius and Yan [Hui]. In the winter, my father passed away. I heard the [*Sutra*] *of the Original Vows of Dizang*[7] and aroused the aspiration to escape the world [of death and rebirth].

At twenty-one years of age, I focused my will on recitation of the Buddha's name (*nianfo*) and completely burned over 2,000 chapters of my schoolboy writings.

When I was twenty-two years old, I heard the *Śūraṃgama-sutra* (Literally: the *Sutra of the Great Buddha Peak*; T. 945) that speaks of the world residing in emptiness and emptiness giving rise to great awakening, and I wondered why there was this great awakening that ultimately becomes the original unfolding of a world of emptiness. My melancholy ceased without my having done anything, but I was extremely confused, and I could not lessen it by my own effort. Thus I decided to become a monk and fully experience the great matter [of life and death].

When I was twenty-three, in a dream I venerated Master Hanshan [Deqing]. I cried and regretted my misfortune that it was too late for us to meet each other. The master said, "This is the suffering resulting [from previous misconduct] (*kuguo*); you must learn the causes of suffering." He had not yet finished speaking, but I abruptly entreated, "Your disciple seeks the higher vehicle. I do not wish to hear the teaching of the Four Noble Truths." The teacher said, "I am delighted that the layman has this higher ambition. Although you cannot be like Huangbo and Linji,[8] you can be like Yantou and Deshan."[9] My mind was still not satisfied, and I planned to ask again but felt and heard [something] and awoke. Then I thought, "How can I place one of the ancients above another? These dreamed thoughts are only deluded discriminations." In one month, I dreamt of Master Han[shan] three times. He went toward Caoxi,[10] but I could not go so far, so I [took the tonsure with] Master Xueling, shaving my head and receiving ordination (in 1622).[11] [Xueling] called me Zhixu. Master Xue[ling] was a disciple of the elder Han[shan].

In the summer and autumn (of 1622), I did service at Yunqi.[12] I heard the Dharma teacher Gude teach on the [*Cheng*] *weishi lun* (T. 1585.31.1a–59a). After hearing it once, I understood completely. I suspected that there was a conflict with the essential purport of the *Śūraṃgama-*[*sutra*] and asked about this. The teacher said, "There are two schools—that of Dharma characteristics (*faxiang*) and that of Dharma nature (*faxing*).[13] One cannot mix them." I was very surprised by this. How could the Buddha's teaching have two divergent views? One day, I asked Master Gu, "I do not fear the arising of thought; I only fear awakening late. Like entering the womb from an intermediate state [between death and rebirth], thoughts arise and one is born. Even if one brings about swift awakening, how can one attain liberation?" The teacher asked, "Have you entered the womb yet?" I smiled. The teacher said, "You have entered the womb." I was speechless. The teacher said, "You are mistaken when you say that there is only this body (*shen*). Are not karmic consequences acquired already when one enters the womb?" Drenched in perspiration, I could not understand. At last, I went to Jingshan and engaged in meditation.

The following summer [in 1623] I pressed on and worked persistently. My body, mind and the outer world suddenly all disappeared. I then knew that my body came from beginningless time and perishes in the very spot it is born.[14] It is only a shadow (*ying*) manifested by entrenched delusion. Instant to instant, thought moment to thought moment, it does not abide. It certainly is not born of a mother or father. From this, the unity of two schools of nature and characteristics became clear. I knew that at their root there was no conflict. It was only that the erroneous teachings of Jiaoguang[15] had greatly confused people. At this time all sutras, *śāstras*, and *gongan* (Jpn. *kōan*) appeared before me, and I soon attained enlightenment. This understanding was not the realization of sages, so I did not tell anyone. After awhile my mind was utterly empty, and I was no longer detained by even the tip of a single brushstroke.

At age twenty-five, I received the bodhisattva precepts.

At age twenty-six, I read the entire Vinaya canon and then knew the mistakes that I had accumulated in all of my lives.

At age twenty-seven, my mother became gravely ill. I cut my arms four [times] but could not save [her]. I was pained to the core. (He already realized that this body is not born from a father and mother, so why did he then cut his arm to save his mother? Examine (*can*) [this as one would a *gongan/kōan*].) After her funeral, I burnt [my writings] and discarded my brush and ink stone. I swore to go deep into the mountains, but my fellow practitioner (*daoyou*) Jiankong[16] detained me at Songling, where during my reclusion I became gravely ill, so I put effort into meditation and sought rebirth in the Pure Land.

At age twenty-nine, I came out of retreat and faced the ocean. I prepared to go toward Zhongnan [Shan]. My fellow practitioner Xuehang wanted [me] to transmit my studies of the Vinaya, so I lived at Longju. I began to write the *Collected Essentials of the Principles and Practicalities of Vinay[a]* and *Occasional [Dharma] talks in the Monastery*. This year I met two friends, Xingyu and Guiyi, and greatly benefited from practicing with them.

At age thirty, I took Xingyu to Boshan to shave his head and went with the meditation master Wuyi to Jinling. I lingered for a hundred and ten days. I was thoroughly familiar with Chan's decadence in recent times, so I decided to promote the Vinaya. But while my understanding of the Vinaya was excellent, my karmic obstructions (*fannao*; Skt. *kleśas*) and karmic impressions (*xiqi*; Skt. *vāsanās*) were strong, my own practice was full of mistakes, and so I vowed not to become a preceptor (*heshang*). (His three karmic activities were not yet pure. He was unjustly famous for his knowledge of the Vinaya—a fame that exceeded reality. This caused him shame throughout his life.)

At age thirty-one, I planned to write a commentary on the *Sutra of Brahma's Net* (*Fanwang jing*) I made four lots asking the Buddha [whether to follow]: (1) the Huayan school, (2) the Tiantai school, (3) the Consciousness-Only school, [or] (4) a self-established school (*zili zong*).[17] Again and again I drew the lot of Tiantai, so I devoted myself to Tiantai texts, but I was not willing to become a member of the Tiantai lineage. This was because in recent times Tiantai, Chan, Huayan, and Consciousness-Only each clung to their own positions and could not get along. (His contemporaries mistook an ear for an eye—they all said he only promoted Tiantai. How false! How false!)

At age thirty-two, in autumn, my two friends Xingyu and Piru passed away. I first entered Lingfeng for the winter to create causes and conditions for obtaining a copy of the canon.

At age thirty-four, I traveled to Xihu Temple and wrote the *Divination Ritual*.

At age thirty-six, I lived at Wushui and wrote the *Fo shuo jie xiaozai jing* (Brief explanation of the [sutra] on the elimination of disaster [through] the precepts; T. 1477), the *Brief Explanation of [Vinaya] Rules and Upholding* the Precepts, and the New Commentary on the Ullambana [All Souls Festival] (yulan pen).

At thirty-seven, I lived at Jiuhua[shan]; the next year [in 1638] I wrote the Fanwang jing (Explanation of the sutra of Brahma's Net).

At age forty, I lived in Wenling [in Fujian] and wrote Verses on the Text Explaining the Profound Meaning of the Śūraṃgama-[sutra].

At age forty-one, I lived at Zhangzhou (in Fujian) and wrote the Treatise on the Vajra Breaking the Sky, the Three Chants of Ouyi, and Zhaijing (An annotation of chapters of the fasting sutra; T. 87.910c25–912a11).

At age forty-three, I lived in Huzhou and wrote the Essential Explanation of Mahāyāna Śamatha and Vipaśyanā [a text written by Huisi].

At age forty-five, I lived at Lingfeng and wrote commentaries on the Sishi'er zhang jing (Sutra in forty-two sections; T. 784.17.722–724), the Yijiao jing (Sutra of the deathbed injunction; T. 389), and Fo shuo ba daren jue jing (An explanation of the [sutra of the] enlightenment of the Eight Mahāsattvas; T. 779.17.715b1–715c3).

At age forty-six, I lived in Shicheng and wrote a Chan Explanation of the Zhouyi. That autumn, I lived at Zutang for more than two years. I wrote The Essentials of the Mind of Consciousness-Only, Direct Explanation of the Eight Essentials of the [Fa]xiang School, The Explanation of the Essentials of Amitabha, and Ouyi's Explanation of the Four Books.

At age fifty, in the winter, I returned to Lingfeng to write the Meaning of the Lotus Assembly. The next year I wrote the Commentary on the Divination [Sutra], and revised the Essentials of the Vinaya.

At age fifty-three (in 1652) I lived at Shengqi. I made a rough draft of Leng qie jing (The Commentary on the Meaning of the Laṅkâ[vatāra-sutra]; T. 670.16; 671.16; 672.16), which I completed only after moving to Changshui. Also there was the Knowing the Fords in Reading the Canon,[18] Watching the Ripples on the Sea of Dharma, and commentaries on the Awakening of Faith (Dasheng qixin lun; T. 1666.32.575b–583b), Vimalakīrti [Sutra] (Weimo jing), and the Yuanjue jing ([Sutra] of perfect enlightenment; T. 842.17.913a–922a).

My vows are unfulfilled; for now I await later [beneficial] conditions. Once in my life I said, "Like a square piece entering a round hole, commentaries from the Han and Song dynasties are plentiful, but the teachings of the mind (xinfa) of the sages is unclear. Like water added to milk, the [Commentary on the Monk's] Behavior According to [the Four-Part Vinaya][19] has been written but study of the Vinaya has declined. Like a hole drilled into primordial chaos (hundun), Zhiyue lu (Records pointing to the moon;

T. 1758.83)[20] circulate freely yet Chan is in shambles.[21] Like someone who treats a critical illness with an outdated prescription, [Zhiyi's] *Doctrine of the Four Teachings* is transmitted but Tiantai is obscured. For this reason, whether it is Confucianism, Chan, Vinaya, or the Teachings, everyone considers it strange or hates it like an enemy." I [now] smile and say, "Only Śākyamuni and Dizang know me; only Śākyamuni and Dizang judge me. I drift away alone, the circumstances of my death unknown."

After the great master passed into extinction, this unworthy disciple Chengshi undeservedly received a serious order from fellow disciples [to] compile the *Lingfeng Zonglun*, and when the compilation was finished, I placed the elder's [i.e., Ouyi's] autobiography at the start of the first fascicle. In consideration of the fact that the elder in the two years of 1653 and 1654 wandered (*xingjiao*) as a hermit in the mountains, and that all of his writings up to the first month of 1655, this last stretch of time, are lacking and not recorded, fellow disciples, because this unworthy disciple accompanied the master on these travels and knows the details, decided that I should compose an appropriate supplementary record. My request to decline this offer was refused. With palms together and a bow of the head I write:

The *Autobiography of the Great Teacher Ouyi of Lingfeng* was completed on the twelfth lunar month of 1652 [i.e., January 1653]. The next year was 1653.

When the elder was fifty-four years old in the fourth month of the summer [of 1653], he entered Xin'an, and later finished a meditation retreat. In the *Tianma yuan* (Heavenly horse cloister) at Shepu he wrote the *Xuanfo pu* (Manual for selection of Buddhas) and read [Yongming Yanshou's (904–976)] *Zongjing lu* (Record of the mirror of orthodoxy; T. 2016.48.417b–957b). He amended the interpolations and mixed theories of Fayong, Yongle, Fazhen, and others, extracted mistakes in the scriptures and commentaries, as well as errors of transcription and carving over time. He settled the essential meaning of more than 360 encounter dialogues (*wenda*), labeling them from start to finish. After he finished reading [Yongming's *Record*], he wrote *Postscript of the Revised Record of the Mirror of Orthodoxy* in four parts. Moreover, he created an abridged version of the *Collected Works of Yuan Hongdao* (1568–1610) in one volume, titled *Master Yuan*. In the eighth month in autumn, he traveled to several places including Baiyue and Huangshan (in Anhui province). In the winter, he again stayed at "Heavenly Horse [Cloister]" during the meditation season (*jiezhi*) and wrote the *Commentary Breaking through the Net [Ensnaring] the Awakening of Faith*.

The next year in 1654 when he was fifty-five, in the first month, he responded to the request of the "Benevolence and Righteousness Cloister" (Renyi Yuan) south of [Xiao]feng [where Lingfeng temple is located]. When the Dharma offering was over, he left Xin'an. Later in the second month, on the day of the *poṣada* (*baosatuo*), he returned to Lingfeng. In the summer, he was bed-ridden with sickness and chose [Siming Zhili's] *Xizhai jing tu shi* (Poems of the Pure Land and western fast; X. 1164.61.725b18–741b6), praising it and adding to the Nine Essentials of the Pure Land [composing a text titled] *The Ten Essentials of the Pure Land*. At the end of the summer, he recovered from his illness.

In the seventh month, he wrote the *Secret Discussion of the Transmissions of the Confucian and Buddhist Schools*. In the eighth month, he finished reading the Tripiṭaka. In the ninth month, he completed the books *Knowing the Fords in Reading the Canon* and *Watching the Ripples on the Sea of Dharma*. In the winter during the tenth month, he became ill.

He also had "Writing about My Feelings in Solitary Meditation," [two] four-line poems in regulated verse. In it, there is a couplet, "There are about two or three disciples, they comfort my lifelong thoughts."[22] On the eighteenth day of the eleventh month (December 26, 1654), there was "Verses Recited during Sickness."[23] On the third day of the twelfth lunar month (January 10, 1655), there was another regulated verse of "Unexpectedly Composed while Free from Illness." In it there is the couplet, "In the places of words and characters are the true eyes of the Buddha; I do not yet know in the end whom I should entrust it to."[24]

On this day (January 10, 1655), he recited his last will and testament and made four vows: that his two disciples Zhaonan and Dengci transmit the five precepts [of not killing, stealing, engaging in licentious behavior, lying, or consuming alcohol] and the bodhisattva precepts; that his three disciples Zhaonan, Lingsheng, and Xingdan replace him in his seat and in responding to any requests; that after his cremation (*duwei*), they grind his bones and mix them with flour and divide it into two groups, one given to birds and beasts, and one given to fishes and shellfish; that they all rejoice in the Dharma and together are born in the Pure Land. On the thirteenth day (January 20, 1655), he formed a Pure [Land] Society (*jingshe*) and wrote votive texts (*yuanwen*). Afterward, he wrote six poems titled "Verses Seeking Rebirth in the Pure Land." On [Chinese] New Year's Eve (January 25, 1655), he wrote "Inscription of Dwelling in the Six *Gen* Trigram."[25] He also wrote verses. On New Year's Day (February 6, 1655), he wrote two poems.

On the twentieth day (February 25, 1655), he again became ill. On the twenty-first day (February 26), in the morning, he awoke and the illness had ceased. At noon, he sat cross-legged on the corner of corded seat, and facing west, he raised his hands and died. At that time, his worldly age (*shengnian*) was fifty-six. His Buddhist age (*fala*)[26] was thirty-four. [He attended] monastic summer [meditation retreats] from the twelfth lunar month of 1623 until the day of the confessional ceremony at the end of the summer retreat in 1633, and again from the spring of 1645 until the first month of the present year 1655 for a total of nineteen summers. In the winter of 1657, his disciples went to cremate (*tupi*) him in accordance with the Dharma. [They found] his hair was long, covering his ears, and his face seemed as if alive. His legs were crossed and dignified. None of his teeth had decayed. Therefore they did not dare proceed to follow his will and testament and grind his bones into powder. They erected a *stūpa* (*guta*) to the left of the Great Buddha Hall at Lingfeng.

At the end of 1657, forty-two characters were [added as] a supplementary record following his cremation in the spring of 1658.) Alas! The eye of the world has disappeared! The banner of the true Dharma is destroyed! [As for] demons with evil intentions toward the Buddha, who will save and correct [them]? [As for] men and women with good minds who encounter poisons, who will support [them]? Indeed, it is because our karma is heavy that we cannot cause sagely people to abide for long. The elder's transmission of [the Dharma] ended.

He also wrote *Knowing the Fords in Reading the Canon*, *Watching the Ripples on the Sea of Dharma*, the *Commentaries on the Awakening of Faith*, *Vimalakīrti [Sutra]*, and the *[Sutra] of Perfect Enlightenment*. His vows were unfulfilled; for the time being, he awaited later [beneficial] conditions. After he finished reading the canon, he burnt incense and [wrote] a votive text that said: "First [if one] peruses the Northern and Southern editions of the canon,[27] [one finds they are] all confused and disordered. Either they do not distinguish between complete and incomplete, or they switch names of sutras and *śastras*, or they do not distinguish between authentic and apocryphal, or they do not differentiate coarse and refined. Although there are Song dynasty catalogues of the Dharma-Treasure and Ming dynasty catalogues and collections [of] particular schools (*yimen*), they are not entirely beautiful or good. Now they are usually not carefully appraised, so I presumed to write two books, *Knowing the Fords in Reading the Canon* [and] *Watching the Ripples on the Sea of Dharma*. If they do not betray the Buddha's intention, I humbly ask that they successfully circulate. Second, [regarding sutras] such as the *Perfect Enlightenment, Vimalakirti, Amitābha, Dizang,* even the *Mahā-parinirvāṇa-sutra,* I have long had a slight hope that I might add another explanatory commentary. I also vow to revise *Precious Instructions from the History of the Sangha.* I pray for protection and aid so that this might be swiftly accomplished."[28]

He also decided to later annotate titles of sutras. These were *Further Commentary on the Practices and Vows [of the Samantabhadra] Chapter [of the Huayan Sutra], New Commentary on the Sutra of Perfect Enlightenment, Commentary on the Assembly of the Tathāgata of the Sukhāvatī-vyūha[-sutra], Essentials of the Recorded Commentaries on the Contemplation Sutra, Explanation of the Daśacakra-kṣitigarbha [sutra], Explanation of the Sutra of Bhadrapāla, Commentary on the [Sutra] of the Seven Medicine Buddhas, Commentary on the Original Vow of Kṣitigarbha, Supplementary Commentary on the Vimalakirti, Further Commentary on the Sutra of the Suvarna-prabhāsa-(uttama)-sutra, Explanation of the Mahāyānâbhisamaya-sutra* (T. 673), *Commentary on the Sutra of the Dharma Gate of No Letters, Commentary on the Sutra of Twelve Austerities, Further Commentary on the [Sutra of] Humane Kings, A Comprehensive Commentary on the Mahā-parinirvāṇa-sutra, Essentials of the Four Āgamas, Essentials of the Sutra on the Path of Ten Good Deeds, Essentials of the Discussion of Bodhicitta, Essentials of the Treatise on the Arousing of Bodhicitta, Essentials of the Record of Supplementary Practices of the Mohe zhiguan,*[29] *An Amended History of the Sangha,* [and] *Precious Instructions for the Sangha,* twenty-one texts in all.

Of the three parts laid out above, only *Knowing the Fords in Reading the Canon, Watching the Ripples on the Sea of Dharma,* and the *Commentary on the Awakening of Faith* were completed. All the remaining texts could not be finished. However, his writings are quite abundant. If one grasps the general principles, then what is lacking? Still more [there is] the great functioning (*dayong*)[30] of [his] new methods, and [his] true turning of the wheel of vows. After receiving the prediction at the precious pool [of the Pure Land], he will immediately enter the *sahā* world, gathering up those who have karmic affinity with him, regretting that he cannot save all, [and] the *gōng'àn* will suddenly be accomplished. When we are [born] in the future, we can all be in his [liberating] presence and engage in practice. Do not [think that] on account of the fact that the body is not here now, one can be disloyal to his mind. The kindness [I] have received is most profound; the kindness he bestowed is most deep. I consider the fact that wise people appear only occasionally, and the wondrous Dharma is difficult to encounter, and I also reflect on the great matter [of life and death] and karmic causes and conditions, and barriers and entanglements of myriad lives. Although the Dharma circulates at times, the difficulties and obstacles of sentient beings are substantial. Therefore I light a thousand incense sticks, abandoning myself to the current [of saving sentient beings]. [I vow] first to repay the kindness of my teacher and help him turn his wheel of vows; second, to make offerings to the wonderful Dharma so that life after life I may encounter it; third, to transform this impure age and save sentient beings who suffer; fourth, to grind my bones into powder in his stead and [thereby] fulfill my teacher's great vows; fifth, to repent of heavy sins and ensure birth in the precious pool [of the Pure Land]. Alas! Those who know me, those who judge me are only the sentient beings of the earth.

Respectfully [offered] with a prostration by the unworthy follower Chengshi on the twelfth day of the twelfth lunar month of 1655 [January 8, 1656].

APPENDIX 2
A MAP OF OUYI'S LIFE

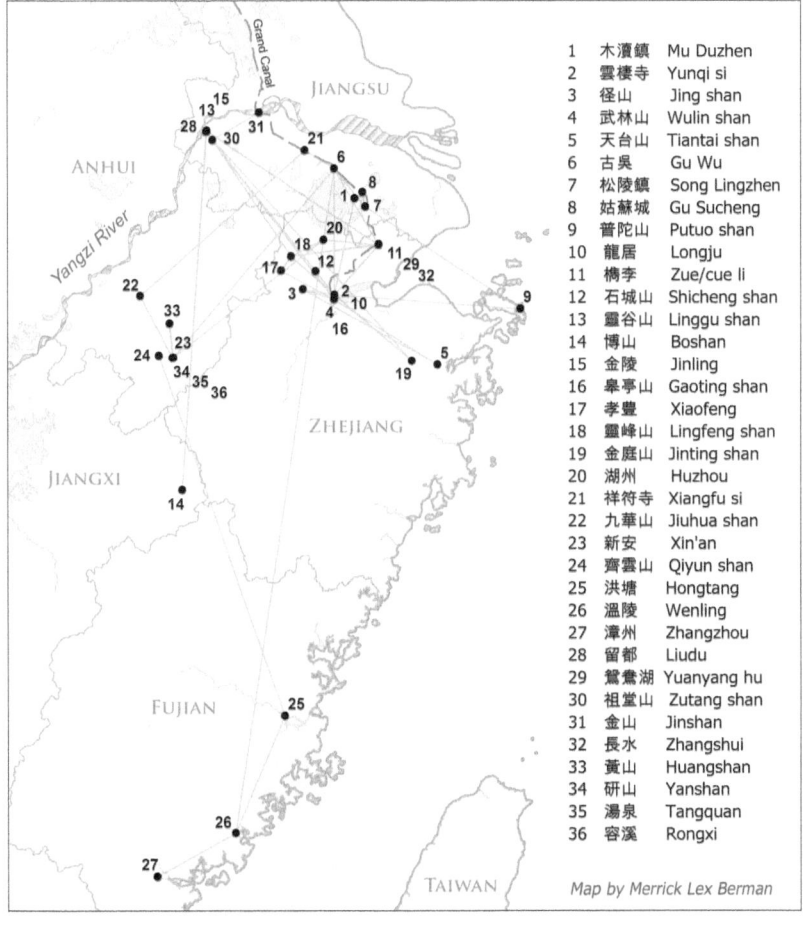

#	中文	Pinyin
1	木瀆鎮	Mu Duzhen
2	雲棲寺	Yunqi si
3	徑山	Jing shan
4	武林山	Wulin shan
5	天台山	Tiantai shan
6	古吳	Gu Wu
7	松陵鎮	Song Lingzhen
8	姑蘇城	Gu Sucheng
9	普陀山	Putuo shan
10	龍居	Longju
11	檇李	Zue/cue li
12	石城山	Shicheng shan
13	靈谷山	Linggu shan
14	博山	Boshan
15	金陵	Jinling
16	皋亭山	Gaoting shan
17	孝豐	Xiaofeng
18	靈峰山	Lingfeng shan
19	金庭山	Jinting shan
20	湖州	Huzhou
21	祥符寺	Xiangfu si
22	九華山	Jiuhua shan
23	新安	Xin'an
24	齊雲山	Qiyun shan
25	洪塘	Hongtang
26	溫陵	Wenling
27	漳州	Zhangzhou
28	留都	Liudu
29	鴛鴦湖	Yuanyang hu
30	祖堂山	Zutang shan
31	金山	Jinshan
32	長水	Zhangshui
33	黃山	Huangshan
34	研山	Yanshan
35	湯泉	Tangquan
36	容溪	Rongxi

Map by Merrick Lex Berman

NOTES

INTRODUCTION

1. Peter Harvey, *An Introduction to Buddhist Ethics: Foundations, Values, and Issues* (New York: Cambridge University Press, 2000), 11–31; Damien Keown, *Buddhist Ethics: A Very Short Introduction* (New York: Oxford University Press, 2005), 5–7; Hammalawa Saddhatissa, *Buddhist Ethics* (Boston: Wisdom, 1997), 10–12; Damien Keown, *The Nature of Buddhist Ethics* (New York: St. Martins, 1992), 179–180.
2. Damien Keown initiated this debate when he argued that Buddhist ethics are best understood as a type of Aristotelian virtue ethics in his *Nature of Buddhist Ethics*, and scholars including Abraham Velez de Cea, Martin Adam, Barbra Clayton, and Charles Goodman have argued for or against this view. As Maria Heim notes in her review of Buddhist ethics, such studies assume that the chief method for understanding Buddhist ethics lies in determining which family of Western ethical theory it might be likened to. Maria Heim, "Buddhist Ethics: A Review Essay," *Journal of Religious Ethics* 39, no. 3 (2011): 576.
3. Charles Hallisey and Anne Hansen, "Narrative, Sub-Ethics, and the Moral Life: Some Evidence from Theravāda Buddhism," *Journal of Religious Ethics* 24, no. 2 (Fall 1996): 317.
4. Heim, "Buddhist Ethics," 583.
5. The phrase "four great masters of the late Ming dynasty" (*mingmo si dashi*) appears in several scholarly studies including: Ming Guo, *Ming Qing Fojiao* (Fujian: Renmin, 1982), 176; and Shengyan, *Minmatsu Chūgoku Bukkyō no kenkyū: toku ni Chigyoku no chūshin to shite* (Tōkyō: Sankibo busshorin, 1975), 30. However, Ouyi Zhixu was not considered one of the four great masters of the Ming during his time. As Jennifer Eichman argues, it was originally Xuelang Hong'en (1545–1608) who was considered the fourth eminent monk alongside Yunqi Zhuhong, Zibo Daguan, and Hanshan Deqing, as evidenced in Qian Qianyi's *Liechao shiji xiaozhuan*

(Short biographies to the poetry collection of successive dynasties). Jennifer Eichman, "Spiritual Seekers in a Fluid Landscape" (PhD diss., Princeton University, 2005), 21, note 24.

6. Chün-fang Yü, *The Renewal of Buddhism in China, Chu-hung and the Late Ming Synthesis* (New York: Columbia University Press, 1981).
7. J. C. Cleary, *Zibo: The Last Great Zen Master of China* (Berkeley: Asian Humanities, 1989).
8. Sung-Peng Hsu, *A Buddhist Leader in Ming China: The Life and Thought of Han-shan Te-ch'ing* (University Park: University of Pennsylvania Press, 1979); Chun-min Yen, "Shadows and Echoes of the Mind—Hanshan Deqing's (1546–1623) Syncretic View and Buddhist Interpretation of the *Daodejing*" (PhD diss., University of Arizona, 2004); Markus Leong, "Hanshan Deqing (1546–1623) on Buddhist Ethics" (PhD diss., California Institute of Integral Studies, 1994).
9. Shengyan, *Minmatsu Chūgoku Bukkyō no kenkyū*.
10. Kenneth Ch'en, *Buddhism in China: A Historical Survey* (Princeton: Princeton University Press, 1964), 439–449; Arthur Wright, *Buddhism in Chinese History* (Stanford, CA: Stanford University Press, 1959). Zhou Qi continues promoting this view, arguing that state selling of ordination certificates led to a decline in the quality of Buddhist clerics and the secularization of Buddhism during this period. Zhou Qi, *Ming dai fo jiao yu zheng zhi wen hua* (Beijing: Renmin, 2005), 104.
11. Chün-fang Yü, *The Renewal of Buddhism in China*; Shi Jianye, *Mingmo fojiao fazhan zhi yanjiu* (Taipei: Faguwenhua, 1994).
12. Chün-fang Yü, *The Renewal of Buddhism in China*; Timothy Brook, *Praying for Power: Buddhism and the Formation of Gentry Society in Late-Ming China* (Cambridge, MA: Harvard University Press, 1993). Although Brook argues that Chinese elites used Buddhist monasteries for civic purposes—as sites to associate and generate cultural capital—rather than religious ones, Jennifer Eichman disagrees and claims that alongside discussions of politics, family, and the classics were constant debates about self-cultivation—including mental concentration, bodily practice, and observance of precepts—that reflected a fluid, changing religious identity as elites tried out a variety of techniques. Eichman, "Spiritual Seekers," 24.
13. Shengyan, "Four Great Thinkers in Modern Chinese Buddhism," in *Buddhist Ethics and Modern Society*, ed. Charles Wei-hsun Fu and Sandra A. Wawrytko (New York: Greenwood, 1991), 55–68.
14. Thomas A. Lewis, Jonathan Wyn Schofer, Aaron Stalnaker, and Mark A. Berkson, "Anthropos and Ethics: Categories of Inquiry and Procedures of Comparison," *Journal of Religious Ethics* 33, no. 2 (2005): 177–185.
15. Aaron Stalnaker, "Comparative Religious Ethics and the Problem of 'Human Nature,'" *Journal of Religious Ethics* 33, no. 2 (2005): 191.
16. Catherine Bell, *Ritual Theory, Ritual Practice* (New York: Oxford University Press, 1992).
17. John Kieschnick, *The Impact of Buddhism on Chinese Material Culture* (Princeton: Princeton University Press, 2003); Gregory Schopen, *Bones, Stones, and Buddhist Monks: Collected Papers on the Archaeology, Epigraphy, and Texts of Monastic Buddhism in India* (Honolulu: University of Hawai'i Press, 1997).
18. Scholars generally agree that because Zhu Xi's commentaries on the Four Books and Five Classics had become part of the orthodox curriculum and assigned for civil service examinations in the Ming dynasty, elites sought ways of reconciling

Buddhism and neo-Confucianism as either complementary or comparable. Erik Zürcher argues this stripped Buddhism of diversity and identity, although Araki Kengo claims it served an important function during a time of significant social, political, and intellectual change. Erik Zürcher, "Beyond the Jade Gate: Buddhism in China, Vietnam, and Korea," in *The World of Buddhism*, ed. Heinz Bechert and Richard Gombrich (London: Thames and Hudson, 1984), 208; Araki Kengo, *Unsei shugō no kenkyū* (Tōkyō: Daizō shuppan kabushiki kaisha, 1985), 55.

19. Chün-fang Yü cites syncretism and emphasis on practice as points that differentiate the four eminent monks of the late Ming from their predecessors. Yü, *The Renewal of Buddhism of China*, 4.

20. Paul Griffiths suggests three features of commentarial writing: it directly relates to some "metawork," the signs of the "metawork" dominate, and its structure and order are determined by the "metawork." Paul Griffiths, *Religious Reading: The Place of Reading in the Practice of Religion* (New York: Oxford University Press, 1999), 81. Jiang Wu describes seventeenth-century Chan monks as cultivating a "textual spirituality" through reading and writing texts rather than engaging in devotional or ritual performances. Jiang Wu, *Enlightenment in Dispute: The Reinvention of Chan Buddhism in Seventeenth-Century China* (New York: Oxford University Press, 2008), 53–59, 246–256. Ouyi similarly cultivates a "textual spirituality," but as a complement to—rather than a substitute for—his religious practice.

21. Daniel Gardner, "Confucian Commentary and Chinese Intellectual History," *The Journal of Asian Studies* 57, no. 2 (May 1998): 397–398.

22. Gardner, "Confucian Commentary," 416.

23. For a discussion, see Beverley Foulks, "Duplicitous Thieves: Ouyi Zhixu's Criticism of Jesuit Missionaries in Late Imperial China," *Chung-Hwa Buddhist Journal* 21 (2008): 55–76. For a translation, see Charles Jones, "*Pie xie ji*: Collected Refutations of Heterodoxy by Ouyi Zhixu," *Pacific World* 3, no. 1 (Fall 2009): 351–408.

24. Foulks, "Duplicitous Thieves," 67–68.

25. Brian Stock, *Listening for the Text: On the Uses of the Past* (Baltimore: Johns Hopkins University Press, 1990), 23.

26. Recent publications include Adam B. Seligman, Robert P. Weller, Michael J. Puett, and Bennett Simon, *Ritual and Its Consequences: An Essay on the Limits of Sincerity* (New York: Oxford University Press, 2008); and Jens Krienath, Jan Snoek, and Michael Stausberg, eds., *Theorizing Rituals* (Boston: Brill, 2006).

27. Michael Puett, "The Haunted World of Humanity: Ritual Theory from Early China," in *Rethinking the Human*, ed. J. Michelle Molina and Donald K. Swearer (Cambridge, MA: Harvard University Press, 2010), 98.

28. Carl Bielefeldt, "Practice," in *Critical Terms for the Study of Buddhism*, ed. Donald Lopez (Chicago: University of Chicago Press, 2005), 233.

29. Bell, *Ritual Theory, Ritual Practice*, ix.

30. As Roy Rappaport notes, these activities can be "performatively stronger" than utterances. Roy Rappaport, *Ritual and Religion in the Making of Humanity* (New York: Cambridge University Press, 1999), 143.

31. For a discussion of *ganying* from the third century B.C.E. to the ninth century C.E., see Robert P. Weller and Peter K. Bol, "From Heaven-and-Earth to Nature: Chinese Concepts of the Environment and Their Influence on Policy Implementation," in *Confucianism and Ecology*, ed. Mary Evelyn Tucker and John Berthrong (Cambridge, MA: Harvard University Press, 1998), 313–341.

32. Weller and Bol, "From Heaven-and-Earth to Nature," 314.
33. John Major, Sarah A. Queen, Andrew Seth Meyer, and Harold D. Roth, trans. and eds., *The Huainanzi: A Guide to the Theory and Practice of Government in Early Han China* (New York: Columbia University Press, 2010), 207.
34. Major, Queen, Meyer, and Roth, *The Huainanzi*, 220; Charles Le Blanc and Huai-nan Tzu, *Philosophical Synthesis in Early Han Thought* (Hong Kong: Hong Kong University Press, 1985), 138–142. For a concise summary of the concept of *ganying* as articulated in the Huainanzi, see Major, Queen, Meyer, and Roth, *The Huainanzi*, 875.
35. Paolo Santangelo, "Destiny and Retribution in Late Imperial China," *East and West* 42, no. 2–4 (December 1992): 390.
36. Robert Sharf, *Coming to Terms with Chinese Buddhism: A Reading of the Treasure Store Treatise* (Honolulu: University of Hawai'i Press, 2002), 125. Sharf discusses the history of stimulus-response in ibid., 119–132.
37. Paolo Santangelo, *Sentimental Education in Chinese History: An Interdisciplinary Textual Research on Ming and Qing Sources* (Boston: Brill, 2003), 151.
38. Puett, "The Haunted World of Humanity," 103.
39. For a study of sincerity (*cheng*) in Confucian texts, see James T. Bretzke, "The Notion of Sincerity (*Ch'eng*) in The Confucian Classics," *Journal of Chinese Philosophy* 21 (1994): 179–212. For a comparative study of Western notions of "sincerity" and Chinese understandings of *cheng*, see Yanming An, "Western 'Sincerity' and Confucian 'Cheng,'" *Asian Philosophy* 14, no. 2 (July 2004): 155–169.
40. Wei-ming Tu, "The Neo-Confucian Concept of Man," *Philosophy East and West* 21, no. 1 (January 1971), 80.
41. On-Cho Ng, "*Hsing* (Nature) as the Ontological Basis of Practicality in Early Ch'ing Ch'eng-Chu Confucianism: Li Kuang-ti's (1642–1718) Philosophy," *Philosophy East and West* 44, no. 1 (January 1994): 90–91; An, "Western 'Sincerity' and Confucian 'Cheng,'" 164–165.
42. Brook Ziporyn, "*Li* (Principle, Coherence) in Chinese Buddhism," *Journal of Chinese Philosophy* 30, no. 3–4 (September 2003): 502.
43. Weller and Bol, "From Heaven-and-Earth to Nature," 322.
44. Ziporyn, "*Li* (Principle, Coherence) in Chinese Buddhism," 504.
45. *Ming ban jiaxing dazangjing* (Taibei Shi: Xin wen feng chu ban gong si, 1987).
46. Ouyi Zhixu, *Ouyi dashi quanji* (Taibei: Fojiao chubanshe, 1989).
47. Fascicle citations include the number of the scroll, followed by the part of that scroll, and finally the section within that part; this is followed by the volume and page number from *Ouyi dashi quanji*.
48. *Oxford English Dictionary Online*, s.v. "Karma," accessed August 13, 2011, http://dictionary.oed.com.
49. In a few instances, the phrase "causes and conditions" (*yinyuan*) also connotes "karma."
50. These two terms can also mean "advantageous" or "beneficial" and "disadvantageous" or "harmful," respectively.
51. *Foguang da cidian* (Gaoxiong Shi: Foguang chuban she, 1989), 5494.
52. *Foguang da cidian*.
53. Scholarship on karmic retribution in China includes the following: Stephen Teiser, *Reinventing the Wheel: Paintings of Rebirth in Medieval Buddhist Temples* (Seattle: University of Washington Press, 2006); Stephen Teiser, *The Scripture on the Ten Kings and the Making of Purgatory in Medieval Chinese Buddhism* (Honolulu: University of

INTRODUCTION 149

Hawai'i Press, 1994); Stephen Teiser, "The Growth of Purgatory," in *Religion and Society in Tang and Song China*, ed. Peter Gregory and Patricia Ebrey (Honolulu: University of Hawai'i Press, 1993), 115–145; Stephen Teiser, "'Having Once Died and Returned to Life': Representations of Hell in Medieval China," *Harvard Journal of Asiatic Studies* 48, no. 2 (December 1988): 433–464; Yün-hua Jan, "The Chinese Understanding and Assimilation of Karma Doctrine," in *Karma and Rebirth: Postclassical Developments*, ed. Ronald W. Neufeldt (Albany: SUNY Press, 1986), 145–167; Robert Campany, "Living off the Books: Fifty Ways to Dodge *Ming* (Preallotted lifespan) in Early Medieval China," in *The Magnitude of Ming: Command, Allotment, and Fate in Chinese Culture*, ed. Christopher Lupke (Honolulu: University of Hawai'i Press, 2005), 129–150. Dan Lusthaus discusses karma briefly, but he focuses more on the notion of karma within Yogācāra Buddhism and does not address it specifically in the context of China. Dan Lusthaus, *Buddhist Phenomenology: A Philosophical Investigation of Yogacara Buddhism and the Ch'eng Wei-shih Lun* (London: Routledge, 2002), 168–199.

54. For a bibliography of scholarship on karma up to 1980 see Karl H. Potter, "The Beginnings of a List of Publications Relating to Karma and Rebirth Compiled by Karl H. Potter, with Supplementary Material by James P. McDermott," in *Karma and Rebirth in Classical Indian Traditions*, ed. Wendy Doniger O'Flaherty (Berkeley: University of California Press, 1980), 319–329. O'Flaherty's edited volume remains seminal in scholarship on karma in Indian Buddhism. Important recent studies include: Charles Prebish, Damien Keown, and Dale S. Wright, eds., *Revisioning Karma—The eBook* (Journal of Buddhist Ethics Online Books, 2005); Gananath Obeyesekere, *Imagining Karma: Ethical Transformation in Amerindian, Buddhist, and Greek Rebirth* (Berkeley: University of California Press, 2002); Bruce R. Reichenbach, *The Law of Karma: A Philosophical Study* (London: Macmillan, 1990); Rajendra Prasad, *Karma, Causation and Retributive Morality* (New Delhi: Munshiram Manoharlal, 1989); Ronald Neufeldt, *Karma and Rebirth: Post Classical Developments* (Albany: SUNY Press, 1986); and James McDermott, *Development in the Early Buddhist Concept of Kamma/Karma* (New Delhi: Munshiram Manoharlal, 1984).

55. Jan, "The Chinese Understanding and Assimilation of Karma Doctrine," 146.

56. Jan, "The Chinese Understanding and Assimilation of Karma Doctrine," 148, 162–165. Stephen Bokenkamp describes how Daoists understood descendants as affected by one's own karma in an earlier period of Chinese history in his *Ancestors and Anxiety: Daoism and the Birth of Rebirth in China* (Berkeley: University of California Press, 2009).

57. Jan, "The Chinese Understanding and Assimilation of Karma Doctrine," 149. This and the following citation are taken from Huiyuan's *Ming baoying lun* (Elucidating karmic retribution).

58. Jan, "The Chinese Understanding and Assimilation of Karma Doctrine," 152.

59. Xi Chao's "Essentials of Religion" is contained in Sengyou's (445–518) *Hongmingji* (T. 2102.52.87a15). Erik Zürcher translates the passage as: "Each and every thought that springs from the mind is subject to retribution; even if the fact (or act) has not yet been realized, the hidden response (of karman) has been built up in the dark." Erik Zürcher, *The Buddhist Conquest of China: The Spread and Adaptation of Buddhism in Early Medieval China* (Leiden: Brill, 1972), 167.

60. One could view Zongmi as a transitional figure, insofar as he adopts the same metaphors used by Xi Chao and Huiyuan, but he does not portray karma as particularly mysterious. He states that "the recompense of the fruit follows of necessity; it is comparable to shadows and echoes following from objects and

sounds. Even with parents and close relatives one cannot stand in for the other." Stephen Teiser, *The Ghost Festival in China* (Princeton: Princeton University Press, 1988), 202.

61. Donald E. Gjertson, *Miraculous Retribution: A Study and Translation of T'ang Lin's "Ming-pao Chi"* (Berkeley: Centers for South and Southeast Asia Studies, University of California at Berkeley, 1989).

62. Robert Campany, *Strange Writing: Anomaly Accounts in Early Medieval China* (Albany: SUNY Press, 1995). Campany also discusses some miracle tales punishing those who have desecrated Buddhist sutras in Campany, "Notes on the Devotional Uses and Symbolic Functions of Sutra Texts as Depicted in Early Chinese Miracle Tales and Hagiographies," *Journal of the International Association of Buddhist Studies* 14 (1991): 28–72.

63. *Baojuan* are long prosimetric narrative texts with Buddhist inspiration, originally performed by nuns. David Johnson, *Ritual and Scripture in Chinese Popular Religion: Five Studies* (Berkeley: University of California Press, 1995).

64. D. Neil Schmid, "Yuanqi: Medieval Buddhist Narratives from Dunhuang" (PhD diss., University of Pennsylvania, 2002). In his dissertation, Schmid argues that such narratives adapt notions of karma and dependent origination to explain and understand otherwise incomprehensible situations in ethical terms so that the reader can morally (re)define his or her self in order to receive a better rebirth and ultimately *parinirvāṇa*. Ibid., 28.

65. Teiser, *The Ghost Festival*, 166–167.

66. Teiser, *The Ghost Festival*, 12.

67. For a concise review of the scholarly debate surrounding how one might classify the genre of "morality books," see Catherine Bell, "A Precious Raft to Save the World: The Interaction of Scriptural Traditions and Printing in a Chinese Morality Book," *Late Imperial China* 17, no. 1 (June 1996): 158–200.

68. Cynthia Brokaw, "Yuan Huang (1533–1606) and The Ledgers of Merit and Demerit," *Harvard Journal of Asiatic Studies* 47, no. 1 (June 1987): 139.

69. Sakai Tadao, *Chūgoku zensho no kenkyu* (Tōkyō: Kobundo, 1960), 356. For late imperial criticism of the notion that moral self-cultivation could be mechanically achieved, see Joanna Handlin Smith, *The Art of Doing Good: Charity in Late Ming China* (Berkeley: University of California Press, 2009), 124–125, 261–262.

70. Judith A. Berling, "Religion and Popular Culture: The Management of Moral Capital in The Romance of the Three Teachings," in Johnson, Nathan, and Rawski, *Popular Culture in Late Imperial China*, 188–218.

71. Smith, *The Art of Doing Good*, 125.

72. Zhuhong divides the meritorious category into four divisions: (1) loyal and filial deeds, (2) altruistic and compassionate deeds, (3) deeds benefiting the Three Jewels of Buddhism, and (4) miscellaneous good deeds; the demeritorous categories are exact opposites.

73. *Foguang Buddhist Dictionary*, Gaoxiong Shi: Foguang chuban she, 1989, 5494.

74. Shengyan, *Minmatsu Chūgoku Bukkyō no kenkyū*, 356. For a discussion about the distinction made between Patriarch Chan and Tathāgata Chan in the seventeenth century, see Jiang Wu, *Enlightenment in Dispute*, 115–117.

75. Shengyan, *Minmatsu Chūgoku Bukkyō no kenkyū*, 355–362.

76. Ying-shan Ch'en, "Ouyi Zhixu sixiang de tezhi ji qi dingwei wenti," *Zhongguo wenzhe yanjiu jikan* 8 (March 1996): 251-252.
77. Eiki Iwaki, "Shuryōgonkyo gengi kara Shuryōgonkyo monku o miru," *Tendai Gakuho (Journal of Tendai Buddhist Studies)* 43 (1 November 2001): 73.
78. Eiki Iwaki, "Shuryōgonkyo gengi," 78-84.
79. Ch'en, "Ouyi Zhixu sixiang de tezhi ji qi dingwei wenti," 246. Interestingly, this tendency to categorize Ouyi as Tiantai goes back to Ouyi's lifetime; as his disciple Jianmi Chengshi notes in a parenthetical comment within Ouyi's autobiography, Ouyi's contemporaries said he only promoted Tiantai, but Jianmi writes "How untrue! How untrue!" (Ouyi 1989a, 16:10225).
80. Ying-shan Ch'en, "Ouyi Zhixu Dashi Xiuxue xinlu licheng zhi tansuo," *Shizi hou* 33, no. 1 (January 1994): 8-14; Ying-shan Ch'en, "Ouyi Zhixu Dashi Xiuxue xinlu licheng zhi tansuo," *Shizi hou* 33, no. 2 (February 1994): 14-20.
81. This is exemplified by Xiaokang Gong, *Rong hui yu guan tong: Ouyi Zhixu sixiang yanjiu* (Chengdu: Ba Shu Shushe, 2009). It also applies to dissertations, with two notable exceptions: Shi Lirong, "Ouyi zhixu zhancha chanfa zhi yanjiu" (PhD diss., Chung-Hwa Buddhist Studies Institute, 2005); Qiuman Yang, "Wanming Ouyi Zhixu zhi Dizang Xinyang" (PhD diss., Huafan University, 2005).
82. Ying Chuan Hung, "Chigyoku no Jōdo nenbutsu shisō tokuni Amidakyō Yōkai chūshintoshite," *Ryūkoku daigaku daigakuin bungaku kenkyūka kiyō* 25 (10 December 2003): 70-84; Eiki Iwaki, "Chigyoku to Chien Shuryōgonkyo kaishaku no hikaku ni shōten o atatte," *Indogaku Bukkyōgaku kenkyū* 54, no. 2 (20 March 2006): 649-654; Iwaki Eiki, "Chigyoku to Sangaiha Shuryōgonkyō kaishaku ni miru renzokusei to hirenzokusei," *Indogaku Bukkyōgaku kenkyū* 50, no. 2 (20 March 2002): 636-641; Iwaki Eiki, "Shuryōgonkyo gengi kara Shuryōgonkyo monku o miru," *Tendai Gakuho* 43 (1 November 2001): 71-80; Iwaki Eiki, "Gūeki Chigyoku no Shuryōgonkyo kaishaku," *Tendai Gakuho* 41 (November 1999): 121-128; "Chigyoku no Okishinron kaishaku ni tsuite," *Tendai Gakuho* 35 (16 October 1992): 98-102; Masayoshi Shinoda, "Chigyoku Senzatsukyō gisho ni okeru 'genzen ichinenshin' ni tsuite," *Komazawa Daigaku Bukkyō Gakubu ronshū* 34 (31 October 2003): 279-290; Masayoshi Shinoda, "'The Dasheng qixinlun liehwang-su' of Zhixu (1599-1655): Quotations from the Awakening of Faith Translated by Paramartha," *Indogaku Bukkyōgaku kenkyū* 52.1 (20 December 2003): 195-197
83. Shi Zidan, "Ouyi Zhixu de jielu guan," *Xiangguang zhuangyan* 57 (March 1999): 140-145; Kōkō Tonegawa, "Gūeki Chigyoku no ingotogaku," *Indogaku Bukkyōgaku kenkyū* 29, no. 1 (December 1980): 350-353.
84. Bau-Ruei Duh, "Ouyi Zhixu goutong rufo de fangfa lun tanjiu," *Zhexue yu wenhua* 30, no. 6 (June 2003): 340-350; Eiki Iwaki, "Chigyoku shūeki zenge ni tsuite," *Indogaku Bukkyōgaku kenkyū* 40, no. 1 (20 December 1991): 121-125; Chün-fang Yü, "Some Ming Buddhist Responses to Neo-Confucianism," *Journal of Chinese Philosophy* 15 (1988): 371-413.
85. Charles Jones, "*Pie xie ji*: Collected Refutations of Heterodoxy by Ouyi Zhixu," *Pacific World* 3, no. 1 (Fall 2009): 351-408; Beverley Foulks, "Duplicitous Thieves, 55-76; Chiko Hoshimiya, "Gūeki Chigyoku no tengaku yihan—akesue ni okeru Shaku ten ronkubiki," *Tendai Gakuho* 29 (1986): 41-46.

1. KARMA AS A NARRATIVE DEVICE IN OUYI'S AUTOBIOGRAPHY

1. Ouyi Zhixu, *Ouyi dashi quanji* (Taibei: Fojiao chubanshe, 1989), 16: 10226.
2. Shengyan, *Minmatsu Chūgoku Bukkyō no kenkyū: toku ni Chigyoku no chūshin to shite* (Tōkyō: Sankibo busshorin, 1975), 356. For cogent criticisms of Shengyan's argument, see Ying-shan Ch'en, "Ouyi Zhixu sixiang de tezhi ji qi dingwei wenti," *Zhongguo wenzhe yanjiu jikan* 8 (March 1996): 227–256; and Eiki Iwaki, "*Shuryōgonkyo gengi* kara Shuryōgonkyo monku o miru," *Tendai Gakuho* 43 (1 November 2001): 71–80.
3. Ch'en, "Ouyi Zhixu sixiang de tezhi ji qi dingwei wenti."
4. For example, see Chun-fang Yü, "Some Ming Buddhist Responses to Neo-Confucianism," *Journal of Chinese Philosophy* 15 (1988): 371–413. Yingshan Ch'en does note that Ouyi's Tiantai influence is not reflected in his autobiography and suggests that Ouyi may have chosen Tiantai (but not officially become a disciple) in order to escape the sectarianism of his age or because it helped him resolve intellectual conflicts, but she does not analyze the rhetorical or literary dimensions of his autobiography.
5. Philippe Lejeune, *L'Autobiographie en France* (Paris: A. Colin, 1971), 14. In his later work, Lejeune admits a variety of modes in which one can engage in referential self-expression. See Lejeune, *Je est un autre: l'autobiographie de la littérature aux medias* (Paris: Seuil, 1980); and Lejeune, *On Autobiography*, trans. Paul John Eakin (Minneapolis: University of Minnesota Press, 1989).
6. Lejeune, *On Autobiography*, 124.
7. Lejeune, *On Autobiography*, 30. The tendency for autobiography to collapse into fiction has led scholars such as Avrom Fleischman to conclude that a generic definition of autobiography is impossible. See Fleischman, *Figures of Autobiography: The Language of Self-Writing in Victorian and Modern England* (Berkeley: University of California Press, 1983), 245, ft. 22. Nevertheless, Lejeune states, "Telling the truth about the self, constituting the self as a complete subject—it is fantasy. In spite of the fact that autobiography is impossible, this in no way prevents it from existing." Lejeune, *On Autobiography*, xiv.
8. Herman Northrop Frye, *Anatomy of Criticism* (Princeton: Princeton University Press, 1957), 307.
9. For example, Avrom Fleischman and Paul Ricoeur adopt a phenomenological conception of narrative, suggesting that the structure of autobiography illustrates the essential narrativity of human experience. Both argue that narratives are the means by which people articulate their sense of self-identity and recount their experiences. Fleischman, *Figures of Autobiography*; and Ricoeur, "Narrative Time" *Critical Inquiry* 7 (1980): 175.
10. Pei-Yi Wu, *The Confucian's Progress: Autobiographical Writings in Traditional China* (Princeton: Princeton University Press, 1990); and Rodney Taylor, "The Centered Self: Religious Autobiography in the Neo-Confucian Tradition," *History of Religions* 17, no. 3–4 (February–May 1978): 266–283. Pei-yi Wu goes so far as to characterize the period from roughly 1565 to 1680 as a "golden age of Chinese autobiography." Wu, *The Confucian's Progress*, 207. Rodney Taylor insists that "the preoccupation with self is not exclusively the prerogative of Western culture, nor for that matter is the occurrence of autobiographical writing." Taylor, "The Centered Self," 267.
11. For example, in footnote 8 of "The Centered Self," Taylor argues that *ji* (records) and *nianpu* (annalistic biography) are two terms for autobiography, but he admits,

"strictly speaking neither need be autobiographical." This contradiction points to the problem of equating them with the genre of "autobiography" as it is understood in the West; the fact that he has to qualify that there are ninety "autobiographical *nianpu*" during the Ming dynasty also illustrates the inadequacy of identifying *nianpu* as a term for autobiography.

12. Yves Hervouet, "L'Autobiographie Dans La Chine Traditionnelle," in *Études d'histoire et de littérature chinoise offertes au Professeur Jaroslav Průšek* (Paris: Presses Universitaires de France, 1976), 111. Hervouet also notes that letters offer autobiographical insight, such as Sima Qian's letter to Ren An, in which he relates his feelings of misfortune and justifies his philosophy of existence. Ibid., 118.
13. Stephen Owen identifies poetry as a genre in which one finds expression of the "individual" or "personality" in a way that is analogous to Western autobiography. He argues that poetry, rather than narrative, was the chief medium for autobiographical self-presentation in traditional Chinese literature. Owen notes that the emphasis of poetry was not on development or change over time but instead on "how a person could be known at all or make himself known." He argues that autobiography requires the ability to see oneself as other, dividing and further subdividing an assumed unity of the self: "To 'know oneself' is to know oneself as other, a disjunction between the knower and the known." Stephen Owen, "The Self's Perfect Mirror: Poetry as Autobiography," in *The Vitality of the Lyric Voice*, ed. Shuen-fu Lin and Stephen Owen (Princeton: Princeton University Press, 1986), 74. Hervouet argues that even though Chinese poetry expresses feelings and occasionally indicates circumstances surrounding its composition, it rarely sheds light on places or people in a person's life, thus it does not qualify as autobiographical. Hervouet, "L'Autobiographie Dans La Chine Traditionnelle," 108.
14. Wolfgang Bauer, "Icherleben und Autobiographie irn Alteren China," *Heidelberger Jahrbücher* 8 (1964): 12–40.
15. Pierre Hadot, *Philosophy as a Way of Life: Spiritual Exercises from Socrates to Foucault*, ed. Arnold I. Davidson, trans. Michael Chase (Oxford: Blackwell, 1995).
16. Aaron Stalnaker, *Overcoming Our Evil: Human Nature and Spiritual Exercises in Xunzi and Augustine* (Washington, DC: Georgetown University Press, 2006), 43.
17. Brian Stock, *Augustine the Reader: Meditation, Self-Knowledge, and the Ethics of Interpretation* (Cambridge, MA: Belknap Press of Harvard University Press, 1996), 14.
18. Karl J. Weintraub, "Autobiography and Historical Consciousness," *Critical Inquiry* 1, no. 4 (June 1975): 828–829.
19. Janet Gyatso, *Apparitions of the Self: The Secret Autobiographies of a Tibetan Visionary* (Princeton: Princeton University Press, 1998), 109.
20. Wendy Larson, *Literary Authority and the Modern Chinese Writer: Ambivalence and Autobiography* (Durham, NC: Duke University Press, 1991), 3.
21. Larson, *Literary Authority*, 11–12.
22. His institutional role within Lingfeng is evidenced in the writings of his disciples, such as Jianmi Chengshi and the Lingfeng temple gazetteer; it is also suggested by the frequency with which he returned to Lingfeng after his initial entry in 1631.
23. The literature on sacred biography in South and Southeast Asian Buddhism is substantial, including: Juliane Schober, ed., *Sacred Biography in the Buddhist Traditions of South and Southeast Asia* (Honolulu: University of Hawai'i Press, 1997); Reginald A. Ray, *Buddhist Saints in India: A Study in Buddhist Values and Orientations* (New York: Oxford University Press, 1994), which provides a summary of some earlier works

on p. 11, ft. 7; John S. Strong, *The Legend and Cult of Upagupta: Sanskrit Buddhism in North India and Southeast Asia* (Princeton: Princeton University Press, 1992); Stanley Tambiah, *The Buddhist Saints of the Forest and the Cult of Amulets* (Cambridge: Cambridge University Press, 1984), especially 113–119; and John S. Strong, *The Legend of King Aśoka: A Study and Translation of the Aśokāvadāna* (Princeton: Princeton University Press, 1983). Examples of East Asian sacred biography appear in *Monks and Magicians: Religious Biographies in Asia*, ed. Phyllis Granoff and Koichi Shinohara (New York: Mosaic, 1988); Matthew Kapstein suggests translating the Tibetan word for sacred biography, *namtar*, as "soteriography" in Kapstein, "The Illusion of Spiritual Progress: Remarks on Indo-Tibetan Buddhist Soteriology," in *Paths to Liberation: The Mārga and Its Transformations in Buddhist Thought*, ed. Robert E. Buswell, Jr. and Robert M. Gimello (Honolulu: University of Hawai'i Press, 1992), 195. Although he surveys French scholarship on Indian Buddhist hagiography, André Couture identifies features of sacred biography that also apply to the Chinese Buddhist context, namely the degree of a saint's individuality, mythic patterns echoed in hagiography, and doctrine implicit in biographical narrative. See Couture, "A Survey of French Literature on Ancient Indian Buddhist Hagiography," in *Monks and Magicians: Religious Biographies in Asia*, ed. Phyllis Granoff and Koichi Shinohara, (New York: Mosaic, 1988), 9–44.

24. James Benn, *Burning for the Buddha: Self-Immolation in Chinese Buddhism* (Honolulu: University of Hawai'i Press, 2007), 20–21. The earliest example of this genre was *Mingseng zhuan* (Biographies of famous monks), compiled by Baochang (462–after 514) beginning in 510, but it is no longer extant in its complete form; next was the *Gaoseng zhuan* (Biographies of eminent monks) by Huijiao (497–554), completed in 531.

25. Gyatso, *Apparitions of the Self*, 103, 116–120.

26. Ouyi, *Ouyi dashi quanji*, 16:10330.

27. His *Pixie ji* (Collected essays refuting heterodoxy) includes an introduction to the engraved edition, two essays, an appendix, and a postscript; it is contained in Ouyi, *Ouyi dashi quanji*, 19:11771–11818.

28. In terms of his Buddhist names, Ouyi calls himself "great lay disciple" (Skt. *upāsaka*) in his earliest votive text titled *Sishi er yuan* (Forty-two vows) written in 1621; the formal Dharma name (*faming*) that he later receives from Master Xueling is Zhixu; he gives himself the name Ouyi, meaning "beneficial lotus," which Shengyan says alludes to Ouyi seeking rebirth in the Pure Land. When he is forty-eight years old, Ouyi uses the name "the *śramaṇa* Ouyi [who believes] in the West there is [Amitābha preaching the Dharma]." In his later years, Ouyi uses the name "Follower of Eight Negations." Shengyan, *Minmatsu Chūgoku Bukkyō*, 143–156.

29. As Evelyn Rawski notes, Suzhou replaced Nanjing as the central metropolis in the Jiangnan region during the late Ming dynasty. Evelyn S. Rawki, "Economic and Social Foundations of Late Imperial Culture," in *Popular Culture in Late Imperial China*, ed. David Johnson, Andrew J. Nathan, and Evelyn S. Rawski, (Taipei: SMC, 1985), 25.

30. This serves as an early indication of his propensity toward Buddhism because vegetarian diets were undertaken not only by Buddhist clerics but also by strict lay practitioners at this time.

31. Kwang-Ching Liu, *Orthodoxy in Late Imperial China* (Taipei: SMC, 1994), 3.

32. In chapter 12 of the *Analects*, Yan Yuan asks Confucius about benevolence (*ren*), and the Master responds: "To conquer oneself and return to ritual is benevolence. If for

one day, one can conquer oneself and return to ritual, the whole world will submit to benevolence. Does being benevolent come from oneself, or from benevolence?" For a discussion of the commentarial tradition surrounding this passage from the *Analects*, see John Kieschnick, "Analects 12.1 and the Commentarial Tradition," *Journal of the American Oriental Society* 112, no. 4 (October–December 1992): 567–576.
33. Ouyi, *Ouyi dashi quanji*, 16:10223.
34. Ouyi, *Ouyi dashi quanji*, 16:10224. Although one might argue that this phrase refers to Chan because his earliest influence was within that tradition, I translate the phrase in this way because it occurs alongside other traditions included within the larger category of "Teachings" (which, in addition to Chan and Vinaya, formed the three established groups in the Ming dynasty). I agree with scholars such as Ch'en Ying-shan who say that Ouyi is indeed referring to the possibility of himself establishing a school. Ch'en, "Ouyi Zhixu Dashi Xiuxue xinlu licheng zhi tansuo" (The quest for the course of the path of cultivating the mind of Master Ouyi Zhixu [Part Two]), *Shizi hou* 33.2 (February): 17.
35. Ouyi's autobiography bears striking resemblance to Hanshan Deqing's autobiography in form and content. Hanshan's autobiography—the first complete autobiography composed by a Chinese Buddhist monk—also follows a chronological format; in it Hanshan describes burning all the works he composed in his teenage years, having a dream when he is nineteen *sui*, and having a series of three dreams when he is thirty-three *sui*, one of the latter including an encounter with a Buddhist master, Qingliang. Hanshan Deqing, *Hanshan dashi nianpu* (Annalistic biography of Great Master Hanshan), ed. Fushan (Taibei: Taiwan yinjing chu, 1954).
36. For example, see Griffith Foulk, "The Ch'an *Tsung* in Medieval China: School, Lineage, or What?" *The Pacific World* 8 (1992): 18–31; and Robert Sharf, "On Pure Land Buddhism and Ch'an/Pure Land Syncretism in Medieval China," *T'oung Pao* 88, no. 4–5 (2002): 282–331.
37. The sole exception would be his entry from the age of twenty-nine, when he relates that he began to write the *Collected Essentials of the Principles and Practicalities of Vinay[a]* and *Occasional [Dharma] talks in the Monastery*. Ouyi, *Ouyi dashi quanji*, 16: 10224.
38. Hayden White, "Introduction: Historical Fiction, Fictional History, and Historical Reality," *Rethinking History* 9, no. 2–3 (June–September 2005): 149.
39. Although Hanshan Deqing lived until 1623, he passed away before Ouyi had the opportunity to meet him. Ouyi refers to letters exchanged between himself and Hanshan Deqing in *Zeng chunru xiong* (A gift for Brother Chunru), *Lingfeng Zonglun* 6.2.12. Ouyi, *Ouyi dashi quanji*, 17:11126.
40. It is interesting to note that dreams appear in the beginning of Ouyi's autobiography but not thereafter, suggesting that they do indeed serve a prognosticatory or legitimizing function. As Pei-Yi Wu notes in his study of spiritual autobiographies, following the transformative experience, autobiographers or diary writers usually follow with more mundane and banal writing. This is also the case for Ouyi Zhixu; in fact, the end of his autobiography is mainly a list of the books he wrote and the years he wrote them.
41. Serinity Young, *Dreaming in the Lotus: Buddhist Dream Narrative, Imagery and Practice* (Boston: Wisdom, 1999), 9. Several scholars point out how dreams can serve as indicators of social status and advance claims to charisma or religious authority. Michel Strickmann describes these dimensions of Daoist dream encounters with

immortals in Strickmann, "Dreamwork of Psycho-Sinologists: Doctors, Taoists, Monks," in *Psycho-Sinology: The Universe of Dreams in Chinese Culture*, ed. Carolyn T. Brown (Lanham, MD: University Press of America, 1988), 34.

42. Serinity Young, *Dreaming in the Lotus*; Serinity Young, "Buddhist Dream Experience: The Role of Interpretation, Ritual, and Gender," in *Dreams: A Reader on Religious, Cultural, and Psychological Dimensions of Dreaming*, ed. Kelly Bulkeley (New York: Palgrave, 2001), 9–28; Alex Wayman, "Significance of Dreams in India and Tibet," *History of Religions* 7, no. 1 (August 1967): 1–12.

43. Roberto Ong, *The Interpretation of Dreams in Ancient China* (Bochum: Studienverlag Brockmeyer, 1985), 66.

44. Dimitri Drettas, "Le rêve mis en ordre: Les traités onirologiques des Ming à l'épreuve des traditions divinatoire, médicale et religieuse du rêve en Chine" (PhD diss., École Pratique des Hautes Études, 2007); Benjamin A. Elman, *A Cultural History of Civil Examinations in Late Imperial China* (Berkeley: University of California Press, 2000), 327; Lien-che Tu Fang, "Ming Dreams," *Tsing Hua Journal of Chinese Studies* 10, no. 1 (June 1973): 61–70.

45. Judith Zeitlin, *Historian of the Strange: Pu Songling and the Chinese Classical Tale* (Stanford, CA: Stanford University Press, 1993), 136. Interestingly, just as Ouyi uses dreams as a vehicle for establishing his religious lineage, Pu Songling (1640–1715) uses the trope of reincarnation to create his literary genealogy, thereby creating an alternative past outside of his family. Ibid., 55.

46. The most comprehensive is *Menglin xuanjie* (The forest of dreams), a huge thirty-four fascicle work by He Dongru (preface dated 1636).

47. For example, some Chinese medical texts said dreams were caused by one of the two souls (*hunpo*) being dislodged by pathogenic agents or by demons that seized the body as it slept. Strickmann, "Dreamwork of Psycho-Sinologists," 29; Rudolf G. Wagner, "Imperial Dreams in China," in *Psycho-Sinology: The Universe of Dreams in Chinese Culture*, ed. Carolyn T. Brown (Lanham, MD: University Press of America, 1988), 11. As Yü Ying-shi notes, the dual-soul theory—which reached its definitive formulation by the second century B.C.E.—conceives of human life as consisting of a bodily and spiritual part, the former nourished by eating and the latter by breathing. The *hun* soul, being more breathlike, was seen to have greater ease of movement while the *po* soul was conceived of as heavier. Thus at death, the *hun* soul was understood to move upward, while the *po* soul sunk downward, and there developed rituals where living relatives would try to summon the *hun* soul back to its *po* soul after death. Yü Yingshi, "'O Soul, Come Back!' A Study in the Changing Conceptions of the Soul and Afterlife in Pre-Buddhist-China," *Harvard Journal of Asiatic Studies* 47, no. 2 (1987): 376–377.

48. Dreams were often attributed with supernatural causes: foreboding future events, delivering messages from spirits (gods, demons, and ghosts), or featuring ancestral spirits. Wai-yee Li notes in the *Zuozhuan* how dreams functioned in a way similar to omens or signs resulting from divination, encounters with spiritual beings, or from natural anomalies, some of which were transparent, others more opaque. Wai-yee Li, "Dreams of Interpretation in Early Chinese Historical and Philosophical Writings," in *Dream Cultures: Explorations in the Comparative History of Dreaming*, ed. David Shulman and Guy G. Stroumsa (New York: Oxford University Press, 1999), 18.

49. His autobiography titled *Hanshan laoren zixu nianpu shilu* was written in 1622, a year before his death. It is included in his collected works and preserved in

the *Xuanzangjing* 127.205a–1001a. Markus Leong includes a translation of the autobiography in his dissertation. Leong, "Hanshan Deqing (1546–1623) on Buddhist Ethics" (PhD diss., California Institute of Integral Studies, 1994), 115–279.
50. Hanshan also uses the popular name for the bodhisattva, "White-Robed Guanyin," in his autobiography.
51. In 1578, when Hanshan is thirty-two years old, he has several dreams, one of which includes an encounter with the Buddhist master Qingliang and another with Maitreya Buddha.
52. In Benedict Anderson's notion of an "imagined community" of a state or nation, the community does not physically gather around a single text or interpreter but nonetheless envisions itself as a coherent unit bound by language, common conviction, or national identity. Anderson, *Imagined Communities: Reflections on the Origin and Spread of Nationalism* (New York: Verso, 2006).
53. Campany, "On the Very Idea of Religions (in the Modern West and in Early Medieval China)," *History of Religions* 42, no. 4 (2003): 317.
54. Ouyi, *Zeng chunru xiong* (A gift for Brother Chunru), *Lingfeng Zonglun* 6.2.12; Ouyi, *Ouyi dashi quanji*, 17:11126.
55. Ouyi, *Shi cangyun* (A teaching for Cangyun), *Lingfeng Zonglun* 2.5.3; Ouyi, *Ouyi dashi quanji*, 16:10556.
56. Because Shengyan argues that Ouyi was more influenced by Chan than by Tiantai, he goes into great detail about the various Buddhist figures that Ouyi mentions and what school or philosophical tenet they represent. Shengyan, *Minmatsu Chūgoku Bukkyō*, 84–92. Here I refer to Ouyi's *Shiba zuxiang zan bing xulüe* (General introduction and praise of the images of the eighteen patriarchs), *Lingfeng Zonglun* 9.4.4–9.4.16; Ouyi, *Ouyi dashi quanji*, 18:11599–11623. Shengyan believes it was written late in Ouyi's life. Shengyan, *Minmatsu Chūgoku Bukkyō*, 88. In this text, Ouyi praises the following eighteen figures: Mahākāśyapa, Upāli, Ānanda, Kāśyapa Mātaṅga, Zhufalan (Gobharana), Kang Senghui, Zhu Shixing, Huiyuan (334–416), Faxian, Bodhidharma, Zhiyi (538–597), Xuanzang (602[0]–664), Guanding (669–741), Chengguan (738–839), Yongming Yanshou (904–975), Yunqi Zhuhong (1535–1615), Zibo Zhenke (1543–1603), and Hanshan Deqing (1546–1623).
57. See Ouyi, *Yuelü lichan zongbie er shu* (Commentary on the distinction of general and specific in reading the canon and performing repentance), *Lingfeng Zonglun* 1.1.15; Ouyi, *Ouyi dashi quanji*, 16:10270. Ouyi praises "the patriarch and teacher Hanshan Deqing who manifested himself in a dream and drew me [to Buddhism]" in his *Li dabei chan yuan wen* (Votive text of the great compassion repentance), *Lingfeng Zonglun* 1.2.9; Ouyi, *Ouyi dashi quanji*, 16:10299. Ouyi praises Hanshan Deqing for having brought him into the Buddhist Dharma, suggesting that his influence preceded that of Master Xueling, in his *Zi xiang zan sanshisan shou* (Thirty-three poems praising images), *Lingfeng Zonglun* 9.4.22; Ouyi, *Ouyi dashi quanji*, 18:11636.
58. Albert Welter, *The Meaning of Myriad Good Deeds: A Study of Yung-ming Yen-shou and the Wan-shan t'ung-kuei chi* (New York: Lang, 1992), 39.
59. John Kieschnick, *The Eminent Monk: Buddhist Ideals in Medieval Chinese Hagiography* (Honolulu: University of Hawai'i Press, 1997); James Benn, *Burning for the Buddha: Self-Immolation in Chinese Buddhism* (Honolulu: University of Hawai'i Press, 2007).
60. Benn, *Burning for the Buddha*, 20–21.

61. For example, many do not even mention his dream of Confucius or his enlightenment experience after reading the *Analects*, thereby minimizing the importance of the Confucian tradition in Ouyi's life.
62. As is illustrated in the volume by Phyllis Granoff and Koichi Shinohara, earlier biographies do not necessarily offer the most reliable accounts (especially if the authors feel constrained by personal relations). Later writers may therefore write more freely and objectively. This is the case with Hongyi's annalistic biography, which draws from material outside of Ouyi's autobiography (such as Ouyi's personal writing); ed. Granoff and Shinohara, *Monks and Magicians*.
63. Albert Welter finds the same in regard to biographies of Yongming Yanshou, which he observes "reflect the aspirations of the Buddhist community contemporary with the respective compilers: these images were cast after models suitable to contemporary religious needs." Welter, *The Meaning of Myriad Good Deeds*, 40.
64. Chengshi, *Babu daoren xuzhuan* (Continued biography of the Follower of Eight Negations). In Ouyi, *Ouyi dashi quanji*, 16:10228.
65. Chengshi, *Babu daoren xuzhuan*, 16:10232.
66. Chengshi, *Babu daoren xuzhuan*, 16:10232.
67. Chengshi, *Babu daoren xuzhuan*, 16:10230.
68. Peng Jiqing, *Jingtu shengxian lu* (Tainan: Heyu Chubanshe, 2001), 202–206. Peng Jiqing is Peng Xisu.
69. Peng, *Jingtu shengxian lu*, 203.
70. Peng, *Jingtu shengxian lu*, 204.
71. Yu Qian, *Xinxu gaoseng zhuan siji* (New continued biographies of eminent monks in four volumes), ed. Yu Mei'an (Taipei: Guangwen, 1977), 1:233–238.
72. Yu, *Xinxu gaoseng zhuan siji*, 1:233.
73. Yu, *Xinxu gaoseng zhuan siji*, 1:236. Because this detail is not included in Ouyi's autobiography, Jianmi Chengshi's biography, or Peng Jiqing's biography (all three of which Yu draws from for his biography), Yu must have had access to the collection of Ouyi's writings contained in the *Lingfeng Zonglun*.
74. Yu, *Xinxu gaoseng zhuan siji*, 1:237. The verses come from his *Zi xiang zan sanshisan shou* (Thirty-three poems praising images), *Lingfeng Zonglun* 9.4.20; Ouyi, *Ouyi dashi quanji*, 18:11631.
75. For a study of Hongyi's autobiography see Raoul Birnbaum, "Master Hongyi Looks Back: A 'Modern Man' Becomes a Monk in Twentieth-Century China," in *Buddhism in the Modern World: Adaptations of an Ancient Tradition*, ed. Steven Heine and Charles S. Prebish (New York: Oxford University Press, 2003), 75–124.
76. Hongyi notes that an engraved edition of the *Lingfeng Zonglun* was published in China in 1659 and additionally in Japan in 1663. He quotes from the preface of the Japanese edition, where Kōken (1652–1739) writes: "In the past I had read the work written by Great Master Ouyi of Lingfeng. Seeing the learning he gained twice over in his study and the severity of his ascetic practices, I privately sighed to myself that it was not even [that which] the great [Tiantai] patriarchs Jingxi [Zhanran] and Siming [Zhili] accomplished. . . . He who reads Ouyi's Zonglun and does not shed tears of blood, that person certainly lacks bodhicitta." Hongyi, *Ouyi dashi nianpu* (Annalistic biography of great master Ouyi), in Ouyi, *Ouyi dashi quanji*, Mulu (Catalogue): 35.
77. For example, he mentions how Ouyi lived at Mount Tiantai in the fall of 1623, which would undermine the role that divination plays in Ouyi's autobiography or would

suggest closer ties to Tiantai that might challenge his harmonization of the various Buddhist traditions. Hongyi also includes excerpts from letters written in 1630, in which Ouyi shares his anxiety about calling himself "Tiantai" but not claiming descent within the Tiantai tradition for fear that it would imply a refusal of Chan; elsewhere, he relates Ouyi's fear that his opinions would render him unorthodox in the Tiantai tradition. In a letter to Dharma master Songxi, Ouyi writes, "I honestly fear that occasionally my writing will be inconsistent, and I will then invite ridicule for being of the Shanwai camp!" Hongyi, *Ouyi dashi nianpu*, 17. Such remarks make one wonder whether Ouyi deliberately omitted details about his time at Tiantai in his autobiography out of fear that it would establish a more solid connection with a particular contemporary Buddhist institution; as we have seen, in his autobiography, he suggests a more tenuous relationship by depicting his choice of Tiantai by lots in 1631.

78. For example, Hongyi notes that the bodhisattva Dizang first prompted Ouyi to arouse *bodhicitta*, that Ouyi recited Dizang's mantra to extinguish fixed karma millions of times, that he went into seclusion (*dunji*) at Jiuhuashan and worshipped at the bodhisattva Dizang tower in 1636, and that generally "during his entire life he exerted himself to promoting worship of the bodhisatva Dizang." Hongyi, *Ouyi dashi nianpu*, 16 and 21. Hongyi includes Ouyi's praises of the bodhisattva Dizang in his own work titled *Dizang pusa shengde daguan* (Great contemplation of the holy bodhisattva Dizang).
79. Hongyi, *Ouyi dashi nianpu*, 26–27.
80. For a discussion of Jiang Qian's attempt to implement Ouyi's vision of uniting the two traditions, see Beverley Foulks McGuire, "Bringing Buddhism into the Classroom: Jiang Qian's (1876–1942) Vision for Education in Republican China," *Journal of Chinese Religions* 39 (forthcoming).
81. The character *ren* has also been translated as "humaneness" and "virtue"; because it combines the characters for "person" (*ren*) and "two" (*er*), some scholars translate it as an "authoritative person" or argue that it signifies those social achievements that distinguish one's entire person. David L. Hall and Roger T. Ames, *Thinking Through Confucius* (Albany: SUNY Press, 1987); and Roger T. Ames, "On Body as Ritual Practice," in *Self as Body in Asian Theory and Practice*, ed. Thomas Kasulis (New York: SUNY Press, 1993), 149–156.
82. Kieschnick, "Analects 12.1," 572.
83. Ouyi, *Ouyi dashi quanji*, 19:12507–12508. Translation slightly adapted from Kieschnick, "Analects 12.1," 572.
84. Ouyi, *Ouyi dashi quanji*, 16:10390.
85. Ouyi, *Ouyi dashi quanji*, 16:10222.
86. Ouyi, *Ouyi dashi quanji*, 16:10223.
87. Gyatso, *Apparitions of the Self*, 268.

2. DIVINATION AS A KARMIC DIAGNOSTIC

1. Ouyi, *Zhancha shan'e yebao jing xingfa* (Rituals of the sutra on the divination of good and bad karmic retribution), SSZZ1485:74.579a14–a16.
2. Divination is proscribed in Daoshi's encyclopedic *Fayuan zhulin*. It is also rejected in Chinese apocryphal scriptures such as the *Fanwang jing* (Sutra of Brahma's net; Skt. *Brahmajāla-sutra*), T. 1484.24.1007a24–26, 1007b16–19; and the *Fo yijiao jing*

(Sutra of the deathbed injunction), T. 289.12.1110c22-23. Whalen Lai, "The Chan-ch'a ching: Religion and Magic in Medieval China," in *Chinese Buddhist Apocrypha*, ed. Robert Buswell (Honolulu: University of Hawai'i Press, 1990), 201, ft. 36; and Shengyan, *Minmatsu Chūgoku Bukkyō no kenkyū: toku ni Chigyoku no chūshin to shite* (Tōkyō: Sankibo busshorin, 1975), 218.

3. These included performing divination by astrology (*zhanxing shu*) when he was twenty years old to determine the life of his mother and to ask that his own life be shortened if his mother's life could be lengthened; engaging in divination twice on occasions tied to one of his friends, Xinggu Daoshou (1583-1631) when he was thirty-one; casting lots to determine which school of Buddhist thought he should follow when writing his commentary on the *Sutra of Brahma's Net*; casting eight lots to determine his karmic status when he was thirty-four; and finally, performing the ritual of divination on New Year's Eve of 1645, at which time he finally received the mark of purity. Ouyi, *Ouyi dashi quanji*, 17:10910; 18:11643; 18:11644; 16:10224; 16:10305-10311; 16:10371.

4. Shengyan, *Minmatsu Chūgoku Bukkyō no kenkyū*, 222; and Yün-hua Jan, "Review of *Minmatsu Chūgoku bukkyō no kenkyū: toku ni Chikyoku o chushin to shite* (A study of Chinese Buddhism during the late Ming dynasty by focusing on the central position of Chih-hsü), by Chang Sheng-yen," *Journal of the American Oriental Society* 99, no. 1 (1979): 131.

5. Michel Strickmann, *Chinese Poetry and Prophecy: The Written Oracle in East Asia* (Stanford, CA: Stanford University Press, 2005), 30-31.

6. Strickmann, *Chinese Poetry and Prophecy*, 58-59.

7. Strickmann, *Chinese Poetry and Prophecy*, 81-85. The oldest surviving printed edition of efficacious lots is the thirteenth-century text titled *Tianzhu lingqian* (Efficacious lots of Tianzhu), discussed in ibid., 40. For a visual cultural analysis of the text, Shih-Shan Susan Huang, "Tianzhu Lingqian: Divination Prints from a Buddhist Temple in Song Hangzhou," *Artibus Asia* 67 (2007): 243-296.

8. Richard Smith notes that techniques such as the casting of lots had an "optimistic thrust" by providing hope in times of uncertainty and fear in his "Divination in Ch'ing Dynasty China," in *Cosmology, Ontology, and Human Efficacy*, ed. Richard Smith and D.W.K. Kwok (Honolulu: University of Hawai'i Press, 1993), 166. Strickmann mentions theorists who share this therapeutic view of casting lots but views their explanations as insufficient in fully capturing the significance of oracular lots in his *Chinese Poetry and Prophecy*, 41-44, 75.

9. Ouyi, *Tuijie yuanqi bing zhuyu*, *Lingfeng Zonglun* 6.1.5; Ouyi, *Ouyi dashi quanji*, 17:11061.

10. *Essentials of the Vinaya* is his earliest dated writing other than letters and votive texts.

11. These include his *Xue pusa jiefa* (Ritual of practicing the bodhisattva precepts, 1628), revisions to his *Pini shiyi ji yao* (Essentials of the collection of the Vinaya rituals, 1630), and his *Chongding xue pusa jiefa* (Revised ritual of practicing the bodhisattva precepts, 1631). The first text contains the vows from his earliest votive text (dated August 27, 1621) titled *Sishiba yuan* (Forty-eight vows) in *Lingfeng Zonglun* 1.1.1-1.1.5; Ouyi, *Ouyi dashi quanji*, 16:10241-10250 and his *Shou pusa jie shiwen* (Votive text on receiving the bodhisattva precepts), dated January 30, 1625, in *Lingfeng Zonglun* 1.1.5-1.1.6; Ouyi, *Ouyi dashi quanji*, 16:10250-10251. His Vinaya writing spanned a decade: he published *Jiexiaozai lüeshi* (Brief explanation of the [sutra] on the elimination of disaster [through] the precepts) in 1636, *Chijie jiandu lüeshi* (Brief

explanation of the collections of rules and precepts) in 1636, and *Fanwang hezhu* (Commentary on the [sutra] of Brahma's net) in 1637.

12. In a votive text describing the divination ritual, Ouyi casts eight lots (*jiu*) to discern whether he has upheld the *bhikṣu* precepts, whether he still has minor transgressions (*qingfan*) that require repentance, whether he has eliminated conventional sins (*zhe*), whether he requires ten years of self-discipline (*bingshou*), whether he needs to perform repentance rituals, or whether he has obstacles limiting him to the role of *bodhisattva śrāmanera, bodhisattva upāsaka*, or only having taken the Three Refuges. Ouyi, *Qian anju ri gongjiu wen, Lingfeng Zonglun* 1.2.12–1.2.14; Ouyi, *Ouyi dashi quanji*, 16:10305–10310.
13. Ouyi, *Qian anju ri gongjiu wen, Lingfeng Zonglun* 1.2.12–1.2.14; Ouyi, *Ouyi dashi quanji*, 16:10305–10310.
14. Hongyi, *Ouyi dashi nianpu*, in Ouyi, *Ouyi dashi quanqi, Mulu* (Catalogue): 24–27.
15. Ouyi Zhixu, *Shi shiwen, Lingfeng Zonglun* 2.3.10; Ouyi, *Ouyi dashi quanqi*, 16:10477.
16. Ouyi Zhixu, *Zhancha shan'e yebao jing xingfa*, SSZZ1485:74.578c16–c18.
17. *Oxford English Dictionary Online*, s.v. "Divination," accessed May 25, 2011, http://dictionary.oed.com.
18. As Shengyan notes, Ouyi draws from three texts in his divination practice, all of which are apocryphal texts: the *Yuanjue jing* (Sutra of perfect enlightenment), the *Zhancha shan'e ye baojing* (Sutra divining good and bad karmic retribution), and the tenth fascicle of the *Guanding jing* (Consecration sutra). Shengyan, *Minmatsu Chūgoku Bukkyō no kenkyū*, 222.
19. For example, in a 1637 votive text, Ouyi offers sticks of incense to the Three Jewels and the bodhisattva Dizang, saying that if he chooses the wheel indicating he has karmic obstacles, he will either repent, live in a quiet place (*alanruo*; Skt. *āraṇya*) to meditate, or try to practice various *samādhi* to establish good roots. See Ouyi, *Mie dingye zhou tan chan yuan wen, Lingfeng Zonglun* 1.3.12; Ouyi, *Ouyi dashi quanji*, 16:10345.
20. Ouyi, *Qian anju ri gongjiu wen, Lingfeng Zonglun* 1.2.12–1.2.14; Ouyi, *Ouyi dashi quanji*, 16:10305–10310.
21. Ouyi, *Dabei tanqian yuanwen, Lingfeng Zonglun* 1.4.10; Ouyi, *Ouyi dashi quanji*, 16:10376.
22. This is not to say that Ouyi solely uses divination for that purpose. We see various instances where he advocates or engages in divination for other purposes. For example, in his *Zhancha shan' e yebao jing xingfa* (Rituals of the sutra on the divination of good and bad karmic retribution), in the fifth section on repentance after a lengthy list of Buddhas that one should worship, he writes "worshipping them all three times would perhaps be too much, rely on lots to make a decision" (SSZZ1485: 74.580a15). Ouyi also describes how he used divination to determine how he should structure his ritual in a votive text written in 1633 titled *Li jingtu chanwen* (Text of performing the Pure Land repentance), *Lingfeng Zonglun* 1.2.15; Ouyi, *Ouyi dashi quanji*, 16:10312.
23. Ouyi, *Qian anju ri gongjiu wen* (Text of drawing lots on the day before the summer retreat), *Lingfeng Zonglun* 1.2.13; Ouyi, *Ouyi dashi quanji*, 16:10307.
24. Ouyi, *Wei rushi shi liuqi li chan shu* (Commentary on six or seven repentance rituals for Master Rushi), written in 1639; *Lingfeng Zonglun* 1.3.15; Ouyi, *Ouyi dashi quanji*, 16:10352.
25. Ouyi, *Zhancha shan'e yebao jing xuanyi* (Profound meaning of the sutra on the divination of good and bad karmic retribution) in Ouyi, *Ouyi dashi quanji*, 4:2364.

26. Richard J. Smith discusses the use of milfoil stalks in his *Fortune-Tellers and Philosophers: Divination in Traditional Chinese Society* (San Francisco: Westview, 1991), 19; for an analysis of the use of milfoil stalks in relation to the Zhouyi, see Edward Louis Shaughnessy, "The Composition of the Zhouyi" (PhD diss., Stanford University, 1983), 75–81; for a study and translation of the Zhouyi, see Richard Gotshalk, *Divination, Order and the Zhouyi* (New York: University Press of America, 1999). Tiziana Lippiello discusses the early history of omens in *Auspicious Omens and Miracles in Ancient China: Han, Three Kingdoms and Six Dynasties* (Sankt Augustin: Monumenta Serica Institute, 2001), 155.
27. Tiziana Lippiello, *Auspicious Omens and Miracles*, 163.
28. Smith, *Fortune-Tellers and Philosophers*, 5.
29. Benjamin A. Elman, *A Cultural History of Civil Examinations in Late Imperial China* (Berkeley: University of California Press, 2000), 311. As Elman notes, mantic techniques in late imperial China took several cultural forms: fate prediction using the Yijing, physiognomy, spirit writing, deciphering of written words, dream interpretation, sighting of portents, and geomancy. Because notions of karma and retribution had become integrated into Ming examination life, candidates would try to calculate their individual fate or "karmic allotment" (*yuanfen*) through fate extrapolation, selection of auspicious and inauspicious days, or the eight characters of a person's birth. In addition, fortune-tellers, Buddhist monks, and Daoist priests widely used astrology, numerology, and milfoil divination based on the Yijing. Ibid., 312.
30. Smith, *Fortune-Tellers and Philosophers*, 44–45.
31. Thomas Cleary excises Confucian or worldly perspectives in his translation. *Chih-hsu Ou-i, The Buddhist I Ching*, trans. Thomas Cleary (Boston: Shambhala, 1987). Although his Buddhist stance often occludes his Confucian interpretation, Ouyi clearly viewed his project as encompassing both worldviews. In fact, toward the end of his commentary, Ouyi omits Buddhist interpretations entirely, for example in the hexagrams for "marrying a young girl" and "richness" in his Zhouyi chanjie 6.32–6.36 and 7.1–7.4; Ouyi, *Ouyi dashi quanji*, 20:12964–12972 and 20:12973–12979. Whether this is due to the secular nature of the hexagrams is a matter of speculation; nevertheless, it suggests that it is not entirely a Buddhist commentary, for these passages are worldly interpretations of the hexagrams.
32. Smith, *Fortune-Tellers and Philosophers*, 13. Scholars agree that the text originated as a book of divination around the second or first millennium before the Common Era, though the earliest reference to the text is in the *Zuozhuan*. The text was used exclusively as a divination manual at its inception, being consulted for battles, rebellions, marriages, as well as for sons and heirs, but by the end of the seventh century, it became cited as a wisdom text. For a study about its composition, see Edward Louis Shaughnessy, "The Composition of the Zhouyi"; for a discussion about the history of the Yijing, see Kidder Smith, Peter Bol, Joseph A. Adler, and Don J. Wyatt, *Sung Dynasty Uses of the I Ching* (Princeton: Princeton University Press, 1990), 11–12.
33. For a history of how scholars and intellectuals talked about and used the Yijing from the Shang dynasty to the present, see Richard J. Smith, *Fathoming the Cosmos and Ordering the World: The Yijing and its Evolution in China* (Charlottesville: University of Virginia Press, 2008). Smith briefly mentions Ouyi's interpretation in ibid., 169–170.

2. DIVINATION AS A KARMIC DIAGNOSTIC 163

34. Ouyi, *Zhouyi chanjie xu; Ouyi dashi quanji*, 20:12569–12571.
35. Ouyi, *Zhouyi chanjie xu*, in *Ouyi dashi quanji*, 20:12572. Although I mostly discuss his Buddhist perspectives in the commentary, it is important to note that Ouyi often speaks of the cultivation of the superior person (*junzi*) alongside his discussion of the path of the bodhisattva. For example, in his discussion of the hexagram "cauldron" (*ding*), Ouyi writes, "To change things, there is nothing like the cauldron; this is the vessel that molds worthies, that casts superior people, boils Buddhas, and transmutes patriarchs. How can it not be very auspicious and good?" *Zhouyi chanjie* 6.20; Ouyi, *Ouyi dashi quanji*, 20:12939.
36. Yuet Keung Lo, "Change Beyond Syncretism: Ouyi Zhixu's Buddhist Hermeneutics of the Yijing," *Journal of Chinese Philosophy* 35, no. 2 (2008): 282.
37. Whalen Lai, "The Chan-ch'a ching: Religion and Magic in Medieval China," in *Chinese Buddhist Apocrypha*, ed. Robert Buswell (Honolulu: University of Hawai'i Press, 1990), 175.
38. Whalen Lai dates the text between 550 and 590 C.E. and notes that, in comparison with other texts tied to the Dizang corpus, specifically the *Dizang benyuan jing* (Sutra on the original vows of Kṣitigarbha Bodhisattva, T. 4120), the Divination Sutra is "more this-worldly and karmatic." Lai, "The Chan-ch'a ching," 177 and 200, note 18.
39. *Zhancha shan'e yebao jing*, T. 839.17.902b28–902c.
40. *Zhancha shan'e yebao jing*, T. 839.17.902c3–7. Although they are not listed in the sutra itself, the wholesome actions are: (1) not to kill, (2) not to steal, (3) not to commit adultery, (4) not to lie, (5) not to use false speech, (6) not to slander, (7) not to have a forked tongue, (8) not to covet, (9) not to become angry, and (10) not to have false views. The unwholesome actions are their opposite.
41. Lai, "The Chan-ch'a ching," 180; Liying Kuo, "Divination, jeux de hazard et purification dans le bouddhisme chinois: Autour d'un sutra apocryhe chinois, le Zhanchajing," in *Bouddhisme et Cultures Locales: Quelques Case de Réciproques Adaptations*, ed. Fukui Fumimasa and Gérard Fussman (Paris: École française d'Extrême-Orient, 1994), 151.
42. *Zhancha shan'e yebao jing*, T. 839.17.903b7–19.
43. *Zhancha shan'e yebao jing*, T. 839.17.905b–905c.
44. *Zhancha shan'e yebao jing*, T. 839.17.906c5. Lai has done a statistical analysis showing that in addition to many overlaps and symmetries, there is approximately a 2:1 ratio of good fortunes to bad. The majority of fates, particularly the middle numbers that are statistically more likely to occur, deal with this-worldly benefits including wealth, official positions, longevity, and immortality. Some prognostications are directed toward stages of religious practice for monks, thus the text reflects both monastic and lay concerns. Lai, "The Chan-ch'a ching," 181; Kuo, "Divination, jeux de hazard et purification," 152.
45. Mengcan, *Zhancha shan'e yebao jing jiangji*, ed. Wu Bitao (Taipei: Fangguang wenhua, 2004).
46. Kuo Liying admits that the use of divination was certainly inspired by analogous Chinese divination practices but also cites divination sections in fifth-century Buddhist texts such as *Fo shuo guanding fan tianshen ce jing*—the tenth fascicle of the Consecration Sutra (*Guanding jing*)—that predates the Divination Sutra by a half-century, as well as the philosophical sophistication of the 189 prognostications that reflects popular Buddhist beliefs at the end of the fifth and beginning of the sixth

century, to argue that "the Divination Sutra offers a résumé of the amalgamation of scholastic Buddhism and popular practice of this period." Kuo, "Divination, jeux de hazard et purification," 154–155. Lai, on the other hand, argues that the Divination Sutra shows more indigenous influence than known Buddhist practice and insists that the use of the "wheel" was simply an adaptation of a Buddhist symbol. Lai, "The Chan-ch'a ching," 155.

47. Lai, "The Chan-ch'a ching," 183.
48. Ouyi Zhixu, Zhancha shan'e yebao jing xingfa, SSZZ1485: 74.579a17.
49. Zhancha shan'e yebao jing, T. 839.17.903c6–10.
50. Zhancha shan'e yebao jing, T. 839.17.903c16–904a24.
51. Zhancha shan'e yebao jing, T. 839.17.904a29-b13.
52. Ouyi, Yu Liaoyin ji yiqie zisu (To Liaoyin and all monks), Lingfeng Zonglun 5.2.8–5.2.9; Ouyi, Ouyi dashi quanji, 17:10974–10975.
53. Gardner, "Confucian Commentary," 404.
54. Gardner, "Confucian Commentary," 405–406.
55. Ouyi, Zhouyi chanjie 1.12; Ouyi, Ouyi dashi quanji, 20:12618.
56. Ouyi, Zhouyi chanjie 1.25; Ouyi, Ouyi dashi quanji, 20:12618.
57. Ouyi, Zhouyi chanjie 2.1; Ouyi dashi quanji, 20:12640.
58. Ouyi, Zhouyi chanjie 2.26; Ouyi dashi quanji, 20:12689.
59. Edward Shaughnessy notes that the character can signal "problems" (hui) and "problems disappearing" (huiwang) in the Zhouyi. Edward Louis Shaughnessy, "The Composition of the Zhouyi," 137. Ouyi does use the latter phrase at certain instances, for example in Chan Explanation of the Zhouyi 5.1; Ouyi, Ouyi dashi quanji, 20:12868.
60. Ouyi, Zhouyi chanjie 1.10; Ouyi, Ouyi dashi quanji, 20:12588.
61. If we consider the definition of "regret" as "to remember, think of (something lost), with distress or longing; to feel (or express) sorrow for the loss of (a person or thing)," we can see how there are certainly elements of regret (remembering sentient beings with distress, feeling sorrow for their loss in the cycle of saṃsāra) motivating bodhisattvas to return to liberate sentient beings. See "Regret," Oxford English Dictionary Online, s.v. "Regret," accessed May 25, 2011, http://dictionary.oed.com.
62. Ouyi, Zhouyi chanjie 3.8; Ouyi, Ouyi dashi quanji, 20:12715. He echoes this sentiment in his discussion of the hexagram "humility," saying that after propagating the Dharma, the practitioner should still observe sentient beings with equanimity and not slight them. Ouyi, Zhouyi chanjie 3.16; Ouyi, Ouyi dashi quanji, 20:12731.
63. Ouyi, Zhouyi chanjie 2.8 and 2.14; Ouyi, Ouyi dashi quanji, 20:12653–12654; 20:12665–12666.
64. Ouyi, Zhouyi chanjie 2.14; Ouyi, Ouyi dashi quanji, 20:12665–12666. Though the translation is my own, I have used Cleary's translation of "stifled" for the character gai. Chih-hsu, The Buddhist I Ching, 42–43.
65. Ouyi, Zhouyi chanjie 2.15; Ouyi, Ouyi dashi quanji, 20:12667. Because of this danger when engaging in self-correction, Ouyi emphasizes the importance of having a good teacher and coming to a proper balance when resolving doubts and eliminating sins.
66. Ouyi, Zhouyi chanjie 2.15; Ouyi, Ouyi dashi quanji, 20:12667.
67. Ouyi, Zhouyi chanjie 5.25; Ouyi, Ouyi dashi quanji, 20:12875.
68. Ouyi, Zhancha shan'e yebao jing xuanyi 1; Ouyi, Ouyi dashi quanji, 4:2273–2274.
69. Ouyi, Zhancha shan'e yebao jing xuanyi 2; Ouyi, Ouyi dashi quanji, 4:2275–2276.

70. Ouyi, *Zhancha shan' e yebao jing xuanyi* 46; Ouyi, *Ouyi dashi quanji*, 4:2363.
71. Ouyi, *Zhancha shan' e yebao jing xuanyi* 45; Ouyi, *Ouyi dashi quanji*, 4:2361-2362.
72. Ouyi, *Zhancha shan' e yebao jing xuanyi* 25; Ouyi, *Ouyi dashi quanji*, 4:2321.
73. Ouyi, *Zhancha shan' e yebao jing xuanyi* 35; Ouyi, *Ouyi dashi quanji*, 4:2342.
74. Ouyi, *Zhancha shan' e yebao jing shu* 1.16; Ouyi, *Ouyi dashi quanji*, 4:2425.
75. Ouyi, *Zhancha shan' e yebao jing shu* 1.35-36; Ouyi, *Ouyi dashi quanji*, 4:2462-2463.
76. Ouyi, *Zhancha shan' e yebao jing shu* 1.38-39; Ouyi, *Ouyi dashi quanji*, 4:2468-2469. It is interesting to note Ouyi's final emphasis on the importance of vows to never commit evil karma again; we will examine this aspect of vows in the fourth chapter.
77. Ouyi, *Zhancha shan' e yebao jing shu* 1.41-42; Ouyi, *Ouyi dashi quanji*, 4:2472-2473.
78. Ouyi, *Zhancha shan' e yebao jing shu* 1.42; Ouyi, *Ouyi dashi quanji*, 4:2473.
79. Ouyi, *Zhouyi chanjie* 5.2; Ouyi, *Ouyi dashi quanji*, 20:12829.
80. Ouyi, *Zhouyi chanjie* 5.3; Ouyi, *Ouyi dashi quanji*, 20:12832.
81. Ouyi, *Zhouyi chanjie* 2.7; Ouyi, *Ouyi dashi quanji*, 20:12652.
82. Ouyi, *Zhouyi chanjie* 2.8; Ouyi, *Ouyi dashi quanji*, 20:12653.
83. Ouyi, *Zhouyi chanjie* 4.25; Ouyi, *Ouyi dashi quanji*, 20:12815.
84. Ouyi, *Zhouyi chanjie* 2.11; Ouyi, *Ouyi dashi quanji*, 20:12659.
85. Ouyi, *Zhancha shan' e yebao jing xuanyi* 61; Ouyi, *Ouyi dashi quanji*, 4:2393.
86. Ouyi, *Zhancha shan' e yebao jing shu* 1.42; Ouyi, *Ouyi dashi quanji*, 4:2475-2476.

3. REPENTANCE RITUALS FOR ELIMINATING KARMA

1. Ouyi, *Da zhuo zuoju mituo shu chao sanshier wen*, *Lingfeng Zonglun* 3.1.11; Ouyi, *Ouyi dashi quanji*, 16:10623. The full passage is in response to the question, "Those who commit the five heinous sins can be reborn [in a Pure Land], why can the Buddha not eliminate fixed karma? Also, people who create karma, if they use this to comfort themselves, would they not prefer not to enter hell [straightaway] like an arrow that is shot?" Ouyi's response reads: "One light can break a thousand years of darkness; the power of repentance can unfix karma. It is like foolish people losing their way and finding a boat but not boarding it, instead clinging to their clothes as a raft or hugging rocks as a boat, and thus not having the power to turn around. Truly fixed karma is difficult to escape."
2. This text is contained in the Xuzangjing, Vol. X74, No. 1485 as well as Ouyi, *Ouyi dashi quanji*, 19:12221-12296.
3. Kumārajīva is attributed with the translation of this sutra (T. 1484.24.997a-1010a) that purports to be the tenth chapter of a longer Sanskrit text titled the *Bodhisattva-śīla-sutra* (*Pusa jie jing*), though scholars consider it an apocryphal text. The first fascicle discusses the stages of the bodhisattva path, and the second fascicle lists the ten grave precepts and the forty-eight minor ones. According to Paul Groner, the second fascicle was circulating in China as an independent text on the precepts by the end of the fifth century. Paul Groner, "The *Fan-wang ching* and Monastic Discipline in Japanese Tendai: A Study of Annen's *Futsuu jubosatsukai kooshaku*," in *Chinese Buddhist Apocrypha*, ed. Robert E. Buswell, Jr. (Honolulu: University of Hawai'i Press, 1990), 253.
4. Ouyi, *Ouyi dashi quanji*, 19:12191-12220.
5. Ouyi, *Ouyi dashi quanji*, 19:12297-12344. This was not the earliest repentance ritual for the Dizang cult; Zhiru discusses the repentance rite *Zanli Dizang pusa chanhui*

fayuan fa that was likely composed in the ninth and tenth centuries. Zhiru, *The Making of a Savior Bodhisattva: Dizang in Medieval China* (Honolulu: University of Hawai'i Press, 2007), 67.
6. Here I adopt three features that Daniel Stevenson identifies as important considerations for those who study devotional and liturgical materials in Chinese Buddhism: (1) the internal form and procedure of a rite (its ritual gestures and liturgical cycle), (2) the contextual setting and pattern of general usage, and (3) broader soteriological themes that inform different currents of devotion. Daniel Stevenson, "The T'ien-T'ai Four Forms of Samādhi and Late North-South Dynasties, Sui, and Early T'ang Buddhist Devotionalism" (PhD diss., Columbia University, 1987), 254.
7. The set of ten grave precepts in the *Sutra of Brahma's Net* includes: no killing, stealing, sexual conduct, lying, selling liquor, talking about the faults of other members of the sangha, harming through stinginess, or slandering the Three Jewels (T. 1484.24.1004b17–1005a25).
8. Shengyan, *Minmatsu Chūgoku Bukkyō no kenkyū: toku ni Chigyoku no chūshin to shite* (Tōkyō: Sankibo busshorin, 1975), 192. Shengyan argues that Ouyi's uniqueness lies in his focusing on Dizang repentance rituals from the Divination Sutra. Shengyan, *Minmatsu Chūgoku Bukkyō no kenkyū*, 202. I agree with Shengyan's argument but here elaborate further on why Ouyi singles out Dizang in particular and the development from his Divination repentance in 1633 to his Dizang repentance in 1637, a diachronic view that is not fully explored in Shengyan's work.
9. The "Ten Mentalities" appear in Ouyi, "Brahma's Net Repentance," *Ouyi dashi quanji*, 19:12201–12202; Ouyi, "Divination Repentance," SSZZ1485:74.581b8–b12; and Ouyi, "Dizang Repentance," *Ouyi dashi quanji*, 19:12324.
10. For a discussion of how Dizang was first associated with the hells in the sixth and seventh centuries and later recognized as "lord of the underworld" in the Ming dynasty, see Zhiru, *The Making of a Savior Bodhisattva*.
11. Zhiru, *The Making of a Savior Bodhisattva*, 6.
12. For a discussion of vows and the specific genre of "votive texts" (*yuanwen*), see the following chapter in this volume.
13. Ouyi, *Yuelü lichan zongbie er shu*, Lingfeng Zonglun 1.1.14; Ouyi, *Ouyi dashi quanji*, 16:10268. For a discussion of the ritual, see David Chapell, "The Precious Scroll of the Liang Emperor: Buddhist and Daoist Repentance to Save the Dead," in *Going Forth: Visions of Buddhist Vinaya*, ed. William Bodiford (Honolulu: University of Hawai'i Press, 2005), 40–67.
14. Ouyi, *Yuelü lichan zongbie er shu*, Lingfeng Zonglun 1.1.14; Ouyi, *Ouyi dashi quanji*, 16:10267. Interestingly, in this votive text written on the occasion of having completed his *Essentials of the Collection of Vinaya Rituals*, Ouyi uses the term *chanmo* for "repentance"—a transliteration of the Sanskrit term kṣama.
15. Ouyi, *Yuelü lichan zongbie er shu*, Lingfeng Zonglun 1.1.15; Ouyi, *Ouyi dashi quanji*, 16:10269.
16. Ouyi, *Jietan shuizhai chi dabeizhou yuanwen*, Lingfeng Zonglun 1.1.18; Ouyi, *Ouyi dashi quanji*, 16:10275–10277. He specifically criticizes himself for slighting others for their mistakes without realizing his own shortcomings, which violates the seventh major precept in the *Sutra of Brahma's Net* (1484.24.1004c19–1004c23).
17. See his *Longju dabei chanwen*, Lingfeng Zonglun 1.2.1–1.2.2; Ouyi, *Ouyi dashi quanji*, 16:10283–10285; *Jietan chi dabei zhou jie*, Lingfeng Zonglun 1.2.2; Ouyi, *Ouyi dashi*

3. REPENTANCE RITUALS FOR ELIMINATING KARMA 167

quanji, 16:10285; Jie tan li dabei chanwen, Lingfeng Zonglun 1.2.3–1.2.4; Ouyi, Ouyi dashi quanji, 16:10288–10289; Li dabei chanwen, Lingfeng Zonglun 1.2.7–1.2.10; Ouyi, Ouyi dashi quanji, 16:10296–10302.
18. Ouyi, Buzong chi shu, Lingfeng Zonglun 1.2.4–1.2.5; Ouyi, Ouyi dashi quanji, 16:10289–10291.
19. Ouyi, Buzong chi shu, Lingfeng Zonglun 1.2.4; Ouyi, Ouyi dashi quanji, 16:10289–10290.
20. Ouyi, Buzong chi shu, Lingfeng Zonglun 1.2.4; Ouyi, Ouyi dashi quanji, 16:10290.
21. Here jia stands for jiachi (Skt. adhiṣṭhāna), which can simply mean "support" but usually means "grace" or "empowerment" in ritual and esoteric contexts in which Buddhas or bodhisattvas are responding to prayers or rituals.
22. Ouyi, Buzong chi shu, Lingfeng Zonglun 1.2.5; Ouyi, Ouyi dashi quanji, 16:10291.
23. Ouyi, Jietan lichan bing hui xiang bu chi zhou wen, Lingfeng Zonglun 1.2.7; Ouyi, Ouyi dashi quanji, 16:10295. Also see Ouyi, Li dabei chanwen, Lingfeng Zonglun 1.2.8; Ouyi, Ouyi dashi quanji, 16:10298.
24. Ouyi, Zai li jinguangming chanwen, Lingfeng Zonglun 1.2.5–1.2.6; Ouyi, Ouyi dashi quanji, 16:10292–10294; Ouyi, Li jingtu chanwen, Lingfeng Zonglun 1.2.10–1.2.11; Ouyi, Ouyi dashi quanji, 16:10302–10303.
25. The word "repent" (ca. 1290) means "sorrow, regret, or contrition for past action or conduct" and ultimately derives from the Latin poenitire ("to make sorry," from the Latin poena, "pain"). The distinction between "repent" and "regret" is a modern one. "Regret," meaning "to remember with distress or longing" (ca. 1300), also entails a certain affective state accompanying remembrance of past actions. Online Etymological Dictionary, s.v. "Repent" and "Regret," accessed July 26, 2011, http://www.etymonline.com.
26. Some early Chinese Buddhists argue that the first character (chan) is a transliteration of the Sanskrit term kṣamā (a term that in Sanskrit originally meant "patience"), while the second (hui) is a translation of the word to "repent," "regret," or "show remorse"; but as Stevenson notes, this etymology was viewed with suspicion as early as the Tang dynasty, and modern scholars have shown that in many Chinese translations of Sanskrit originals, the term pāpa-deśanā or āpatti-deśanā ("confession or exposing of sins or misdeeds") appears in lieu of kṣamā. Stevenson, "The T'ien-T'ai Four Forms of Samādhi," 403.
27. Liying Kuo, Confession et contrition dans le bouddhisme chinois du Ve au Xe siècle (Paris: Publications de l'École Française d'Extrême-Orient [Monographies, no. 170], 1994).
28. Stevenson, "The T'ien-T'ai Four Forms of Samādhi."
29. This future commitment often appears in sections on "professing vows" (fayuan). This is explored in the next chapter, which examines Ouyi's votive texts (yuanwen).
30. As a verb, guo means "to pass through" or "to surpass"; the English term "transgression" serves as an apt translation because it carries both the nominal and verbal connotations.
31. In Chinese Buddhism, the "five heinous sins" (Skt. pañcānantarya) are commonly understood to be: (1) matricide, (2) patricide, (3) killing an arhat, (4) harming or spilling the blood of the Buddha, and (5) destroying the harmony of the sangha.
32. Avīci means "endless hell" or "hell of unremitting pain." It is the eighth of the eight burning hells; those who commit the five wicked actions will be reborn here and undergo continuous suffering.
33. The ten evil deeds are killing, stealing, adultery, lying, using immoral language, slandering, equivocating, coveting, anger, and false views.

34. The four grave sins (Skt. *pārājika*) are those offenses that result in expulsion of a monk from the sangha, and for which one will fall into hell. Soothill lists the following four: (1) sexual immorality (Skt. *abrahmacarya*); (2) stealing (Skt. *adattādāna*), (3) killing (Skt. *vadhahiṃsa*); and (4) lying (Skt. *uttaramanuṣyadharma-prālapa*).
35. The eight *pārājika* (*boluoyi* 波羅夷) or grave offenses for nuns include the four grave sins as well as (5) libidinous contact with a male; (6) any sort of improper association (leading to adultery); (7) concealing the misbehavior (of an equal, or inferior); and (8) improper dealings with a monk.
36. For example, Ouyi includes all of these lists in his votive text *Sishiba yuan, Lingfeng Zonglun* 1.1.1–1.1.5; Ouyi, *Ouyi dashi quanji*, 16:10241–10250.
37. Amitai Etzioni and David E. Carney, eds., *Repentance: A Comparative Perspective* (New York: Rowman & Littlefield, 1997), 8–14.
38. Daniel Stevenson similarly emphasizes that repentance does not simply involve admission of guilt but instead a substantive conversion (*hua*) where the practitioner renounces his sinful status and accepts an entirely new state of being. Stevenson, "The T'ien-T'ai Four Forms of Samādhi," 409.
39. This is the ceremony that occurs on the last day of the rains retreat, which brings itinerant monks together during three months of rain in the summer. On the last day, an assembly would be held that included a *maigre* feast (*dazhai*) at noon, followed by a gathering in which monks would repent of their mistakes and then be given offerings by the laity. For a discussion of the ritual, see Kuo, *Confession et contrition*, 19.
40. This is an assembly held every fifteen days, when monks confess their infractions in the presence of other monks according to the rules of the Vinaya, or monastic code. The word *poṣadha* (or *upoṣadha*) is often transliterated in Chinese as *busa* or translated as *zhai* ("fast") or *shuojie* ("to recite the precepts"). The actual recitation of the rules of the Vinaya is called *prātimokṣa*, which Daoxuan (596–667) calls *lüchan*, "confession according to the rules of the Vinaya." The monastic rules stipulated that twice a month—on the day of the new moon and the full moon—monks should come together to fast, make sacrifices, and to read the monastic rules. The latter were divided into sections, and guilty monks confessed their offenses accordingly.
41. Pei-yi Wu notes that it is impossible to determine when the *poṣadha* first appeared in China because it required the participation of a certain number of monks to be performed, and early translators of Buddhist sutras were primarily interested in doctrine rather than monastic rules. Dharmakala was the first to translate part of the monastic rules (the *Mahāsāṅghika Vinaya*) into Chinese, but his translation covered only the precepts themselves (*jieben*; Skt. *prātimokṣa*); it did not include the confession ceremony (*busa*; Skt. *poṣadha*). Pei-Yi Wu, *The Confucian's Progress: Autobiographical Writings in Traditional China* (Princeton: Princeton University Press, 1990), 212. For a detailed study of the evolution of monastic regulations in China, see Yifa, *The Origins of Buddhist Monastic Codes in China* (Honolulu: University of Hawai'i Press, 2002), 3–52.
42. Compilations include Sengyou's (445–518) *Fayuan zayuan yuanshi ji mu lu* and Daoxuan's (596–667) *Guang Hongming ji* (T. 2103.52.97–363). Stevenson, "The T'ien-T'ai Four Forms of Samādhi," 238–243. Stevenson stresses the need to recognize the diversity of liturgical traditions and particular perspectives in the history of repentance rituals, noting that Xiao Ziliang and Xiao Yan (as Emperor Wu of the Liang) influenced metropolitan Buddhism in the south, but that their

perspective as laypeople and part of the ruling aristocracy did not necessarily represent the monastic tradition in the south. Stevenson, "The T'ien-T'ai Four Forms of Samādhi," 306.

43. Heinrich Dumoulin regards this as a general feature of *Mahayāna* Buddhist repentance rites—that none include a detailed list of transgressions but instead refer primarily to "the general sinful condition of man." Dumoulin, *Christianity Meets Buddhism*, trans. John C. Maraldo (La Salle, IL: Open Court, 1974), 123.
44. Stevenson, "The T'ien-T'ai Four Forms of Samādhi," 401.
45. Paolo Santangelo contends that they developed in response to Daoism, although Shengyan argues they may have originated from Buddhist esoteric rituals or from both Daoism and Buddhism, but not solely Daoism. Santangelo, "Human Conscience and Responsibility in Ming-Qing China," Trans. Mark Elvin, *East Asian History* 4 (1992): 31–80; Shengyan, *Minmatsu Chūgoku Bukkyō no kenkyū*, 200. For a discussion of Confucian and Daoist predecessors such as the Taipingdao, see Kuo, *Confession et contrition*, 8–12.
46. Stevenson remarks that what is astonishing is their lack of originality—the degree to which they conform to the preferences of their contemporaries and the devotional foci of such texts as Daoshi's *Fayuan zhulin* (Dharma park and precious forest) T. 2122.53.346c–349c; and Daoxuan's Continued Biographies of Eminent Monks (Xu gaoseng zhuan) T. 2060.50.425a–707a (Stevenson 1987, 236, 248).
47. Stevenson, "The T'ien-T'ai Four Forms of Samādhi," 350–351.
48. Stevenson, "The T'ien-T'ai Four Forms of Samādhi," 354. These two types of repentance continued to be a feature of repentance in Tiantai in the Song dynasty. As Zanning notes, by the tenth century the rite of repentance practiced six times a day (*liushi lichan*) was well known in religious and lay circles (T. 2126.54.241b2).
49. As Stevenson notes, the *Procedure for Performing the Lotus Samādhi Repentance* appears to be one of Zhiyi's earlier works, slightly later than his oldest work, *Procedure for Performing the Fangdeng Repentance*, which dates from the first years of Zhiyi's time in Jinling (568–575). Stevenson, "The T'ien-T'ai Four Forms of Samādhi," 613, note 74.
50. For annotated translations of both texts, see Stevenson, "The T'ien-T'ai Four Forms of Samādhi," 468–537 and 538–596. For a discussion of his other rituals, see Stevenson, "The T'ien-T'ai Four Forms of Samādhi," 60–130.
51. Stevenson discusses the Fangdeng repentance at length in "The T'ien-T'ai Four Forms of Samādhi," 82–92. He notes its use as a preliminary confession ritual to prepare students for ordination in the bodhisattva precepts and Zhiyi's characterization of the master of the sanctuary as both confessor and ordination preceptor to argue for the existence of a preceptural tradition based on the *Fangdeng dhāraṇī sutra* (*Fangdeng tuoluoni jing*). Stevension, "The T'ien-T'ai Four Forms of Samādhi," 187–188.
52. Stevenson, "The T'ien-T'ai Four Forms of Samādhi," 85.
53. In his translation of Zhiyi's *Mohe zhiguan*, Paul Swanson translates the former "actual repentance" and the latter "ideal repentance." In his dissertation, Stevenson translates the former "repentance [based on] phenomenal features" and the latter "repentance that accords with principle." I have opted for "practice" and "principle" to translate *shi* and *li* to avoid possible misconceptions deriving from Western philosophical assumptions about "ideal" or "phenomenal."
54. Though Zhiyi notes that practical techniques are intended for novices who are less disciplined in meditative practice or experienced individuals whose meditative

powers have become disrupted by obstacles, as Stevenson notes, the effectiveness of such techniques depends on the ability of the practitioner to maintain a meditative concentration or one-pointedness in order to invoke the Buddha's response. Stevenson, "The T'ien-T'ai Four Forms of Samādhi," 355.
55. Stevenson, "The T'ien-T'ai Four Forms of Samādhi," 97–98.
56. Zhiyi discusses the "five-fold repentance" in his *Mohe zhiguan* (Great calming and contemplation) (T. 1911.46.98a14–c16). Although Zhiyi is later attributed with the invention of the "fivefold repentance" (*wu hui*), Stevenson highlights evidence in a diverse range of texts from the late North–South dynasties and early Tang dynasty that suggest the fivefold sequence was already widely used by the time of Zhiyi, and that he likely borrowed it rather than created it. Stevenson, "The T'ien-T'ai Four Forms of Samādhi," 421–423.
57. The Sanskrit term for the six perfections is *pāramitā*; these are considered perfections in virtue, typically including giving (*dāna*), morality (*śīla*), forbearance (*kṣānti*), effort (*vīrya*), meditation (*dhyāna*), and wisdom (*prajñā*).
58. Kuo Liying seems to draw this conclusion, suggesting "theoretical confession" and "confession by meditating on non-production" are superior to all others, which leads her to conclude that sin is an abstract idea or philosophical notion in Chinese Buddhism: "sin is created by false thought, by the illusion of 'ordinary men.' In the eyes of 'learned and intelligent men,' it simply does not exist." Kuo, *Confession et contrition*, 169 (my translation). As we will see, Ouyi suggests that this type of confession can actually be quite destructive if undertaken by one with insufficient discernment.
59. This is the notion that the three truths—of emptiness (*kong*), conventional designation (*jia*), and the middle (*zhong*)—are mutually contained in each other. For a discussion of this aspect of Zhiyi's philosophy, see Paul Swanson, *Foundations of T'ien-t'ai Philosophy* (Berkeley: Asian Humanities, 1989), 150–156.
60. This notion refers to the ten realms of reality (hells, hungry ghosts, animals, asuras, humans, gods, *śrāvakas*, pratyekas, bodhisattvas, and Buddhas), each of which includes all the others. Each of these also contains the ten suchlike characteristics (*zhenru xiang*): appearance, nature, substance, powers, functions, causes, conditions, effects, retributions, and the ultimate identity of beginning and end. Because each realm can be viewed from the perspective of skandhas, sentient beings, and lands, there are a total of 3,000 worlds or aspects of reality, each of which contain others.
61. Stevenson, "The T'ien-T'ai Four Forms of Samādhi," 401.
62. Daniel A. Getz, "Siming Zhili and Tiantai Pure Land in the Song Dynasty" (PhD diss., Yale University, 1994), 66.
63. Daniel Getz notes that Zhili performed five repentance rituals over the course of his life: he performed Zhiyi's *Fahua chanfa* five times, Zhiyi's *Qing Guanyin chanfa* eight times, Zhiyi's *Jin guangming chanfa* ten times, his own *Dabei chanfa* ten times, and Zunshi's *Mituo chanfa* fifty times. Not only did he perform repentance with Zunshi to alleviate drought in Mingzhou in 1000, but he also famously made a pact with ten other companions in 1017 to perform the Lotus repentance for three years, after which they were to immolate themselves, from which he was eventually dissuaded. Getz, "Siming Zhili and Tiantai Pure Land," 62, 67–68.
64. Getz, "Siming Zhili and Tiantai Pure Land," 168.
65. Zunshi's *Qing Guanyin yi* (Emended invocation of Guanyin repentance), *Jinguangming buzhu yi* (Emended golden light repentance), and *Wansheng jingtu jueyi xingyuan*

3. REPENTANCE RITUALS FOR ELIMINATING KARMA 171

ermen (Two teachings for resolving doubts and establishing the practice and vow to be reborn in the Pure Land) are discussed in Stevenson 1999, 358-363.

66. Daniel Stevenson, "Protocols of Power: Tz'u-yun Tsun-shih (964-1032) and T'ien-t'ai Lay Buddhist Ritual in the Sung," in *Buddhism in Sung Dynasty China*, ed. Peter N. Gregory and Daniel A. Getz, Jr. (Honolulu: University of Hawai'i Press, 1999), 358-363.
67. Daniel Stevenson is currently conducting research concerning the curricula of Tiantai public monasteries during the late Song and Yuan dynasties; Shi Darui includes a few pages on repentance in the Yuan dynasty that, although scarce, suggests that their repentance rituals continued to be promoted in the Yuan. Shi Darui, *Tiantai chanfa zhi yanjiu* (Taibei: Fagu wenhua, 2000), 335-339.
68. Shi Shengkai, *Zhongguo fojiao chan fa yanjiu* (Beijing: Zong jiao wen hua chu ban she, 2004), 342-345.
69. These were set within his rubric of the four *samādhi* system of constant sitting, constant walking, part walking and part sitting, and neither walking nor sitting. For a discussion of this fourfold rubric and the repertoire of rites, see Daniel Stevenson, "Where Meditative Theory Meets Practice," *Tendai Gakuho* (October 2007): 74-86.
70. Stevenson, "Where Meditative Theory Meets Practice," 90, 95.
71. Stevenson, "Where Meditative Theory Meets Practice," 101-102, 141-142.
72. Zunshi's *Qing guanshiyin pusa xiao fu duhai tuoluoni sanmei yi* (Rite for the samādhi involving the invocation of Guanyin), T. 1949.46.969b13-9b14 and Siming Zhili, *Qianshou qianyan dabeixin zhou xingfa* (Procedure for performing the great compassion dhāraṇī of the thousand armed and eyed [Guanyin]), T. 1950.46.974b21-974b22.
73. *Fanwang jing chanhui xingfa* in Ouyi, *Ouyi dashi quanji*, 19:12198 and *Zhancha shan'e yebao jing xingfa*, 1489.X74.580a22-a23. This conceptualization of ritual space appears in Ouyi's writings as early as 1628, in his *Xue pusa jiefa* (Ritual of practicing the bodhisattva precepts).
74. Stevenson notes that Huisi was averse to populated cultural centers and disdained fraternization, although Zhiyi's estimation for solitary and self-reliant lifestyles of mountain hermits is reflected in texts such as his *Lizhi fa* (Establishing the regulations), written circa 595, in which he distinguishes among three grades of practitioners, encouraging communal practice for the lowest grade but allowing an eremetic lifestyle of mountain retreat or solitary wandering and renunciation for the superior and middle grades. Stevenson, "The T'ien-T'ai Four Forms of Samādhi," 44.
75. Ouyi, *Xihu si anju shu*, *Lingfeng Zonglun* 1.2.11; Ouyi, *Ouyi dashi quanji*, 16:10304.
76. Ouyi, *Xihu si anju shu*, *Lingfeng Zonglun* 1.2.11-12; Ouyi, *Ouyi dashi quanji*, 16:10304-10305.
77. Ouyi, *Qian anju ri gongjiu wen*, *Lingfeng Zonglun* 1.2.12; Ouyi, *Ouyi dashi quanji*, 16:10306.
78. Ouyi specifically lists the *Fanwang jing*, the *Pusa yingluo benye jing* (T. 1485.24.1010b-1023a), the *Bodhisattvabhūmi-sutra* (*Pusa dichi jing*; T. 1581.30.888-959), the *Pusa shanjie jing* (T. 1582.30.960a1-1013c14), as well as the *Xindi guan jing* (T. 159.3.291a2-331c11). In regard to the reception of the bodhisattva precepts, Paul Groner identifies three ritual manuals as especially influential: the Yogacāra master Huizhao's (650-714) *Shou pusa jie fayi*, Tiantai patriarch Huiwei's (ca. late 7th century) *Shou pusa jie yi*, and Tiantai patriarch Zhanran's (711-782) *Shou pusa jie yi*. Paul Groner, "The *Fan-wang ching* and Monastic Discipline in Japanese Tendai: A Study of Annen's *Futsuu jubosatsukai kooshaku*," in *Chinese Buddhist Apocrypha*, ed. Robert E. Buswell, Jr. (Honolulu: University of Hawai'i Press, 1990), 297-301.

79. Ouyi claims that the pattern is "largely the same and rarely different" between the five versions of the Vinaya—that is, the Dharmagupta Vinaya (Sifen lü), Sarvāstivādin Vinaya (Shisong lü), Mahīśāsaka Vinaya (Wufen lü), Prātimokṣa-sutra (Jietuo jie jing), and Vātsīputrīya Vinaya. Ouyi ultimately advocates the Sifen lü (Four-Part Vinaya) because it is pared down and is not plagued by excessive formalities.
80. Fanwang jing, T. 1484.24.1008c14–1008c19. For those who have violated the forty-eight minor precepts, the sutra states that their transgressions can be expiated by simply confessing them one by one to a superior monk (T. 1484.24.1008c20).
81. Ouyi, Fanwang jing chanhui xingfa 1; Ouyi, Ouyi dashi quanji, 19:12191.
82. Ouyi, Fanwang jing chanhui xingfa 1; Ouyi, Ouyi dashi quanji, 19:12191.
83. Ouyi, Fanwang jing chanhui xingfa 2; Ouyi, Ouyi dashi quanji, 19:12193.
84. Ouyi, Fanwang jing chanhui xingfa 2; Ouyi, Ouyi dashi quanji, 19:12194.
85. Ouyi, Fanwang jing chanhui xingfa 2; Ouyi, Ouyi dashi quanji, 19:12194.
86. Ouyi, Fanwang jing chanhui xingfa 3; Ouyi, Ouyi dashi quanji, 19:12195.
87. Here I adopt Stevenson's translation of "mentality" for xin instead of "mindfulness." Stevenson, "The T'ien-T'ai Four Forms of Samādhi," 413.
88. It is interesting to note that Zhiyi in the Mohe zhiguan (Great calming and contemplation) suggests that if the practitioner in his repentance conceals his sins, he will develop abscesses or carbuncles that may result in death if he continues his dissemblance. Stevenson, "The T'ien-T'ai Four Forms of Samādhi," 413–414.
89. Ouyi, Fanwang jing chanhui xingfa 6; Ouyi, Ouyi dashi quanji, 19:12202.
90. Fanwang jing, T. 1484.24.1004c22.
91. Ouyi, Fanwang jing chanhui xingfa 6–7; Ouyi, Ouyi dashi quanji, 19:12202–12203.
92. Ouyi, Fanwang jing chanhui xingfa 7; Ouyi, Ouyi dashi quanji, 19:12203.
93. Ouyi, Fanwang jing chanhui xingfa 7; Ouyi, Ouyi dashi quanji, 19:12203.
94. Ouyi follows the general outlines in the original sutra for (1) purifying the place of practice (which is entirely from 839.17.903c16–903c18), (2) purifying the three karmic activities (839.17.903c16–903c18–19), (3) offerings of flower and incense (839.17.903c23), (6) practicing repentance (839.17.903c26), (7) exhortation and prayers (839.17.904a4–904a6), (8) sympathetic joy, (9) profession of vows, and (10) sitting still and engaging in name recitation (839.17.904a7-a8), but he adds the sections on (4) urgent summons and (5) rituals of praise.
95. These defilements are trends of the present age, mistaken views, afflictions, being a sentient being, and having a lifetime.
96. Ouyi, Zhancha shan'e yebao jing xingfa, SSZZ1485: 74.578c7-c11.
97. It is interesting to consider this in light of Alan Cole's argument that Chinese Buddhism fashioned new filial relationships, supplanting the father–son relationship with that of mother and son. Alan Cole, Mothers and Sons in Chinese Buddhism (Stanford, CA: Stanford University Press, 1998).
98. As Robert Sharf notes, although "stimulus-response" in morality books connotes a type of divine retribution in which the stimulus of bad deeds prompts the response of a shortened or lengthened life, in Buddhist texts, it can represent the interaction in which humans "stimulate" (gan) Buddhas and bodhisattvas, which elicits a compassionate "response" (ying). Robert Sharf, Coming to Terms with Chinese Buddhism: A Reading of the Treasure Store Treatise (Honolulu: University of Hawai'i Press, 2002) 94, 120. For a general discussion of "sympathetic resonance" see Paolo Santangelo, "Destiny and Retribution in late imperial China," East and West 42, no. 2–4 (1992): 386–388.

3. REPENTANCE RITUALS FOR ELIMINATING KARMA 173

99. Ouyi, *Zhancha shan'e yebao jing xingfa*, SSZZ1485: 74.578c13–c15.
100. *Avīci* means "endless hell" or "hell of unremitting pain." It is the eighth of the eight burning hells where those who commit the five wicked actions are reborn and undergo continuous suffering.
101. Ouyi, *Zhancha shan'e yebao jing xingfa*, SSZZ1485: 74.578c20–579a3.
102. Ouyi, *Zhancha shan'e yebao jing xingfa*, SSZZ1485: 74.579a3–a4.
103. Ouyi, *Zhancha shan'e yebao jing xingfa*, SSZZ1485: 74.579a8.
104. Ouyi, *Zhancha shan'e yebao jing xingfa*, SSZZ1485: 74.579a9–10.
105. Ouyi, *Zhancha shan'e yebao jing xingfa*, SSZZ1485: 74.579a8.
106. Ouyi, *Zhancha shan'e yebao jing xingfa*, SSZZ 1485:74.579a12.
107. Ouyi, *Zhancha shan'e yebao jing xingfa*, SSZZ1485: 74.579b3.
108. Ouyi, *Zhancha shan'e yebao jing xingfa*, SSZZ1485: 74.579c24–580a2.
109. Ouyi, *Zhancha shan'e yebao jing xingfa*, SSZZ1485: 74.580a12–13.
110. Ouyi, *Zhancha shan'e yebao jing xingfa*, SSZZ1485: 74.581a24–581b1.
111. Ouyi, *Zhancha shan'e yebao jing xingfa*, SSZZ1485: 74.581b3–b5.
112. The word *xunxi* literally means "permeating" or "perfuming," but it metaphorically describes the functioning of karma, in which activities inevitably leave impressions on one's consciousness.
113. Ouyi, *Zhancha shan'e yebao jing xingfa*, SSZZ1485: 74.581b23.
114. Ouyi, *Zhancha shan'e yebao jing xingfa*, SSZZ1485: 74.581b24–c1.
115. Ouyi, *Zhancha shan'e yebao jing xingfa*, SSZZ1485: 74.581c2.
116. Ouyi, *Zhancha shan'e yebao jing xingfa*, SSZZ1485: 74.581c4.
117. Ouyi, *Zhancha shan'e yebao jing xingfa*, SSZZ1485: 74.581c6–8.
118. With the exception of a trip to Fujian, his trip to Jiuhuashan is the farthest that Ouyi travels from the main sites of his religious activity—the vicinities of Hangzhou and Nanjing.
119. Ouyi, *Zanli Dizang pusa chan yuan yi* 4; Ouyi, *Ouyi dashi quanji*, 19:12300–12303.
120. Ouyi, *Zanli Dizang pusa chan yuan yi* 19; Ouyi, *Ouyi dashi quanji*, 1919:12315.
121. For a discussion of Ouyi's criticism of Jesuit missionaries whose description of God eliminating sins bears striking resemblance to his own characterization of Dizang, see Beverley Foulks, "Duplicitous Thieves: Ouyi Zhixu's Criticism of Jesuit Missionaries in Late Imperial China," *Chung-Hwa Buddhist Journal* 21 (2008): 67–68.
122. Ouyi, *Zanli Dizang pusa chan yuan yi* 32; Ouyi, *Ouyi dashi quanji*, 1919:12328.
123. Ouyi, *Zanli Dizang pusa chan yuan yi* 33–34; Ouyi, *Ouyi dashi quanji*, 1919:12329–12330.
124. Ouyi, *Zanli Dizang pusa chan yuan yi* 35–36; Ouyi, *Ouyi dashi quanji*, 1919:12331–12332.
125. See *Buzong chi shu*, *Lingfeng Zonglun* 1.2.4–1.2.5; Ouyi, *Ouyi dashi quanji*, 16:10289–10291. Ouyi praises Dizang's divine mantra for its ability to extinguish fixed karma and universally save people from boundless suffering because of the five defilements (*wuzhuo*). Ouyi recalls how sentient beings have lost their originally pure mind and created fixed karma such that they are obscured (*fu*) by ignorance. He likens them to infants, having demonic and mistaken views (*moxie*), and slandering the Dharma, so that they have little merit. Ouyi suggests that only by relying on the compassion of Dizang and his mantra can one destroy such karma.
126. Bruce Williams, "Mea Maxima Vikalpa: Repentance, Meditation, and the Dynamics of Liberation in Medieval Chinese Buddhism, 500–650 CE" (PhD diss., University of California–Berkeley, 2002), 18.
127. Although the physical acts of kneeling and prostrating may seem quite simple, when extended over several hours of a ritual they certainly strain one's lower back;

moreover, the expectation that one will maintain purity of body, speech, and mind throughout the ritual and be singly focused with "one mind" as one recites the names of dozens of Buddhas is also a challenging task.

128. Ouyi, *Zanli Dizang pusa chan yuan yi* 29–30; Ouyi, *Ouyi dashi quanji*, 1919:12325–12326.
129. Ouyi, *Zanli Dizang pusa chan yuan yi* 29; Ouyi, *Ouyi dashi quanji*, 1919:12325.
130. Ouyi, *Zanli Dizang pusa chan yuan yi* 39; Ouyi, *Ouyi dashi quanji*, 1919:12335.

4. VOWING TO ASSUME THE KARMA OF OTHERS

1. Ouyi, *Jiuhua Dizang ta qian yuanwen, Lingfeng Zonglun* 1.3.1; Ouyi, *Ouyi dashi quanji*, 16:10324.
2. Stephen Owen, "The Self's Perfect Mirror: Poetry as Autobiography," in *The Vitality of the Lyric Voice*, ed. Shuen-fu Lin and Stephen Owen (Princeton: Princeton University Press, 1986), 74.
3. This notion of "substitution" does appear in the writings of earlier Buddhist figures, such as Śāntideva's *Bodhicaryāvatāra* (The way of the bodhisattva) in Chapter 10, Verse 56, where Śāntideva offers to exchange himself for others according to their various needs and vows, "Whatever suffering is in store for the world, may it all ripen in me. May the world find happiness through all the pure deeds of the Bodhisattvas." Śāntideva, *The Bodhicaryāvatāra*, trans. Kate Crosby and Andrew Skilton (Oxford: Oxford University Press, 1998), 143. Although he does not explicitly mention suffering karmic retribution in another person's stead, he does suggest that he will personally take on the suffering of the world. Such vows accord with the general theme presented in the section on the "Perfection of Meditative Absorption" in Chapter 8, Verse 120 where Śāntideva states: "Whoever longs to rescue quickly both himself and others should practice the supreme mystery: exchange of self and other." Ibid., 99.
4. This theory originated with lectures delivered by J. L. Austin at Harvard in 1962 and later published in J. L. Austin, *How to Do Things with Words*, ed. J. O. Urmson and Marina Sbisà (Cambridge, MA: Harvard University Press, 1975). It was further developed by John Searle in *Speech Acts* (Cambridge: Cambridge University Press, 1969); and in *Expression and Meaning* (Cambridge: Cambridge University Press, 1979). Austin distinguished between the locutionary act (uttering a set of words), the illocutionary act (creating a certain force; for example, a promise, threat, or suggestion), and a perlocutionary act (an effect resulting from the communication of the first two acts). Although subsequent theorists have usually adopted the notion of "performativity" as a category of analysis, Austin actually refutes the hypothesis of a constative/performative distinction in his lectures, opting for the distinction between locutionary/illocutionary/perlocutionary acts. For an intelligent critique of the recent trend in literary theory toward "performativity," see David Gorman, "The Use and Abuse of Speech-Act Theory in Criticism," *Poetics Today* 20, no. 1 (1999): 93–119. Gorman issued a corrective note that continues his complaint against the "critical fetishization of the 'performative'" in "The Use and Abuse of Speech-Act Theory in Criticism: A Corrective Note," *Poetics Today* 22, no. 3 (2001): 669–670. He exempts a few literary scholars from his critique, notably Mary Louise Pratt and Wendell Harris: Mary Louise Pratt, *Towards a Speech-Act Theory of Literary Discourse* (Bloomington: Indiana University Press, 1977); and Wendell Harris, *Interpretive Acts: In Search of Meaning* (Oxford: Clarendon, 1988).

4. VOWING TO ASSUME THE KARMA OF OTHERS 175

5. In the Hebrew Bible, people frequently make vows to God in exchange for some request—Jacob vows that the Lord will be his God if he watches over him in his journey (Genesis 28:20–21); Israel makes vows to the Lord to deliver its people (Numbers 21:2). The solemnity of such oaths is emphasized throughout (see Numbers 30:2; Ecclesiastes 5:4–5), and several psalms are in fact praises offered in fulfillment of a vow (Psalm 22:25; Psalm 56:12; Psalm 61:8; Psalm 116:14–18).
6. The ten stages (*bhūmi*) of the bodhisattva path as set out in the *Daśabhūmika* (On the ten levels) are: generosity (*dāna*), good conduct (*śīla*), patient acceptance (*kṣānti*), vigor (*vīrya*), meditation (*dhyāna*), wisdom (*prajñā*), skillful means (*upāya-kauśalya*), determination (*praṇidhāna*), strength (*bala*), and knowledge (*jñāna*). For a general introduction to the bodhisattva path, see Rupert Gethin, *The Foundations of Buddhism* (New York: Oxford University Press, 1998), 226–230.
7. Luis Gómez, trans., *Land of Bliss: The Paradise of the Buddha of Measureless Light: Sanskrit and Chinese Versions of the Sukhāvatīvyūha Sutras* (Honolulu: University of Hawai'i Press, 1996), 334.
8. It recounts how bodhisattvas can travel to countless Buddha lands virtually instantaneously; have adamantine bodies, the divine eye, and have sutras memorized; and can bring forth limitless inspired speech. The sutra even embellishes details such as the bodhisattvas being able to see the radiance of Amitābha's Tree of Awakening standing four million leagues high (vow 28), finding that "as their bodies are exposed to my radiant light, [they] feel their body and mind become soft and pliant to a degree surpassing anything in the human or celestial realms" (vow 33), and that neither humans nor gods ever again have to perform mundane tasks such as sewing, bleaching, dying, or washing their garments (vow 38). Gómez, *Land of Bliss*, 170.
9. Liu Benzun (844–907) purportedly repeated each of Dharmākara's forty-eight vows as he sliced off pieces of flesh from his shoulder—one of his ten austerities depicted at Baodingshan. Teiser argues that such austerities not only demonstrate his resolve and spiritual standing but also bring benefits to others because they are accompanied by vows dedicated to other sentient beings. Teiser, *Reinventing the Wheel: Paintings of Rebirth in Medieval Buddhist Temples* (Seattle: University of Washington Press, 2006), 225–228. As we will see in this chapter and the next, Ouyi combines bodily practices with the profession of vows in similar ways.
10. Gómez, *Land of Bliss*, 167.
11. Gómez, *Land of Bliss*, 168.
12. Ouyi, *Yu Liaoyin ji yiqie zisu*, Lingfeng Zonglun 5.2.8; Ouyi, *Ouyi dashi quanji*, 17:10973. The text is undated but mentions that for the past twenty years he has promoted the Dharma and hoped to eliminate sin, which suggests it was written approximately ten years after the composition of his "Forty-Eight Vows," around 1631.
13. Ouyi, *Sishiba yuan*, Lingfeng Zonglun 1.1.1–1.1.5; Ouyi, *Ouyi dashi quanji*, 16: 10241–10250.
14. Ouyi, *Sishiba yuan*, Lingfeng Zonglun 1.1.2; Ouyi, *Ouyi dashi quanji*, 16:10244. These two particular *bodhisattvas* are renown for vowing to satisfy hungry ghosts with streams bursting from within (Guanyin/Avalokiteśvara in the *Kāraṇḍavyūha Sutra*) and vowing to save those in hell (Dizang/Kṣitigarbha in the *Kṣitigarbha Sutra*).
15. Ouyi, *Sishiba yuan*, Lingfeng Zonglun 1.1.1; Ouyi, *Ouyi dashi quanji*, 16:10242.
16. Ouyi, *Sishiba yuan*, Lingfeng Zonglun 1.1.4; Ouyi, *Ouyi dashi quanji*,16:10248.

17. See his *Sishiba yuan, Lingfeng Zonglun* 1.1.1–1.1.5; Ouyi, *Ouyi dashi quanji*, 16:10241–10250; *Jisi chuxi bai sanbao wen, Lingfeng Zonglun* 1.1.13; Ouyi, *Ouyi dashi quanji*, 16:10266, and *Li dabei chan yuan wen, Lingfeng Zonglun* 1.2.7; Ouyi, *Ouyi dashi quanji*, 16:10296.
18. Ouyi, *Sishiba yuan, Lingfeng Zonglun* 1.1.1; Ouyi, *Ouyi dashi quanji*, 16:10242; Ouyi, *Ci xue shujing yuanwen, Lingfeng Zonglun* 1.1.6; Ouyi, *Ouyi dashi quanji*, 16:10252, the votive texts written on the anniversary of his mother's death titled *Wei mu sanzhou qiu baji qi, Lingfeng Zonglun* 1.1.9; Ouyi, *Ouyi dashi quanji*, 16:10257–10258 and *Wei mu sizhou yuanwen, Lingfeng Zonglun* 1.1.17; Ouyi, *Ouyi dashi quanji*, 16:10273–10274, and the votive texts written on the anniversary of his father's death titled *Wei fu shier zhounian qiu jian ba qi, Lingfeng Zonglun* 1.1.18; Ouyi, *Ouyi dashi quanji*, 16:10275 and *Wei fu huixiang wen, Lingfeng Zonglun* 1.1.19; Ouyi, *Ouyi dashi quanji*, 16:10277–10278.
19. Ouyi, *Sishiba yuan, Lingfeng Zonglun* 1.1.2; Ouyi, *Ouyi dashi quanji*, 16:10243 and Ouyi, *Li da bao'enta jie, Lingfeng Zonglun* 1.1.8–1.1.9; Ouyi, *Ouyi dashi quanji*, 16:10256–10257.
20. Ouyi, *Sishiba yuan, Lingfeng Zonglun* 1.1.1–1.1.5; Ouyi, *Ouyi dashi quanji*, 16:10241–10250 and Ouyi, *Ci xue shujing yuanwen, Lingfeng Zonglun* 1.1.6; Ouyi, *Ouyi dashi quanji*, 16:10252.
21. Ouyi, *Sishiba yuan, Lingfeng Zonglun* 1.1.2–1.1.3; Ouyi, *Ouyi dashi quanji*, 16:10244–10246, Ouyi, *Shu foming jing huixiang wen, Lingfeng Zonglun* 1.1.6–1.1.7; Ouyi, *Ouyi dashi quanji*, 16:10252–10253, and Ouyi, *Chizhou xian baiwen, Lingfeng Zonglun* 1.1.8; Ouyi, *Ouyi dashi quanji*, 16:10255–10256.
22. Ouyi, *Wei fumu pu qiu baji qi, Lingfeng Zonglun* 1.2.5; Ouyi, *Ouyi dashi quanji*, 16:10292, Ouyi, *Sishiba yuan, Lingfeng Zonglun* 1.1.2; Ouyi, *Ouyi dashi quanji*, 16:10243, Ouyi, *Chizhou xian baiwen, Lingfeng Zonglun* 1.1.8; Ouyi, *Ouyi dashi quanji*, 16:10255–10256, Ouyi, *Li dabei tongdian jie, Lingfeng Zonglun* 1.1.12; Ouyi, *Ouyi dashi quanji*, 16:10264, Ouyi, *Qizhou wen, Lingfeng Zonglun* 1.1.13; Ouyi, *Ouyi dashi quanji*, 16:10265, Ouyi, *Jisi chuxi bai sanbao wen, Lingfeng Zonglun* 1.1.14; Ouyi, *Ouyi dashi quanji*, 16:10267, Ouyi, *Anju lun lü gaowen, Lingfeng Zonglun* 1.1.16; Ouyi, *Ouyi dashi quanji*, 16:10271–10272, Ouyi, *Wei mu sizhou yuanwen, Lingfeng Zonglun* 1.1.17; Ouyi, *Ouyi dashi quanji*, 16:10274, Ouyi, *Jie tan shuizhai chi dabeizhou yuanwen, Lingfeng Zonglun* 1.1.18; Ouyi, *Ouyi dashi quanji*, 16:10275–10277, Ouyi, *Weifu huixiang wen, Lingfeng Zonglun* 1.1.19; Ouyi, *Ouyi dashi quanji*, 16:10277–10278, Ouyi, *Lengyan tan qizhou ji huixiang wen er jie, Lingfeng Zonglun* 1.1.19–1.1.20; Ouyi, *Ouyi dashi quanji*, 16:10278–10280, Ouyi, *Xu chi huixiang jie, Lingfeng Zonglun* 1.1.20–1.1.21; Ouyi, *Ouyi dashi quanji*, 16:10280–10282, Ouyi, *Longju dabei chanwen, Lingfeng Zonglun* 1.2.1–1.2.2; Ouyi, *Ouyi dashi quanji*, 16:10283–10285, Ouyi, *Jie tan chi dabei zhou jie, Lingfeng Zonglun* 1.2.2; Ouyi, *Ouyi dashi quanji*, 16:10285, Ouyi, *Jie tan chi wangsheng zhoujie, Lingfeng Zonglun* 1.2.2–1.2.3; Ouyi, *Ouyi dashi quanji*, 16:10285–10287, Ouyi, *Jie tan li dabei chanwen, Lingfeng Zonglun* 1.2.3–1.2.4; Ouyi, *Ouyi dashi quanji*, 16:10288–10289, Ouyi, *Buzong chi shu, Lingfeng Zonglun* 1.2.4–1.2.5; Ouyi, *Ouyi dashi quanji*, 16:10289–10291, Ouyi, *Jie tan nianfo huixiang wen, Lingfeng Zonglun* 1.2.3; Ouyi, *Ouyi dashi quanji*, 16:10287–10288, Ouyi, *Zai li jinguangming chan wen, Lingfeng Zonglun* 1.2.5–1.2.6; Ouyi, *Ouyi dashi quanji*, 16:10292–10294, Ouyi, *Jie tan lichan bing hui xiang bu chi zhou wen, Lingfeng Zonglun* 1.2.6–1.2.7; Ouyi, *Ouyi dashi quanji*, 16:10294–10296, Ouyi, *Li dabei chan yuanwen, Lingfeng Zonglun* 1.2.7–1.2.10; Ouyi, *Ouyi dashi quanji*, 16:10296–10302, Ouyi, *Li jingtu chanwen, Lingfeng Zonglun* 1.2.10–1.2.11; Ouyi, *Ouyi dashi quanji*, 16:10302–10303, Ouyi, *Li jinguangming chanwen, Lingfeng Zonglun* 1.2.16–1.2.17; Ouyi, *Ouyi dashi quanji*, 16:10314–10316, Ouyi, *Jiang jinguangming*

chan gaowen, Lingfeng Zonglun 1.2.17–1.2.20; Ouyi, *Ouyi dashi quanji*, 16:10316–10321, Ouyi, *Jiuhua Dizang ta qian yuanwen, Lingfeng Zonglun* 1.3.1; Ouyi, *Ouyi dashi quanji*, 16:10324, Ouyi, *Qizhou wen, Lingfeng Zonglun* 1.1.13; Ouyi, *Ouyi dashi quanji*, 16:10265, Ouyi, *Yuezang chanwen, Lingfeng Zonglun* 1.3.4.–1.3.5; Ouyi, *Ouyi dashi quanji*, 16:10330–10331, Ouyi, *Mie dingye zhou tan chan yuanwen, Lingfeng Zonglun* 1.3.8–1.3.12; Ouyi, *Ouyi dashi quanji*, 16:10337–10346, Ouyi, *Chenzui qiu'ai shu, Lingfeng Zonglun* 1.3.12–1.3.15; Ouyi, *Ouyi dashi quanji*, 16:10346–10351, Ouyi, *Wei rushi si liuqi li chan shu, Lingfeng Zonglun* 1.3.15–1.3.16; Ouyi, *Ouyi dashi quanji*, 16:10351–10354, Ouyi, *Yulanpen dazhai bao'en pu du daochang zongbie heshu, Lingfeng Zonglun* 1.3.16–1.3.17; Ouyi, *Ouyi dashi quanji*, 16:10354–10356, Ouyi, *Tiefosi lichan wen, Lingfeng Zonglun* 1.4.1; Ouyi, *Ouyi dashi quanji*, 16:10357–10358, Ouyi, *Fo pusa shangzuochan yuanwen, Lingfeng Zonglun* 1.4.3.–1.4.4; Ouyi, *Ouyi dashi quanji*, 16:10361–10363, Ouyi, *Dabei xingfa daochang yuanwen, Lingfeng Zonglun* 1.4.4–1.4.5; Ouyi, *Ouyi dashi quanji*, 16:10363–10366, Ouyi, *Zutang jie dabei tan chanwen, Lingfeng Zonglun* 1.4.6–1.4.9; Ouyi, *Ouyi dashi quanji*, 16:10368–10373, Ouyi, *Zhancha xingfa yuanwen, Lingfeng Zonglun* 1.4.9–1.4.10; Ouyi, *Ouyi dashi quanji*, 16:10373–10376, Ouyi, *Dabei tanqian yuanwen, Lingfeng Zonglun* 1.4.10–1.4.11; Ouyi, *Ouyi dashi quanji*, 16:10376–10378, Ouyi, *Dabing zhong jian jingshe yuanwen, Lingfeng Zonglun* 1.4.13–1.4.14; Ouyi, *Ouyi dashi quanji*, 16:10382–10384.

23. Ouyi, *Shou pusa jie shiwen, Lingfeng Zonglun* 1.1.5; Ouyi, *Ouyi dashi quanji*, 16:10250; Ouyi, *Wei Xue Hangji jianglü ci xieshu yuanwen, Lingfeng Zonglun* 1.1.7; Ouyi, *Ouyi dashi quanji*, 16:10254, Ouyi, *Wei mu fayuan huixiang wen, Lingfeng Zonglun* 1.1.10; Ouyi, *Ouyi dashi quanji*, 16:10260, Ouyi, *Chi zhunti zhou, Lingfeng Zonglun* 1.1.12–1.1.13; Ouyi, *Ouyi dashi quanji*, 16:10262–10263, Ouyi, *Wei fumu pu qiu baji qi, Lingfeng Zonglun* 1.2.5; Ouyi, *Ouyi dashi quanji*, 16:10292, Ouyi, *Li jinguangming chanwen, Lingfeng Zonglun* 1.2.17; Ouyi, *Ouyi dashi quanji*, 16:10315, Ouyi, *Jiang jinguangming chan gao wen, Lingfeng Zonglun* 1.2.18; Ouyi, *Ouyi dashi quanji*, 16:10318, and Ouyi, *Wan fanwang gaowen, Lingfeng Zonglun* 1.3.7; Ouyi, *Ouyi dashi quanji*, 16:10335.
24. Ouyi, *Ci xue shujing yuanwen, Lingfeng Zonglun* 1.1.6; Ouyi, *Ouyi dashi quanji*, 16:10252.
25. Ouyi, *Wei mu sanzhou qiu baji qi, Lingfeng Zonglun* 1.1.9; Ouyi, *Ouyi dashi quanji*, 16:10258.
26. Ouyi, *Sishiba yuan, Lingfeng Zonglun* 1.1.2; Ouyi, *Ouyi dashi quanji*, 16:10243. It is interesting to note the connection between Ouyi's discussion of divination and repentance being means of "revealing" (*fa*) karma, and the compound "to make a vow" (*fayuan*). Both are means of opening, disclosing, or making manifest. Scattered throughout Ouyi's writing is the notion that religious practice entails a certain disclosure—both about one's own shortcomings and faults, and also about one's commitment to the bodhisattva path. It raises the question over whether the transparency of such acts may be the very challenge to sin—the tendency to hide one's faults—as well as karma, which is inscrutable and hidden.
27. He uses the word "touch" (*chu*) in the case of those in hell or ghosts and spirits, and "receive" (*meng*) in the case of those in all other realms.
28. Ouyi, *Sishiba yuan, Lingfeng Zonglun* 1.1.2–1.1.3; Ouyi, *Ouyi dashi quanji*, 16:10244–10245.
29. Ouyi, *Sishiba yuan, Lingfeng Zonglun* 1.1.4; Ouyi, *Ouyi dashi quanji*, 16:10248.
30. Ouyi, *Li da bao'enta jie, Lingfeng Zonglun* 1.1.8; Ouyi, *Ouyi dashi quanji*, 16:10256. Here Ouyi emphasizes that bodhisattvas can take recourse not only in the mechanism of stimulus-response (*ganying*), but also in their wonder-working abilities to "liberate everyone like a magical display."

31. For an example of the former see Ouyi, *Wei mu sizhou yuanwen, Lingfeng Zonglun* 1.1.17; Ouyi, *Ouyi dashi quanji*, 16:10274, Ouyi, *Wei fu huixiang wen, Lingfeng Zonglun* 1.1.19; Ouyi, *Ouyi dashi quanji*, 16:10278, Ouyi, *Lengyan tan qizhou ji huixiang wen er jie, Lingfeng Zonglun* 1.1.20; Ouyi, *Ouyi dashi quanji*, 16:10279; for an example of the latter see Ouyi, *Yuelü lichan zongbie er shu, Lingfeng Zonglun* 1.1.14; Ouyi, *Ouyi dashi quanji*, 16:10268.
32. Ouyi, *Anju lun lü gaowen, Lingfeng Zonglun* 1.1.16; Ouyi, *Ouyi dashi quanji*, 16:10272: "I only hope that the Three Jewels in the *dharma-dhātu*, by the force of their original vows, realize, know, and pity me, causing my evil karma to forever be eliminated, the good Dharma to thrive, so that I together with virtuous friends, can overcome, purify, and perfect [ourselves]."
33. Ouyi, *Li dabei tongdian jie, Lingfeng Zonglun* 1.1.12; Ouyi, *Ouyi dashi quanji*, 16:10264 and Ouyi, *Yuezang chanwen, Lingfeng Zonglun* 1.3.5; Ouyi, *Ouyi dashi quanji*, 16:10331.
34. Ouyi, *Jiang jinguangming chan gao wen, Lingfeng Zonglun* 1.2.19; Ouyi, *Ouyi dashi quanji*, 16:10319. In this text, Ouyi vows that "all will awaken and enter the sea of Golden Light, and with their pure actions they will stimulate (*gan*) the auspicious *devas* to embrace (*yong*) the groups and always protect them."
35. Ouyi, *Li dabei tongdian jie, Lingfeng Zonglun* 1.1.12; Ouyi, *Ouyi dashi quanji*, 16:10264. Here Ouyi recounts how he was born from a mantra recited by his father, how he felt like he had been summoned by Dizang in a dream as a youth but because of evil karma, he followed heterodox teachings, maligned the Buddha, and reviled Dizang. He writes: "The *mahāsattva* took pity on me, and his marvelous virtue secretly empowered me, causing me to at last attain a firm faith." He then emphasizes that he has now given rise to *bodhicitta* and says, "I regret that my obstacles are heavy and my karmic afflictions are deep-rooted; they are eternally separate from the compassionate marks of the *mahāsattva*." He admits that the three outflows (*sanlou*; Skt. *traya-āsravāḥ*) of desire, existence, and ignorance and the three pollutions (*sangou*; Skt. *tri-mala*) of desire, hate, and ignorance burn within him, but similarly, that the virtues and three bodies of the Buddha cover him.
36. Ouyi, *Li dabei tongdian jie, Lingfeng Zonglun* 1.1.12; Ouyi, *Ouyi dashi quanji*, 16:10264.
37. Ouyi, *Yuelü lichan zongbie er shu, Lingfeng Zonglun* 1.1.15; Ouyi, *Ouyi dashi quanji*, 16:10269.
38. Ouyi, *Jie tan shuizhai chi dabeizhou yuanwen, Lingfeng Zonglun* 1.1.18; Ouyi, *Ouyi dashi quanji*, 16:10276.
39. Ouyi, *Zai li jinguangming chan wen, Lingfeng Zonglun* 1.2.6; Ouyi, *Ouyi dashi quanji*, 16:10293.
40. Ouyi, *Jie tan li dabei chanwen, Lingfeng Zonglun* 1.2.3–1.2.4; Ouyi, *Ouyi dashi quanji*, 16:10288–10289.
41. Ouyi, *Jie tan chi dabei zhou jie, Lingfeng Zonglun* 1.2.2; Ouyi, *Ouyi dashi quanji*, 16:10285. Here he seeks rebirth in the Pure Land but admits that if he abandons his original mind of *bodhicitta*, he will instead fall into joyless hell.
42. Ouyi, *Zutang jie dabei tan chanwen, Lingfeng Zonglun* 1.4.7; Ouyi, *Ouyi dashi quanji*, 16:10369.
43. Ouyi, *Zutang jie dabei tan chanwen, Lingfeng Zonglun* 1.4.8; Ouyi, *Ouyi dashi quanji*, 16:10371.
44. Ouyi, *Chenzui qiu'ai shu, Lingfeng Zonglun* 1.3.13–1.3.14; Ouyi, *Ouyi dashi quanji*, 16:10347–10349.
45. Specifically, Ouyi says that although he has upheld basic precepts, he has committed many serious offenses, his mind is scattered and "completely lacks proper *samādhi*,"

and his reputation and fame for intelligence does not even match the five types of practitioners. See Ouyi, *Chenzui qiu'ai shu*, *Lingfeng Zonglun* 1.3.13; Ouyi, *Ouyi dashi quanji*, 16:10347.

46. Specifically, Ouyi recounts how meeting false *kalyāṇamitra* (*shan zhishi*) and disordered schools and lineages in the Chan tradition prompted him to become a monk, but that he finds it difficult to distinguish true and false, feels he lacks the strength to continue on the Buddhist path, and laments the fact that he does not have a school that might "mend his empty speech." Ouyi, *Chenzui qui'ai shu*, *Lingfeng Zonglun* 1.3.13; Ouyi, *Ouyi dashi quanji*, 16:10347.

47. Here Ouyi refers to his failure to bring together a community of monks as he writes, "When I first read the precepts, I knew that in the latter day there were various false teachings. I vowed to gather five people with a similar ambition, and if it exceeded five people, to live together according to the Dharma, causing the Tathāgata's true Dharma to be renewed. Yet my own obstacles were profound and my *karma* heavy. I could not align myself with *bhikkhus*, lost my expedient means, and came into conflict with my good friends." Ouyi, *Chenzui qui'ai shu*, *Lingfeng Zonglun* 1.3.13; Ouyi, *Ouyi dashi quanji*, 16:10348.

48. Here Ouyi refers to the fall of the Ming dynasty as he says, "I first saw rampant bandits and heretics as numerous as a flood, pestilence, or famine, the perversity of the national government, and our vigor being eroded away, I vowed to cultivate the strength of the Way, [make] prosperous the true Dharma, and tacitly support the fate of the emperor. Now I cannot save myself. I sit and observe enemies and evil spirits within [our country]. How is it not possible to dismiss them?" Ouyi, *Chenzui qui'ai shu*, *Lingfeng Zonglun* 1.3.13; Ouyi, *Ouyi dashi quanji*, 16:10348.

49. In this phrase, I take *xie* as its variant *ye*, which can be used in an interrogatory way or to express doubt; the compound (*qianmao*) means "vanguard," but I have translated it liberally as "the gates of hell" to avoid an awkward translation.

50. Ouyi, *Chenzui qui'ai shu*, *Lingfeng Zonglun* 1.3.14; Ouyi, *Ouyi dashi quanji*, 16:10349.

51. Ouyi, *Shou pusa jie shiwen*, *Lingfeng Zonglun* 1.1.5–1.1.6; Ouyi, *Ouyi dashi quanji*, 16:10250–10251. In fact, it is the second earliest votive text to the aforementioned "Forty-Eight Vows." The next extant votive text dates to 1628, several years after these first two texts.

52. Ouyi, *Shou pusa jie shiwen*, *Lingfeng Zonglun* 1.1.6; Ouyi, *Ouyi dashi quanji*, 16:10251.

53. Although this notion of "substitution" is not unprecedented in Chinese Buddhism, it is very rare and seems to have caused a fair amount of controversy. It appears in the Huayan text titled *Beihua jing* (T. 157.3.167–233), translated by Dharmakṣema (ca. 385–433 or 436), which gives a list of fifty-one of Amitābha's vows, one of which is "I will abandon my life and enter into Avīci Hell to substitute in suffering" (T. 3.157p212c22). Yet the notion of "substitution" is discussed by a later Huayan figure, Chengguan (738–839), in his *Dafangguang fo huayanjing shu* (T. 1735.35.503a–963a), where he dismisses the notion that bodhisattvas can substitute in the stead of sentient beings. Referring to the claim that "bodhisattvas cultivate worldly purity, they themselves amass virtue, and they cultivate pity for the manifold suffering of sentient beings, considering them ceaselessly. Owing to this cultivation, they use the joy of their pity and compassion to benefit sentient beings in evil realms of rebirth, vowing to dwell in that evil realm, making it like their home. Living in the evil realm, they are able to attest to *bodhi* and also practice forbearance. In order to eliminate the various sufferings, they vow

themselves to substitute (*daishou*), causing that evil karma to never manifest itself" (T. 35.1735.699a24–a29). In his explanation, Chengguan maintains that although such bodhisattvas can have compassionate vows, they cannot themselves substitute and offers four alternate interpretations: (1) they can themselves increase their merit (which presumably they could transfer to sentient beings); (2) they can themselves engage in ascetic practices thereby substituting by ameliorating karmic conditions; (3) they can remain among delusion, thereby receiving a body that suffers, in order to preach the Dharma and cause sentient beings not to create further causes for suffering; or (4) they can end the lives of those beings who wish to created endless bad karma for themselves, and then suffer the karmic retribution for having committed murder (T. 35.1735.699b3–b10). Ouyi acknowledges Chengguan as one of his own teachers in his constructed lineage, so he may have known that these types of vows were controversial.

54. Ouyi, *Li jinguangming chanwen*, Lingfeng Zonglun 1.2.17; Ouyi, *Ouyi dashi quanji*, 16:10315. This also appears in a votive text in which Ouyi asks that the stimulated response of the Three Jewels penetrate (*gantong*) those who have fallen into heterodoxy but then adds, "If the power of obstacles from evil sins cannot be eliminated or dissipated by regret and awakening, I vow to substitute for them." Ouyi, *Jiang jinguangming chan gao wen*, Lingfeng Zonglun 1.2.18–1.2.19; Ouyi, *Ouyi dashi quanji*, 16:10318–10319.
55. Ouyi, *Wei Xue Hangji jianglü ci xieshu yuanwen*, Lingfeng Zonglun 1.1.8; Ouyi, *Ouyi dashi quanji*, 16:10255.
56. Ouyi, *Wei mu fayuan huixiang wen*, Lingfeng Zonglun 1.1.10; Ouyi, *Ouyi dashi quanji*, 16:10260.
57. Ouyi, *Wei fumu pu qiu baji qi*, Lingfeng Zonglun 1.2.5; Ouyi, *Ouyi dashi quanji*, 16:10292.
58. Ouyi, *Wan fanwang gaowen*, Lingfeng Zonglun 1.3.7; Ouyi, *Ouyi dashi quanji*, 16:10335–10336.
59. This character—which can mean "to atone for, redeem, ransom"—appears in the *Sutra of Brahma's Net* (T. 1484.24.1007b9), but there it refers to monks, nuns, or bodhisattvas atoning for their own sins to avoid committing any minor or defiling transgression; it does not refer to atoning for someone else's karma.
60. Ouyi, *Chi zhunti zhou yuanwen*, Lingfeng Zonglun 1.1.12–1.1.13; Ouyi, *Ouyi dashi quanji*, 16:10262–10263.
61. Ouyi, *Jiu hua Dizang ta qian yuan wen* (Votive text before the Dizang Tower at Jiuhuashan), Lingfeng Zonglun 1.3.2; Ouyi, *Ouyi dashi quanji*, 16:10325.

5. SLICING, BURNING, AND BLOOD WRITING

1. Susanne Mrozik opts to use the term "body" in lieu of "the body" because the latter implies a generic body when in fact bodies are always marked by various physical differences. She agrees with Margaret R. Miles, who says, "While 'bodyness,' the condition of being body, is a universal trait of humanness, bodies are invariably gendered. They are also young or old, healthy or ill; they are socially located, along with other factors that loudly and intimately affect the experience of body." Margaret Miles, *Plotinus on Body and Beauty: Society, Philosophy, and Religion in Third-Century Rome* (Malden, MA: Blackwell, 1999), xii. Although I agree with Miles and Mrozik, I use the term "bodies" because it is less awkward and more in keeping with

the plurality of different bodies. When referring to Ouyi's body, I specify "his body" to emphasize its corporeal specificity, the way he is bodied.
2. Paul Williams, "Some Mahāyāna Buddhist Perspectives on the Body," in *Religion and the Body*, ed. Sarah Coakley (New York: Cambridge University Press, 1997), 228.
3. Suzanne Mrozik, *Virtuous Bodies: The Physical Dimensions of Morality in Buddhist Ethics* (New York: Oxford University Press, 2007), 46–47.
4. Mark Csikszentmihalyi argues that in the fourth and third centuries B.C.E., there emerged a similar notion of "material virtue" of embodiment in China, wherein self-cultivation was understood as an observable physical process. Mark Csikszentmihalyi, *Material Virtue: Ethics and the Body in Early China* (Leiden: Brill, 2004), 86.
5. Mrozik, *Virtuous Bodies*, 3–6.
6. I use the term "bodily practice" to avoid immediate connotations of "asceticism" within Western religious traditions, but I would admit that insofar as the latter connotes rigorous self-discipline and austerity, there is certainly overlap.
7. As Charlotte Furth notes, "the term *shen* (the closest classical approximation to our English word 'body') sometimes referred to the physical form of the human being, that which could be weighed, measured, or covered with clothing, and sometimes to the 'self' as a sentient person with a lived history and subjective consciousness." Charlotte Furth, *A Flourishing Yin: Gender in China's Medical History, 960-1665* (Berkeley: University of California Press, 1999), 19. Both connotations are reflected by Elvin's rendering of *shen* as "body-person." Mark Elvin, "Tales of *Shen* and *Xin*: Body-Person and Heart-Mind in China during the Last 150 Years," in *Fragments for a History of the Human Body*, ed. Michel Feher with Ramona Naddaff and Nadia Tazi (New York: Zone, 1989), 275.
8. Roger Ames argues that ritual practice enables people to assume roles and to determine their appropriate position in relation to others, and that anatomical language suggests the intimate relationship between one's physical figure and one's interpersonal or social configuration. Roger Ames, "The Meaning of the Body in Classical Chinese Philosophy," in *Self as Body in Asian Theory and Practice*, ed. Thomas P. Kasulis (New York: SUNY Press, 1993), 157–178. I find this particularly true in the case of "filial slicing."
9. Jimmy Yu, *Sanctity and Self-Inflicted Violence in Chinese Religions, 1500-1700* (New York: Oxford University Press, 2012), 62.
10. Although some modern scholars attribute the spread of filial slicing to the impact of Indian Buddhism in China, Jimmy Yu contends it is difficult to demonstrate conclusively. Yu, *Sanctity and Self-Inflicted Violence*, 69–73.
11. Keith Nathaniel Knapp, *Selfless Offspring: Filial Children and Social Order in Medieval China* (Honolulu: University of Hawai'i Press, 2005), 4.
12. Knapp, *Selfless Offspring*, 37.
13. This character—meaning "ulcer," "tumor," or "abscess"—may connote Buddhist notions of bodies as defiled, or it could reflect Ouyi's estimation of his body as diseased and rotten. Although the character could be translated "wound," given its parallel construction with the joining of illusory conditions in the previous verse, I have translated it as "sore" and interpret it as reflecting Buddhist understandings of bodies as defiled. As James Benn notes, the only bodies in Buddhism free of "cankers" or outflows are those of Buddhas. James Benn, "Where Text Meets Flesh:

Burning the Body as an Apocryphal Practice in Chinese Buddhism," *History of Religions* 37, no. 4 (May 1998): 300.

14. Ouyi, *Gegu jiu Xinggu xiong, Lingfeng Zonglun* 10.1.9; Ouyi, *Ouyi dashi quanji,* 18:11656. For a study of "filial slicing" in late imperial Chinese literature, see Yenna Wu, "Moral Ambivalence in the Portrayal of *Gegu* in Late Imperial Chinese Literature," in *Ming Qing wenhua xinlun,* ed. Wang Chengmian (Taipei: Wenjin chubanshe, 2000), 247–274.

15. Alan Cole frequently draws attention to the use of familial idioms or a type of fictive family structure in Buddhist organizations modeled on Confucian family structures. Alan Cole, "Upside Down/Right Side Up: A Revisionist History of Buddhist Funerals in China," *History of Religions* 35, no. 4 (May 1996): 308, 336.

16. For a list of all the instances of burning that appear in his writing, see Shengyan, *Minmatsu Chūgoku Bukkyō no kenkyū: toku ni Chigyoku no chūshin to shite* (Tōkyō: Sankibo busshorin, 1975), 234–236. For a study of two well-known apocryphal Chinese Buddhist texts that recommended burning the body—the *Sutra of Brahma's Net* (*Fanwang jing*; T. 1484.24.997a–1010a) and *Śūraṃgama-sutra* (*Shoulengyan jing*; T. 642.15.629–644), which were particularly influential for Ouyi—see Benn, "Where Text Meets Flesh." In his article, Benn admits uncertainty surrounding when it became established practice for monks to burn their heads at ordination, noting that the earliest reference to such a practice dates to the Yuan dynasty (1271–1368) in the biography of Zhide (1235–1322), but the practice does not become an empire-wide phenomenon until the early Qing. He notes that ordination manuals for the bodhisattva precepts are frustratingly silent on the matter, and the earliest references he finds are those in a Qing commentary by Chaoyuan (1631–1687) and an ordination manual completed in 1650 by Duti (1601–1679), a year after the Qing regulation that speaks of burning at ordination; he introduces Ouyi as a potential suspect because he is said to have burned his head on six occasions and his arms twenty-eight times, but he admits it remains unclear whether his personal practice had any effect on ordination in general. Benn, "Where Text Meets Flesh," 310.

17. Shengyan, *Minmatsu Chūgoku Bukkyō no kenkyū*, 237.

18. See James Benn, *Burning for the Buddha: Self-Immolation in Chinese Buddhism* (Honolulu: University of Hawai'i Press, 2007); Reiko Ohnuma, *Head, Eyes, Flesh, and Blood: Giving Away the Body in Indian Buddhist Literature* (New York: Columbia University Press, 2007); and Reiko Ohnuma, "The Gift of the Body and the Gift of the Dharma," *History of Religions* 37, no. 4 (1998): 323–359. Ohnuma argues that the latter "gift-of-the-body" stories constitute a discrete subgenre of Indian Buddhist narrative literature, and she distinguishes these stories—which feature bodhisattvas as heroes, conceive of bodily sacrifice as a gift, and emphasize the physical body as that which is given away—from devotional tales in which bodhisattvas burn their bodies as offerings or copy the Buddhist teachings using their own skin as parchment, own bones as pens, or blood and marrow as ink. Ohnuma, *Head, Eyes, Flesh, and Blood,* 50.

19. See Benn, *Burning for the Buddha*; and John Kieschnick, *The Eminent Monk: Buddhist Ideals in Medieval Chinese Hagiography* (Honolulu: University of Hawai'i Press, 1997), 35–50.

20. Ouyi, *Wei mu fayuan huixiang wen, Lingfeng Zonglun* 1.1.10; Ouyi, *Ouyi dashi quanji,* 16:10259; Ouyi, *Xu chi huixiang jie, Lingfeng Zonglun* 1.1.21; Ouyi, *Ouyi dashi quanji,* 16:10281.

5. SLICING, BURNING, AND BLOOD WRITING   183

21. Ouyi, *Wei mu fayuan huixiang wen*, Lingfeng Zonglun 1.1.10; Ouyi, *Ouyi dashi quanji*, 16:10259 and Ouyi, *Li dabei chan yuanwen*, Lingfeng Zonglun 1.2.8; Ouyi, *Ouyi dashi quanji*, 16:10297–10298.
22. Ouyi, *Shu foming jing huixiang wen*, Lingfeng Zonglun 1.1.7; Ouyi, *Ouyi dashi quanji*, 16:10253.
23. Ouyi, *Shu foming jing huixiang wen*, Lingfeng Zonglun 1.1.6–1.1.7; 16:10252–10253.
24. Ouyi, *Jiuhua Dizang ta qian yuanwen*, Lingfeng Zonglun 1.3.1; Ouyi, *Ouyi dashi quanji*, 16:10324.
25. Ouyi, *Jiuhua Dizang ta qian yuanwen*, Lingfeng Zonglun 1.3.1; Ouyi, *Ouyi dashi quanji*, 16:10324.
26. Ouyi, *Jiuhua Dizang ta qian yuanwen*, Lingfeng Zonglun 1.3.1; Ouyi, *Ouyi dashi quanji*, 16:10324.
27. Ouyi, *Qizhou wen*, Lingfeng Zonglun 1.1.13; Ouyi, *Ouyi dashi quanji*, 16:10265.
28. Ouyi, *Xu chi huixiang jie*, Lingfeng Zonglun 1.1.21; Ouyi, *Ouyi dashi quanji*, 16:10281.
29. Ouyi, *Jietan chi dabei zhou jie*, Lingfeng Zonglun 1.2.2; Ouyi, *Ouyi dashi quanji*, 16:10285.
30. These ten afflictions are: a view of self, extreme views, evil views, a view of attachment to views, a view of attachment to the precepts, desire, hatred, ignorance, pride, and doubt.
31. Ouyi, *Lengyan tan qizhou ji huixiang wen er jie*, Lingfeng Zonglun 1.1.19–1.1.20; Ouyi, *Ouyi dashi quanji*, 16:10279–10280.
32. Ouyi, *Li jingtu chanwen*, Lingfeng Zonglun 1.2.15; Ouyi, *Ouyi dashi quanji*, 16:10312.
33. Roy A. Rappaport, *Ritual and Religion in the Making of Humanity* (New York: Cambridge University Press, 1999), 147.
34. Ouyi, *Longju dabei chanwen*, Lingfeng Zonglun 1.2.1; Ouyi, *Ouyi dashi quanji*, 16:10283–10284.
35. Ouyi, *Longju dabei chanwen*, Lingfeng Zonglun 1.2.1–1.2.2; Ouyi, *Ouyi dashi quanji*, 16:10284–10285.
36. For a study of the bodhisattva as wonder worker, see Luis Gómez, "The Bodhisattva as Wonder Worker," in *Prajnaparamita and Related Systems*, ed. Lewis Lancaster (Berkeley: University of California Press, 1977), 221–262.
37. Ouyi, *Yuelü lichan zongbie er shu*, Lingfeng Zonglun 1.1.14; Ouyi, *Ouyi dashi quanji*, 16:10267.
38. Ouyi, *Yuelü lichan zongbie er shu*, Lingfeng Zonglun 1.1.14–1.1.15; Ouyi, *Ouyi dashi quanji*, 16:10268–10269.
39. Ouyi, *Yuelü lichan zongbie er shu*, Lingfeng Zonglun 1.1.15–1.1.16; Ouyi, *Ouyi dashi quanji*, 16:10269–10271. The figures include Śākyamuni the preserver of the true Dharma, the seven past Buddhas who transmitted the Dharma, Amitābha Buddha the eliminator of karmic obstacles, Ākāśagarbha the extinguisher of heavy karma, Dizang the transformer of fixed karma and his main object of veneration (*benzun*), Mañjuśrī and Samantabhadra who protect wisdom and practice, Guanyin and Mahāsthāmaprāpta who take refuge in joy, Bhaiṣajya-rāja (the Medicine King) and Bhaiṣajya-samudgata who cultivate Dharma offerings, Vajragarbha bodhisattva, Zhunti, and other *dhāraṇī* kings who obtain great *dhāraṇīs*, Upāli the Vinaya master, Kāśyapa and Ānanda the translation and *dhāraṇī* masters, Zibo Zhenke who published the canon and renewed the sangha, Yunqi Zhuhong whom Ouyi calls his personal master (*sishu*), Hanshan Deqing whom Ouyi calls his first cause (*chuyuan*) for giving rise to *bodhicitta*, Xueling whom Ouyi calls his strict tonsure master (*tidu*),

Gude who clarified the precepts, Wuyi for encouraging Ouyi to print his *Essential Collection*, his Dharma brothers Biru Gao and Guiyi Shou for revising and correcting the text, six present teachers and all virtuous friends who will similarly practice in the future, whom Ouyi vows to assist in the turning of the wheel of the Dharma, and finally Masters Lixian Xian and Jingkong Miao, with whom Ouyi vows to enter the stream of the Dharma.

40. For studies of the scriptural precedent, merit-making function, and ascetic dimensions of blood writing in Chinese Buddhism see Yu, *Sanctity and Self-Inflicted Violence*, 37–61; and John Kieschnick, "Blood Writing in Chinese Buddhism," *Journal of the International Association of Buddhist Studies* 23, no. 2 (2000): 177–194.
41. Shigehisa Kuriyama, *The Expressiveness of the Body and the Divergence of Greek and Chinese Medicine* (New York: Zone, 2002), 229.
42. Kieschnick, "Blood Writing in Chinese Buddhism," 187.
43. Yu, *Sanctity and Self-Inflicted Violence*, 45–47, 50–55.
44. Yu essentially agrees with Shengyan, who claims that Ouyi (alongside other Ming monks such as Zibo and Hanshan) engaged in blood writing to express the utmost sincerity towards the true Dharma. Shengyan, *Minmatsu Chūgoku Bukkyō no kenkyū*, 229. In this section on blood writing, I am simply clarifying that Ouyi did not *solely* use blood writing as a remedy for the crisis of spiritual deterioration at the time. Yu, *Sanctity and Self-Inflicted Violence*, 53.
45. Yu, *Sanctity and Self-Inflicted Violence*, 55. For a discussion of blood writing and its Buddhist doctrinal genesis, see Jimmy Yu, "Bodies and Self-Inflicted Violence in Sixteenth- and Seventeenth-Century China" (PhD diss., Princeton University, 2008), 29–95; Kieschnick, "Blood Writing in Chinese Buddhism"; Shengyan, *Minmatsu Chūgoku Bukkyō no kenkyū*, 234–240; and Holmes Welch, *The Practice of Chinese Buddhism: 1900–1950* (Cambridge, MA: Harvard University Press, 1967), 323.
46. Yu, *Sanctity and Self-Inflicted Violence*, 55–56.
47. Charlotte Furth, *A Flourishing Yin: Gender in China's Medical History, 960–1665* (Berkeley: University of California Press, 1999), 92. Yu argues that red symbolized *yang* (the light, male, creative principle) in the *yin-yang* taxonomy, having a strong exorcistic or liminal significance, and that blood was considered ultra-*yang*, representing the element of fire and the source of life or creative power. Yu, *Sanctity and Self-Inflicted Violence*, 56. However, in my own research, I have never seen blood represented as "ultra-*yang*"; since the Yellow Emperor's *Inner Canon*, *yin* and *yang* were understood as regulating the movement of bodily *qi* and by extension, the path, momentum, and direction of normal and pathological change in the body; in the cosmology of the *Book of Changes*, blood was receptive, following *qi*. In Song medical texts for women, Furth shows how blood and *qi* as *yin* and *yang* dominated in females and males, respectively, and that the metaphor of *yin* and *yang* was both hierarchical and encompassing, with blood feminized as secondary and dependent in the hierarchy of bodily energies, and unlike *qi*, unable to stand alone. Furth, *A Flourishing Yin*, 21–28, 74.
48. Yu, *Sanctity and Self-Inflicted Violence*, 41.
49. Yu, "Bodies and Self-Inflicted Violence," 39, 59.
50. Ouyi, *La xieshu huayanjing shu*, *Lingfeng Zonglun* 10.3.3–10.3.4; Ouyi, *Ouyi dashi quanji*, 18:11328–11329.
51. Indeed, if we consider the variety of texts that Ouyi mentions in connection with blood writing—the Lotus Sutra, Huayan Sutra, *Sutra of Brahma's Net*, and Dizang

Sutra—we find that they all relate to bodhisattvahood. We will discuss blood texts of the Lotus Sutra later; Ouyi mentions the last two scriptures in Ouyi, *Xieshu jingpin ba*, *Lingfeng Zonglun* 7.1.2; Ouyi, *Ouyi dashi quanji*, 18:11241. He mentions blood writing of the Diamond Sutra in *Xieshu jingangjing ba*, *Lingfeng Zonglun* 7.1.17; Ouyi, *Ouyi dashi quanji*, 18:11271–11272.

52. Ouyi, *Sanxue xieshu huayanjing ba*, *Lingfeng Zonglun* 7.1.12; yi, *Ouyi dashi quanji*, 18:11261.
53. Yu, "Bodies and Self-Inflicted Violence," 49–60.
54. Yu, "Bodies and Self-Inflicted Violence," 59.
55. Yu, "Bodies and Self-Inflicted Violence," 58–60.
56. Yu, *Sanctity and Self-Inflicted Violence*, 45–46.
57. Yu, *Sanctity and Self-Inflicted Violence*, 46–47.
58. Yu, *Sanctity and Self-Inflicted Violence*, 52–53.
59. These themes also appear in Ouyi, *Xieshu fahuajing ba*, *Lingfeng Zonglun* 7.1.8–7.1.9; Ouyi, *Ouyi dashi quanji*, 18:11254–11255.
60. Ouyi, *Ji nankai shi xieshu fahuajing ba*, *Lingfeng Zonglun* 7.1.4–7.1.5; Ouyi, *Ouyi dashi quanji*, 18:11246–11248.
61. Ouyi, *Shi benguang*, *Lingfeng Zonglun* 2.2.8; Ouyi, *Ouyi dashi quanji*, 16:10441.
62. Kieshnick discusses Ouyi's blood letter to his mother but characterizes it as an oath of sincerity, which does not fully capture its import. Kieschnick, "Blood Writing in Chinese Buddhism," 192.
63. Alan Cole, *Mothers and Sons in Chinese Buddhism* (Stanford, CA: Stanford University Press, 1998), 2.
64. Ouyi, *Jimu*, *Lingfeng Zonglun* 5.1.1–5.1.2; Ouyi, *Ouyi dashi quanji*, 17:10909–10911.
65. Cole, *Mothers and Sons*, 223.
66. In this sense, Ouyi seeks to accomplish what some sought through women's funeral rites such as "Breaking the Blood Bowl" (*xuepen*), where men drink wine dyed red to symbolize birth blood, which Gary Seaman argues is not meant to show pity on mothers for the pollution of childbirth or feelings of gratitude but has a degree of self-interest because of the karmic consequences: "if he does not make amends for the pain he has caused his mother at his birth, he will be forced to live with this wrong in his future lives. Thus, he drinks the blood of his birth to free himself (and his mother) from future karmic conflict." Gary Seaman, "The Sexual Politics of Karmic Retribution," in *The Anthropology of Taiwanese Society*, ed. Emily Ahern and Hill Gates (Stanford, CA: Stanford University Press, 1981), 389. In an analogous way, Ouyi uses blood writing to sever ties with his mother.
67. Ouyi, *Wuchen chun cishe duan liu bie zhuyou ba jie zhi er*, *Lingfeng Zonglun* 10.1.3; Ouyi, *Ouyi dashi quanji*, 18:11643.
68. Ouyi, *Fu songxi fazhu*, *Lingfeng Zonglun* 5.2.13; Ouyi, *Ouyi dashi quanji*, 17:10984. For a brief discussion of Youxi Chuandeng, see Shengyan, *Minmatsu Chūgoku Bukkyō no kenkyū*, 110. Shengyan admits that he has scant information about Guiyi Shouchou. Shengyan, *Minmatsu Chūgoku Bukkyō no kenkyū*, 115–116.
69. Ouyi, *Fu songxi fazhu*, *Lingfeng Zonglun* 5.2.14; Ouyi, *Ouyi dashi quanji*, 17:10985.
70. Ouyi, *Tuijie yuanqi bing zhuyu*, *Lingfeng Zonglun* 6.1.6; Ouyi, *Ouyi dashi quanji*, 17:11063.
71. Ouyi, *Tuijie yuanqi bing zhuyu*, *Lingfeng Zonglun* 6.1.4–6.1.7; Ouyi, *Ouyi dashi quanji*, 17:11060–11066.
72. Ouyi, *Tuijie yuanqi bing zhuyu*, *Lingfeng Zonglun* 6.1.7; Ouyi, *Ouyi dashi quanji*, 17:11065.
73. Ouyi, *Tuijie yuanqi bing zhuyu*, *Lingfeng Zonglun* 6.1.7; Ouyi, *Ouyi dashi quanji*, 17:11065.

74. Ouyi, *Wei Xue Hangji jianglü ci xieshu yuanwen*, Lingfeng Zonglun 1.1.7–1.1.8; Ouyi, *Ouyi dashi quanji*, 16:10253–10255. In the text, Ouyi mentions preaching the Four Part Vinaya to his fellow practitioner and cleric Xuehang Zhiji, and he professes ten vows and hopes that the accrued merit would enable him to uproot any mistaken views, uphold the correct teachings, and prompt him to pity and liberate sentient beings; if he has any evil karma that demands retribution, Ouyi vows to substitute in his place.
75. Ouyi, *Ti duifeng chanshi xieshu shoujie wen hou*, Lingfeng Zonglun 7.1.1; Ouyi, *Ouyi dashi quanji*, 18:11240.
76. Ouyi, *Guan quankai shi xie shu fahuajing ba*, Lingfeng Zonglun 7.1.15; Ouyi, *Ouyi dashi quanji*, 18:11267.
77. Ouyi, *Guan quankai shi xie shu fahuajing ba*, Lingfeng Zonglun 7.1.10; Ouyi, *Ouyi dashi quanji*, 18:11258.
78. Ouyi, *Da lianshao*, Lingfeng Zonglun 5.2.10; Ouyi, *Ouyi dashi quanji*, 17:10978–10979.
79. Ouyi, *Shi jingchan*, Lingfeng Zonglun 2.2.8; Ouyi, *Ouyi dashi quanji*, 16:10441–10442.
80. Ouyi, *Zhouyi chanjie* 6.26; Ouyi, *Ouyi dashi quanji*, 20:12951.
81. Furth, *A Flourishing Yin*, 28.
82. Ouyi, *Zhouyi chanjie* 6.26; Ouyi, *Ouyi dashi quanji*, 20:12952.
83. Ouyi, *Shi miyi*, Lingfeng Zonglun 2.2.6; Ouyi, *Ouyi dashi quanji*, 16:10437.
84. Furth, *A Flourishing Yin*, 187.
85. Christoph Kleine, "'The Epitome of the Ascetic Life': The Controversy over Self-Mortification and Ritual Suicide as Ascetic Practices in East Asian Buddhism," in *Asceticism and Its Critics: Historical Accounts and Comparative Perspectives*, ed. Oliver Freiberger (New York: Oxford University Press, 2006), 164.
86. Furth, *A Flourishing Yin*, 307.
87. Ouyi, *Shi yuanyin*, Lingfeng Zonglun 2.2.6; Ouyi, *Ouyi dashi quanji*, 16:10437.
88. Ouyi, *Shi yangde*, Lingfeng Zonglun 2.4.8; Ouyi, *Ouyi dashi quanji*, 16:10522.
89. Ouyi, *Shi yuanbai*, Lingfeng Zonglun 2.1.11; Ouyi, *Ouyi dashi quanji*, 16:10405.
90. Ouyi, *Shi yuanbai*, Lingfeng Zonglun 2.1.11; Ouyi, *Ouyi dashi quanji*, 16:10405.
91. Ohnuma, *Head, Eyes, Flesh, and Blood*, 202.
92. Ohnuma, *Head, Eyes, Flesh, and Blood*, 203.
93. Ohnuma, *Head, Eyes, Flesh, and Blood*, 209.
94. Mrozik, *Virtuous Bodies*, 31.
95. Mrozik, *Virtuous Bodies*, 32.
96. Ouyi, *Shi chuping*, Lingfeng Zonglun 2.1.2; Ouyi, *Ouyi dashi quanji*, 16:10387.
97. Ouyi, *Shi zhilin*, Lingfeng Zonglun 2.4.1; Ouyi, *Ouyi dashi quanji*, 16:10508.
98. Ouyi, *Fu hu shanzhu*, Lingfeng Zonglun 5.1.17; Ouyi, *Ouyi dashi quanji*, 17:10941. Ouyi literally writes he cannot "remain pure while asleep" or "not tell lies with a forked tongue."
99. Ouyi, *Fu hu shanzhu*, Lingfeng Zonglun 5.1.17; Ouyi, *Ouyi dashi quanji*, 17:10942.
100. Ouyi, *Shi xizhan*, Lingfeng Zonglun 2.1.12; Ouyi, *Ouyi dashi quanji*, 16:10408.
101. Ouyi, *Shi cunpu*, Lingfeng Zonglun 2.1.5: Ouyi, *Ouyi dashi quanji*, 16:10394. The latter phrase about "lowering one's robe and losing one's human form" also appears in *Shi yuwu*, Lingfeng Zonglun 2.2.9; Ouyi, *Ouyi dashi quanji*, 16:10444.
102. Ouyi, *Shi huihan*, Lingfeng Zonglun 2.1.8; Ouyi, *Ouyi dashi quanji*, 16:10400.
103. Elaine Scarry, *The Body in Pain: The Making and Unmaking of the World* (New York: Oxford University Press, 1985), 5–6.
104. Ariel Glucklich, *Sacred Pain: Hurting the Body for the Sake of the Soul* (New York: Oxford University Press, 2001), 47.

105. It is interesting to note that the three practices we have studied—filial slicing, burning, and blood writing—induce several, if not all, of the sensations of pain that neurophysiologists have identified: throbbing, burning, and piercing, which they argue correspond to distinct neurological events. Glucklich, *Sacred Pain*, 74.
106. Glucklich, *Sacred Pain*, 61.
107. As Glucklich notes, when the human is bombarded with incoming signals from the periphery to center (from self-inflicted pain), it can produce a virtual shutdown of outgoing signals, resulting in dissociative states or a weakening of the body-self template. Glucklich, *Sacred Pain*, 58. Certain levels of pain can have analgesic qualities or even induce euphoric states because of the triggering of beta-endorphins. Glucklich, *Sacred Pain*, 33.
108. Ouyi, *Zi xiang zan sanshisan shou*, Lingfeng Zonglun 9.4.22; Ouyi, *Ouyi dashi quanji*, 18:11635.
109. Ouyi, *Rushan er jie*, Lingfeng Zonglun 10.1.18; Ouyi, *Ouyi dashi quanji*, 18:11673.
110. Ouyi, *Shanju liu shi er jie (youxu)*, Lingfeng Zonglun 10.2.1; Ouyi, *Ouyi dashi quanji*, 18:11675.
111. Scholars such as Paul Demiéville have noted this connection between illness and sanctity, illustrated by bodhisattvas frequently generating physical illness as a means of compassionately instructing sentient beings. Mark Tatz, trans., *Buddhism and Healing: Demiéville's Article "Byō" from Hōbōgirin* (Lanham, MD: University Press, 1985).
112. Ouyi, *Da han fuyuan*, Lingfeng Zonglun 5.2.11; Ouyi, *Ouyi dashi quanji*, 17:10979.
113. Ouyi, *Fu wang sigu*, Lingfeng Zonglun 5.1.24; Ouyi, *Ouyi dashi quanji*, 17:10955–10956.
114. Ouyi, *Shi shiwen*, Lingfeng Zonglun 2.3.10–2.3.11; Ouyi, *Ouyi dashi quanji*, 16:10478–10479.
115. Ouyi, *Shi erjie*, Lingfeng Zonglun 2.3.9–2.3.10; Ouyi, *Ouyi dashi quanji*, 16:10476–10477.
116. Ouyi, *Shi youruo*, Lingfeng Zonglun 2.4.3; Ouyi, *Ouyi dashi quanji*, 16:10511.
117. Ouyi, *Shi youruo*, Lingfeng Zonglun 2.4.3; Ouyi, *Ouyi dashi quanji*, 16:10511.
118. Alan Cole, "Upside Down/Right Side Up: A Revisionist History of Buddhist Funerals in China," *History of Religions* 35, no. 4 (May 1996): 327.
119. The term *duwei* is a transliteration of the Pali *jhāpeti* and Sanskrit *jhāpita*; as Anna Seidel notes, it is one of the oldest transcriptions in Chinese versions of the *Mahāparinirvāṇa-sutra* (Seidel 2007, 573b). Anna Seidel, "Dabi (Cremation)," *Hōbōgirin* Vol. 6 (Paris: L'Académie des Inscriptions et Belles-Lettres, Institute de France, 1983), 573b.
120. Jianmi Chengsi, *Babu daoren xuzhuan*, in Ouyi, *Ouyi Dashi Quanji*, 16:10229.
121. As Susanne Mrozik notes, the word for ripening or "cooking" bodhisattva bodies is also used to describe transformative process such as sacrifice, cremation, digestion, aging, and yogic austerities. Mrozik, *Virtuous Bodies*, 51. For a study of the Chinese Buddhist practice of exposing the corpse to feed animals and insects, see Liu Shufen, "Death and Degeneration of Life: Exposure of the Corpse in Medieval Chinese Buddhism," *Journal of Chinese Religions* 28 (2000): 1–30.
122. Seidel, "Dabi," 579a. The Buddha's own cremation, described in the *Mahāparinirvāṇa sutra*, serves as a prototype for such cremation in India. Seidel notes that cremation met with resistance in China because of the reticence to damage one's body inherited from one's parents, but that it gradually became accepted by Chinese monks after the seventh century C.E. She relates five stages of the Buddha's cremation as described in the *Mahāparinirvāṇa sutra*: wrapping the body in pieces

of fabric, putting it in a coffin (a trough filled with oil), performing cremation, collecting the relics, and depositing relics in reliquaries set up beside routes. Seidel, "Dabi," 575b.
123. Patricia Ebrey, "Cremation in Sung China," *The American Historical Review* 95, no. 2 (April 1990): 419. Ebrey speculates that cremation became more acceptable because of extensive warfare and forced migration at the end of the ninth and tenth centuries; cremation allowed one to transport deceased relatives from ancestral graveyards into new contexts that were likely to be less spacious. Ebrey, "Cremation in Sung China," 420–421.
124. Stephen Teiser, "The Growth of Purgatory," in *Religion and Society in Tang and Song China*, ed. Peter Gregory and Patricia Ebrey (Honolulu: University of Hawai'i Press, 1993). Teiser identifies three factors contributing to the new purgatorial system: a deinstitutionalization of mortuary ritual circumventing Buddhist and Daoist institutions that were previously consulted to improve the fate of the deceased, a new social order and government administration that prompted a bureaucratization of purgatory, and use of token paper money instead of material offerings that contributed to a commercialization of purgatory.
125. Daniel Stevenson, "Protocols of Power: Tz'u-yun Tsun-shih (964–1032) and T'ien-t'ai Lay Buddhist Ritual in the Sung," in *Buddhism in Sung Dynasty China*, ed. Peter N. Gregory and Daniel A. Getz, Jr. (Honolulu: University of Hawai'i Press, 1999), 390.
126. Daniel Stevenson, "Text, Image, and Transformation in the History of the Shuilu fahui, the Buddhist Rite for Deliverance of Creatures of Water and Land," in *Cultural Intersections in Later Chinese Buddhism*, ed. Marsha Weidner (Honolulu: University of Hawai'i Press, 2001), 31.
127. Ouyi, *Ouyi dashi quanji*, 16:10229.
128. As scholars note, such signs of a corpse defying corruption—understood as indicating the sanctity of the deceased—were typically given as reasons for mummification; the fact that hair and nails would grow while corpses were stored in jugs indicated that in some sense the body was considered alive. See Justin Ritzinger and Marcus Bingenheimer, "Whole-Body Relics in Chinese Buddhism—Previous Research and Historical Overview," *The Indian International Journal of Buddhist Studies* 7 (2006): 74. Although this suggests Ouyi may have been mummified, the text suggests that they did cremate the body but did not scatter the ashes according to Ouyi's will, instead putting the cremated remains into a *stūpa*. Having visited the present site of the reliquary at Lingfeng Mountain, the size of the *stūpa* (which purportedly dates to the Qing dynasty) also suggests that Ouyi was cremated.
129. As Gregory Schopen notes, two Sanskrit terms for relics are *śarīra*, meaning "the body, bodily frame" or *dhātu*, meaning "constituent part," "ingredient," "element," "primitive matter," or "constituent element or essential ingredient." Schopen, Gregory Schopen, "Relic," in *Critical Terms for Religious Studies*, ed. Mark C. Taylor (Chicago: University of Chicago Press, 1998), 256.
130. Bernard Faure documents a similar use of relics in the Buddhist "conquest" of Sung Shan and the establishment of Ts'ao-ch'i as a major pilgrimage site. Bernard Faure, "Relics and Flesh Bodies: The Creation of Ch'an Pilgrimage Sites," in *Pilgrims and Sacred Sites in China*, ed. Susan Naquin and Chün-fang Yü (Taipei: SMC, 1992), 150–189.
131. As Robert Sharf notes, the idea that relics denote "the Buddha's enduring presence in his very absence" has been argued by many scholars of Buddhist relics such as

himself, David Eckel, and John Strong. Robert Sharf, "The Allure of Buddhist Relics," *Representations* 66 (1999): 78.
132. Sharf, "The Allure of Buddhist Relics," 86.
133. Sharf, "The Allure of Buddhist Relics," 89.
134. Schopen, "Relic," 260.
135. They show concern for where Ouyi's remains should be deposited, which Patricia Ebrey argues was one of the main reasons why cremation became acceptable in the tenth century; people seem to have found it more important to deposit the deceased in the right place instead of worrying about the particular method through which they were reduced to bones. Ebrey, "Cremation in Sung China," 415.
136. Republican era and contemporary (2007) gazetteers of Lingfeng Temple highlight the connection between their temple and Ouyi, an association that is also reflected in temple architecture and activities; to celebrate the 1100th anniversary of the building of Lingfeng Temple, they constructed a new reliquary courtyard and memorial hall for Ouyi, and they also hosted a forum on the "Buddhist Studies of Great Master Ouyi" in October 2007. The commemoration of the 1100th anniversary of the temple included not only speeches by high-ranking members of the Chinese Buddhist Association as well as local government officials but also a procession of Ouyi's relics to its newly constructed reliquary courtyard. See Guanqi Ruan and Shi Ciman, eds., *Bei tianmu shan lingfeng si zhi* (Beijing: Zhongguo wenshi chubanshe, 2007). The website of Lingfeng Temple visually connects its monastery with Ouyi by superimposing the image of Ouyi and his writings over a natural landscape painting, which appears just above a picture of the present abbot of the monastery, Ven. Ciman. See "Zhejiang Anji Beitianmu Lingfeng Si," accessed June 9, 2011, http://www.btmlfs.org.

CONCLUSION

1. The September 2010 issue of the *Journal of Religious Ethics* was devoted to this very issue. See Donald Swearer, "Focus Editor's Comments on 'Ethnography, Anthropology, and Comparative Religious Ethics' Essays," *Journal of Religious Ethics* 38, no. 3 (September 2010): 393–394. John Kelsay argues that descriptive scholarship characteristic of the "third wave" of Comparative Religious Ethics has little to contribute to constructive or explanatory discourse. See John Kelsay, "The Present State of the Study of Comparative Religious Ethics," *Journal of Religious Ethics* 40, no. 4 (December 2012): 597. For a discussion of the "third wave" of Comparative Religious Ethics, see Elizabeth M. Bucar, "Methodological Invention as a Constructive Project," *Journal of Religious Ethics* 36, no. 3 (2008): 355–373.
2. Specifically, it addresses some concerns raised about karma in the 2005 conference "Revisioning Karma," sponsored by the *Journal of Buddhist Ethics*.
3. Dale Wright, "Critical Questions Towards a Naturalized Concept of Karma in Buddhism," in *Revisioning Karma—The eBook*, ed. Charles Prebish, Damien Keown, and Dale S. Wright (Journal of Buddhist Ethics Online Books, 2005), 28. Jessica Main explores the ethical implications when strict divisions are not made between karma and rebirth in the context of Theravada Buddhism in the same volume. See Jessica Main, "The Karma of Others: Stories from the *Milindapañha* and the *Petavatthuaṭṭhakathā*," in Prebish, Keown, and Wright, *Revisioning Karma*, 303–358.

4. Brandon Cokelet, Jim Deitrick, and Peter Hershock underscore the practical and motivational role of karma and rebirth. See Brandon Cokelet, "Reflections on Kant and Karma," in Prebish, Keown, and Wright, *Revisioning Karma*, 101–132; Jim Deitrick, "Can American Buddhism Accommodate Karma?" in Prebish, Keown, and Wright, *Revisioning Karma*, 155–174; Peter Hershock, "Valuing Karma," in Prebish, Keown, and Wright, *Revisioning Karma*, 175–228.
5. Peter Hershock, "Valuing Karma," 183.
6. Peter Hershock, "Valuing Karma," 186.
7. Eric Sean Nelson, "Questioning Karma: Buddhism and the Phenomenology of the Ethical," in Prebish, Keown, and Wright, *Revisioning Karma*, 368.
8. Brian Victoria, "The Reactionary Use of Karma in Twentieth-Century Japan," in Prebish, Keown, and Wright, *Revisioning Karma*, 433.

APPENDIX 1. A TRANSLATION OF OUYI'S AUTOBIOGRAPHY

1. *Daoren* could have a variety of translations, including "practitioner," "person on the path," or the more lofty "person of the Way." Although the latter two translations include a term for *dao*—which Robert Campany notes has an analogous usage as "religion" in the West—I have opted for "follower" because it does not sound grandiose; and it conveys the most general sense of a religious person, which I argue is Ouyi's underlying project in the text—to criticize sectarianism and portray himself as a religious person in the broadest sense. Robert Campany, "On the Very Idea of Religions (in the Modern West and in Early Medieval China)," *History of Religions* 42, no. 4 (2003): 300.
2. The phrase "eight negations" (*babu*) also alludes to Nāgārjuna's eight negations of neither arising nor ceasing, neither eternal nor permanent, neither one nor many, and neither coming nor going.
3. This refers to the threefold division of Buddhism into Chan, Vinaya (*lü*), and Teachings (*jiao*) during the Ming dynasty. The "Teachings" division encompassed Huayan, Tiantai, and Consciousness-Only (*weishi*) schools of thought.
4. This title refers to Ouyi's famous non-sectarianism—he did not affiliate with any one particular school of thought or tradition but instead drew from all of them.
5. I take "Old Wu" (*guwu*) to refer to Wu County, which was part of Suzhou from 591 to 1911. See "CHGIS, Version 4" (Cambridge: Harvard Yenching Institute, January 2007).
6. This comes from chapter 12 of the *Analects*, where Yan Yuan (otherwise known as Yan Hui) asks Confucius about humaneness, and the Master responds: "To conquer oneself and return to ritual is humaneness. If for one day, one can conquer oneself and return to ritual, the whole world will submit to humaneness. Does being humane come from oneself, or from humaneness?"
7. The full title is *Dizang pusa benyuan jing* (Sutra on the fundamental vows of the Bodhisattva Dizang) (T. 412.13.777c–790a); it was translated by Śikṣānanda. The sutra describes how Dizang became a bodhisattva by making great vows to rescue other sentient beings.
8. Huangbo Xiyun (d. 850) was the student and Dharma successor of Baizhang Huaihai; Linji Yixuan (d. 866–7) was Huangbo's student and Dharma successor, and he is the ancestor of the Linji school of Chan Buddhism.

9. Deshan Xuanjian (782–865) is a legendary figure in the Chan tradition famous for his understanding of the Diamond Sutra and renowned for his approach of threatening to beat his students in order to put them in a state in which they could attain awakening. Yantou Quan (828–887) was Deshan's student and Dharma successor.
10. Caoxi was the place where Hanshan Deqing (1546–1623) died, and it is considered a holy place by Chan Buddhists because it is where the Sixth Patriarch Huineng preached for several decades.
11. Unlike Theravada Buddhist traditions were no one enters the sangha until receiving one's first ordination (taking ten vows of a novice), Chinese Buddhist tonsure did not entail ordination or taking vows, which came years later. For a discussion of the practice of receiving tonsure or Dharma names, see Holmes Welch, *The Practice of Chinese Buddhism: 1900–1950* (Cambridge, MA: Harvard University Press, 1967), 269–282.
12. This was the monastery of Yunqi Zhuhong.
13. The school of Dharma characteristics (*faxiang*) is also called the Consciousness-Only (*weishi*) school. They hold that there is nothing cognized independently from transformations within one's consciousness; various schools espouse the notion of the original nature of *dharma*s (*faxing*), a concept equivalent to thusness (*zhenru*) or the ultimate nature of all *dharma*s, including Huayan and Tiantai.
14. This is a quote from the *Śūraṃgama-sutra* (T. 945.19.114a20): "Ananda, you still do not yet understand: all phenomena (lit: floating dust) are characteristics of illusory transformation. In the very spot they arise, they cease. This illusion one falsely calls characteristics."
15. Jiaoguang is the style name (*zi*) of a Ming dynasty monk named Zhenjian (tonsure 1576) who was a correspondent of Zhuhong, Deqing, and Zibo, and author of the Proper Logic of the Śūraṃgama-[sutra]. Zhenhua, ed., *Zhongguo fojiao renming da cidian* (Shanghai: Shanghai cishu chubanshe, 1999), 558.
16. Elsewhere Ouyi describes Jiankong Ning, who lives in Songling, as a virtuous friend (*shan zhishi*; Skt. *kalyāṇa-mitra*) who gave him external support. Ouyi, *Zeng chunru xiong xu, Lingfeng Zonglun*, 6.2.13; Ouyi, *Ouyi dashi quanji*, 17:11127.
17. The Chinese terms Huayan and Weishi do not appear in the text, but Xianshou and Ci'en refer to Fazang, the third patriarch of the Huayan School, and Kuiji, the scholar-monk of the school of Weishi or Faxiang, respectively.
18. The phrase "knowing the fords" comes from *Analects* 18.6, where Confucius asks his disciple Zilu to ask two farmers whether the river could be forded. When one of the farmers learns it is Confucius driving the carriage, he responds, "then he already knows where the river can be forded!"
19. The full title is *Sifenlü shan bu suiji jiemo shu* (Commentary on monastic behavior according to the supplemented four-part Vinaya), a text written by Daoxuan between 626 and 630 (T. 1804).
20. The metaphor of "pointing to the moon" is a stock phrase within the Chan tradition.
21. This image of "opening primordial chaos" appears in one of the Chan transmissions of the lamps, describing how Bodhidharma "opened up primordial chaos and revealed the hidden" to Wudi (X. 1559.79.467b18).
22. Ouyi, *Duzuo shu huai er shou, Lingfeng Zonglun* 10.4.15; Ouyi, *Ouyi dashi quanji*, 18:11762.

23. Ouyi, *Bing zhong kouhao*, Lingfeng Zonglun 10.4.15; Ouyi, *Ouyi dashi quanji*, 18:11762.
24. Ouyi, *Bing jian ou cheng*, Lingfeng Zonglun 10.4.15; Ouyi, *Ouyi dashi quanji*, 18:11762.
25. Ouyi, *Gen liu ju ming*, Lingfeng Zonglun 9.2.15; Ouyi, *Ouyi dashi quanji* 18:11557. The inscription reads: "With a single thought of delusion, the six fields suddenly appear. Becoming intertwined with the roots, they rush towards defilement. Creating karma and inviting suffering, one loiters about the three realms [of desire, form, and formlessness]. One then experiences vast kalpas [of rebirth] and does not ask about the fording [across the river to enlightenment]. Meeting unexpectedly with this suffering, I realize that my body is not my body. By uprooting delusion and conquering [myself] within, I do not see that person. I think of not leaving my position and hope to return to the truth."
26. Buddhist age refers to the number of years since a monk's ordination; each year is calculated at the end of the summer retreat.
27. Yongle ordered two editions of the canon, a Northern and Southern edition. What follows is Ouyi's dissatisfaction with them.
28. Ouyi, *Yuezang bi yuanwen*, Lingfeng Zonglun 1.4.12; Ouyi, *Ouyi dashi quanji*, 16:10380.
29. This is the abbreviated name of a text by Zhanran.
30. As Robert Sharf notes, this term appears in early Chinese works such as the *Zhuangzi*; but in Buddhist texts, the term referred to the powers of skillful means at the disposal of Buddhas or bodhisattvas—specifically the impersonal and spontaneous aspects of those skillful means. Robert Sharf, *Coming to Terms with Chinese Buddhism: A Reading of the Treasure Store Treatise* (Honolulu: University of Hawai'i Press, 2002), 208.

GLOSSARY OF TERMS, PEOPLE, PLACES, AND TITLES OF TEXTS

TERMS

aimin	哀愍	chan	禪
alanruo	阿蘭若	chanfa	懺法
an	暗	chanhui	懺悔
ba	拔	chanmo	懺摩
bailian	百煉	chanwen	懺文
bao'en	報恩	chanzhu	懺主
baoji	報記	chenbai	陳白
baojuan	寶卷	chenhui	瞋恚
baosatuo	褒灑陀	chi	癡
baotai	胞胎	chu	觸
baoying	報應	chuang	瘡
baozhang	報障	chuanghou	創後
baqi	八棄	chushi	出世
benzun	本尊	chuyi	除疑
bie chang chanhui	別場懺悔	chuyuan	初緣
bingshou	秉受	ci	刺
biqiu	比丘	cishe	刺舌
biqiu moumou	比丘某某	dai	代
busa	布薩	dai shou	代受
can	參	dangti	當體
canjiu	參究	dao	道
cankui	慚愧	daochang	道場
cankui yi	慚愧衣	daojiao	道交
chan	懺	daoren	道人

daoxue	道學	gua	卦
daoyou	道友	guo	果
dawu	大悟	guo	過
dayong	大用	guobao wuyin	果報五陰
dazhai	大齋	guta	骨塔
dazhangfu xiang	大丈夫相	hao	號
diandao	顛倒	heshang	和尚
ding	定	hua	化
dingshi	定式	huanye	幻業
dingye	定業	hui	悔
duan	段	huiguo	悔過
dunji	遁跡	huizuo	悔罪
duwei	闍維	huiwang	悔亡
e	惡	huixiang	迴向
ewan	扼腕	huixiang wen	回向文
ezhang	惡障	hun	昏
fa	發	hundun	混沌
fa	法	hunpo	魂魄
fala	法臘	huo fo	活佛
falu	發露	huowei	或謂
faming	法名	ji	機
fangsheng	放生	ji	記
fangwai	方外	ji	即
fangzhang	方丈	jia	假
fannao	煩惱	jiachi	加持
fannao zhang	煩惱障	jiahu	加護
fanxing	梵行	jianyuan	監院
faqi	法器	jiao	教
fashen	法身	jiba	濟拔
fashen fumu	法身父母	jie	解
faxiang	法相	jie	偈
faxing	法性	jie	戒
fayuan	發願	jieben	戒本
fazhi	法執	jiemo	羯磨
fose	佛色	jieti	戒體
fu	孚	jiezhi	結制
fu	覆	jin	今
fu	負	jingshe	淨社
fubi	覆蔽	jingye	淨業
fuhu	覆護	jiu	鬮
gai	蓋	juan	卷
gantong	感通	jue	決
ganying	感應	juku ji	劇苦機
gaowen	告文	junzi	君子
gegu	割股	kanming	看命
gong'an	公案	kehuo	尅獲
gongguo ge	功過格	keji	克己
gou	垢	keze	尅責

kong	空	pusa shami	菩薩沙彌
kuang chan	狂禪	puti zhongzi	菩提種子
kuguo	苦果	qi	豈
kuigong	刲肱	qian	籤
ku ju	苦具	qian	乾
kun	坤	qianmao	前茅
kuxing	苦行	qianmo	千磨
lanruo	蘭若	qingfan	輕犯
li	里	qiu	求
li	理	qiwen	啟文
liaoyin	了因	qi yu	氣欲
li chan	禮懺	quanqing	勸請
li chanhui	理懺悔	ran	然
liguan	理觀	ranbi	然臂
liuchen	六塵	rantou	然頭
liugen liuchen liuyi	六根	ranxiang	然香
liushi lichan	六時禮懺	rao	繞
liushi li fo	六時禮佛	ren	仁
liuyi	六識	renti	仁體
lou	漏	risong foming	日誦佛名
lü	律	rulai chan	如來禪
lüchan	律懺	rulai zang	如來藏
lun	輪	sajiaye	薩迦耶
lunxiang	輪相	sangou	三垢
meng	蒙	sanjiao heyi	三教合一
mengwang	夢王	sanlou	三漏
menxin	捫心	sanmei	三昧
miaoli	妙理	sanshen	三身
mieye	滅業	sanshi weixin	三界惟心
miezui	滅罪	santu	三塗
ming	名	sanxue	三學
ming	命	sanye	三業
ming	冥	sanzhang	三障
minggou	冥構	shami	沙彌
mingjia	冥加	shami youpose	沙彌優婆塞
mofa	末法	shan	善
moshi	末世	shangen	善根
moxie	魔邪	shanmeng	善夢
moye	魔業	shanshu	善書
moyun	末運	shanxiang	善相
mulun xiang	木輪相	shanyou	善友
neng	能	shan zhishi	善知識
nian	念	shao	燒
nianfo	念佛	she	捨
nianfo jingshe	念佛淨社	sheli	舍利
nianpu	年譜	shen	身
pi chen	披陳	shen	神
poluotimucha	波羅提木叉	shengnian	生年

shenjian	身見	tidu	剃度
shen qu	神軀	tixing zui	體性罪
sheng'en	生恩	tongren	同人
shengsi	生死	tui	退
shenxiang	身相	tuijie	退戒
sheshen	捨身	tun	屯
shi	事	tupi	荼毗
shi	誓	wai	外
shi chanhui	事懺悔	wangshen	亡身
shi'e	十惡	wangye	往業
shi'egen	十惡根	weishi	唯識
shi li chan	事理懺	weixi	微細
shi ni xin	十逆心	weiyi	威儀
shishan	十善	wenda	問答
shishen	捨身	wozhi	我執
shi shun xin	十順心	wuai	無礙
shiwen	誓文	wuguan	五官
shixin	十心	wu hui	五悔
shi yi	十翼	wuji ye	無記業
shiyi	事儀	wulou	無漏
shi zhong jie	十重戒	wuming	無明
shou	受	wuming fannao gen benzui	無明煩惱根本罪
shu	疏	wuni	五逆
shu	舒	wusuode	無所得
shu	贖	wutong	五通
shuilu hui	水陸會	wuyuan	無緣
shuojie	說戒	wuyuan ci	無緣慈
shuozui	說罪	wuzang	五臟
si da	四大	wuzhuo	五濁
siju	四句	xian	咸
sinian	四念	xian	線
siqi	四棄	xiangxu xin	相續心
sishi	四誓	xiangying	相應
sishu	私淑	xiaomie	消滅
si xitan	四悉檀	xie	邪
sui	歲	xieshu	血書
suixi	隨喜	xin	信
suiyuan	隨緣	xin	心
suo	所	xinfa	心法
suopo	娑婆	xin gan	心感
sushan	夙善	xingjiao	行腳
suzhang	夙障	xinfa	心法
tanyu	貪欲	xingfa	行法
tao	陶	xinggong	省躬
ti	體	xingling	性靈
tianding	天定	xingmen	行門
tianxia guiren	天下歸仁		

GLOSSARY OF TERMS, PEOPLE, PLACES, AND TITLES OF TEXTS

xiqi	習氣	yuanwen	願文
xiu	修	yuanyin	緣因
xiuchi fa	羞恥法	yuchi	愚癡
xiushen	修身	yue fo fa	約佛法
xu	畜	yue guanxin	約觀心
xu	蓄	yue shi fa	約世法
xue	學	yuezhi yi li	約之以禮
xuepen	血盆	yulan pen	盂蘭盆
xun	熏	yun	運
xunxi	熏習	yunxiang	運想
xunxiu	熏修	yuposai	優婆塞
xun zhongzi	熏種子	zaoming	造命
xuwang	虛妄	zhai	齋
xuwang xingzhi	虛妄形質	zhan	占
yang	陽	zhan	展
yangde	養德	zhangdao zui	障道罪
yao	爻	zhanxing shu	占星術
ye	耶	zhe	遮
ye	業	zhengbao	正報
yejing	業境	zhengyin	正因
yexi	業習	zhengzhi	證知
yeyong	業用	zhenming	證明
yezhang	業章	zhenru	眞如
yi	義	zhenru xiang	真如相
yibao	依報	zhenxing	振興
yiduan	異端	zhi	志
yimen	義門	zhi	智
yin	陰	zhi	旨
yin	因	zhiguai	志怪
yinian	一念	zhiguan	止觀
yinian sanqian	一念三千	zhixin	至心
ying	應	zhi yu	志欲
ying	影	zhong	中
ying shou bao	應受報	zhuan	傳
yinguo	因果	zhuan	轉
yinyuan	因緣	zhuzong ronghe	諸宗融合
yishen	遺身	zi	字
yong	擁	zili zong	自立宗
youdui	幽對	zixing	自性
youxiang	有相	zixu	自序
yuan	緣	zixu	自叙
yuan	願	zizai	自在
yuan	愛	zizhuan	自傳
yuandun xinzong	圓頓心宗	zongmen	宗門
yuanfen	緣分	zui	罪
yuanrong sandi	圓融三諦	zuo	作
yuanqi	緣起	zuo chan	作懺

| zuofa chanhui | 作法懺悔 |
| zushi chan | 祖師禪 |

PEOPLE & PLACES

Baochang	寶唱
Biru Gao	壁如鎬
Chengguan	澄觀
Cheyin Hai	徹因海
Ci'en	慈恩
Ciman	慈滿
Ciyun Zunshi	慈雲尊式
Dajie	達階
Dalang	大朗
Dao'an	道安
Daoshi	道世
Daoxuan	道宣
Dayuan	達緣
Dengci	等慈
Deshan Xuanjian	德山宣鑑
Dizang	地藏
Faxian	法顯
Guanding	灌頂
Guanyin	觀音
Gude	古德
Guiyi Shou	歸一籌
Hanshan Deqing	憨山德清
He Dongru	何棟如
Hongyi	弘一
Huangbo Xiyun	黃檗希運
Huiyuan	慧遠
Jiang Qian	江謙
Jiang Yiyuan	江易園
Jianmi Chengshi	堅密成時
Jingshan	徑山
Jiuhuashan	九華山
Huijiao	慧皎
Huiyuan	慧遠
Jiaoguang	交光
Jin	金
Jin Dalian	金大蓮
Jingkong Miao	淨空妙
Jiming	隙明
Jiqing	隙清
Jiuhuashan	九華山
Kang Senghui	康僧會

Lingfeng Shan	靈峰山
Lingsheng	靈晟
Linji Yixuan	臨濟義玄
Lixian Xian	季賢獻
Mengcan	夢參
Mingxue	明學
Mudu Zhen	木瀆鎮
Ouyi Zhixu	藕益智旭
Peng Xisu	彭希涑
Qizhong	岐仲
Renyi Yuan	仁義院
Rushi Daofang	如是道昉
Ru Xing	如惺
Sengyou	僧祐
Shangchou	尚籌
Shicheng Shan	石城山
Siming Zhili	四明知禮
Songxi	松溪
Tang Zhongxiang	唐中祥
Tianma yuan	天馬院
Tiantai Shan	天台山
Wu	吳
Wuyi	無異
Xianshou	賢首
Xiaofeng	孝豐
Xi Chao	郗超
Xingdan	性旦
Xinggu Daoshou	性谷道壽
Xuanzang	玄奘
Xuehang Zhiji	雪航智機
Xueling	雪嶺
Yantou Quan	巖頭全奯
Yixing	一行
Yongming Yanshou	永明延壽
Yuan Hongdao	袁宏道
Yunqi Zhuhong	雲棲袾宏
Yu Qian	喻謙
Zhanran	湛然
Zhaonan	照南
Zhenjian	真鑒
Zhenzhi	振之
Zhiyi	智顗
Zhong	鍾
Zhong Zhifeng	鍾之鳳
Zhufalan	竺法蘭
Zhu Shixing	朱士行
Zibo Zhenke	紫柏真可
Zutang Shan	祖堂山

TEXTS

Anju lun lü gaowen	安居論律告文
Babu daoren zhuan	八不道人傳
Beihua jing	悲華經
Bing jian ou cheng	病閒偶成
Bing zhong kouhao	病中口號
Buzong chi shu	補總持疏
Chan boluomi cidi famen	禪波羅密次第法門
Chenzui qiu'ai shu	陳罪求哀疏
Chijie jiandu lüeshi	持戒犍度略釋
Chizhou xian baiwen	持呪先白文
Chi zhunti zhou yuanwen	持準提呪願文
Chongding xue pusa jiefa	重定學菩薩戒法
Cibei daochang chanfa	慈悲道場懺法
Cixie shujing yuanwen	刺血書經願文
Ci xue shujing yuanwen	刺血書經願文
Dabei chanfa	大悲懺法
Dabei tanqian yuanwen	大悲壇前願文
Dabei xingfa daochang yuanwen	大悲行法道場願文
Dabing zhong jian jingshe yuanwen	大病中啟建淨社願文
Dacheng daji dizang shilun jing	大乘大集地藏十輪經
Dafangguang fo huayanjing shu	大方廣佛華嚴經疏
Da han fuyuan	荅韓服遠
Da lianshao	荅蓮勺
Dasheng qixin lun	大乘起信論
Deyu Longhua xiu zheng chan yi	得遇龍華修證懺儀
Dizang pusa benyuan jing	地藏菩薩本願經
Dizang pusa shengde daguan	地藏菩薩聖德大觀
Duzuo shu huai er shou	獨坐書懷二首
Fahua sanmei chanyi	法華三昧懺儀
Fahua sanmei xingshi yunxiang buzhu yi	法華三昧行事運想補助儀
Fangdeng sanmei xingfa	方等三昧行法
Fangdeng tuoluoni jing	方等陀羅尼經
Fanwang hezhu	梵網合註
Fanwang jing	梵網經
Fanwang jing chanhui xingfa	梵網經懺悔行法
Fayuan zhulin	法苑珠林
Fengfa yao	奉法要
Fo pusa shangzuochan yuanwen	佛菩薩上座懺願文
Fo shuo ba daren jue jing	佛說八大人覺經
Fo shuo jie xiaozai jing	佛說戒消災經
Fo yijiao jing	佛遺教經
Foxue banyue kan	佛學半月刊
Fu hu shanzhu	復胡善住
Fu songxi fazhu	復松溪法主
Fu wang sigu	復王思鼓
Gaoseng zhuan	高僧傳
Gegu jiu Xinggu xiong	割股救惺谷兄
Gen liu ju ming	艮六居銘
Guanding jing	灌頂經
Guan quankai shi xie shu fahuajing ba	觀泉開士血書法華經跋
Guan wuliangshou jing	觀無量壽經
guan wusheng chanhui	觀無生懺悔
guanxiang chanhui	觀相懺悔
Hanshan laoren zixu nianpu shilu	憨山老人自序年譜實錄
Hongming ji	弘明集
Jiang jinguangming chan gaowen	講金光明懺告文
Jie tan chi dabei zhou jie	結壇持大悲呪偈
Jie tan chi wangsheng zhoujie	結壇持往生呪偈

Jie tan lichan bing hui xiang bu chi zhou wen	結壇禮懺并回向補持呪文	Pixie ji	闢邪集
		Pusa dichi jing	菩薩地持經
		Pusa jie jing	菩薩戒經
Jie tan li dabei chanwen	結壇禮大悲懺文	Pusa shanjie jing	菩薩善戒經
		Pusa yingluo benye jing	菩薩瓔珞本業經
Jie tan nianfo huixiang wen	結壇念佛回向文		
		Qian anju ri gongjiu wen	前安居日供關文
Jie tan shuizhai chi dabeizhou yuanwen	結壇水齋持大悲呪願文		
		Qizhou wen	起呪文
		ren	忍
Jietuo jie jing	解脫戒經	Rufo heyi jiujie bian	儒佛合一救劫編
Jiexiaozai lüeshi	戒消災略釋	Rufo zong chuan qieyi	儒佛宗傳竊議
Jimu	寄母		
Ji nankai shi xieshu fahua jing ba	寄南開士血書法華經跋	Rushan er jie	入山二偈
		Sanxue xieshu huayanjing ba	三學血書華嚴經跋
Jinguangming chan	金光明懺		
Jisi chuxi bai sanbao wen	己巳除夕白三寶文	Shanju liu shi er jie (youxu)	山居六十二偈 (有序)
Jiuhua Dizang ta qian yuanwen	九華地藏塔前願文	Shiba zuxiang zan bing xulüe	十八祖像贊並序略
La xieshu huayanjing shu	剌血書華嚴經疏	Shou pusa jie shiwen	受菩薩戒誓文
Leng qie jing	楞伽經	Shou pusa jie yi	受菩薩戒儀
Lengyan tan qizhou ji huixiang wen er jie	楞嚴壇起呪及回向二偈	Shi benguang	示本光
		Shi cangyun	示蒼雲
		Shi chuping	示初平
Li da bao'enta jie	禮大報恩塔偈	Shi cunpu	示存朴
li dabei chan yuanwen	禮大悲懺願文	Shi erjie	示爾階
		Shi huihan	示慧含
Li dabei tongdian jie	禮大悲銅殿偈	Shi jingchan	示淨禪
Li jingtu chanwen	禮淨土懺文	Shi jing jian youpoti	示淨堅優婆夷
Li jinguangming chanwen	禮金光明懺文	Shi ju fangming zhaonan	示巨方名照南
Lingfeng Zonglun	靈峰宗論	Shi shiwen	示世聞
Longju dabei chanwen	龍居禮大悲懺文	Shisong lü	十誦律
		Shi wang sihu	示王思湖
Menglin xuanjie	夢林玄解	Shi xizhan	示西瞻
Mie dingye zhou tan chan yuanwen	滅定業呪壇懺願文	Shi yangde	示養德
		Shiyi yaolüe	事義要略
Ming ban jiaxing dazingjing	明版嘉興大藏經	Shi youruo	示幽若
		Shi yuanyin	示元印
Ming baoying lun	明報應論	Shi yuanbai	示元白
Mingseng zhuan	名僧傳	Shi yuwu	示毓悟
Mituo chanfa	彌陀懺法	Shi zhilin	示智林
Mohe zhiguan	摩訶止觀	Shi ziruo	示自若
Pini shiyi ji yao	毘尼事義要略	Shu foming jing huixiang wen	書佛名經回向文
Pini shiyi yaolüe	毘尼事義要略		

GLOSSARY OF TERMS, PEOPLE, PLACES, AND TITLES OF TEXTS 201

Shou pusa jie fayi	受菩薩戒法儀	Xu chi huixiang jie	續持回向偈
Shou pusa jie shiwen	受菩薩戒誓文	Xue pusa jiefa	學菩薩戒法
Shoulengyan jing	首楞嚴經	Xuanfo pu	選佛譜
Shi miyi	示密詣	Xuanfo tu	選佛圖
Sifen lü	四分律	Xue pusa jiefa	學菩薩戒法
Sifenlü shan bu suiji jiemo shu	四分律刪補隨機羯磨疏	Yijiao jing	遺教經
		Yijing	易經
Sishiba yuan	四十八願	Yuanjue jing	圓覺經
Sishi er wen	四十二願	Yuelü lichan zongbie er shu	閱律禮懺總別二疏
Sishi'er zhang jing	四十二章經		
Ti duifeng chanshi xieshu shoujie wen hou	題對峰禪師血書受戒文後	Yuezang bi yuanwen	閱藏畢願文
		Yuezang chanwen	閱藏願文
		Yulanpen dazhai bao'en pu du daochang zongbie heshu	盂蘭盆大齋報恩普度道場總別合疏
Tiefosi lichan wen	鐵佛寺禮懺文		
Tuijie yuanqi bing zhuyu	退戒緣起并囑語		
		Yu Liaoyin ji yiqie zisu	與了因及一切緇素
Wan fanwang gaowen	完梵網告文		
		Zai li jinguangming chan wen	再禮金光明懺文
Wangsheng jingtu chanyuan yi	往生淨土懺願儀		
		Zan jingtu chan wen	讚淨土懺文
Wei fu shier zhounian qiu jian ba qi	為父十二周年求薦拔啟	Zanli Dizang pusa chan yuan yi	讚禮地藏菩薩懺願儀
		Zeng chunru xiong	贈純如兄
Wei fu huixiang wen	為父回向文	Zhaijing	齋經
Wei fumu pu qiu baji qi	為父母普求拯拔啟	Zhancha shan'e yebao jing	占察善惡業報經
Weimo jing	維摩經		
Wei mu fayuan huixiang wen	為母發願回向文	Zhancha shan'e yebao jing shu	占察善惡業報經疏
Wei mu sanzhou qiu baji qi	為母三周求拔濟啟	Zhancha shan'e yebao jing xingfa	占察善惡業報經行法
Wei mu sizhou yuanwen	為母四周願文	Zhancha shan'e yebao jing xuanyi	占察善惡業報經玄義
Wei rushi shi liuqi li chan shu	為如是師六七禮懺疏	Zhancha xingfa yuanwen	占察行法願文
Wei Xue Hangji jianglü ci xieshu yuanwen	為雪航機公講律刺血書願文	Zhiyue lu	指月錄
		Zhonglun	中論
		Zhouyi	周易
Wuchen chun cishe duan liu bie zhuyou ba jie zhi er	戊辰春刺舌端雷別諸友八偈之二	Zhouyi chanjie	周易禪解
		Zi xiang zan sanshisan shou	自像贊三十三首
Wufen lü	五分律	Zizhi lu	
Xiaojing	孝經	Zizi ri nian jiu wen	自恣日拈鬮文
Xieshu fahuajing ba	血書法華經跋	Zongjing lu	宗鏡錄
Xieshu jingangjing ba	血書金剛經跋	Zuozhuan	左傳
Xieshu jingpin ba	血書經品跋	Zutang jie dabei tan chanwen	祖堂結大悲壇懺文
Xindi guan jing	心地觀經		
Xizhai jing tu shi	西齋淨土詩		

BIBLIOGRAPHY

Allen, Sarah. *The Shape of the Turtle: Myth, Art, and Cosmos in Early China*. New York: SUNY Press, 1991.
Ames, Roger T. "On Body as Ritual Practice." In Kasulis, *Self as Body*, 149–156.
———. "The Meaning of the Body in Classical Chinese Philosophy." In Kasulis, *Self as Body*, 157–178.
An, Yanming. "Western 'Sincerity' and Confucian 'Cheng.'" *Asian Philosophy* 14, no. 2 (July 2004): 155–169.
Anderson, Benedict. *Imagined Communities: Reflections on the Origin and Spread of Nationalism*. Rev. ed. New York: Verso, 2006.
Andō Toshio 安藤俊雄. "Gūeki Chigyoku no shōgu shisō" 藕益智旭の性具思想 (Ouyi Zhixu's thoughts on intrinsic inclusiveness). *Indogaku Bukkyōgaku kenkyū* 印度学仏教学研究 (*Journal of Indian and Buddhist Studies*) 3, no. 1 (September 1954): 273–276.
Araki Kengo 荒木見悟. *Unsei shugō no kenkyū* 雲棲株宏の研究 (*A Study of Yunqi Zhuhong*). Tōkyō: Daizō shuppan kabushiki kaisha, 1985.
———. "Confucianism and Buddhism in the Late Ming." In de Bary, *The Unfolding of Neo-Confucianism*, 39–66.
———. "Chigyoku no shisō to Yōmeigaku—aru bukkyō shingakusha no ayunda michi" 智旭の思想と陽明学—ある仏教心学者の歩んだ道 (The thought of Zhixu and Wang Yangming's teachings—the road tread by a certain Buddhist Confucian). *Bukkyo Shigaku* 仏教史学 (*Buddhist Historical Studies*) 13, no. 3 (November 1967): 1–15.
Austin, J. L. *How to Do Things with Words*, ed. J. O. Urmson and Marina Sbisà. Cambridge, MA: Harvard University Press, 1975.
Bauer, Wolfgang. "Icherleben und Autobiographie irn Alteren China." *Heidelberger Jahrbücher* 8 (1964): 12–40.
Bell, Catherine. "A Precious Raft to Save the World: The Interaction of Scriptural Traditions and Printing in a Chinese Morality Book." *Late Imperial China* 17, no. 1 (June 1996): 158–200.
———. *Ritual Theory, Ritual Practice*. New York: Oxford University Press, 1992.

Benn, James. *Burning for the Buddha: Self-immolation in Chinese Buddhism*. Honolulu: University of Hawai'i Press, 2007.

———. "Where Text Meets Flesh: Burning the Body as an Apocryphal Practice in Chinese Buddhism." *History of Religions* 37, no. 4 (May 1998): 295–322.

Berling, Judith A. "Religion and Popular Culture: The Management of Moral Capital in The Romance of the Three Teachings." In Johnson, Nathan, and Rawski, *Popular Culture in Late Imperial China*, 188–218.

Bielefeldt, Carl. "Practice." In *Critical Terms for the Study of Buddhism*, ed. Donald Lopez, 229–244. Chicago: University of Chicago Press, 2005.

Birnbaum, Raoul. "Master Hongyi Looks Back: A 'Modern Man' Becomes a Monk in Twentieth-Century China." In *Buddhism in the Modern World: Adaptations of an Ancient Tradition*, ed. Steven Heine and Charles S. Prebish, 75–124. New York: Oxford University Press, 2003.

Bokenkamp, Stephen R. *Ancestors and Anxiety: Daoism and the Birth of Rebirth in China*. Berkeley: University of California Press, 2009.

Bretzke, James T. "The Notion of Sincerity (Ch'eng) in the Confucian Classics." *Journal of Chinese Philosophy* 21 (1994): 179–212.

Brokaw, Cynthia J. *The Ledgers of Merit and Demerit: Social Change and Moral Order in Late Imperial China*. Princeton: Princeton University Press, 1991.

———. "Yuan Huang (1533–1606) and The Ledgers of Merit and Demerit." *Harvard Journal of Asiatic Studies* 47, no. 1 (June 1987): 137–195.

Brook, Timothy. *Praying for Power: Buddhism and the Formation of Gentry Society in Late-Ming China*. Cambridge, MA: Harvard University Press, 1993.

Bucar, Elizabeth M. "Methodological Invention as a Constructive Project." *Journal of Religious Ethics* 36, no. 3 (2008): 355–373.

Burkert, Walter. *Creation of the Sacred: Tracks of Biology in Early Religions*. Cambridge, MA: Harvard University Press, 1996.

Campany, Robert Ford. "Living off the Books: Fifty Ways to Dodge Ming [Preallotted Lifespan] in Early Medieval China." In *The Magnitude of Ming: Command, Allotment, and Fate in Chinese Culture*, ed. Christopher Lupke, 129–150. Honolulu: University of Hawai'i Press, 2005.

———. "On the Very Idea of Religions (in the Modern West and in Early Medieval China)." *History of Religions* 42, no. 4 (2003): 287–319.

———. *Strange Writing: Anomaly Accounts in Early Medieval China*. Albany: SUNY Press, 1995.

———. "Notes on the Devotional Uses and Symbolic Functions of Sutra Texts as Depicted in Early Chinese Miracle Tales and Hagiographies." *Journal of the International Association of Buddhist Studies* 14 (1991): 28–72.

Chappell, David. "The Precious Scroll of the Liang Emperor: Buddhist and Daoist Repentance to Save the Dead." In *Going Forth: Visions of Buddhist Vinaya*, ed. William Bodiford, 40–67. Honolulu: University of Hawai'i Press, 2005.

———. "Formless Repentance in Comparative Perspective." In *Report of International Conference on Ch'an Buddhism*, 251–267. Taiwan: Foguangshan, 1990.

Chen, Jidong. "The Zhujing Risong Jiyao of the Late Ming." *Indogaku Bukkyōgaku kenkyū* 印度学仏教学研究 (*Journal of Indian and Buddhist Studies*) 55, no. 2 (March 20, 2007): 552–558.

Ch'en, Kenneth. *Buddhism in China: A Historical Survey*. Princeton: Princeton University Press, 1964.

Ch'en, Ying-shan 陳英善. "Ouyi Zhixu sixiang de tezhi ji qi dingwei wenti" 蕅益智旭思想的特質及其定位問題 (The characteristics of Ouyi Zhixu's thought and an appraisal of his status). *Zhongguo wenzhe yanjiu jikan* 中國文哲研究集刊 (*Bulletin of the Institute of Chinese Literature and Philosophy*) 8 (March 1996): 227–256. Taibei: Zhongyang yanjiuyuan zhongguo wenzhe yanjiusuo.

——. "Ouyi Zhixu Dashi Xiuxue xinlu licheng zhi tansuo" 蕅益智旭大師修學心路歷程之探索 (上) (The quest for the course of the path of cultivating the mind of Master Ouyi Zhixu [Part one]. *Shizi hou* 獅子吼 (*Lion's Roar*) 33, no. 1 (January 1994): 8–14.

——. "Ouyi Zhixu Dashi Xiuxue xinlu licheng zhi tansuo" 蕅益智旭大師修學心路歷程之探索 (下) (The quest for the course of the path of cultivating the mind of Master Ouyi Zhixu [Part two]. *Shizi hou* 獅子吼 (*Lion's Roar*) 33, no. 2 (February 1994): 14–20.

Chiang, I-pin 蔣義斌. "Tiantai zong chanyi yu shenti" 天台宗懺儀與身體 (Ritual and body in the repentance rites of Tiantai Buddhism). *Foxue Yanjiu Zhongxin Xuebao* 佛學研究中心學報 (*Journal of the Center for Buddhist Studies*), 13 (1 June 2007): 55–96. Taibei: Guoli Taiwan Daxue Foxue Yanjiu Zhongxin 國立台灣大學佛學研究中心 (The Center for Buddhist Studies, National Taiwan University).

Chih-hsu Ou-i. *The Buddhist I Ching*. Trans. Thomas Cleary. Boston: Shambhala, 1987.

Chow, Kai-wing. *The Rise of Confucian Ritualism in Late Imperial China: Ethics, Classics, and Lineage Discourse*. Stanford, CA: Stanford University Press, 1994.

Chu, William. "Bodhisattva Precepts in the Ming Society: Factors behind Their Success and Propagation." *Journal of Buddhist Ethics* 13 (2006): 1–36.

Cleary, J. C. *Zibo: The Last Great Zen Master of China*. Berkeley: Asian Humanities, 1989.

Cole, Alan. *Mothers and Sons in Chinese Buddhism*. Stanford, CA: Stanford University Press, 1998.

——. "Upside Down/Right Side Up: A Revisionist History of Buddhist Funerals in China." *History of Religions* 35, no. 4 (May 1996): 307–338.

Couture, André. "A Survey of French Literature on Ancient Indian Buddhist Hagiography." In Granoff and Shinohara, *Monks and Magicians*, 9–44.

Cox, Harvey. "Repentance and Forgiveness: A Christian Perspective." In Etzioni and Carney, *Repentance*, 21–30.

Csikszentmihalyi, Mark. *Material Virtue: Ethics and the Body in Early China*. Leiden: Brill, 2004.

De Bary, Wm. Theodore. *The Unfolding of Neo-Confucianism*. New York: Columbia University Press, 1975.

Doniger O'Flaherty, Wendy, ed. *Karma and Rebirth in Classical Indian Traditions*. Berkeley: University of California Press, 1980.

Drège, Jean-Pierre, and Dimitri Drettas, "Oniromancie." In *Divination et société dans la Chine médiévale: Étude des manuscrits de Dunhuang de la Bibliothèque nationale de France et de la British Library*, ed. Marc Kalinowski, 368–404. Paris: Bibliothèque nationale de France, 2003.

Drettas, Dimitri. "Le rêve mis en ordre. Les traités onirologiques des Ming à l'épreuve des traditions divinatoire, médicale et religieuse du rêve en Chine." PhD diss., École Pratique des Hautes Études, 2007.

Duh, Bau-Ruei 杜保瑞. "Ouyi Zhixu goutong rufo de fangfa lun tanjiu" 蕅益智旭溝通儒佛的方法論探究 (A methodological study of Master Ouyi Zhixu's works integrating Buddhism and Confucianism). *Zhexue yu wenhua* 哲學與文化 (*Monthly Review of Philosophy and Culture*) 30, no. 6 (June 2003): 340–350. Taipei: Zhexue yu wenhua yuekan zazhishi.

Dumoulin, Heinrich. *Christianity Meets Buddhism*. Trans. John C. Maraldo. La Salle, IL: Open Court, 1974.

Ebrey, Patricia. "Cremation in Sung China." *The American Historical Review* 95, no. 2 (April 1990): 406–428.

Eckel, Malcolm David. "A Buddhist Approach to Repentance." In Etzioni and Carney, *Repentance*, 122–142.

Eichman, Jennifer. "Spiritual Seekers in a Fluid Landscape: A Chinese Buddhist Network in the Wanli Period (1573–1620)." PhD diss., Princeton University, 2005.

Elman, Benjamin A. *A Cultural History of Civil Examinations in Late Imperial China*. Berkeley: University of California Press, 2000.

Elvin, Mark. "Tales of Shen and Xin: Body-Person and Heart-Mind in China during the Last 150 Years." In *Fragments for a History of the Human Body*, ed. Michel Feher with Ramona Naddaff and Nadia Tazi, 267–349. New York: Zone, 1989.

Etzioni, Amitai, and David E. Carney, eds. *Repentance: A Comparative Perspective*. New York: Rowman & Littlefield, 1997.

Fang, Lien-che Tu. "Ming Dreams." *Tsing Hua Journal of Chinese Studies* 10, no. 1 (June 1973): 61–70.

Faure, Bernard. "Relics and Flesh Bodies: The Creation of Ch'an Pilgrimage Sites." In *Pilgrims and Sacred Sites in China*, ed. Susan Naquin and Chün-fang Yü, 150–189. Taipei: SMC, 1992.

Fleischman, Avrom. *Figures of Autobiography: The Language of Self-Writing in Victorian and Modern England*. Berkeley: University of California Press, 1983.

Foguang Buddhist Dictionary (Foguang da cidian 佛光大辭典). Gaoxiong Shi: Foguang chuban she, 1989.

Foulk, Griffith. "The Ch'an Tsung in Medieval China: School, Lineage, or What?" *The Pacific World* 8 (1992): 18–31.

Foulks, Beverley. "Living Karma: The Religious Practices of Ouyi Zhixu (1599–1655)." PhD diss., Harvard University, May 2009.

———. "Duplicitous Thieves: Ouyi Zhixu's Criticism of Jesuit Missionaries in Late Imperial China." *Chung-Hwa Buddhist Journal* 21 (2008): 55–76.

Frye, Northrop. *Anatomy of Criticism*. Princeton: Princeton University Press, 1957.

Furth, Charlotte. *A Flourishing Yin: Gender in China's Medical History, 960–1665*. Berkeley: University of California Press, 1999.

Gardner, Daniel. "Confucian Commentary and Chinese Intellectual History." *The Journal of Asian Studies* 57, no. 2 (May 1998): 397–422.

Gernet, Jacques. *China and the Christian Impact: A Conflict of Cultures*. Trans. Janet Lloyd. Cambridge: Cambridge University Press, 1985.

Gethin, Rupert. *The Foundations of Buddhism*. New York: Oxford University Press, 1998.

Getz, Daniel A. "T'ien-t'ai Pure Land Societies and the Creation of the Pure Land Patriarchate." In *Buddhism in the Sung*, ed. Peter N. Gregory and Daniel A. Getz, Jr., 477–523. Honolulu: University of Hawai'i Press, 1999.

———. "Siming Zhili and Tiantai Pure Land in the Song Dynasty." PhD diss., Yale University, 1994.

Gjertson, Donald E. *Miraculous Retribution: A Study and Translation of T'ang Lin's "Ming-pao Chi."* Berkeley: Centers for South and Southeast Asia Studies, University of California at Berkeley, 1989.

———. "The Early Chinese Buddhist Miracle Tale: A Preliminary Survey." *Journal of the American Oriental Society* 101 (1981): 287–301.

Glucklich, Ariel. *Sacred Pain: Hurting the Body for the Sake of the Soul*. New York: Oxford University Press, 2001.
Goffman, Erving. *Frame Analysis: An Essay on the Organization of Experience*. New York: Harper & Row, 1974.
Gómez, Luis, trans. *Land of Bliss: The Paradise of the Buddha of Measureless Light: Sanskrit and Chinese Versions of the Sukhāvatīvyūha Sutras*. Honolulu: University of Hawai'i Press, 1996.
——. "The Bodhisattva as Wonder Worker." In *Prajnaparamita and Related Systems*, ed. Lewis Lancaster, 221–262. Berkeley: University of California Press, 1977.
Gong, Xiaokang 龔曉康. *Rong hui yu guan tong: Ouyi Zhixu sixiang yanjiu* 融会与贯通：蕅益智旭思想研究 (*Harmonization and penetration: an examination of Ouyi Zhixu's Thought*). Chengdu: Ba Shu Shushe, 2009.
Gorman, David. "The Use and Abuse of Speech-Act Theory in Criticism: A Corrective Note." *Poetics Today* 22, no. 3 (2001): 669–670.
——. "The Use and Abuse of Speech-Act Theory in Criticism." *Poetics Today* 20, no. 1 (1999): 93–119.
Gotshalk, Richard. *Divination, Order and the Zhouyi*. New York: University Press, 1999.
Granoff, Phyllis, and Koichi Shinohara, eds. *Monks and Magicians: Religious Biographies in Asia*. New York: Mosaic, 1988.
Gregory, Peter N., and Daniel A. Getz, eds. *Buddhism in the Sung*. Honolulu: University of Hawai'i Press, 1999.
Griffiths, Paul. *Religious Reading: The Place of Reading in the Practice of Religion*. New York: Oxford University Press, 1999.
Groner, Paul. "The *Fan-wang ching* and Monastic Discipline in Japanese Tendai: A Study of Annen's *Futsuu jubosatsukai kooshaku*." In *Chinese Buddhist Apocrypha*, ed. Robert E. Buswell, Jr., 251–290. Honolulu: University of Hawai'i Press, 1990.
Guo Ming 郭明. *Ming Qing Fojiao* 明清佛教 (*Ming and Qing Buddhism*). Fujian: Renmin, 1982.
Gyatso, Janet. *Apparitions of the Self: The Secret Autobiographies of a Tibetan Visionary*. Princeton: Princeton University Press, 1998.
Hadot, Pierre. *Philosophy as a Way of Life: Spiritual Exercises from Socrates to Foucault*, ed. Arnold I. Davidson, trans. Michael Chase. Oxford: Blackwell, 1995.
Hall, David L., and Roger T. Ames. *Thinking through Confucius*. Albany: SUNY Press, 1987.
Hallisey, Charles, and Anne Hansen. "Narrative, Sub-Ethics, and the Moral Life: Some Evidence from Theravāda Buddhism." *Journal of Religious Ethics* 24, no. 2 (Fall 1996): 305–327.
Hanshan Deqing. *Hanshan dashi nianpu* 憨山大師年譜 (*Annalistic Biography of Great Master Hanshan*), ed. Fushan. Taibei: Taiwan yinjing chu, 1954.
Harpham, Geoffrey Galt. *Getting It Right: Language, Literature, and Ethics*. Chicago: University of Chicago Press, 1992.
Harris, Wendell. *Interpretive Acts: In Search of Meaning*. Oxford: Clarendon, 1988.
Heim, Maria. "Buddhist Ethics: A Review Essay." *Journal of Religious Ethics* 39, no. 3 (2011): 571–584.
——. "The Aesthetics of Excess." *Journal of the American Academy of Religion* 71, no. 3 (September 2003): 531–554.
Hershock, Peter. "Valuing Karma." in Prebish, Keown, and Wright, *Revisioning Karma*, 175–228.
Hervouet, Yves. "L'Autobiographie Dans La Chine Traditionnelle." In *Études d'histoire et de littérature chinoise offertes au Professeur Jaroslav Průšek*, 107–141. Paris: Presses Universitaires de France, 1976.

Hongyi 弘一. "Ouyi dashi nianpu" 蕅益大師年譜 (Annalistic Biography of Great Master Ouyi). In Ouyi, *Ouyi dashi quanqi, Mulu* 目錄 (Catalogue): 7–35.

Hoshimiya, Chiko 星宮智光. "Gūeki Chigyoku no tengaku yihan—akesue ni okeru Shaku ten ronkubiki" 蕅益智旭の天學批判—明末における釋天論衡 (Ouyi Zhixu's criticism of Jesuit interpretations of "Tian" in the late Ming). *Tendai Gakuho* 天台学報 (*Journal of Tendai Buddhist Studies*) 29 (1986): 41–46.

Hsu Sung-Peng. *A Buddhist Leader in Ming China: The Life and Thought of Han-shan Te-ch'ing*. University Park: University of Pennsylvania Press, 1979.

Huang, Shih-Shan Susan. "Tianzhu Lingqian: Divination Prints from a Buddhist Temple in Song Hangzhou." *Artibus Asia* 67 (2007): 243–296.

Hung, Ying Chuan 洪桜娟. "Chigyoku no Jōdo nenbutsu shisō tokuni Amidakyō Yōkai chūshintoshite" 智旭の浄土念仏思想特に『阿弥陀経要解』を中心として (The thought of the Pure Land and Nianfo in the Amituojing Yaojie of Zhixu). *Ryūkoku daigaku daigakuin bungaku kenkyūka kiyō* 龍谷大学大学院文学研究科紀要 (*Ryukoku University, Bulletin of the Graduate School of Letters*) 25 (December 10, 2003): 70–84.

Hurvitz, Leon. "Chu-hung's One Mind of Pure Land and Ch'an Buddhism." In *Self and Society in Ming Thought*, ed. William Theodore de Bary, 451–481. New York: Columbia University Press, 1970.

Ikeda Rosan 池田魯参. "Chigyoku Kyōgaku to Tendai Kyōhan" 智旭教学と天台教判 (Zhixu's teachings and Tiantai classification of teaching). *Indogaku Bukkyōgaku kenkyū* 印度学仏教学研究 (*Journal of Indian and Buddhist Studies*) 25, no. 1 (December 1976): 234–238.

Iwaki, Eiki 岩城英規. "Chigyoku to Chien Shuryōgonkyo kaishaku no hikaku ni shōten o atatte" 智旭と智円『首楞厳経』解釈の比較に焦點を当てて (Zhixu and Zhiyuan's commentaries on the Shoulengyan jing). *Indogaku Bukkyōgaku kenkyū* 印度学仏教学研究 (*Journal of Indian and Buddhist Studies*) 54, no. 2 (March 20, 2006): 649–654.

——. "Chigyoku to Sangaiha Shuryōgonkyō kaishaku ni miru renzokusei to hirenzokusei" 智旭と山外派『首楞厳経』解釈に見る連続性と非連続性 (Continuities and discontinuities between [Ouyi] Zhixu and the Shanwai sect's interpretation of Śūraṃgamasamādhi sutra). *Indogaku Bukkyōgaku kenkyū* 印度学仏教学研究 (*Journal of Indian and Buddhist Studies*) 50, no. 2 (March 20, 2002): 636–641.

——. "Shuryōgonkyo gengi kara Shuryōgonkyo monku o miru" 『首楞厳経玄義』から『首楞厳経文句』をみる (A study of Zhixu's Shoulengyanjing-wenju). *Tendai Gakuho* 天台学報 (*Journal of Tendai Buddhist Studies*) 43 (November 1, 2001): 71–80.

——. "Chigyoku no kyōhanron tsūno goji jūshi to iu tokuchō ni jōten o ate" 智旭の教判論「通の五時重視」という特徴に焦点を当てて (Zhixu's Tiantai thought). *Tendai Gakuho* 天台学報 (*Journal of Tendai Buddhist Studies*) 42 (November 2000): 78–84.

——. "Gūeki Chigyoku no Shuryōgonkyo kaishaku" 蕅益智旭の『首楞厳経』解釈 (Ouyi Zhixu's interpretation of the Shoulengyan jing). *Tendai Gakuho* 天台学報 (*Journal of Tendai Buddhist Studies*) 41 (November 1999): 121–128.

——. "Chigyoku no kairitsu shisō—shinseiron to no kanrensei o chūshin ni shite" 智旭の戒律思想-心性論との関連性を中心にして」 (The precept thought of Zhixu). *Tendai Gakuho* 天台学報 (*Journal of Tendai Buddhist Studies*) 40 (November 1998): 74–81.

——. "Chigyoku no Okishinron kaishaku ni tsuite" 智旭の起信論解釈について (Zhixu's interpretation of Dashengqixinlun). *Tendai Gakuho* 天台学報 (*Journal of Tendai Buddhist Studies*) 35 (October 16, 1992): 98–102.

———. "Chigyoku shūeki zenge ni tsuite" 智旭『周易禅解』について (On Zhixu's Zhouyi Chanjie). *Indogaku Bukkyōgaku kenkyū* 印度学仏教学研究 (*Journal of Indian and Buddhist Studies*) 40, no. 1 (December 20, 1991): 121–125.
Jan Yün-hua. "The Chinese Understanding and Assimilation of Karma Doctrine." In *Karma and Rebirth: Postclassical Developments*, ed. Ronald W. Neufeldt, 145–167. Albany: SUNY Press, 1986.
———. "Review of Minmatsu Chūgoku bukkyō no kenkyū: toku ni Chikyoku o chushin to shite" (A study of Chinese Buddhism during the late Ming dynasty by focusing on the central position of Chih-hsü, by Chang Sheng-yen). *Journal of the American Oriental Society* 99, no. 1 (1979): 131.
Jiang, Qian 江謙. *Ru fo heyi jiujie pian* 儒佛合一救劫編 (Uniting Confucianism and Buddhism to save our kalpa). Shanghai: Zhongguo rufo heyi jiujie hui, 1936.
Jianmi Chengshi. "Babu daoren xuzhuan" 八不道人續傳 (Continued biography of the follower of Eight Negations). In Ouyi, *Ouyi Dashi Quanji*, 16: 10227–10232.
Johnson, David. *Ritual and Scripture in Chinese Popular Religion: Five Studies*. Berkeley: University of California Press, 1995.
———. "Communication, Class, and Consciousness in Late Imperial China." In Johnson, Nathan, and Rawski, *Popular Culture in Late Imperial China*, 34–74.
Johnson, David, Andrew J. Nathan, and Evelyn S. Rawski, eds. *Popular Culture in Late Imperial China*. Taipei: SMC, 1985.
Jones, Charles. "Pie xie ji: Collected Refutations of Heterodoxy by Ouyi Zhixu." *Pacific World* 3, no. 1 (Fall 2009): 351–408.
Kapstein, Matthew. "The Illusion of Spiritual Progress: Remarks on Indo-Tibetan Buddhist Soteriology." In *Paths to Liberation: The Mārga and Its Transformations in Buddhist Thought*, ed. Robert E. Buswell, Jr. and Robert M. Gimello, 193–224. Honolulu: University of Hawai'i Press, 1992.
Kasulis, Thomas P., ed. *Self as Body in Asian Theory and Practice*. New York: SUNY Press, 1993.
Keitley, David N. "The Shang: China's First Historical Dynasty." In *From the Origins of Civilization to 221 B.C.*, ed. Michael Loewe and Edward L. Shaughnessy. Cambridge Histories Online. New York: Cambridge University Press, 1999. doi: 10.1017/CHOL9780521470308.006.
Kelsay, John. "The Present State of the Study of Comparative Religious Ethics." *Journal of Religious Ethics* 40, no. 4 (December 2012): 583–602.
Keown, Damien. "Karma, Character, and Consequentialism." *Journal of Religious Ethics* 24 (1996): 329–350.
Kieschnick, John. *The Impact of Buddhism on Chinese Material Culture*. Princeton: Princeton University Press, 2003.
———. "Blood Writing in Chinese Buddhism." *Journal of the International Association of Buddhist Studies* 23, no. 2 (2000): 177–194.
———. *The Eminent Monk: Buddhist Ideals in Medieval Chinese Hagiography*. Honolulu: University of Hawai'i Press, 1997.
———. "Analects 12.1 and the Commentarial Tradition." *Journal of the American Oriental Society* 112, no. 4 (October–December 1992): 567–576.
Klein, Anne Carolyn. "Buddhist Understandings of Subjectivity." In *Buddhist Women and Social Justice*, ed. Karma Lekshe Tsomo, 23–34. New York: SUNY Press, 2004.
Kleine, Christoph. "'The Epitome of the Ascetic Life': The Controversy over Self-Mortification and Ritual Suicide as Ascetic Practices in East Asian Buddhism." In

Asceticism and Its Critics: Historical Accounts and Comparative Perspectives, ed. Oliver Freiberger, 153–177. New York: Oxford University Press, 2006.

Knapp, Keith Nathaniel. *Selfless Offspring: Filial Children and Social Order in Medieval China.* Honolulu: University of Hawai'i Press, 2005.

Kreinath, Jens, Jan Snoek, and Michael Stausberg, eds. *Theorizing Rituals.* Boston: Brill, 2006.

Kuo, Liying. *Confession et contrition dans le bouddhisme chinois du Ve au Xe siècle.* Paris: Publications de l'École Française d'Extrême-Orient (Monographies, no. 170), 1994.

——. "Divination, jeux de hazard et purification dans le bouddhisme chinois: Autour d'un sutra apocryhe chinois, le Zhanchajing." In *Bouddhisme et cultures locales: Quelques case de réciproques adaptations*, ed. Fukui Fumimasa and Gérard Fussman, 145–167. Paris: École française d'Extrême-Orient, 1994.

——. "La confession dans le bouddhisme mahayanique: théories et pratiques." La pensée et les hommes, 37e année, Nouvelle série 25: *Enquêtes sur le Bouddhisme*, 17–26. Bruxelles: Éditions de l'Université de Bruxelles, 1994.

Kuriyama, Shigehisa. *The Expressiveness of the Body and the Divergence of Greek and Chinese Medicine.* New York: Zone, 2002.

LaCapra, Dominick. *Rethinking Intellectual History: Texts, Contexts, Language.* Ithaca: Cornell University Press, 1983.

Lai, Whalen. "The Chan-ch'a ching: Religion and Magic in Medieval China." In *Chinese Buddhist Apocrypha*, ed. Robert Buswell, 175–206. Honolulu: University of Hawai'i Press, 1990.

Larson, Wendy. *Literary Authority and the Modern Chinese Writer: Ambivalence and Autobiography.* Durham, NC: Duke University Press, 1991.

Le Blanc, Charles. *Huai-nan Tzu: Philosophical Synthesis in Early Han Thought: The Idea of Resonance (Kan-Ying 感應) with a Translation and Analysis of Chapter Six.* Hong Kong: Hong Kong University Press, 1985.

Lejeune, Philippe. *On Autobiography.* Trans. Paul John Eakin. Minneapolis: University of Minnesota Press, 1989.

——. *Je est un autre: l'autobiographie de la littérature aux médias.* Paris: Seuil, 1980.

——. *L'Autobiographie en France.* Paris: A. Colin, 1971.

Leong, Markus. "Hanshan Deqing (1546–1623) on Buddhist ethics." PhD diss., California Institute of Integral Studies, 1994.

Lewis, Thomas A., Jonathan Wyn Schofer, Aaron Stalnaker, and Mark A. Berkson. "Anthropos and Ethics: Categories of Inquiry and Procedures of Comparison." *Journal of Religious Ethics* 33, no. 2 (2005): 177–185.

Li, Wai-yee. "Dreams of Interpretation in Early Chinese Historical and Philosophical Writings." In *Dream Cultures: Explorations in the Comparative History of Dreaming*, ed. David Shulman and Guy G. Stroumsa, 17–42. New York: Oxford University Press, 1999.

Lippiello, Tiziana. *Auspicious Omens and Miracles in Ancient China: Han, Three Kingdoms and Six Dynasties.* Monumenta Serica Monograph Series 39. Sankt Augustin: Monumenta Serica Institute, 2001.

Liu, Kwang-Ching. *Orthodoxy in Late Imperial China.* Taipei: SMC, 1994.

Liu, Shufen. "Death and Degeneration of Life: Exposure of the Corpse in Medieval Chinese Buddhism." *Journal of Chinese Religions* 28 (2000): 1–30.

Lo, Yuet Keung. "Change Beyond Syncretism: Ouyi Zhixu's Buddhist Hermeneutics of the Yijing." *Journal of Chinese Philosophy* 35, no. 2 (2008): 273–295.

Lusthaus, Dan. *Buddhist Phenomenology: A Philosophical Investigation of Yogacara Buddhism and the Ch'eng Wei-shih Lun*. London: Routledge, 2002.
Main, Jessica. "The Karma of Others: Stories from the Milindapañha and the Petavatthuaṭṭhakathā." In Prebish, Keown, and Wright, *Revisioning Karma*, 303–358.
Major, John, Sarah A. Queen, Andrew Seth Meyer, and Harold D. Roth, trans. and eds. *The Huainanzi: A Guide to the Theory and Practice of Government in Early Han China*. New York: Columbia University Press, 2010.
McDermott, James. *Development in the Early Buddhist Concept of Kamma/Karma*. New Delhi: Munshiram Manoharlal, 1984.
McGuire, Beverley Foulks. "Bringing Buddhism into the Classroom: Jiang Qian's 江謙 (1876–1942) Vision for Education in Republican China." *Journal of Chinese Religions* 39 (2011): 33–54.
Mengcan 夢參. *Zhancha shan'e yebao jing jiangji* 占察善惡業報經講記 (*Recorded talks on the Divination Sutra*), ed. Wu Bitao 吳碧濤. Rev. ed. Taipei: Fangguang wenhua, 2004.
Miles, Margaret. *Plotinus on Body and Beauty: Society, Philosophy, and Religion in Third-Century Rome*. Malden, MA: Blackwell, 1999.
Mote, Frederick. *Imperial China 900–1800*. Cambridge, MA: Harvard University Press, 1999.
Mrozik, Susanne. *Virtuous Bodies: The Physical Dimensions of Morality in Buddhist Ethics*. New York: Oxford University Press, 2007.
——. "Cooking Living Beings: The Transformative Effects of Encounters with Bodhisattva Bodies." *Journal of Religious Ethics* 32 (March 2004): 175–194.
Nattier, Jan. *Once Upon a Future Time: Studies in a Buddhist Prophecy of Decline*. Berkeley: Asian Humanities, 1991.
Nelson, Eric Sean. "Questioning Karma: Buddhism and the Phenomenology of the Ethical." In Prebish, Keown, and Wright, *Revisioning Karma*, 359–380.
Neufeldt, Ronald. *Karma and Rebirth: Post Classical Developments*. Albany: SUNY Press, 1986.
Ng, On-Cho. "Hsing (Nature) as the Ontological Basis of Practicality in Early Ch'ing Ch'eng-Chu Confucianism: Li Kuang-ti's (1642–1718) Philosophy." *Philosophy East and West* 44, no. 1 (January 1994): 79–109.
Ngai, May-Ying Mary. "From Entertainment to Enlightenment: A Study on a Cross-Cultural Religious Board Game with an Emphasis on the Table of Buddha Selection Designed by Ouyi Zhixu of the Late Ming Dynasty." PhD diss., University of British Columbia, January 2011.
Obeyesekere, Gananath. *Imagining Karma: Ethical Transformation in Amerindian, Buddhist, and Greek Rebirth*. Berkeley: University of California Press, 2002.
Ohnuma, Reiko. *Head, Eyes, Flesh, and Blood: Giving Away the Body in Indian Buddhist Literature*. New York: Columbia University Press, 2007.
——. "The Gift of the Body and the Gift of the Dharma." *History of Religions* 37, no. 4 (1998): 323–359.
Ong, Roberto K. *The Interpretation of Dreams in Ancient China*. Bochum: Studienverlag Brockmeyer, 1985.
Ouyi dashi foxue luntan lunwen huibian 蕅益大师佛学论坛论文汇编 (*Collected papers from the forum on Master Ouyi's Buddhist studies*). Anji, Zhejiang: 2007.
Ouyi Zhixu. "Babu daoren zhuan" 八不道人傳 ([Auto]biography of the follower of Eight Negations). In Ouyi, *Ouyi dashi quanji*, 16: 10219–10226.
——. *Ouyi dashi quanji* 蕅益大師全集 (The collected works of Great Master Ouyi). Taibei: Fojiao chubanshe, 1989.

Owen, Stephen. "The Self's Perfect Mirror: Poetry as Autobiography." In *The Vitality of the Lyric Voice*, ed. Shuen-fu Lin and Stephen Owen, 71–102. Princeton: Princeton University Press, 1986.

Peng Jiqing 彭際清. *Jingtu shengxian lu* 淨土聖賢録 (*Record of Pure Land Sages*). Tainan: Heyu Chubanshe, 2001.

Potter, Karl H. "The Beginnings of a List of Publications Relating to Karma and Rebirth Compiled by Karl H. Potter, with Supplementary Material by James P. McDermott." In *Karma and Rebirth in Classical Indian Traditions*, ed. Wendy Doniger O'Flaherty, 319–329. Berkeley: University of California Press, 1980.

Prasad, Rajendra. *Karma, Causation and Retributive Morality*. New Delhi: Munshiram Manoharlal, 1989.

Pratt, Mary Louise. *Towards a Speech-Act Theory of Literary Discourse*. Bloomington: Indiana University Press, 1977.

Prebish, Charles, Damien Keown, and Dale S. Wright, eds. *Revisioning Karma—The eBook*. Journal of Buddhist Ethics Online Books, 2005.

Puett, Michael. "The Haunted World of Humanity: Ritual Theory from Early China." In *Rethinking the Human*, ed. J. Michelle Molina and Donald K. Swearer, 95–111. Cambridge, MA: Harvard University Press, 2010.

Qiu, Zhonglin 邱仲麟. "Buxiao zhi xiao—Tang yilai gegu laioqin xianxiang di shehiushi chutan" 不孝之孝 隨唐以來割股療親現象的社會史初探 (The filiality of non-filiality: a sociohistorical study of the phenomenon of "slicing the flesh to heal parents" from the Tang dynasty to the modern era). *Xin shixue* 新史學 (*New Historical Studies*) 6, no. 1 (1995): 49–94.

Rappaport, Roy A. *Ritual and Religion in the Making of Humanity*. New York: Cambridge University Press, 1999.

Rawski, Evelyn S. "Economic and Social Foundations of Late Imperial Culture." In Johnson, Nathan, and Rawski, *Popular Culture in Late Imperial China*, 3–33.

Ray, Reginald A. *Buddhist Saints in India: A Study in Buddhist Values and Orientations*. New York: Oxford University Press, 1994.

Reichenbach, Bruce R. *The Law of Karma: A Philosophical Study*. London: Macmillan, 1990.

Rhi, Ki-yong. *Aux Origines Du "Tch'an Houei": Aspects Bouddhiques de la Pratique Penitentielle*. Seoul: The Korean Institute for Buddhist Studies, 1982.

Rhodes, Robert. "The Four Modes of Interpretation of the Lotus Sutra: A Note on Tendai Hermeneutics." *Tendai Gakuho* 天台学報 (*Journal of Tendai Buddhist Studies*) Special Issue (October 2007): 59–69.

Richard, Timothy. *Guide to Buddhahood: Being a Standard Manual of Chinese Buddhism*. Shanghai: Christian Literature Society, 1907.

Ricoeur, Paul. "Narrative Time." *Critical Inquiry* 7 (1980): 169–190.

Ritzinger, Justin, and Marcus Bingenheimer. "Whole-Body Relics in Chinese Buddhism— Previous Research and Historical Overview." *The Indian International Journal of Buddhist Studies* 7 (2006): 37–93.

Ruan, Guanqi 阮观其, and Shi Ciman 释慈满, eds. *Bei tianmu shan lingfeng si zhi* 北天目山灵峰寺志 (*The gazetteer of Lingfeng temple on North Tianmu mountain*). Beijing: Zhongguo wenshi chubanshe, 2007.

Santangelo, Paolo. *Sentimental Education in Chinese History: An Interdisciplinary Textual Research on Ming and Qing Sources*. Boston: Brill, 2003.

——. "Human Conscience and Responsibility in Ming-Qing China." Trans. Mark Elvin, *East Asian History* 4 (1992): 31–80.

———. "Destiny and Retribution in Late Imperial China." *East and West* 42, no. 2-4 (1992): 377-442.
Śāntideva. *The Bodhicaryāvatāra*. Trans. Kate Crosby and Andrew Skilton. Oxford: Oxford University Press, 1998.
Scarry, Elaine. *The Body in Pain: The Making and Unmaking of the World*. New York: Oxford University Press, 1985.
Schechner, Richard. *The Future of Ritual: Writings on Culture and Performance*. New York: Routledge, 1993.
Schmid, D. Neil. "Yuanqi: Medieval Buddhist Narratives from Dunhuang." PhD diss., University of Pennsylvania, 2002.
Schober, Juliane, ed. *Sacred Biography in the Buddhist Traditions of South and Southeast Asia*. Honolulu: University of Hawai'i Press, 1997.
Schopen, Gregory. "Relic." In *Critical Terms for Religious Studies*, ed. Mark C. Taylor, 256-268. Chicago: University of Chicago Press, 1998.
———. *Bones, Stones, and Buddhist Monks: Collected Papers on the Archaeology, Epigraphy, and Texts of Monastic Buddhism in India*. Honolulu: University of Hawai'i Press, 1997.
Seaman, Gary. "The Sexual Politics of Karmic Retribution." In *The Anthropology of Taiwanese Society*, ed. Emily Ahern and Hill Gates, 381-396. Stanford, CA: Stanford University Press, 1981.
Searle, John. *Expression and Meaning*. Cambridge: Cambridge University Press, 1979.
———. *Speech Acts*. Cambridge: Cambridge University Press, 1969.
Seidel, Anna. *Dabi* 茶毗 (Cremation). *Hōbōgirin* 法寶義林: *Dictionnaire Encyclopédique du Bouddhisme D'Après Les Sources Chinoises et Japonaises*. Vol. 6, 573-585. Paris: L'Académie des Inscriptions et Belles-Lettres, Institute de France, 1983.
Seligman, Adam B., Robert P. Weller, Michael J. Puett, and Bennett Simon. *Ritual and Its Consequences: An Essay on the Limits of Sincerity*. New York: Oxford University Press, 2008.
Sharf, Robert. *Coming to Terms with Chinese Buddhism: A Reading of the Treasure Store Treatise*. Honolulu: University of Hawai'i Press, 2002.
———. "On Pure Land Buddhism and Ch'an/Pure Land Syncretism in Medieval China." *T'oung Pao* 88, no. 4-5 (2002): 282-331.
———. "The Allure of Buddhist Relics." *Representations* 66 (1999): 75-99.
Shaughnessy, Edward Louis. "The Composition of the Zhouyi." PhD diss., Stanford University, 1983.
Shek, Richard Hon-chun. "Religion and Society in Late Ming: Sectarianism and Popular Thought in Sixteenth-Seventeenth Century China." PhD diss., University of California at Berkeley, 1980.
Shengkai, Shi. *Zhongguo fo jiao chan fa yanjiu* 中国佛教忏法研究 (*Research on Chinese Buddhist Repentance Rituals*). Beijing: Zong jiao wen hua chu ban she, 2004.
Shengyan 聖嚴. *Mingmo fojiao yanjiu* 明末佛教研究 (*Studies in Late Ming Buddhism*). Taibei: Dongchu, 1992.
———. "The Renaissance of Vinaya Thought During the Late Ming Dynasty of China." In *Buddhist Ethics and Modern Society: An International Symposium*, ed. Charles Wei-hsun Fu and Sandra A. Wawrytko, 41-53. New York: Greenwood, 1991a.
———. "Four Great Thinkers in Modern Chinese Buddhism." In *Buddhist Ethics and Modern Society*, ed. Charles Wei-hsun Fu and Sandra A. Wawrytko, 55-68. New York: Greenwood, 1991b.
———. "Ouyi dashi de jingtu sixiang" 藕益大師的淨土思想 (The Pure Land thought of Master Ouyi). *Xiandai Fojiao Xueshu Congkan* 現代佛教學術叢刊 (*Academic Studies of Modern Buddhism*) 65 (October 1980): 331-342.

———. *Minmatsu Chūgoku Bukkyō no kenkyū: toku ni Chigyoku no chūshin to shite* 明末中國佛教の研究：特に智旭を中心として (*A study of late Ming Buddhism: focusing especially on [Ouyi] Zhixu*). Tōkyō: Sankibo busshorin, 1975.

———. "Chigyoku no shisō to tendaigaku" 智旭の思想と天台学 (Zhixu's thought and Tiantai). *Indogaku Bukkyōgaku kenkyū* 印度学仏教学研究 (*Journal of Indian and Buddhist Studies*) 23, no. 1 (December 1975): 326–329.

———. "Chigyoku no chosaku ni arawareta hitobito no keihu" 智旭の著作にあらわれた人びとの系譜 (Genealogy of people in Zhixu's writings). *Indogaku Bukkyōgaku* kenkyū 印度学仏教学研究 (*Journal of Indian and Buddhist Studies*) 22, no. 1 (December 1973): 285–290.

Shi Darui 釋大叡. *Tiantai chanfa zhi yanjiu* 天台懺法之研究 (*Study in Tiantai Repentance Rituals*). Taibei: Fagu wenhua, 2000.

Shi Jianye 釋見曄. "Yi Ouyi Zhixu wei lie tanjiu wanming fojiao zhi 'Fuyu' neihan" 以藕益智旭為例探究晚明佛教之「復興」內函 (The Buddhist revival in late Ming China: A study with special reference to Ouyi Zhixu). *Chung-Hwa Buddhist Studies* 中華佛學研究 3 (March 1999): 207–250.

Shi Jianye. *Mingmo fojiao fazhan zhi yanjiu* 明末佛教發展之研究 (Research on the development of late Ming dynasty Buddhism). Zhonghua foxue yanjiusuo luncong (Collection of Dissertations from the Chunghwa Institute of Buddhist Studies). Taipei: Faguwenhua, 1994.

Shi Lirong 釋立融. "Ouyi zhixu zhancha chanfa zhi yanjiu" 藕益智旭占察懺法之研究 (Study of repentance rituals and divination of Ouyi Zhixu). PhD diss., Chung-Hwa Buddhist Studies Institute, 2005.

Shi Zidan 釋自澹. "Ouyi Zhixu de jielu guan" 藕益智旭的戒律觀 (Ouyi Zhixu's view of the Vinaya). *Xiangguang zhuangyan* 香光莊嚴 57 (March 1999): 140–145.

Shinoda, Masayoshi 篠田昌宜. "Chigyoku Senzatsukyō gisho ni okeru 'genzen ichinen-shin' ni tsuite" 智旭『占察経義疏』に於ける「現前一念心」について」 (A study of "The Mind of the Present Moment" [現前一念心] in Zhixu's Zhancha shan'e yebao jing shu). *Komazawa Daigaku Bukkyō Gakubu ronshū* 駒沢大学仏教学部論集 (*Collected Essays of the Buddhist Studies Department at Komazawa University*) 34 (October 31 2003): 279–290.

———. "'The Dasheng qixinlun liehwang-su' (大乘起信論裂網疏) of Zhixu (1599–1655): Quotations from the Awakening of Faith Translated by Paramartha." *Indogaku Bukkyōgaku kenkyū* 印度学仏教学研究 (*Journal of Indian and Buddhist Studies*) 52, no.1 (December 20, 2003b): 195–197.

Shioiri, Ryodo 塩入良道. "Chūgoku shoki bukkyō ni okeru raisan—Ritsu ni kankei nai zange no jirei" 中国初期仏教における礼懺—律に関係ない懺悔の事例 (Repentance in early Chinese Buddhism). *Bukkyō shisō ronshū* 仏教思想論集 Narita (1984): 531–544.

———. "Zange no nai kyōten ni ikyōshita zenbō" 懺悔のない経典に依拠した懺法 (Repentance rituals based on scriptures without repentance). In *Chūgoku no shūkyō shisō to kagaku: Makio Ryōkai Hakushi shōju kinen ronshū* 中国の宗教・思想と科学：牧尾良海博士頌寿記念論集 (*Religion, thought, and science in China: A festschrift in honor of Professor Makio Ryōkai*), 189–202. Tōkyō: Kokusho kankōkai, 1984.

———. "Shishū-sammai ni atsukawareta Chigi no zenbō" 四種三昧に扱われた智顗の懺法 (Zhiyi's repentance rituals treating four kinds of samādhi). *Indogaku bukkyōgaku kenkyū* 印度学仏教学研究 (*Journal of Indian and Buddhist Studies*) 8, no. 2 (1960): 269–274.

———. "Zenbō no seritsu to Chigi no tachiba" 懺法の成立と智顗の立場 (The establishment of repentance rituals and Zhiyi's position). *Indogaku bukkyōgaku kenkyū* 印度学仏教学研究 (*Journal of Indian and Buddhist Studies*) 7, no. 2 (1959): 45-55.
Skinner, G. William. "Social Mobility Strategies in Late Imperial China: A Regional Systems Analysis." In *Regional Analysis*, ed. Carol A. Smith, 327-364. New York: Academic, 1976.
Smith, Joanna Handlin. *The Art of Doing Good: Charity in Late Ming China*. Berkeley: University of California Press, 2009.
———. "Liberating Animals in Ming-Qing: Buddhist Inspiration and Elite Imagination." *Journal of Asian Studies* 58, no. 1 (February 1999): 51-84.
Smith, Jonathan Z. "The Bare Facts of Ritual." In *Imagining Religion: From Babylon to Jonestown*, 53-65. Chicago: University of Chicago Press, 1982.
Smith, Kidder, Jr., Peter K. Bol, Joseph A. Adler, and Don J. Wyatt, eds. *Sung Dynasty Uses of the I Ching*. Princeton: Princeton University Press, 1990.
Smith, Richard J. *Fathoming the Cosmos and Ordering the World: The Yijing and Its Evolution in China*. Charlottesville: University of Virginia Press, 2008.
———. "Divination in Ch'ing Dynasty China." In *Cosmology, Ontology, and Human Efficacy*, ed. Richard Smith and D. W. K. Kwok, 141-178. Honolulu: University of Hawai'i Press, 1993.
———. *Fortune-Tellers and Philosophers: Divination in Traditional Chinese Society*. San Francisco: Westview, 1991.
Songhua 松華, and Zhaoyuan Chen 陈兆元. *Dong Tianmu Zhao ming chan si zhi* 東天目昭明禅寺志 (*The gazetteer of Zhaoming Chan temple on East Tianmu mountain*). Reprint. Yangzhou Shi: Jiangsu Guangling gu ji ke yin she, 1996.
Sørensen, Henrik. "Optional Causality: Karma, Retribution, and the Transference of Merit in the Context of Popular Chinese Buddhism." *Horin* 6 (1999): 171-189.
Stalnaker, Aaron. *Overcoming Our Evil: Human Nature and Spiritual Exercises in Xunzi and Augustine*. Washington, DC: Georgetown University Press, 2006.
———. "Comparative Religious Ethics and the Problem of 'Human Nature.'" *Journal of Religious Ethics* 33, no. 2 (2005): 187-225.
Stevenson, Daniel. "Where Meditative Theory Meets Practice." *Tendai Gakuho* 天台學報 (*Journal of Tendai Buddhist Studies*) Special Issue (October 2007): 71-142.
———. "The 'Hall for the Sixteen Contemplations' as a Distinctive Institution for Pure Land Practice in Tiantai Monasteries of the Song (960-1279)." In *Buddhism in Global Perspective*, ed. Kalpakam Sankaranarayan, Ravindra Panth, and Ichigo Ogawa, Vol. 2, 147-204. Mumbai: Somaiya, 2004.
———. "Text, Image, and Transformation in the History of the Shuilu fahui, the Buddhist Rite for Deliverance of Creatures of Water and Land." In *Cultural Intersections in Later Chinese Buddhism*, ed. Marsha Weidner, 30-70. Honolulu: University of Hawai'i Press, 2001.
———. "Protocols of Power: Tz'u-yun Tsun-shih (964-1032) and T'ien-t'ai Lay Buddhist Ritual in the Sung." In *Buddhism in Sung Dynasty China*, ed. Peter N. Gregory and Daniel A. Getz Jr., 340-408. Honolulu: University of Hawai'i Press, 1999.
———. "The T'ien-T'ai Four Forms of Samādhi and Late North-South Dynasties, Sui, and Early T'ang Buddhist Devotionalism." PhD diss., Columbia University, 1987.
Stock, Brian. *Augustine the Reader: Meditation, Self-Knowledge and the Ethics of Interpretation*. Cambridge, MA: Belknap Press of Harvard University Press, 1996.

———. *Listening for the Text: On the Uses of the Past*. Baltimore: Johns Hopkins University Press, 1990.
Strickmann, Michel. *Chinese Poetry and Prophecy: The Written Oracle in East Asia*. Stanford, CA: Stanford University Press, 2005.
———. "Dreamwork of Psycho-Sinologists: Doctors, Taoists, Monks." In *Psycho-Sinology: The Universe of Dreams in Chinese Culture*, ed. Carolyn T. Brown, 25–46. Lanham, MD: University Press, 1988.
Strong, John S. *The Legend and Cult of Upagupta: Sanskrit Buddhism in North India and Southeast Asia*. Princeton: Princeton University Press, 1992.
———. *The Legend of King Aśoka: A Study and Translation of the Aśokāvadāna*. Princeton: Princeton University Press, 1983.
Sullivan, Lawrence E. "Body Works: Knowledge of the Body in the Study of Religion." *History of Religions* 30, no. 1 (1990): 86–99.
Swanson, Paul. *Foundations of T'ien-t'ai Philosophy*. Berkeley: Asian Humanities, 1989.
Swearer, Donald. "Focus Editor's Comments on 'Ethnography, Anthropology, and Comparative Religious Ethics' Essays." *Journal of Religious Ethics* 38, no. 3 (September 2010): 393–394.
Tadao Sakai 酒井忠夫. *Chūgoku zensho no kenkyu* 中國善書の研究 (Studies of Chinese Morality Books). Tōkyō: Kobundo, 1960.
Tambiah, Stanley. *The Buddhist Saints of the Forest and the Cult of Amulets*. Cambridge: Cambridge University Press, 1984.
Tatz, Mark, trans. *Buddhism and Healing: Demiéville's Article "Byō" from Hōbōgirin*. Lanham, MD: University Press, 1985.
Taylor, Rodney. "The Centered Self: Religious Autobiography in the Neo-Confucian Tradition." *History of Religions* 17, no. 3–4 (February–May 1978): 266–283.
Teiser, Stephen. *Reinventing the Wheel: Paintings of Rebirth in Medieval Buddhist Temples*. Seattle: University of Washington Press, 2006.
———. *The Scripture on the Ten Kings and the Making of Purgatory in Medieval Chinese Buddhism*. Honolulu: University of Hawai'i Press, 1994.
———. "The Growth of Purgatory." In *Religion and Society in Tang and Song China*, ed. Peter Gregory and Patricia Ebrey, 115–145. Honolulu: University of Hawai'i Press, 1993.
———. "'Having Once Died and Returned to Life': Representations of Hell in Medieval China." *Harvard Journal of Asiatic Studies* 48, no. 2 (December 1988): 433–464.
———. *The Ghost Festival in China*. Princeton: Princeton University Press, 1988.
Tonegawa Kōkō 利根川浩行. "Gūeki Chigyoku no ingotogaku" 藕益智旭の戒学 (Ouyi Zhixu's Vinaya thought). *Indogaku Bukkyōgaku kenkyū* 印度学仏教学研究 (Journal of Indian and Buddhist Studies) 29, no. 1 (December 1980): 350–353.
Tu, Wei-ming. "The Neo-Confucian Concept of Man." *Philosophy East and West* 21, no. 1 (January 1971), 79–87.
Twitchett, Denis. "Problems of Chinese Biography." In *Confucian Personalities*, ed. Arthur F. Wright and Denis Twitchet, 24–42. Stanford, CA: Stanford University Press, 1962.
Victoria, Brian. "The Reactionary Use of Karma in Twentieth-Century Japan." In Prebish, Keown, and Wright, *Revisioning Karma*, 411–434.
Wagner, Rudolf G. "Imperial Dreams in China." In *Psycho-Sinology: The Universe of Dreams in Chinese Culture*, ed. Carolyn T. Brown, 11–24. Lanham, MD: University Press, 1988.

Wang, Hua 王华. *Bei Tianmu Lingfeng si zhi* 北天目灵峰寺志 (*The gazetteer of Lingfeng temple on North Tianmu mountain*). Yangzhou Shi: Jiangsu Guangling guji keyin she, 1996.

Wang, Juan 汪娟. "Lidai dizang chanyi xilun" 歷代地藏懺儀析論 (Examination of confession liturgies of Ksitigarbha), *Foxue yanjiu zhongxin xuebao* 佛學研究中心學報 (*Journal of the Center for Buddhist Studies*) 4 (July 1999): 169–207. Taibei: Guoli Taiwan daxue foxue yanjiu zhongxin 國立台灣大學佛學研究中心 (The Center for Buddhist Studies, National Taiwan University).

Watson, James L., and Evelyn S. Rawski, eds. *Death Ritual in Late Imperial and Modern China*. Berkeley: University of California Press, 1988.

Wayman, Alex. "Significance of Dreams in India and Tibet." *History of Religions* 7, no. 1 (August 1967): 1–12.

Weintraub, Karl J. "Autobiography and Historical Consciousness." *Critical Inquiry* 1, no. 4 (June 1975): 821–848.

Welch, Holmes. *The Practice of Chinese Buddhism: 1900–1950*. Cambridge, MA: Harvard University Press, 1967.

Weller, Robert P., and Peter K. Bol. "From Heaven-and-Earth to Nature: Chinese Concepts of the Environment and Their Influence on Policy Implementation." In *Confucianism and Ecology: The Interrelation of Heaven, Earth, and Humans*, ed. Mary Evelyn Tucker and John Berthrong, 313–341. Cambridge, MA: Harvard University Press, 1998.

Welter, Albert. *The Meaning of Myriad Good Deeds: A Study of Yung-ming Yen-shou and the Wan-shan t'ung-kuei chi*. New York: Lang, 1992.

———. "The Contextual Study of Chinese Buddhist Biography: The Example of Yung-ming Yen-shou (904–975)." In Granoff and Shinohara, *Monks and Magicians*, 247–268.

White, Hayden. "Introduction: Historical Fiction, Fictional History, and Historical Reality." *Rethinking History* 9, no. 2–3 (June–September): 147–157.

Williams, Bruce. "Mea Maxima Vikalpa: Repentance, Meditation, and the Dynamics of Liberation in Medieval Chinese Buddhism, 500–650 C.E." PhD diss., University of California–Berkeley, 2002.

Williams, Paul. "Some Mahāyāna Buddhist Perspectives on the Body." In *Religion and the Body*, ed. Sarah Coakley, 205–230. New York: Cambridge University Press, 1997.

Wright, Arthur. *Buddhism in Chinese History*. Stanford, CA: Stanford University Press, 1959.

———. "Values, Roles and Personalities." In *Confucian Personalities*, ed. Arthur F. Wright and Denis Twitchet, 2–23. Stanford, CA: Stanford University Press, 1962.

Wright, Dale. "Critical Questions Towards a Naturalized Concept of Karma in Buddhism." In Prebish, Keown, and Wright, *Revisioning Karma*, 9–34.

Wu, Jiang. *Enlightenment in Dispute: The Reinvention of Chan Buddhism in Seventeenth-Century China*. New York: Oxford University Press, 2008.

Wu, Pei-Yi. *The Confucian's Progress: Autobiographical Writings in Traditional China*. Princeton: Princeton University Press, 1990.

———. "Self-Examination and Confession of Sins in Traditional China." *Harvard Journal of Asiatic Studies* 39, no. 1 (June 1979): 5–38.

———. "The Spiritual Autobiography of Te-ch'ing." In de Bary, *The Unfolding of Neo-Confucianism*, 67–91.

Wu, Yenna. "Moral Ambivalence in the Portrayal of Gegu in Late Imperial Chinese Literature." In *Ming Qing wenhua xinlun*, ed. Wang Chengmian, 247–274. Taipei: Wenjin chubanshe, 2000.

Yang Qiuman 杨秋满. "Wanming Ouyi Zhixu zhi Dizang Xinyang" 晚明蕅益智旭之地藏信仰 (The Dizang worship of Ouyi Zhixu in the late Ming). PhD diss., Huafan University, 2005.

Yen, Chun-min. "Shadows and Echoes of the Mind—Hanshan Deqing's (1546–1623) Syncretic View and Buddhist Interpretation of the Daodejing." PhD diss., University of Arizona, 2004.

Yetts, Perceval. "Notes on the Disposal of Buddhist Dead in China." *Journal of the Royal Asiatic Society* (1991): 699–725.

Yifa. *The Origins of Buddhist Monastic Codes in China*. Honolulu: University of Hawai'i Press, 2002.

Young, Serinity. "Buddhist Dream Experience: The Role of Interpretation, Ritual, and Gender." In *Dreams: A Reader on Religious, Cultural, and Psychological Dimensions of Dreaming*, ed. Kelly Bulkeley, 9–28. New York: Palgrave, 2001.

———. *Dreaming in the Lotus: Buddhist Dream Narrative, Imagery and Practice*. Boston: Wisdom, 1999.

Yü Chün-fang. "Some Ming Buddhist Responses to Neo-Confucianism." *Journal of Chinese Philosophy* 15 (1988): 371–413.

———. *The Renewal of Buddhism of China: Chu-hung and the Late Ming Synthesis*. New York: Columbia University Press, 1981.

———. "Ming Buddhism." In *The Cambridge History of China*, ed. Denis Twitchett and Frederick W. Mote, Vol. 8, 893–952. Cambridge: Cambridge University Press, 1978.

———. "Chu-hung and Lay Buddhism in the Late Ming." In de Bary, *The Unfolding of Neo-Confucianism*, 93–140.

Yu, Jimmy. *Sanctity and Self-Inflicted Violence in Chinese Religions. 1500–1700*. New York: Oxford University Press, 2012.

———. "Bodies and Self-Inflicted Violence in Sixteenth- and Seventeenth-Century China." PhD diss., Princeton University, 2008.

Yu Qian 喻謙. *Xinxu gaoseng zhuan siji* 新續高僧傳四集 (New continued biographies of eminent monks in four volumes), ed. Yu Mei'an 喻昧庵. Taipei: Guangwen, 1977.

Yü, Ying-shi. "'O Soul, Come Back!' A Study in the Changing Conceptions of the Soul and Afterlife in Pre-Buddhist-China." *Harvard Journal of Asiatic Studies* 47, no. 2 (1987): 363–395.

Zeitlin, Judith. *Historian of the Strange: Pu Songling and the Chinese Classical Tale*. Stanford, CA: Stanford University Press, 1993.

"Zhejiang Anji Beitianmu Lingfeng Si." Accessed June 9, 2011. http://www.btmlfs.org.

Zhenhua, ed. *Zhongguo fojiao renming da cidian* 中國佛教人名大辭典 (Chinese Buddhist biographical dictionary). Shanghai: Shanghai cishu chubanshe, 1999.

Zhiru Ng. *The Making of a Savior Bodhisattva: Dizang in Medieval China*. Honolulu: University of Hawai'i Press, 2007.

———. "The Formation and Development of the Dizang 地藏 Cult in Medieval China." PhD diss., University of Arizona, 2000.

Zhou Qi 周齐. *Ming dai fo jiao yu zheng zhi wen hua* 明代佛教与政治文化 (*Ming dynasty Buddhism and political culture*). Beijing: Renmin, 2005.

———. "Ouyi Zhixu yu Tiantai zong yi Lingfeng zonglun wei zhongxin" 蕅益智旭与天台宗——以〈灵峰宗论〉为中心 (Ouyi Zhixu and the Tiantai tradition—focusing on the Lingfeng Zonglun). *Dongnan wenhua* 东南文化 (*Southeast Culture Journal*) 1 (1998): 70–75.

Ziporyn, Brook. "Li (Principle, Coherence) in Chinese Buddhism." *Journal of Chinese Philosophy* 30, no. 3–4 (September 2003): 501–524.

Zürcher, Erik. "The Jesuit Mission in Fukien in Late Ming Times: Levels of Response." In *Development and Decline of Fukien Province in the 17th and 18th Centuries*, ed. E. B. Vermeer, 417–458. Leiden: Brill, 1990.

———. "Beyond the Jade Gate: Buddhism in China, Vietnam, and Korea." In *The World of Buddhism*, ed. Heinz Bechert and Richard Gombrich, 193–211. London: Thames and Hudson, 1984.

———. *The Buddhist Conquest of China: The Spread and Adaptation of Buddhism in Early Medieval China*. Leiden: Brill, 1972.

INDEX

action (*ye*): karma and, 12–13; in *Lingfeng Zonglun*, 12; terminology, 12; wholesome and unwholesome, 43, 163*n*40
afflictions: mental, 70; ten, 100, 183*n*30; three poisons and, 59, 99–100
Ames, Roger, 181*n*8
Amitābha Buddha: forty-eight vows of, 84–85; Hanshan's dream of, 28; king of vows, 92; in name of Ouyi, 154*n*28; vows to, 86
Amitābha repentance (*Mituo chanfa*), 62–63
Analects, 25, 33–34, 127, 154*n*32, 190*n*6
Anderson, Benedict, 157*n*52
anxiety: filiality and, 86; karma and, 39; lots and, 40; mother and, 107; precepts and, 36, 70, 99–100; punishment and, 13; role in ritual, 60
apocrypha: burning and, 182*n*16; divination and, 5, 45, 161*n*18; repentance rituals and, 53, 80
Araki Kengo, 147*n*18
asceticism. *See* bodily practices
attachment: to *dharma*s/phenomena, 105; illness and, 117; to self, 50–51, 105, 117
autobiography: Augustine's *Confessions* and, 20; "autobiographical pact" of, 19; Chinese, 19–22; fiction and, 19–20; individuality and, 19–20; literary dimensions of, 18; of Ouyi Zhixu, 17–19, 33–36; retrospection in, 20; rhetoric of, 22–23; spiritual formation and, 20; Western, 19, 32
[Auto]biography of the Follower of Eight Negations (*Babu daoren zhuan*), 23–29, 33–36, 133–42; nonsectarian message of, 22–26; summary of, 24–26
Awakening of Faith, 43

Bell, Catherine, 4, 6
Benn, James, 30, 182*n*16
Bielefeldt, Carl, 6
Biographies of Eminent Monks, 22, 31, 113, 154*n*24
biography (*zhuan*): bias of, 30; Buddhist, 22, 25, 28; Chinese (*zhuan*), 21, 25; conventions of, 25; elements of, 21; exemplars in, 22; genre of, 30; institutions and, 21; officials and, 21; of Ouyi Zhixu, 29–33; reliability of, 158*n*62; religious/sacred, 22, 28, 153*n*23. *See also* hagiography
blood, 184*n*47
blood writing (*xieshu*), 103–12; Buddhist precedent for, 95; ethics and, 94; function of, 103; Huayan Sutra and, 104; mechanics of, 104–5; mother and, 106–8; origins of, 103–4; pain and, 111; writing and, 111–12

INDEX

bodhicitta: Dizang and, 159n78, 178n35; in Ouyi's vows, 86-87; as protection from hell, 89
bodhisattva: bodies of, 93-94, 104; capacity to eliminate sins, 87-88; emotions and, 7, 10, 47-48, 54-58, 65; Ouyi's vision of himself as, 82-83, 86-92; path, 84, 175n6; precepts, 38-39, 67-68, 171n78; Pure Land and, 85; shame/sincerity, 7, 10; stimulus-response and, 6, 51-52, 60, 72, 80; supernatural powers of, 40, 175n8; vow of, 84, 90
bodily practices, 181n6; pain and, 117, 187n105
body, 112-16, 124; of bodhisattvas, 93-94, 104; of Buddhas, 115-16; Buddhist view of, 112-13, 115-16; filial piety and, 106-7; Four Noble Truths and, 118; generation and, 113-14; human, 112, 116; as karmic product, 34-35, 106, 114-15; karmic retribution and, 94; karmic transformation and, 94, 104; medical view of, 112; spiritual development and, 94; suffering and, 118-19; three karmic activities and, 106
Book of Changes: prominence of, 40. See also *Yijing*, *Zhouyi*
Brahma's Net repentance, 53, 65, 66-71
Brook, Timothy, 146n12
Buddha: body of, 115-16; nature, 47-48; role in stimulus-response, 51-52; supernatural powers of, 40
Buddhist studies: Protestant bias in, 4
burning, 96-103; bodhisattvahood and, 103; creativity of, 99; (Buddhist) doctrine and, 100-101; ethics and, 94; function of, 97-98, 102-3; ordination and, 182n16; punishment and, 99; transformation and, 98

Carney, David, 57
cause and effect: karma and, 7, 54; linchpin for transformation, 54, 69-71; retribution and, 12
Chan: "Crazy Chan," 105, 108-9; Ouyi's autobiography and, 25-27; Ouyi's connection to, 13-14; Chan of the Patriarchs (*zushi chan*), 18; Tathāgata Chan (*rulai chan*), 13, 18
Ch'en, Ying-shan, 14, 152n4
Chengshi. *See* Jianmi Chengshi
Cheng weishi lun, 34

Cheng Yi, 7
Ch'en Ying-shan, 14
Cheyin Hai, 110
Ciyun Zunshi, 53, 62-65, 71
Cole, Alan, 106-8
Collected Essays Refuting Heterodoxy (*Pixie ji*), 5; audience of, 5, 24; epithets in, 23; genre of, 5; Jesuits and, 5
commentary (*shu*): on *Analects*, 33-34; Chinese literati and, 5; on *Divination Sutra*, 45-46; Ouyi casting lots to determine, 38; three features of, 147n20, on *Zhouyi*, 41-42, 46
community: "imagined," 28; nonsectarian, 21, 29; religious, 21, 29; "textual," 5-6, 21, 26
compassion: stimulus-response and, 72, 87-92; substitution and, 83
confession: Chinese Buddhist term for, 57; generic, 58; individualized, 70-71; Jesuit, 5; Ouyi's own, 77-78; repentance rituals and, 57
confidence: divination and, 39, 49; Dizang and, 74-75, 88; stimulus-response and, 51-52
Confucius, 25, 28, 33, 41, 134
consciousness: Consciousness-Only (*weishi*), 25, 191n13; storehouse, 50-51
Couture, André, 154n23
cremation, 30, 119-20; of Buddha, 187n122; Chinese acceptance of, 188n123, 189n135; Chinese term for, 187n119; history of, 120
crimes (*zui*), 57. *See also* sins, transgressions
Csikszentmihalyi, Mark, 181n4

Daoan, 58
death: illness and, 89-90; of parents, 25, 86; practices, 119-20; trope of, 27-29; universality of, 105-7
decline of the Dharma, 43, 54, 65, 71-72, 110, 125
defilement: body and, 96, 181n13; five, 72, 172n95; illness and, 117-19
devotion: of Ouyi to Dizang, 55, 64, 76; role in eliminating karma, 80; role in rituals, 57-58, 62; stimulus-response and, 87
dhāraṇī: of Dizang, 55, 77; Fangdeng, 59; of Great Compassion, 55-56; of Guanyin, 24; Ouyi's karma and, 100

dharma-dhātu, 86, 91–92
Dharmākara, 84, 85
dharmakāya, 77, 119
dharmas: attachment to, 48; emptiness of, 50, 69, 70–72; of transformation, 102
disciples: of Ouyi Zhixu, 30–31
divination, 37–52; belief and, 4; Buddhist, 44, 163*n*46; Chinese types of, 40–44; cognition and, 4; confidence and, 39, 49; as a karmic diagnostic, 37–38, 40, 46–52, 82, 92–93; Ouyi's performance of, 25–26, 38–40, 160*n*3, 161*n*22; prohibition of, 37, 160*n*2; self-understanding and, 40; spiritual formation and, 47–49; stimulus-response and, 41; trope of, 27
Divination repentance, 53, 65, 71–75, 77; role of Dizang in, 72; ten mentalities in, 75
Divination Sutra, 42–46; 44, 55, 66, 71, 77; commentary on, 45; confidence and, 39, 49; karma and, 37; origin of, 44; Ouyi's performance of, 46; summary of, 45; wheels in, 43
Dizang: *dhāraṇī* of, 55, 77, 99; *Divination Sutra* and, 42, 45; fixed karma and, 54–55, 78–79; as judge, 17–18, 131; as mother, 72, 92; Ouyi Zhixu and, 25, 55, 83, 159*n*78; as savior of the penitent, 55, 74, 76–77; tower of, 55, 56, 92, 98; vow of, 52
Dizang repentance, 75–80; Dizang as savior figure, 76–77; ritual protocol of, 77
dreams: causes of, 156*n*48; function of, 155*n*40, 155*n*41; trope of, 27–29; two souls and, 156*n*47
Duke of Zhou, 41
Dumoulin, Heinrich, 169*n*43

Ebrey, Patricia, 188*n*123
Eichman, Jennifer, 145*n*5, 146*n*12
eight negations (*babu*), 23–24
Elman, Benjamin, 162*n*29
emotions: confession and, 70–71; role in ritual, 7, 62, 68, 80; stimulus-response and, 87; ten mentalities and, 69–70
Emperor Wen of the Chen, 58
Emperor Wu of the Liang, 55, 58
emptiness: cause and effect and, 79; of *dharmas*, 71; erroneous conception of, 79–80; ethics and, 79–80; interdependence

and, 79–80; of karma, 61, 72, 128; karmic retribution and, 72; principle of, 8, 54, 60–61; ritual and, 68; of sin, 75, 79
enlightenment: bodily practices and, 106, 114–19; Buddhist, 25–26, 33–35, 94; Confucian, 24–25, 33–34; *Divination Sutra* and, 49; religious biographies and, 22
epithets. *See* names
ethics: Buddhist, 1, 145*n*2; comparative religious, 3, 13; constructive discourse and, 130, 189*n*1; descriptive, 1; emptiness and, 79–80; virtue, 1, 145*n*2
Etzioni, Amitai, 57
evil: deeds, 167*n*33

Fahua sanmei chanyi. *See Lotus Samādhi Repentance*
failure: illness and, 88; to uphold precepts, 39, 45–46, 82
faith: in cause and effect, 69–70; divination and, 39, 49; repentance and, 72–73
Fangdeng dhāraṇī sutra (*Fangdeng tuoluoni jing*), 59
Fangdeng sanmei xingfa (Fangdeng repentance), 59–61, 67
Fanwang jing chanhui xingfa. *See* Brahma's Net repentance
fate: extrapolation, 162*n*29; Ming dynasty and, 41; morality books and, 11–12
faults: concealing of, 69, 177*n*26. *See also* sins, transgressions
Faure, Bernard, 188*n*130
filial piety, 95–96; Ouyi's vows and, 86–87
filial slicing, 95–96; filial piety and, 95; literati and, 95; social purpose of, 96; spread of, 181*n*10
fixed karma: definition of, 12; of Ouyi Zhixu, 53–55, 78–79
Fleischman, Avrom, 152*n*7, 152*n*9
friends, 29, 39, 108–9, 179*n*47
Frye, Northrop, 19
Fujian province, 45, 46
Furth, Charlotte, 113, 181*n*7, 184*n*47
Fu Xi, 41

ganying. *See* stimulus-response
Gardner, Daniel, 5, 46
Getz, Daniel, 62, 63
Glucklich, Ariel, 117

goodness (ren), 159n81; in Analects, 34; use in repentance, 50
Great Compassion repentance, 55–56, 62
Griffiths, Paul, 147n20
Guanding jing (Consecration sutra), 38
Guan wuliangshou jing (Contemplation sutra), 63
Guanyin: in Hanshan Deqing's autobiography, 28; in Ouyi's biography, 22, 24–25; Ouyi's repentance rituals to, 55, 74; Ouyi's vows and, 85–86
Gude, 109; in autobiography, 135
Guiyi Shouchou, 108–9
Gyatso, Janet, 22

hagiography: Augustine's Confessions and, 19; Buddhist, 19, 22; of eminent monks, 22; exemplars in, 22; Ouyi's autobiography and, 25, 28; religious development and, 19; tropes of, 28
Hallisey, Charles, 1
Hansen, Anne, 1
Hanshan Deqing, 2, 25, 27–29; autobiography of, 28, 155n35, 155n39, 156n49–51; Caoxi and, 191n10; Ouyi's praise of, 157n57
Han Wudi, 41
Heim, Maria, 1, 2, 145n2
hell: Avīci, 167n32, 173n100; as Ouyi's karmic retribution, 77–78, 85; Ouyi's vows to those in, 87
Hershock, Peter, 130
Hervouet, Yves, 20, 153n12–13
Hongyi, 2, 30; biography of Ouyi, 32
Huayan Sutra, 104
Huisi, 58
Huiyuan, 10–11, 128–29
humility, 128

illness, 116–19; benefits of, 117–18; bodhisattvas and, 94; forbearance and, 117–18; karma and, 94, 99–100; moral failures and, 88; of Ouyi Zhixu, 89–90; pain and, 117
impermanence: of body, 94, 113, 115; illness and, 117–18, 124; life and death and, 74, 107
interdependence: emptiness and, 79–80
Iwaki Eiki, 14

Jan Yün-hua, 10, 38
Jesuits, 5, 15, 35
Jiang Qian, 32–33, 159n80

Jiangsu Province, 24
Jianmi Chengshi, 8, 81, 95, 119, 121; biography of Ouyi, 30–31
Jiangnan, 25
Jingshan, 25, 34
Jiuhuashan, 40, 46, 55, 56, 76, 92, 98; lot chosen at, 40

Kang Senghui, 41
karma: action and, 12–13; body and, 34–35, 94; Chinese Buddhist ideas of, 10–11; Chinese terms for, 9; causes and conditions (yinyuan), 35, 49–50, 72, 148n49; as a comparative category, 3, 131; constructive discourse about, 130; definition of, 9; divination of, 40; elimination of, 9–10, 13, 54–55, 69–70, 73, 78–79; emptiness and, 128; internal rewards of, 130; interpretation of, 125; "lived karma," 4, 130; "living karma," 13; mechanistic view of, 9–10, 127–28; morality and, 131; motivating force of, 130; as narrative device, 33–36; naturalized concept of, 130; opacity of, 10–11, 128; organic view of, 9–10, 50–51; Ouyi's depiction of, 3–4; relationships and, 126; religious practices and, 129; repentance and, 54; retribution and, 9–10, 49–50; revelation of, 50, 177n26; terminology, 12–13; transformative potential of, 130–31; translations of, 9. See also action, fixed karma, retribution
karmic activities (body, speech, and mind): burning and, 99–100; purification of, 63; ten mentalities and, 69; wheels and, 43
Kelsay, John, 189n1
Keown, Damien, 145n2
Kieschnick, John, 30, 34
King Wen, 41
Knapp, Keith, 95
Kuo Liying, 61, 163n46, 170n58

Lai, Whalen, 42, 44, 163n44, 164n46
Larson, Wendy, 21
latter-day (moshi), 73, 88. See also decline of the Dharma
ledgers of merit and demerit (gongguo ge), 11–12
Lejeune, Philip, 19, 152n5, 152n7

Li, Wai-yee, 156*n*48
lineage: dreams and, 28–29; Ouyi's autobiography and, 17–18, 21–22, 29; Tiantai and, 109
Lingfeng Mountain, 21, 30, 121–22
Lingfeng Temple, 121–22; memorial hall, *124*; Ouyi's role in, 153*n*22, 189*n*136; stupa, *123*; stupa pillar, *121*
Lingfeng Zonglun: compilation of, 8, 81; editions of, 158*n*76; karma and, 12; vows in, 86
Longju, 109
lots, 160*n*7–8; Buddhist practice of, 38; Ouyi's casting of, 25, 38–39, 45, 161*n*12
Lotus Samādhi Repentance, 59–62; as template for Tiantai ritual, 64; ten stages of, 60
Lotus Sutra, 60, 97; blood writing and, 104–5, 111

Madhyamaka-kārikā (*Zhonglun*), 23; eight negations and, 23
Mādhyamika, 42
Mahāprajñāparamitā-sutra, 116
Maitreya, 64
Mara, 88
master: "four great masters of the Ming dynasty," 2, 145*n*5; Ouyi as, 30–32, 122
Mengcan, 44
merit: morality books and, 11–12
Miles, Margaret, 180*n*1
mind: karma and, 10–11, 48–51, 88; suffering and, 118; ten mentalities and, 69; vows and, 100–101
Ming dynasty: Buddhism in, 4; divination in, 41; dreams in, 28; examination system of, 41; fall of, 42, 179*n*48; filiality in, 95; four great masters of, 2, 145*n*5; karmic interpretation of, 125; rituals in, 63; scholastic activity in, 24; syncretism in, 4; threefold division of Buddhism in, 23, 190*n*3
mistakes (*guo*): of Ouyi Zhixu, 32, 89, 109; repentance and, 74–75; ten mentalities and, 69–70; terminology, 57. See also transgression
Mohe zhiguan (Great calming and contemplation), 61
moral agency: Buddhist view of, 2
morality books (*shanshu*), 11–12
Mrozik, Susanne, 93, 180*n*1, 187*n*121

Mudu Zhen, 24
mummification, 188*n*128

Nāgārjuna, 23
names: of Ouyi Zhixu, 23–24, 154*n*28
narrative: devices, 33–36; ethics and, 1–2
Nelson, Eric Sean, 131
neo-Confucianism: sectarianism of, 33–34
nonsectarianism: filial slicing and, 95; message of Ouyi's autobiography, 22–26, 29, 35

obstacles, 75, 127–28; three poisons and, 101; three types of (*sanzhang*), 59; revealed in divination, 46–47
Ohnuma, Reiko, 115, 182*n*18
omens: karma and, 41. See also signs
Ouyang Jingwu, 2
Owen, Stephen, 82–83, 153*n*13

pārājika, 57, 85, 87, 168*n*35
*pāramitā*s, 45, 170*n*57
Peng Xisu, 30; biography of Ouyi Zhixu, 31–32
penitence: attachment to self and, 51; blood writing and, 108–9; ritual efficacy and, 68; stimulus-response and, 87
Pini shiyi yaolüe (Essentials of the Vinaya), 38
poetry: vows and, 82, 86
poṣadha, 58, 168*n*40; in China, 168*n*41
practice (*shi*), 126–27; principle (*li*) and, 7–8, 102; repentance in, 59–61
practices, religious: definition of, 6; purpose of, 130; ritualization and, 6
prātimokṣa (*jiemo*), 66
pravāraṇā, 58, 168*n*39
precepts (*jie*): bodhisattva, 38–39, 67–68, 171*n*78; divination and, 38–39; karma and, 12; obstacles to, 116; Ouyi's reception of, 38–39; repentance and, 66–68; ten grave/major, 54, 67–68, 166*n*7; Ouyi's upholding of, 46; Ouyi's violation of, 53–55, 89
principle (*li*): Buddhist view of, 8; definition of, 7; discernment of (*liguan*), 60; neo-Confucian view of, 7–8; practice (*shi*) and, 7–8, 102; *qi* and, 7–8; repentance in, 59–61
Puett, Michael, 6
Pure Land: Chan versus, 108; deathbed practices, 85, 119–20; Ouyi Zhixu and, 14, 27, 31, 92; precepts and, 66–67; votive texts and, 82, 87, 97–99

qi, 7–8
Qin dynasty, 41
Quanzhou, 45

Rappaport, Roy, 101
reading: ritual and, 33–36
realm: "three thousand realms in a moment of thought" (*yinian sanqian*), 61, 170n60
regret: bodhisattva path and, 48; definition of, 164n61; function of, 47–48; humility and, 48; role in ritual, 62; role in spiritual formation, 47–49; stimulus-response and, 62. *See also* remorse
relics, 121–22; presence and, 188n131; terms for, 188n129; use of, 188n130
remorse: of Ouyi Zhixu, 3; repentance rituals and, 57, 68; stimulus-response and, 62. *See also* regret
repentance (*chan*), 53–80, 65; Buddhas and bodhisattvas' role in, 61–62; in Chinese Buddhism, 58; Chinese Buddhist terms for, 57, 167n26; crux of, 54; devotion and, 57–58; etymology of, 167n25; elements of, 57–58; emotions and, 62, 68; fivefold repentance (*wuhui*), 60; in Indian Buddhism, 58; Jesuit confession and, 5; Mahāyāna Buddhist, 37, 61; Maitreya and, 64; Ouyi's practice of, 55; in practice and principle, 59–61, 68–69, 169n53; sight and, 98; spiritual formation and, 47–49; stimulus-response and, 58, 60; ten stages of, 60; three types of (monastic, separate, public), 58–59; three types of (*zuofa, guanxiang, guan wuxiang*), 61; Tiantai Buddhist, 59–61
response. *See* stimulus-response
retribution: Chinese Buddhist views of, 10–12; circumstantial, 125–26; direct, 126; determining factors of, 50; karma and, 7, 9–12; of Ouyi Zhixu, 88–89, 91–92; stimulus-response and, 7, 41
ritual: aims, 68, 73–74; practitioners, 68, 73–74; texts, 5; studies, 4, 6; theory, 4–8; writing and, 33–36
rūpakāya, 85, 87
Rushi Daofang, 109
Ru Xing, 64

Śākyamuni Buddha: compassion of, 73; as judge, 17–18, 33, 131; repentance and, 77; vows and, 92

samādhi: Buddhas and bodhisattvas and, 40, 87–88; Dizang and, 76; fourfold, 58, 64; karma and, 73, 92; precepts and, 66; repentance and, 63; stimulus-response and, 52, 60
Samantabhadra, 60, 104, 105
saṃsāra, bodhisattvas and, 47–48, 72; confession and, 70; Ouyi's decision to escape, 79; repentance and, 60, 75; ten mentalities and, 69
saṃskāras, 86
sangha: harm of, 33, 62, 78, 85; importance of, 66
Santangelo, Paolo, 169n45
scars, 101; symbolism of, 101
Schmid, Neil, 150n64
Schopen, Gregory, 122, 188n129
Seaman, Gary, 185n66
Seidel, Anna, 187n119
shadow: metaphor for the body, 25, 34, 94; metaphor for karma, 11, 50
shame: Buddha-nature and, 48; cloak of, 97; Dizang and, 76–77; Ouyi's vows and, 86–87; repentance rituals of, 70–71; role in ritual, 7, 54–55, 68; ten mentalities and, 69–70; Zhiyi's emphasis on, 60
Shang dynasty, 40
Sharf, Robert, 7, 122, 172n98, 188n131, 192n30
Shengkai, 63
Shengyan: burning incense, 96; Chan argument of, 13–14, 18, 157n56; divination and, 37–38; estimation of Ouyi, 2; fixed karma and, 54
Shuangjing, 109
Shuilu hui (Assembly of Water and Land), 120
siddhantas, 42
signs: dreams and, 27, 59; reading fate and, 41; repentance and, 45, 54, 67–68
śīla, 66, 73, 76, 170n57, 175n6
Sima Qian, 19
Siming Zhili, 53, 62–65, 71, 170n63
sincerity (*cheng*): blood writing and, 103–8, 184n44, 185n62; burning and, 99; Confucian view of, 148n39; neo-Confucian view of, 7; religious practice and, 7; repentance rituals and, 68; vows and, 88
sins: Chinese Buddhist term for, 57; consequences of, 70–71; elimination of, 68–70, 73–75, 87–88; emptiness of, 75,

79; five heinous, 57, 84–85, 167n31; four grave, 57, 168n34; of Ouyi Zhixu, 70, 77–78, 82–83, 89–90; repentance of, 74–75; revelation of, 50, 69; of sense faculties, 61; ten mentalities and, 69; types of sins, 61–62, 69. *See also* crimes, transgressions

slander: of the Buddhist teachings, 55, 62, 77–78, 85, 98; ten evil deeds and, 167n33; ten wholesome actions and, 163n40; of the Three Jewels, 81, 85, 98, 166n7

slicing. *See* filial slicing

Smith, Richard, 160n8

Song dynasty: commentary on *Yijing* in, 46; Tiantai Buddhism and, 14, 63–65, 169n48

speech-act theory, 83, 174n4

Stalnaker, Aaron, 3

Stevenson, Daniel, 58, 61–62, 64, 166n6, 168n42

stimulus-response (*ganying*): Buddhist depictions of, 7, 172n98; description of, 6–7; omens and, 41; *qi* and, 7; retribution and, 7, 41; ritual efficacy and, 7; stimulating Buddhas and bodhisattvas, 51–52, 54–55; students and teachers and, 52

Strickmann, Michel, 38

stūpa (*guta*), 30, *121*, 121–22

substitution (*dai*), 90–92; in Buddhist texts, 174n3; in Chinese Buddhism, 179n53; in Ouyi's bodhisattva vows of, 83, 90–92

Sudhana, 104

suffering: body and, 118–19; obstacles and, 75; stimulus of, 54–55, 72–73; Ouyi's vows and, 91–92

Sukhāvatīvyūha-sutra, 83–84

Śūraṃgama-sutra, 51, 99, 105; importance in Chan and Huayan, 13–14; notion of Dharma nature, 34

Sutra of Brahma's Net, 104; eight negations and, 23; Ouyi's commentary on, 38; Ouyi's repentance ritual on, 53–55, 65, 66–71

Suzhou, 24

sympathetic resonance. *See* stimulus-response

syncretism (*sanjiao heyi*), 4, 26

Taixu, 2

Tathāgata, 73; womb of, 97

Taylor, Rodney, 152n10–11

teachers: dearth of, 29; precepts as, 55, 66; relationship with students, 52

Teiser, Stephen, 11, 175n9, 188n124

ten mentalities (*shixin*), 69–70, 166n9

thought: and practice, 129; turning of (*yunxiang*), 69

three jewels: Ouyi's criticism of, 12, 53–54, 64; Ouyi's ritual and, 65, 77; Ouyi's votive texts and, 86; Tiantai repentance and, 59–60

three karmic activities (body, speech, and mind): burning and, 99–100; classification of, 9; obstructions of, 74; rebirth and, 35; to stimulate Buddhas and bodhisattvas, 13, 68–69; wheel marks and, 43

three poisons, 59, 99–101

Tiantai Buddhism: Ouyi and, 14, 108–9, 152n4, 159n77; repentance and, 59–61

Tiantai Mountain, 109

tonsure: in Chinese Buddhism, 191n11

tops, 43, *44*, 45

traditions (*zong*): Chinese term for, 26; harmonization of (*zhuzong ronghe*), 14, 25–27; Ouyi's eschewing of, 17–18; schools versus, 26

transformation (*hua, zhuan*), 102; autobiography and, 34; body and, 16, 93–94; burning and, 98–99; religious practices and, 6, 102; repentance and, 69–71; of seeds of evil, 50–51; vows and, 89–90

transgressions: Buddhas and bodhisattvas salvific power and, 61–62, 67–68; Chinese Buddhist terms for, 57; emptiness and, 79–80; of Ouyi Zhixu, 70, 77–78, 82–83, 89–90; of precepts, 67–68; retribution for, 74–75, 79, 88–89; revelation of, 70–71. *See also* crimes, sins

tropes, 22, 27–29; hagiographic, 28; poetic function of, 27

uncertainty: divination and, 43; karma and, 17, 33, 39; precepts and, 36, 38; vows and, 90

Vairocana Buddha, 92, 104, 116

vegetarianism, 22, 24, 31, 154n30

Victoria, Brian, 131

Vinaya: brothers, 39, 110; disregard for, 38; Ouyi and, 38–39, 109–10; Ouyi's writings on, 160n11; versions of, 172n79

virtue: "embodied," 93–94

votive texts (*yuanwen*), 81–92; function of, 82, 94; future and, 82; genre of, 83–84; poetry and, 82; structure of, 81–82, *Sukhāvatīvyūha Sutra* and, 5, 83–84 vows (*yuan*): of bodhisattva, 84, 90; body and, 97–104; of Christian sacraments, 84; of Dharmākara, 84–85; of Dizang, 18, 52, 55; to eliminate karma, 87–88; four extensive, 89; of Hebrew Bible, 83, 175n5; to sinners, 85; speech-act theory and, 83; translation of, 84; types of Ouyi's vows, 86

Welter, Albert, 158n63
Wenling, 45
wheel marks (*lunxiang*): definition of, 38; in Divination repentance, 74; in *Divination Sutra*, 43–44, 71
wheels (*lun*), 43–44, 44
White, Hayden, 27
Williams, Bruce, 78
Williams, Paul, 93
Wright, Dale, 130
writing: karma and, 33–36; lineage and, 29; ritual and, 33–36
Wu, Jiang, 147n20
Wu, Pei-yi, 152n10
Wuyi, 109

Xiaojing, 95
Xiao Ziliang, 58
Xi Chao, 10, 128–29
Xinggu Daoshou, 96, 109
Xuanzong, 41
Xuehang Zhiji, 109, 110
Xueling, 13, 29
Xue pusa jiefa (Ritual of practicing the bodhisattva precepts), 67

Yan Hui, 25, 134
Yijing, 40, 127, 162n32; interpretation of, 46; Ouyi's commentary on, 162n31. See also *Zhouyi*, *Book of Changes*
Yinshun, 2
Yixing, 41
Yongming Yanshou, 13, 29
Young, Serenity, 28
Youxi Chuandeng, 108
Yü, Chün-fang, 147n19

Yu, Jimmy, 95, 103–5, 184n44, 184n47
Yuan dynasty, 63
Yuet Keung Lo, 41
Yunqi, 38, 109
Yunqi Zhuhong, 2, 24, 26, 29, 35, 38, 109; in autobiography, 134; division of merit, 12, 150n72; writings, 12, 24
Yu Qian, 30; biography of Ouyi, 31–32
Yü Ying-shi, 156n47

Zanli Dizang pusa chan yuan yi (Dizang repentance). See Dizang repentance
Zhancha shan'e yebao jing (Sutra on the divination of good and bad karmic retribution), 42–46, 163n44; Ouyi's promotion of, 39. See also *Divination Sutra*
Zhancha shan'e yebao jing shu (Commentary on the divination sutra), 45
Zhancha shan'e yebao jing xingfa (Rituals of the divination sutra). See Divination repentance
Zhancha shan'e yebao jing xuanyi (Profound meaning of the divination sutra), 49–51
Zhanran, 53, 62, 64, 65
Zhili. See Siming Zhili
Zhiyi, 53, 58–64, 69–72, 170n56; eremitic lifestyle of, 171n74; repentance texts, 59; stimulus-response and, 7; ten mentalities, 69–70; three types of repentance (*zuofa*, *guanxiang*, *guan wuxiang*), 61, 79; two approaches to repentance (*shi* and *li*), 59–61
Zhou Qi, 146n10
Zhouyi, 40; interpretation of, 46. See also *Yijing*, *Book of Changes*
Zhouyi chanjie (Chan explanation of the Zhouyi), 41–42; three interpretive stances in, 42
Zhuhong. See Yunqi Zhuhong
Zhu Xi, 7, 34, 146n18
Zhu Yuanzhang (Ming Taizu), 41
Zibo Zhenke, 2, 13, 29
Zongmi, 149n60
Zunshi. See Ciyun Zunshi
Zürcher, Erik 147n18

GPSR Authorized Representative: Easy Access System Europe, Mustamäe tee 50, 10621 Tallinn, Estonia, gpsr.requests@easproject.com

www.ingramcontent.com/pod-product-compliance
Lightning Source LLC
Chambersburg PA
CBHW021402290426
44108CB00010B/348